John Ray

Sams **Teach Yourself**

iPad™
Application Development

in **24**
Hours

SAMS   800 East 96th Street, Indianapolis, Indiana, 46240 USA

Sams Teach Yourself iPad™ Application Development in 24 Hours

Copyright © 2011 by Pearson Education, Inc.

ISBN-13: 978-0-672-33339-2
ISBN-10: 0-672-33339-2

Library of Congress Cataloging-in-Publication Data:

Ray, John, 1971-

  Sams teach yourself iPad application development in 24 hours / John Ray.

    p. cm.

  Includes index.

  ISBN 978-0-672-33339-2

  1. iPad (Computer)—Programming. 2. Application software—Development. I. Title.

  QA76.8.I863R392 2011

  005.3—dc22

                    2010023693

Printed in the United States of America

First Printing July 2010

Trademarks

All terms mentioned in this book that are known to be trademarks or service marks have been appropriately capitalized. Sams Publishing cannot attest to the accuracy of this information. Use of a term in this book should not be regarded as affecting the validity of any trademark or service mark.

Warning and Disclaimer

Every effort has been made to make this book as complete and as accurate as possible, but no warranty or fitness is implied. The information provided is on an "as is" basis. The author and the publisher shall have neither liability nor responsibility to any person or entity with respect to any loss or damages arising from the information contained in this book.

Bulk Sales

Sams Publishing offers excellent discounts on this book when ordered in quantity for bulk purchases or special sales. For more information, please contact

  U.S. Corporate and Government Sales
  1-800-382-3419
  corpsales@pearsontechgroup.com

For sales outside of the U.S., please contact

  International Sales
  international@pearson.com

Associate Publisher
Greg Wiegand

Acquisitions Editor
Laura Norman

Development Editor
Keith Cline

Managing Editor
Kristy Hart

Project Editor
Lori Lyons

Indexer
Angela Martin

Proofreader
Kathy Ruiz

Technical Editor
Matthew David

Publishing Coordinator
Cindy Teeters

Multimedia Developer
Dan Scherf

Book Designer
Gary Adair

Compositor
Gloria Schurick

Contents at a Glance

Table of Contents

About the Author

John Ray is currently serving as a Senior Business Analyst and Development Team Manager for the Ohio State University Research Foundation. He has written numerous books for Macmillan/Sams/Que, including *Using TCP/IP: Special Edition, Sams Teach Yourself Dreamweaver MX in 21 Days, Mac OS X Unleashed*, and *Sams Teach Yourself iPhone Development in 24 Hours*. As a Macintosh user since 1984, he strives to ensure that each project presents the Macintosh with the equality and depth it deserves. Even technical titles such as *Using TCP/IP* contain extensive information on the Macintosh and its applications—and have garnered numerous positive reviews for its straightforward approach and accessibility to beginning and intermediate users.

Dedication

This book is dedicated to everyone who can see beyond the count of USB ports, RAM slots, and technical jargon to recognize the beauty of a platform as a whole. I'm excited to see what you create.

Acknowledgments

Thank you to the group at Sams Publishing—Laura Norman, Kristy Hart, Lori Lyons, Keith Cline, Matthew David, Gloria Schurick, Kathy Ruiz—for recognizing the importance of the iPhone OS/iPad platform, and helping to create this book. Skilled editors make authors coherent.

As always, thanks to my family and friends for keeping me sane for the duration of the project. It wasn't that bad, was it?

We Want to Hear from You!

As the reader of this book, *you* are our most important critic and commentator. We value your opinion and want to know what we're doing right, what we could do better, what areas you'd like to see us publish in, and any other words of wisdom you're willing to pass our way.

You can email or write me directly to let me know what you did or didn't like about this book—as well as what we can do to make our books stronger.

Please note that I cannot help you with technical problems related to the topic of this book, and that due to the high volume of mail I receive, I might not be able to reply to every message.

When you write, please be sure to include this book's title and author as well as your name and phone or email address. I will carefully review your comments and share them with the author and editors who worked on the book.

E-mail: feedback@samspublishing.com

Mail: Greg Wiegand
          Associate Publisher
          Sams Publishing
          800 East 96th Street
          Indianapolis, IN 46240 USA

Reader Services

Visit our website and register this book at informit.com/register for convenient access to any updates, downloads, or errata that might be available for this book.

Introduction

"It's just a big iPod Touch."

Few words have puzzled me more during the weeks leading up to the iPad launch. Let's break down exactly what it means to be a "big iPod Touch."

First, it means a large, bright, colorful display, coupled with an amazingly thin enclosure and amazing battery life. Second, it means a user experience based on the world's most popular portable Internet device.

Perhaps the most important aspect of being a "big iPod touch" is that it is a device designed to be controlled by human fingers. Every aspect of development is centered on touch interactions. Quite simply, the iPad is a multitouch device that is 100% dedicated to running applications that you control with your fingers.

Terrible, isn't it?

Less than a month after the iPad launched, Apple has sold more than a million units. It's reassuring that people still recognize and embrace innovation. It also means that there is no end to the opportunity that the iPad affords to you, the developer.

The iPad is an open canvas. On the iPhone, there are plenty of apps, but less of an opportunity to experiment with user interfaces. On the iPad, apps take on new life. The display begs to be touched, and complex gestures are fun and easy to implement. Computing truly becomes a personal experience, similar to curling up with a good book.

Our hope is that this book will bring iPad development to a new generation of developers who want to create large-scale multitouch applications. *Sams Teach Yourself iPad Application Development in 24 Hours* provides a clear natural progression of skills development—from installing developer tools and registering with Apple, to submitting an application to the App Store. It's everything you need to get started in just 24 hour-long lessons.

Who Can Become an iPad Developer?

If you have an interest in learning, time to invest in exploring and practicing with Apple's developer tools, and an Intel Macintosh computer, you have everything you need to begin developing for the iPad.

Developing an application won't happen overnight, but with dedication and practice, you can be writing your first applications in a matter of days. The more time you spend working with the Apple developer tools, the more opportunities you'll discover for creating new and exciting projects.

You should approach iPad application development as creating software that *you* want to use, not what you think others want. If you're solely interested in getting rich quick, you're likely to be disappointed. (The App Store is a crowded marketplace—albeit one with a lot of room—and competition for top sales is fierce.) However, if you focus on building useful and unique apps, you're much more likely to find an appreciative audience.

Who Should Use This Book?

This book targets individuals who are new to development for the iPhone OS and have experience using the Macintosh platform. No previous experience with Objective-C, Cocoa, or the Apple developer tools is required. Of course, if you do have development experience, some of the tools and techniques may be easier to master, but this book does not assume that you've coded before.

That said, some things are expected from you, the reader. Specifically, you must be willing to invest in the learning process. If you just read each hour's lesson without working through the tutorials, you will likely miss some fundamental concepts. In addition, you need to spend time reading the Apple developer documentation and researching the topics covered in this book. A vast amount of information on iPhone development is available, but only limited space is available in this book. However, this book does cover what you need to forge your own path forward.

What Is (and Isn't) in This Book?

This book targets the initial release of the iPad OS 3.2. Much of what you'll be learning is common to all iPhone OS releases (the iPad is built on top of the iPhone OS), but we also cover several important advances, such as popovers, modal views, and more!

Unfortunately, this is not a complete reference for the iPhone OS application programming interfaces. Some topics require much more space than the format of this book allows. Thankfully, the Apple developer documentation is available directly within the free tools you'll be downloading in Hour 1, "Preparing Your System and iPad for Development." Many lessons include a section titled "Further Exploration" that will guide you toward additional related topics of interest. Again, a willingness to explore is an important quality in becoming a successful developer!

Each coding lesson is accompanied by project files that include everything you need to compile and test an example or, preferably, follow along and build the application yourself. Be sure to download the project files from the book's website at http://teachyourselfipad.com.

In addition to the support website, you can follow along on Twitter! Search for #iPadIn24 on Twitter to receive official updates and tweets from other readers. Use the hashtag #iPadIn24 in your tweets to join the conversation. To send me messages via Twitter, begin each tweet with @johnemeryray.

HOUR 1

Preparing Your System and iPad for Development

What You'll Learn in This Hour:

▶ What makes an iPad an iPad
▶ Where to get the tools you need to develop for the iPad
▶ How to join the iPhone OS Developer Program
▶ The need for (and use of) provisioning profiles
▶ What to expect during the first few hours of this book

The iPad is the next step in Apple's touch-based platform, iPhone OS. Sporting a larger screen and faster processor than the iPhone, the iPad brings desktop-level computing to a very portable and flexible platform. If you're an iPhone developer, the iPad gives you the ability to think bigger—to imagine your applications in a whole new way. For those just starting out, it offers a robust toolset for realizing your touch-enabled computing ideas.

This hour will get you prepared for iPad development. You're about to embark on the road to becoming an iPad developer, but there's a bit of prep work before you start coding.

Welcome to the iPad Platform

If you're reading this book, you probably already have an iPad, and that means you already understand how to interact with its interface. Crisp graphics, amazing responsiveness, multitouch, and thousands of apps—this just begins to scratch the surface. As a developer, however, you'll need to get accustomed to dealing with a platform that, to borrow a phrase from Apple, forces you to "think different."

Display and Graphics

The iPad screen is 1024x768 pixels—giving you a large amount of space to present
your application's content and interface (see Figure 1.1). Although this resolution
might seem limiting, consider that desktop computers only recently exceeded this
size and many websites are still designed for 800x600. In addition, the iPad's display
is dedicated to the currently running application. You will have one window to work
in. You can change the content within that window, but the desktop and multiwindow application metaphors are gone.

FIGURE 1.1
The iPad has a
screen resolu-
tion of
768x1024
(portrait),
1024x768
(landscape).

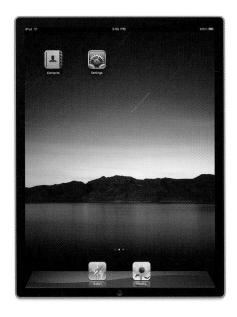

The lack of multiple windows shouldn't be considered a flaw, however. Apple provides plenty of interface alternatives that will help you display just as much information as a traditional multiwindow desktop application, but in a more structured
way.

The graphics that you display on your screen can include complex animated 2D
and 3D displays thanks to the OpenGL ES implementation. OpenGL, an industry
standard for defining and manipulating graphic images, is widely used to create
games.

Application Resource Constraints

The iPad, by all accounts, is a snappy device. It is also the first device in many years to use an Apple-branded processor: the A4. The A4 is a "system on a chip" that provides CPU, GPU, and other capabilities to the device. The specs of the processor will eventually become clearer, but are still mostly guesswork at the time of this writing.

Apple has gone to great lengths to keep the iPad responsive, no matter what you're doing. Unfortunately, this has led to one of the biggest drawbacks of the system—only a single *third-party* application can run at a time. This means that your program must provide the features users need without forcing them to jump into other apps. It also means that your application must remain active to communicate with the user. Although push notifications are possible, no actual processing can take place when your application has exited. The good news? This will change in late 2010 when the iPad adopts iPhone OS 4.0.

Another constraint that you need to be mindful of is the available memory. The iPad contains 256MB of dedicated application RAM—hardly astronomical, and no chance for an upgrade in the future!

> Throughout the book, you'll see reminders to "release" memory when you're done using it. Even though you might get tired of seeing it, this is a very important process to get used to.

By the Way

Connectivity

The iPad's connectivity options mirror the iPhone and iPod Touch. The 3G iPad, for example, has the ability to always be connected via a cellular provider (such as AT&T in the United States). This wide-area access is supplemented with built-in WiFi and Bluetooth in all iPad models. WiFi can provide desktop-like browsing speeds within the range of a wireless hot spot. BlueTooth, on the other hand, can be used to connect a variety of peripheral devices to your iPad, including a keyboard!

As a developer, you can make use of the Internet connectivity to update the content in your application, display web pages, or create multiplayer games. The only drawback is that applications that rely heavily on 3G data usage stand a greater chance of being rejected from the App Store. These restrictions have been lessened in recent months, but it is still a point of frustration for developers.

Input and Feedback

The iPad shines when it comes to input and feedback mechanisms and your ability to work with them. You can read the input values from the capacitive multitouch (four-finger!) screen, sense motion and tilt via the accelerometer, determine where you are using the GPS (3G model), and even determine which way you're facing with the digital compass (3G model). The iPad itself can provide so much data to your application about how and where it is being used that the device itself truly becomes a controller of sorts—much like the Nintendo Wii.

Finally, for each action your user takes when interacting with your application, you can provide feedback. This, obviously, can be visible text on the screen, or it can be high-quality audio and video. As a developer, you can incorporate all of these capabilities, and in this book you'll learn how!

That wraps up our quick tour of the iPad platform. After years of feeling cramped by the iPhone's display, developers can now explore full-screen high-resolution applications—all with the same capabilities found on the successful iPhone platform.

Although this book targets the iPad specifically, much of the information also applies to the iPhone and iPod Touch. These systems differ in capabilities, such as support for a camera and GPS, but the development techniques are otherwise identical.

Becoming an iPad Developer

Obviously, there is more to being an iPad developer than just sitting down and writing a program. You need a modern Intel Macintosh desktop or laptop running Snow Leopard, and at least 6GB of free space on your hard drive. The more screen space you have on your development system, the easier it will be to switch between the coding, design, simulation, and reference tools that you'll need to be using. That said, I've worked perfectly happily on a 13" MacBook Pro, so an ultra-HD multi-monitor setup certainly isn't necessary.

So, assuming you already have a Mac, what else do you need? The good news is that there isn't *much* more, and it won't cost you a cent to write your first application.

Joining the Apple Developer Program

Despite somewhat confusing messages on the Apple website, there really is no fee associated with joining the Apple Developer Program, downloading the iPhone OS SDK (Software Development Kit), writing iPad applications, and running them on Apple's iPhone OS simulator.

There are limitations, however, to what you can do for free. If you want to have early access to beta versions of the iPhone OS and SDK, you'll need to be a paid member. If you want to load the applications you write on a physical iPad device or distribute them on the App Store, you'll also need to pay the membership fee. Most of the applications in this book will work just fine on the simulator provided with the free tools, so the decision on how to proceed is up to you.

> If you aren't yet sure if the paid program is right for you, you can upgrade at any time. I recommend starting out with the free program and upgrading after you've had a chance to write a few sample applications and to run them in the simulator.
>
> Obviously, things such as motion sensor input and GPS readings can't be accurately presented in the simulator, but these are special cases and won't be needed until later in this book.

Did you Know?

If you choose to pay, the paid Developer Program offers two levels: a standard program ($99) for those who will be creating applications that they want to distribute from the App Store, or an enterprise program ($299) for larger companies wanting to develop and distribute applications in-house but *not* through the App Store. Chances are, the standard program is what you want.

> The standard ($99) program is available for both companies and individuals. If you want to publish to the App Store with a business name, you'll be given the option of choosing a standard "individual" or "company" program during the registration.

By the Way

Registering as a Developer

Big or small, free or paid, your venture into iPad development begins on Apple's website. To start, visit the Apple iPhone Dev Center (http://developer.apple.com/iphone), shown in Figure 1.2.

If you already have an Apple ID from using iTunes or other Apple services, congratulations, you're almost done! Use the Log In link to access your account, agree to Apple's developer terms, and provide a few pieces of additional information for your developer profile. You'll immediately be granted access to the free developer resources!

If you don't yet have an Apple ID, click the Register link, followed by Get Started on the subsequent page. When the registration starts, choose Create an Apple ID in the first step, as shown in Figure 1.3.

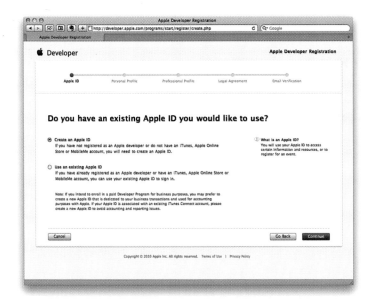

The registration process walks you through the process of creating a new Apple ID, and collects information about your development interests and experience, as shown in Figure 1.4.

After the registration is complete, Apple will verify your email address by sending you a clickable link to activate your account.

FIGURE 1.4
The multistep registration process collects a variety of information about your development experience.

Joining a Paid Developer Program

Once you have a registered and activated Apple ID, you can make the decision to join a paid program, or continue using the free resources. If you choose to join a paid program, again point your browser to the iPhone Dev Center (http://developer. apple.com/iphone) and click the Register button. Choose Use an Existing Apple ID for the Developer Program option, visible in Figure 1.3.

On the page that appears, look for the Join Today link and click it. The registration tool will now guide you through applying for the paid programs, including choosing between the standard and company options, as shown in Figure 1.5.

FIGURE 1.5
Choose the paid
program that
you want to
apply for.

Unlike the free Developer Membership, the paid Developer Program does not take effect immediately. When the App Store first launched, it took months for new developers to join and be approved into the program. Today, it may take hours or a few days—just be patient. You can check your current status at any time by logging in to the iPhone Dev Center and following the Check Your Enrollment Status Now link.

Use the Register link to create a new free Developer Membership, or follow the links in the iPhone OS Developer Program section (currently http://developer.apple.com/iphone/program) to join a paid program.

Installing the iPhone OS Developer Tools

After you've registered your Apple ID, you can immediately download the current release version of the iPhone OS developer tools directly from the iPhone Dev Center (http://developer.apple.com/iphone). Just click the Download link and sit back while your Mac downloads the massive (~2.5GB) SDK disk image.

If you have the free Developer Membership, you'll likely only see a single SDK to download—the current release version of the development tools. If you've become a paid program member, you may see additional links for different versions of the SDK (3.2, 3.5, 4.0, and so on). The examples in this book are based on the 3.2+ series of SDKs, so be sure to choose that option if presented.

When the download completes, open the resulting disk image, and double-click the Xcode and iPhone SDK for Snow Leopard icon. This will launch the Mac OS X Installer application and assist you in the installation. There is no need to change any of the defaults for the installer, so just read and agree to the software license and click Continue to proceed through the steps.

Unlike most applications, the Apple developer tools are installed in a folder called Developer located at the root of your hard drive. Inside the Developer folder are dozens of files and folders containing developer frameworks, source code files, examples, and of course, the developer applications themselves. Nearly all your work in this book will start with the application Xcode, located in the Developer/Applications folder (see Figure 1.6).

FIGURE 1.6
Most of your work with the developer tools will start in the Developer/Applications folder.

Although we won't get into real development for a few more hours, we will be configuring a few options in Xcode in the next section, so don't forget where it is!

Creating a Development Provisioning Profile

Even after you've obtained an Apple Developer Membership, joined a paid Developer Program, and downloaded and installed the iPhone OS development tools, you *still* won't be able to run applications that you write on your iPad! The reason for this is that you haven't created a development provisioning profile.

In many development guides, this step isn't covered until after development begins. In my mind, once you've written an application, you're going to want to immediately run it on the iPad. Why? Because it's just cool to see your own code running on your own device!

What Is a Development Provisioning Profile?

Like it or not, Apple's current approach to iPhone OS development is to make absolutely certain that the development process is controlled—and that groups can't just distribute software to anyone they please. The result is a rather confusing process that ties together information about you, any development team members, and your application into a "provisioning profile."

A development provisioning profile identifies the developer who may install an application, an ID for the application being developed, and the "unique device identifiers" for each iPad that will run the application. This is *only* for the development process. When you are ready to distribute an application via the App Store or to a group of testers (or friends!) via ad hoc means, you'll need to create a separate "distribution" profile. Because we're just starting out, this isn't something you'll need right away. We talk more about distribution profiles in Hour 24, "Distributing Applications Through the App Store."

Generating and Installing a Development Provisioning Profile

Creating a provisioning profile can be frustrating and seem outrageously convoluted. Apple has streamlined the process tremendously with an online Development Provisioning Assistant, but we still have to jump through some hoops. Let's bite the bullet, and get through this!

Getting Your iPad Unique Device Identifier

To run your application on a real iPad, you'll need the ID that uniquely identifies your iPad from the thousands of other iPads. To find this, first make sure that your device is connected to your computer, and then launch Xcode from the Developer, Applications folder. When Xcode first launches, immediately choose Window, Organizer from the menu. The Organizer utility slightly resembles iTunes in its layout. You should see your iPad listed in the far left column of the Organizer under the Devices section. Click the icon to select it, then click the "Use for Development" button. Your screen should now resemble Figure 1.7.

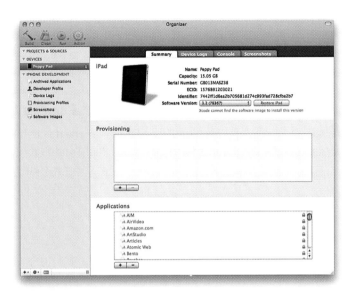

FIGURE 1.7
First, grab the
ID of your iPad.

The Identifier field is the unique device ID that we're looking for. Go ahead and copy it to the Clipboard. You'll need to paste it into the Provisioning Assistant shortly.

Starting the Provisioning Assistant

Next, head to the Apple website and the iPhone Dev Center (http://developer.apple.com/iphone). Make sure that you've logged in to the site, and then click the iPhone Provisioning Portal link, currently located in the upper-right side of the page. The Provisioning Portal is designed to give you access to the tools you need to create provisioning and distribution profiles. It also includes the Development Provisioning Assistant, which is the web utility that will make our lives much easier. Click the Launch Assistant button (see Figure 1.8).

FIGURE 1.8
Head to the
iPhone
Provisioning
Portal, and then
launch the
Development
Provisioning
Assistant.

The assistant will launch in your web browser and display a short splash screen. Click the Continue button to begin.

Choosing an App ID

Your first step is to choose an App ID. This ID will identify a shared portion of the keychain that your application will have access to.

Come again?

The keychain is a secure information store on the iPad that can be used to save passwords and other critical information. Most apps don't share a keychain space (and therefore can't share protected information). If you use the same App ID for multiple applications, however, they *can* share keychain data.

For the purposes of this book, there's no reason the tutorial apps can't share a single App ID, so create a new ID named anything you want. If you have already created App IDs in the past, you'll be given the option to choose an existing ID. I'm creating a new App ID, Tutorials, as shown in Figure 1.9. Enter the ID and click Continue to move on.

FIGURE 1.9
An App ID can be used for a single application or group of applications.

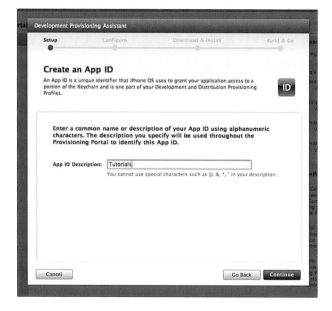

Assigning a Development Device

Next you are asked to assign a development device, as shown in Figure 1.10. This is the device ID that identifies which iPad will be allowed to run the applications you create. Enter a meaningful description for the device (Johns WiFi iPad, for example), and then paste the string you copied from the Xcode organizer into the Device ID field. Click Continue to move on.

FIGURE 1.10
Assign a device that can run your application.

Note that as with the App IDs, if you've already used a device ID in the past, you will be given the option of simply selecting it from a drop-down list.

Generating a Certificate Signing Request

Now things are getting fun. The next step takes place outside of your browser. Leaving the Development Provisioning Assistant open, go to the Applications, Utilities folder on your hard drive and open the Keychain Access utility. Choose Keychain Access, Certificate Assistant, Request a Certificate from a Certificate Authority from the menu (see Figure 1.11).

FIGURE 1.11
In this step, you create a certificate request that is uploaded to Apple.

The Keychain Access Certificate Assistant will start. Thankfully, this is a pretty short process. You just need to enter your email address, name, and highlight the Saved to Disk option, as shown in Figure 1.12.

FIGURE 1.12
Enter the infor-
mation needed
for the certifi-
cate request.
You can leave
the CA Email
Address field
empty.

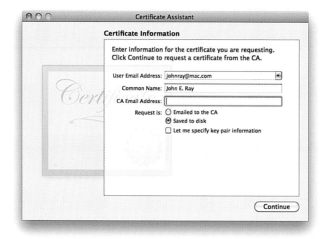

Click Continue to save the certificate to your disk. Make sure you make a note of where you save the certificate, because you're going to be uploading it to Apple back in the Development Provisioning Assistant. Once you save it, you can close the Certificate Assistant window.

Uploading the Certificate Signing Request

Return to the Development Provisioning Assistant in your web browser. Click continue until you are prompted to submit the certificate signing request that you just
generated (see Figure 1.13). Use the Choose File button to select the request file, and
then click Continue to upload it.

Naming and Generating the Provisioning Profile

We're almost done! After uploading the request, you'll be prompted to name the
provisioning profile (see Figure 1.14). Because this profile contains information that
can potentially identify individual phones and applications, you should choose
something relevant to how you intend to use it. In this case, I'm only interested in
using it as a generic development profile for all of my apps, so I'm naming it iPad
Development Profile. Not very creative, but it works.

FIGURE 1.13
Upload the certificate signing request to Apple.

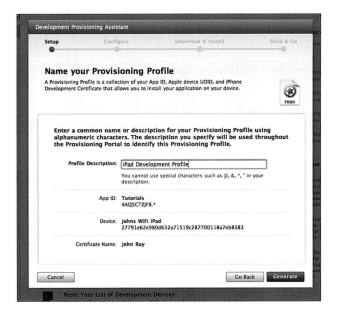

FIGURE 1.14
Name the profile to reflect how you intend to use it.

Click the Generate button to create your provisioning profile. This may take 20 to 60 seconds, so be patient. The screen will eventually refresh to show the final profile information, as shown in Figure 1.15.

FIGURE 1.15
After several
seconds, the
profile is gener-
ated.

Our final steps will be downloading and installing the profile, and downloading and installing a security certificate that will be associated with the profile.

Downloading the Development Provisioning Profile and Certificate

At this point, your profile has been generated, along with a security certificate that can be used to uniquely associate your applications with that profile. All that remains is downloading and installing them. Click the Continue button to access the provisioning profile download screen, as shown in Figure 1.16. Click the Download Now button to save the profile to your Downloads folder (file extension .mobileprovision).

As much as I hate to say it, the next thing to do is to ignore the onscreen instructions—the installation process that Apple describes in the assistant isn't the most efficient route. Instead, click the Continue button until you are given the option of downloading the development certificate, as shown in Figure 1.17.

Click the Download Now button to download the certificate file (file extension .cer) to your Downloads folder. You are now finished with the Provisioning Assistant and can safely exit.

FIGURE 1.16
Download the provisioning profile.

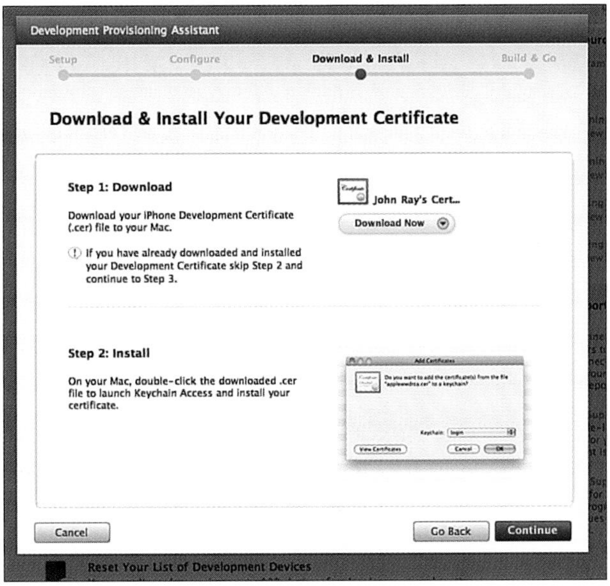

FIGURE 1.17
Download the development certificate.

Installing the Development Provisioning Profile and Certificate

To install the profile and certificate, we just need to exercise our double-click skills.
First, install the development certificate by double-clicking it. Doing so opens

Keychain Access and prompts you for the keychain where the certificate should be installed. Choose the login keychain, and then click OK, as demonstrated in Figure 1.18.

FIGURE 1.18
Choose the login keychain to hold your development certificate.

After adding the certificate, you should be able to browse through your login keychain for a key labeled with your name that contains the certificate.

To install the development profile, double-click the downloaded .mobileprovision file. Xcode will launch—if it isn't already running—and silently install the profile. You can verify that it has been successfully installed by launching the Organizer within Xcode (Window, Organizer) and then clicking the Provisioning Profiles item within the iPhone Development section, as shown in Figure 1.19.

FIGURE 1.19
If the profile has been successfully installed, it should be listed in the Xcode Organizer.

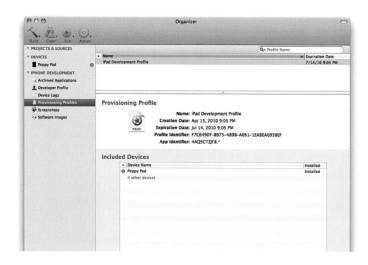

Once you have a development machine configured, you can easily configure other computers using the "Developer Profile" item in the Xcode organizer. The "Export Developer Profile" and "Import Developer Profile" buttons will export (and subsequently import) all your developer profiles/certificates in a single package.

But Wait...I Have More Than One iPhone OS Device!

The Development Provisioning Assistant helps you create a provisioning profile for a single iPad, iPhone, or iPod Touch device. But, what if you have multiple devices that you want to install onto? No problem. You'll need to head back to the iPhone Provisioning Portal and click the Devices link listed on the left side of the page. From there, you can add additional devices that will be available to your profile.

Next, click the Provisioning link, also on the left side of the page, and use the Edit link to modify your existing profile to include another iPad, as demonstrated in Figure 1.20.

Finally, you'll need to use the Download link to redownload the modified profile and then import it into Xcode so that the additional device is available.

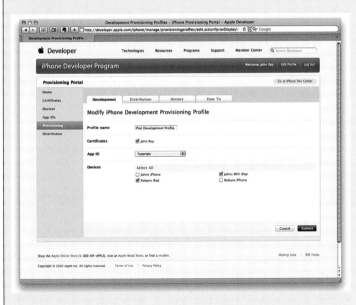

FIGURE 1.20
Add additional devices to a provisioning profile within the web portal. Remember to redownload the profile and install it!

Testing the Profile with an iPad App

It seems wrong to go through all of that work without some payoff, right? For a real-world test of your efforts, let's actually try to run an application on your iPad. If you haven't downloaded the project files to your computer, now would be a good time to visit http://www.teachyourselfipad.com and download the archives.

Within the Hour 1 Projects folder, open the Welcome folder. Double-click Welcome.xcodeproj to open a very simple application in Xcode. After the project opens, your display should be similar to Figure 1.21.

FIGURE 1.21
Open the Welcome.xcode-proj in Xcode.

Next, make sure that your iPad is plugged into your computer. Using the menu in the upper-left corner of the Xcode window, choose iPhone Device 3.2 (or a later version, if available). This will tell Xcode that when the project is built, it should be installed on your iPad. Finally, click Build and Run.

After a few seconds, the application should be installed and launched on your iPad, as you can see in Figure 1.22.

FIGURE 1.22
Congratulations,
you've just
installed your
first home-
grown iPad
application!

You can now exit Xcode and quit the Welcome application on your iPad.

When you clicked Build and Run, the Welcome application was installed and started on your iPad. It will remain there until you remove it manually. Just touch and hold the Welcome icon until it starts wiggling, then delete the application as you would any other.

By the Way

Developer Technology Overview

Over the course of the next few hours, you will be introduced to the technologies that you'll be using to create iPad applications. Our goal is to get you up to speed on the tools and technology, and then you can start actively developing. This means you're still a few hours away from writing your first app, but when you start coding, you'll have the necessary background skills and knowledge to successfully create a wide variety of applications.

The Apple Developer Suite

In this chapter, you downloaded and worked with the Xcode application. This is just one piece (albeit a very important piece) of the developer suite that you will be using throughout this book. Xcode, coupled with Interface Builder and the iPhone

Simulator, will make up your development environment. These three applications are so critical, in fact, that we've devoted two hours (2 and 4) to covering them.

It's worth mentioning that almost every iPad, iPhone, iPod, and Macintosh application you run, whether created by a single developer at home or a huge company, is built using the Apple developer tools. This means that you have everything you need to create software as powerful as any you've ever run.

Later in the book, you'll be introduced to additional tools in the suite that can help you debug and optimize your application.

Objective-C

Objective-C is the language that you'll be using to write your applications. It will provide the structure for our applications, and be used to control the logic and decision making that goes on when an application is running.

If you've never worked with a programming language before, don't worry. We cover everything you need to get started in Hour 3, "Discovering Objective-C." Developing for the iPad in Objective-C is a unique programming experience, even if you've used other programming languages in the past. The language is unobtrusive and structured in a way that makes it easy to follow. After your first few projects, Objective-C will fade into the background, letting you concentrate on the specifics of your application.

Cocoa Touch

While Objective-C defines the structure for iPad applications, Cocoa Touch defines the functional building blocks, called *classes*, that can make the iPad do certain things. Cocoa Touch isn't a "thing," per se, but a collection of interface elements, data storage elements, and other handy tools that you can access from your applications.

As you'll learn in Hour 4, "Inside Cocoa Touch," you can access literally hundreds of different Cocoa Touch classes and you can do thousands of things with them. We cover quite a few of the most useful classes in this book and give you the pointers you need to explore even more on your own.

Model-View-Controller

The iPhone OS platform and Macintosh use a development approach called Model-View-Controller (MVC) to structure applications. Understanding why MVC is used and the benefits it provides will help you make good decisions in structuring your most complex applications. Despite the potentially complicated-sounding name, MVC is really just a way to keep your application projects arranged so that you can easily update and extend them in the future. We look more at MVC in Hour 6, "Model-View-Controller Application Design."

Summary

This hour introduced you to the iPad, its capabilities, and its limitations. You learned about the iPad's display, networking, and other features that can be used to create unique user experiences. We also discussed the Apple developer tools, how to download and install them, and the differences between the varying pay-for developer programs. To prepare you for actual on-device development, you explored the process of creating and installing a development provisioning profile in Xcode and even installed an application on your iPad.

The hour wrapped up with a quick discussion of the development technologies that will make up the first part of the book and form the basis for all the iPad development you'll be doing.

Q&A

Q. *I thought the iPad had at minimum 16GB of RAM in the low-end and 64GB on the high-end model. Doesn't it?*

A. The "memory" capabilities for the iPad that are advertised to the public are the storage sizes available for applications, songs, and so forth. It is separate from the RAM that can be used for executing programs. If Apple implements virtual memory in a future version of iPhone OS, it is possible that the larger storage could be used for increasing available RAM.

Q. *What platform should I target for development?*

A. That depends on your goals. If you want to reach the largest audience, consider a universal application that works on the iPad, iPhone, and iPod Touch. We examine this development possibility later in Hour 22, "Building Universal Applications." If you want to make use of the most capable hardware, you can certainly target the unique capabilities of the 3G iPad, but you will potentially be limiting the size of your customer base.

Q. *Why isn't the iPad (and iPhone OS platform) open?*

A. Great question. Apple has long sought to control the user experience so that it remains "positive" regardless of how users have set up their device, be it a Mac, an iPad, or an iPhone. By ensuring that applications can be tied to a developer and enforcing an approval process, Apple attempts to limit the potential for a harmful application to cause damage to data or otherwise negatively impact the user. Whether this is an appropriate approach, however, is open to debate.

Workshop

Quiz

1. What is the resolution of the iPad screen?

2. What is the cost of joining an individual iPhone OS Developer Program?

3. What language will you use when creating iPad applications?

Answers

1. 1024x768. The iPad screen resolutions are identical across the platform variants.

2. The Developer Program costs $99 a year for the individual option.

3. Objective-C will be used for iPad development.

Activities

1. Establish an Apple Developer Membership and download and install the developer tools. This is an important activity that, if you didn't follow along in the course of the hour, should be completed before starting the next hour's lesson.

2. Review the resources available in the iPhone Dev Center. Apple has published several introductory videos and tutorials that helpfully supplement what you'll learn in this book.

HOUR 2

Introduction to Xcode and the iPhone Simulator

What You'll Learn in This Hour:

▶ How to create new projects in Xcode
▶ Code editing and navigation features
▶ Where to add classes and resources to a project
▶ How to modify project properties
▶ Compiling for the iPad and the iPhone Simulator
▶ How to interpret error messages
▶ Features and limitations of the iPhone Simulator

The core of your work in the Apple Developer Suite will be spent in three applications: Xcode, Interface Builder, and the iPhone Simulator. This trio of apps provides all the tools that you need to design, program, and test applications for the iPad. And, unlike other platforms, the Apple Developer Suite is entirely free!

This hour walks you through the basics you need to work within two of the three components—Xcode and the iPhone Simulator—and you'll get some hands-on practice working with each. We cover the third piece, Interface Builder, in Hour 5, "Exploring Interface Builder."

Using Xcode

When you think of coding—actually typing the statements that will make your iPad meet Apple's "magical" mantra—think Xcode. Xcode is the IDE, or integrated development environment, that manages your application's resources and lets you edit the code that ties the different pieces together.

By the
Way

iPhone? I'm Using an iPad!

Let's get this out of the way upfront. When you see a reference to the iPhone, you're not reading the wrong book! Apple refers to the development platform using terms like the *iPhone OS* and *iPhone SDK*, and the simulator tool is named the iPhone Simulator. We're using these tools to develop for the iPad, but they also apply to the iPhone. Instead of changing all the terminology, Apple has stuck with *iPhone* to refer to many of the pieces in the developer toolset.

After you install the developer tools, as described in Hour 1, "Preparing Your System and iPad for Development," you should be able to find Xcode in the /Developer/Applications folder located at the root level of your hard drive. We'll be walking through the day-to-day use of Xcode in this hour, so if you haven't installed the tools yet, do so now!

Launch Xcode from the /Developer/Applications folder. After a few moments, the Welcome to Xcode screen will display, as shown in Figure 2.1.

FIGURE 2.1
Explore Apple's developer resources, right from the Xcode Welcome screen.

You can choose to disable this screen by unchecking the Show This Window When Xcode Launches check box, but it does provide a convenient "jumping-off" point for sample code, tutorials, and documentation. In Hour 4, "Inside Cocoa Touch," we take a detailed look at the documentation system included in Xcode, which is quite extensive. For now, click Cancel to exit the Welcome screen.

Creating and Managing Projects

Most of your iPad work will start with an Xcode project. A project is a collection of all the files that are associated with an application, along with the settings that are needed to "build" a working piece of software from the files. This includes images, source code, and a file that describes the appearance and objects that make up the interface.

Choosing a Project Type

To create a new project, choose File, New Project (Shift+Command+N) from the Xcode menu. Do this now. Xcode will prompt you to choose a template for your application, as shown in Figure 2.2. The Xcode templates contain the files you need to quickly start on a new development effort. Although it is possible to build an application completely from scratch, the time saved by using a template is pretty significant. We'll use several templates throughout the book, depending on what type of application we're building.

FIGURE 2.2
To create a new project, start by choosing an appropriate template.

Along the left side of the Template window are the categories of templates you can choose from. Our focus will be on the iPhone OS Application category, so be sure that it is selected.

On the right side of the display are the templates within the category, with a description of the currently highlighted template. For this tutorial, click the Window-Based Application template. Be sure that the Product selected is the iPad, and then click the Choose button.

After choosing the template, you'll be prompted for a location and a name to use when saving the project. Name the test project for this hour **HelloXcode** and click Save. Xcode will automatically create a folder with the name of the project and place all the associated files within that folder.

Within your project folder, you'll find a file with the extension .xcodeproj. This is the file you need to open to return to your project workspace after exiting Xcode.

Project Groups

After you've created or opened a project in Xcode, the interface displays an iTunes-like window for navigating the project's files. On the left side of the window, the Groups & Files list contains a logical grouping of the files within your project. Clicking the top group, called the "project group" (and named after the project), updates the list to the right and shows all the files associated with the application, as shown in Figure 2.3.

FIGURE 2.3
Use the Groups & Files list to navigate through your project resources.

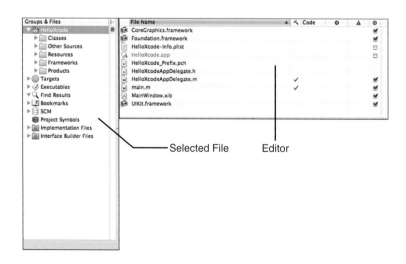

By the Way

Keep in mind that these are logical groupings. You won't find all of these files in your project directory, nor will you find the same folder structure. The Xcode layout is designed to help you find what you're looking for easily—not to mirror a file system structure.

Within the project group are five subgroups that you may find useful:

Classes: As you'll learn in the next hour, classes group together application features that complement one another. Most of your development will be within a class file.

Other Sources: These are any other source code files that are associated with the application. You'll rarely need to touch these files.

Resources: The Resources group contains the files that define the user interface, application properties, and any images, sounds, or other media files that you want to make use of within the project.

Frameworks: Frameworks are the core code libraries that give your application a certain level of functionality. By default, Xcode includes the basic frameworks for you, but if you want to add special features, such as sound or vibration, you may need an additional framework. We'll walk through the process of adding frameworks in Hour 10, "Getting the User's Attention."

Products: Anything produced by Xcode is included here (typically, the executable application).

Outside of the project group are additional groups, most of which you won't need to touch for the purposes of learning iPad development—but a few can come in handy. The Find Results group, for example, contains all the searches you execute, and the files that match. The Bookmarks group enables you to mark specific lines in your code and quickly jump to them. Finally, two smart groups (denoted by the violet folder with the gear icon) are defined by default: Implementation Files and NIB Files. Smart groups cluster together files of a particular type from throughout a project. These groups, in particular, provide quick access to the files where you'll be adding your application logic (known as *implementation files*), and the files which define your interface (NIB "now known as XIB" files).

By the Way

Didn't You Just Say My Work Would Be with the Class Files? What's This About Implementation Files?

As you'll learn in the next hour, classes are made up of two files: a header, or interface file that describes the features a class will provide; and an implementation file that actually contains the logic that makes those features work. When we say "implementation file," we're just referring to one of the two files in a class.

> If you find that you want additional logical groupings of files, you can define your own smart groups via Project, New Smart Group.

Adding New Code Files to a Project

Even though the Apple iPad templates do give you a great starting point for your development, you'll find, especially in more advanced projects, that you need to add additional code classes or interface files to supplement the base project. To add a new file to a project, choose File, New. In an interface very similar to the project templates, Xcode will prompt you, as shown in Figure 2.4, for the category and type of file that you want to add to the project. We'll be guiding you throughout the book, so don't worry if the options in the figure look alien.

FIGURE 2.4
Use Xcode to add new files to a project.

> ### Can I Add Empty Files Manually?
>
> Yes, you could drag your own files into one of the Xcode group folders and copy them into the project. However, just as a project template gives you a head start on implementation, Xcode's file templates do the same thing. They frequently include an outline for the different features that you'll need to implement to make the code functional.

Adding Existing Resources to a Project

Many applications will require sound or image files that you'll be integrating into your development. Obviously Xcode can't help you "create" these files, so you'll need to add them by hand. To do this, just click and drag the file from its location into the Resources group in Xcode. You will be prompted to copy the files. Always make sure the "copy" check box is selected so that Xcode can put the files where they need to go within your project directory.

In the downloadable project folder that corresponds with what you're building this hour, an Images folder contains a file named Icon.png. Drag this file from the Finder into to the Xcode Resources folder. Choose to copy if needed, as shown in Figure 2.5.

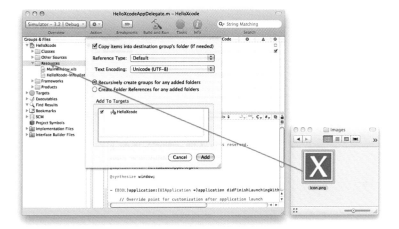

FIGURE 2.5
Drag the icon.png file into the Resources folder and choose to copy if needed.

This file will ultimately serve as the icon for the HelloXcode app.

Removing Files and Resources

If you've added something to Xcode that you decide you don't want, you can delete it easily. To remove a file or resource from your project, simply select it within one of the Xcode groups where it appears, and then press the Delete key. Xcode gives you the option to delete any references to the file from the project and move the file to the trash or just to delete the references (see Figure 2.6).

If you choose to delete references, the file itself will remain, but will no longer be visible in the project.

If Xcode can't find a file that it expects to be part of a project, that file will be highlighted in red in the Xcode interface. This might happen if you accidentally delete a file from the project folder within the Finder. It also occurs when Xcode knows that an application file will be created by a project, but the application hasn't been generated yet. In this case, you can safely ignore the red .app file within the Xcode groups.

FIGURE 2.6
Deleting a file's references leaves the actual file untouched.

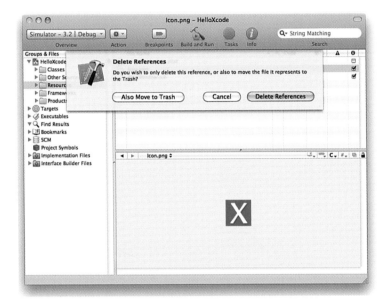

Editing and Navigating Code

To edit code in Xcode, just click the group that contains the file, and then click the filename. The editable contents of the file are shown in the lower-right pane of the Xcode interface (see Figure 2.7).

Selected File   Editor

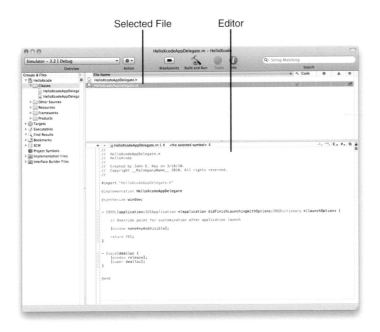

FIGURE 2.7
Choose the group, then the file, then edit!

The Xcode editor works just like any text editor, with a few nice additions. To get a feel for how it works, click the Classes group within the HelloXcode project, then HelloXcodeAppDelegate.m to begin editing the source code.

For this project, we're going to use an interface element called a label to display the text Hello Xcode on the iPad screen. This application, like most that you write, will use a method to show our greeting. A method is just a block of code that executes when something needs to happen. In this sample, we'll use an existing method called application:didFinishLaunchingWithOptions that runs as soon as the iPad application starts.

Jumping to Methods with the Symbol Menu

The easiest way to find a method or property within a source code file is to use the symbol pop-up menu, located above the editing pane. This menu, shown in Figure 2.8, will automatically show all the methods and properties available in the current file, and enables you to jump between them by selecting them.

Find and select `application:didFinishLaunchingWithOptions` from the pop-up
menu. Xcode will select the line where the method begins. Click the *next* line, and
let's start coding!

Code Completion

Using the Xcode editor, type the following text to implement the
`application:didFinishLaunchingWithOptions` method. You should only need to
enter the bolded code lines, as shown in Listing 2.1.

LISTING 2.1

```
- (BOOL)application:(UIApplication *) application
    didFinishLaunchingWithOptions:(NSDictionary *)launchOptions {

    // Override point for customization after application launch
    UILabel *myMessage;
    UILabel *myUnusedMessage;
    myMessage=[[UILabel alloc] initWithFrame:CGRectMake(190,300,500,75,50)];
    myMessage.text=@"Hello Xcode";
    myMessage.font=[UIFont systemFontOfSize:72];
    [window addSubview:myMessage];
    [myMessage release];
    [window makeKeyAndVisible];

    return YES;
}
```

As you type, you should notice something interesting happening. As soon as you get to a point in each line where Xcode thinks it knows what you intend to type, it displays an autocompleted version of the code, as demonstrated in Figure 2.9.

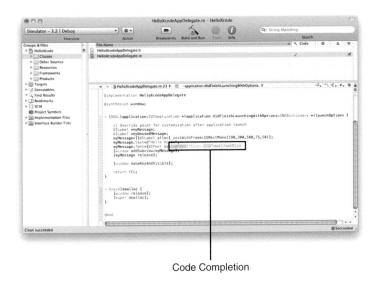

Code Completion

FIGURE 2.9
Xcode automatically completes the code as you type!

To accept an autocompletion suggestion, just press Tab, and the code will be inserted, just as if you typed the whole thing. Xcode will try to complete method names, variables that you've defined, and anything else related to the project that it might recognize.

After you've made your changes, you can save the file by choosing File, Save.

> It's not important to understand exactly what this code does—we just want to make sure you get experience in the Xcode editor. The "short and sweet" description of this fragment, however, is that it creates a label object roughly in the center of the iPad screen, sets the label's text, font, and size, and then adds it to the application's window.

Using Snapshots

If you're planning to make many changes to your code and you're not quite sure you'll like the outcome, you might want to take advantage of the "snapshot" feature. A code snapshot is, in essence, a copy of all your source code at a particular moment in time. If you don't like changes you've made, you can revert to an earlier snapshot. Snapshots are also helpful because they show what has changed between multiple versions of an application.

To take a snapshot, choose File, Make Snapshot. That's all there is to it!

To view the available snapshots, choose File, Snapshots. The snapshot viewer displays available snapshots. Clicking Show Files displays a list of changed files to the right, and, if a file is selected, the changes that were made between the selected snapshot and the preceding one. Figure 2.10 shows all of these elements.

FIGURE 2.10
Use a snapshot to figure out what changes you've made between different versions of your application.

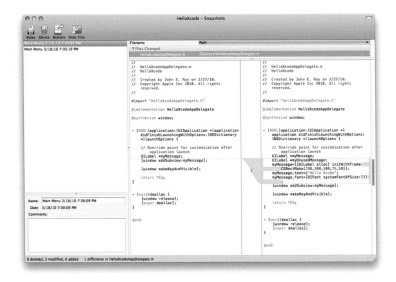

To restore to a specific snapshot, select it in the list, and then click the Restore button.

You can also use the Name and Comments fields at the bottom of the snapshot viewer to provide a meaningful name and relevant comments for any snapshot in the list.

Adding Bookmarks and Pragma Marks

Earlier in the hour, you read about the Bookmarks group, which displays bookmarks within your project and allows for simple navigation within and between files. To create a new bookmark, position your cursor in whatever portion of a file you want to mark, and then choose Add to Bookmarks from the Action menu in the toolbar (see Figure 2.11).

FIGURE 2.11
Create your own code bookmarks.

You'll be prompted for a title for the bookmark, just like in Safari. After you've saved your bookmark, you can access it from the Bookmarks group in the Groups and Files list.

Not only are the bookmarks Safari-like, but you'll also notice a History pop-up menu beside the symbol jump-to menu, and, to the left of that, forward and backward arrows to take you back and forward in the history.

Another way to mark points in your code is by adding a `#pragma mark` directive. Pragma marks do not add any features to your application, but they can be used to create sections within your code that are displayed within the symbol menu. There are two types of pragma marks:

```
#pragma mark -
```

and

```
#pragma mark <label name>
```

The first inserts a horizontal line in the symbol menu; the second inserts an arbitrary label name. You can use both together to add a section heading to your code. For example, to add a section called "Methods that update the display" followed by a horizontal line, you could type the following:

```
#pragma mark Methods that update the display
#pragma mark -
```

Once the pragma mark is added to your code and saved, the symbol menu will update appropriately.

Building Applications

After you've completed your source code, it's time to build the application. The build process encompasses several different steps, including compiling and linking. Compiling translates the instructions you type into something that the iPad understands. Linking combines your code with the necessary frameworks the application needs to run. During these steps, Xcode displays any errors that it might find.

Before building an application, you must first choose what it is being built to run on: the iPad Simulator or a physical iPad device.

Configuring the Build Output

To choose how your code will be built, use the Overview pop-up menu at the upper left of the Xcode window. There are two main settings within this menu that you may want to change: the Active SDK and the Active Configuration, visible in Figure 2.12.

Use the Active SDK setting to choose between the iPhone Device SDK and the iPhone Simulator (which we'll be exploring shortly). For most day-to-day development, you'll want to use the simulator—it is faster than transferring an application to the iPad each time you make a simple change.

By default, you have two configurations to choose from: Release and Debug. The Debug configuration adds additional debugging code to your project to help in the debugging process; we take a closer look at this in Hour 23, "Application Debugging and Optimization." The Release configuration leaves debugging code out and is what you eventually submit to the App Store.

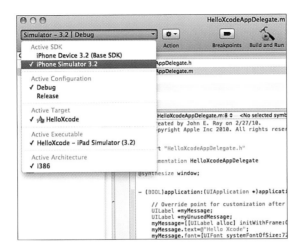

FIGURE 2.12
Change the
active SDK and
configuration
before building.

For most development, you can set the SDK to the iPhone Simulator and the Active Configuration to Debug unless you want to try real-world performance testing. Choose these options in Xcode now.

Building and Executing the Application

To build and run the application, click the Build and Run button from the Xcode toolbar (Command+R). Depending on the speed of your computer, this may take a minute or two for the process to complete. Once done, the application will be transferred to your iPad and started (if selected in the build configuration and connected) or started in the iPhone Simulator.

To just build without running the application (useful for checking for errors), choose Build from the Build menu. To run the application without building, choose Run from the Run menu.

Quite a few intermediate files are generated during the build process. These take up space and aren't needed for the project itself. To clean out these files, choose Clean All Targets from the Build menu.

The HelloXcode application is shown running in the iPhone Simulator in Figure 2.13. Try building and running your version of the application now.

FIGURE 2.13
The iPhone Simulator is a quick and easy way to test your code.

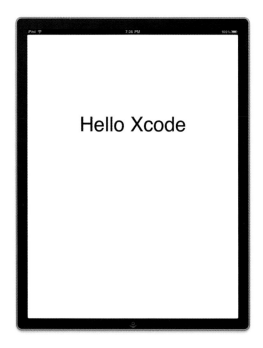

If you've been following along, your application should... *not* work! There are two problems with the code you were asked to type in earlier. Let's see what they are.

Correcting Errors and Warnings

You may receive two types of feedback from Xcode when you build an application: errors and warnings. Warnings are potential problems that may cause your application to misbehave; they are displayed as yellow caution signs. Errors, on the other hand, are complete showstoppers. You can't run your application if you have an error. The symbol for an error, appropriately enough, is a stop sign. A count of the warnings and errors is displayed in the lower-right corner of the Xcode window after the build completes.

If you are viewing the code that contains the error or warning, the error message is visible directly after the line that caused the problem. If you're in another file, you can quickly jump to a list of the errors (with links to the source code in which they occurred) by clicking the error or warning count in the Xcode window. Figure 2.14 shows an error and a warning you should be receiving in the HelloXcode app.

The warning points out that we have an unused variable, myUnusedMessage, in the code. Remember, this is just a helpful warning, not necessarily a problem. If we choose to remove the variable, the message will go away; but even if we don't, the application will still run. Go ahead and delete the line that reads UILabel *myUnusedMessage; in HelloXcodeAppDelegate.m. This fixes the warning, but there's still an error to correct.

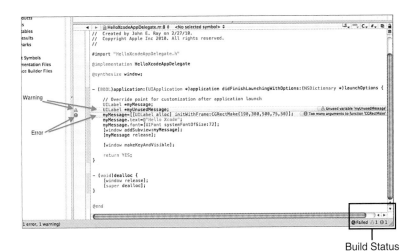

Build Status

The error message reads "too many arguments to function 'CGRectMake'." The reason for this is that the function takes four numbers and uses them to make a rectangle for the label—we've typed in five numbers. Delete the fifth number and preceding comma from the CGRectMake function.

Click Build and Run. HelloXcode should now start in the iPhone Simulator, just like what we saw in Figure 2.12.

Project Properties

Before finishing our brief tour of the Xcode interface, quickly turn your attention to a specific project component: the Info property list resource. This file, found in the Xcode Resources folder, is created automatically when you create a new project, is prefixed with the project name, and ends in Info.plist. This file contains settings that, while you won't need right away, will be necessary for deploying an application to the App Store and configuring some functionality in later hours. Click the HelloXcode-Info.plist file in Xcode now. Your display should resemble Figure 2.15.

To change a property value, double-click the right column and type your changes.

FIGURE 2.15
Project proper-
ties control a
few important
settings for your
application.

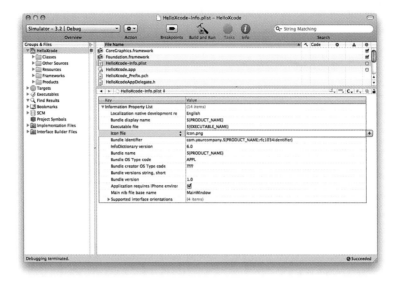

Setting an Application Icon

If you look closely at the Info properties for your project, you'll notice an Icon File property that is completely blank. To set the property to the icon that you added to the project earlier this hour, double-click the right side to enter edit mode, and then type in **Icon.png**. Ta da! You've just set the icon for your iPad application.

We've included icon files with many of the projects in this book. You're welcome to use ours, or create new icons on your own. iPad icons should be 72x72 PNG images with no special rounding or effects applied. The "glossy look" will automatically be applied to the icons for you! Apple also stresses that you should not manually add a black background to your icons. Unlike the iPhone, the iPad allows custom back-grounds on its home screens, making it likely that an icon with custom shadows or black backgrounds will clash with the display.

Setting a Project ID

Another property that you'll want to keep in the back of your mind is the Bundle Identifier. This unique ID becomes critical when publishing to the iTunes App Store. You'll learn more about this process in Hour 24, "Distributing Applications Through the App Store."

Setting the Status Bar Display

Another interesting property that you may want to explore controls the status bar (the thin line with the WiFi and battery status at the top of the iPad display). By default, this property isn't present in the Info.plist file, so you'll need to add a new row. Right-click one of the existing lines and choose Add Row.

Once a new row has appeared, click the far left column to display all the available properties. You'll notice that Status Bar Is Initially Hidden is an option. If selected, this property adds a check box in the far right column that, if checked, automatically hides the iPad status bar for your application.

Setting a Launch Image

You can also add a "launch image" option to your project that enables you to choose a "splash-screen" image that will display as your application loads. To access this setting, again, add a new row to the Info.plist file, this time choosing Launch Image (iPad) in the column on the left. You can then configure the image using the same technique used for adding an application icon, the only difference being a launch image should be sized to fit the iPad's screen.

That's it for Xcode! There's plenty more that you'll find as you work with the software, but these should be the foundational skills you need to develop apps for your iPad. We'll round out this hour by looking at the next best thing to your iPad: the Apple iPhone Simulator.

> **By the Way**
>
> Note that although we haven't covered it here, Xcode includes a wonderful documentation system. We look at this in depth as we start to get our feet wet with the Cocoa framework in Hour 4.

Using the iPhone Simulator

In Hour 1, you learned that you don't even need an iPad to start developing for the platform. The reason for this is the iPhone Simulator included with the Apple developer tools. Despite the name, the iPhone Simulator does a great job of simulating the Apple iPad, with the Safari, Contacts, Settings, and Photos apps available for integration testing, as shown in Figure 2.16.

Targeting the simulator for the early stages of your development can save you a great deal of time; you won't need to wait for apps to be installed on your physical device before seeing the effects of changes in your code. In addition, you don't need to buy and install a developer certificate to run code in the simulator.

FIGURE 2.16
The iPhone
Simulator
includes a
stripped-down
version of the
iPad apps.

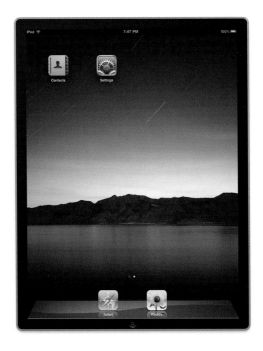

The simulator, however, is not a *perfect* iPad. It can't display OpenGL graphics, simulate complex multitouch events, or provide readings from some of the iPad sensors (GPS, accelerometer, and so on). The closest it comes on these counts is the ability to rotate to test landscape interfaces and a simple "shake" motion simulation. That said, for most apps, it has enough features to be a valuable part of your development process.

Watch
Out!

> One thing that you absolutely *cannot* count on in the simulator is that your simulated app performance will resemble your real app performance. The simulator tends to run silky smooth, whereas real apps might have more limited resources and not behave as nicely. Be sure to occasionally test on a physical device so that you know your expectations are in line with reality.

Launching Applications in the Simulator

To launch an application in the simulator, open the project in Xcode, make sure that the active SDK is set to iPhone Simulator, and then click Build and Run. After a few seconds, the simulator will launch and the application will be displayed. You can test this using the HelloSimulator project included in this hour's Projects folder.

Once up and running, the HelloSimulator app should display a simple line of text (see Figure 2.17).

When an application is running, you can interact with it using your mouse as if it were your fingertip. Click buttons, drag sliders, and so on. If you click into a field where input is expected, the iPad keyboard will display. You can "type" using your Mac keyboard, or click the keyboard's buttons onscreen. The iPhone OS's Copy and Paste services are also simulated by clicking and holding on text until the familiar loupe magnifier appears.

Clicking the virtual Home button, or choosing Hardware, Home from the menu, exits the application.

Launching an application in the simulator installs it in the simulator, just like installing an app on the iPad. When you exit the app, it will still be present on the simulator until you manually delete it.

To remove an installed application from the simulator, click and hold the icon until it starts "wiggling," and then click the X that appears in the upper-left corner. In other words, remove apps from the simulator in the exact same way you would remove them from a physical iPad!

To quickly reset the simulator back to a clean slate, choose Reset Content and Settings from the iPhone Simulator menu.

FIGURE 2.17
Click Build and Run in Xcode to launch and run your application in the simulator.

Generating Multitouch Events

Even though you have only a single mouse, simple multitouch events, such as two-finger pulls and pinches, can be simulated by holding down Option when your cursor is over the iPhone Simulator "screen." Two circles, representing fingertips, will be drawn and can be controlled with the mouse. To simulate a touch event, click and drag while continuing to hold down Option. Figure 2.18 shows the "pinch" gesture.

Try this using the HelloSimulator app. You should be able to use the simulator's multitouch capabilities to shrink or expand the onscreen text and image.

Rotating the Simulated iPad

To simulate a rotation on the iPad, choose Rotate Right or Rotate Left from the Hardware menu (see Figure 2.19). You can use this to rotate the simulator window through all four possible orientations and view the results onscreen.

FIGURE 2.18
Simulate simple multitouch with the Option key.

FIGURE 2.19
Rotate the inter-
face through the
possible orien-
tations.

Again, test this with HelloSimulator. The app will react to the rotation events and orient the text properly.

Simulating Other Conditions

You will want to test against a few other esoteric conditions in the simulator. Using the Hardware menu, you can access these additional features:

Version: Check to see how your app will behave on earlier versions of the iPhone OS. This option enables you to choose from many of the recent versions of the operating system. The earliest version of the iPad-compatible iPhone OS is 3.2.

Shake Gesture: Simulate a quick shake of the iPad.

Lock: Simulates the condition of a locked iPad. Because a user can lock an iPhone while an application is running, some developers choose to have their programs react uniquely to this situation.

Simulate Memory Warning: Triggers an application's low-memory event. Useful for testing to make sure your application exits gracefully if resources run low.

Test a few of these out on the HelloSimulator application. Figure 2.20 shows the application's reaction to a simulated memory warning.

FIGURE 2.20
The iPhone
Simulator can
test for applica-
tion handling in
several unique
conditions.

Further Exploration

You're not quite at the stage yet where we can ask you to go off and read some code-related tutorials, but if you're interested, you may want to take some time to look into more of the features offered in Xcode. Our introduction was limited to roughly a dozen pages, but entire volumes can (and have) been written about this unique tool. Anything else you need will be covered in the lessons in this book, but we still recommend reviewing Apple's *Xcode Workspace Guide*. You can find this document by choosing Help, Xcode Help from the menu while in the Xcode application.

Summary

This hour introduced you to the Xcode development environment and the core set of tools that you'll be using to create your applications. You learned how to create projects using Apple's iPad templates and how to supplement those templates with new files and resources. You also explored the editing and navigation capabilities of Xcode that you'll come to depend on every day. To illustrate the concepts, you wrote and built your first iPad application—and even corrected a few errors that we added to try to trip you up!

We finished up this hour by walking through the use of the iPhone Simulator. This tool will save wear and tear on your iPad (and your patience) as it provides a quick and easy way to test code without having to install applications on your phone.

Q&A

Q. *What is Interface Builder, and how does it fit in?*

A. Interface Builder is a very important tool that gets its own lesson in Hour 5. As the name implies, Interface Builder is mostly about creating the user interface for your applications. It is an important part of the development suite, but your interactions with it will be very different from those in Xcode.

Q. *Do I have to worry about constantly saving if I'm switching between files and making lots of changes in Xcode?*

A. No. If you switch between files in the Xcode editor, you won't lose your changes. Xcode will even prompt you to save, listing all the changed project files, if you attempt to close the application.

Q. *I notice that there are Mac OS X templates that I can access when creating a project. Can I create a Mac application?*

A. Almost all the coding skills you learn in this book can be transferred to Mac development. The iPad, however, is a somewhat different piece of hardware than the Mac, so you'll need to learn the Mac model for windowing, UI, and so on.

Q. *Can I run commercial applications on the iPhone Simulator?*

A. No. You can only run apps that you have built within Xcode.

Workshop

Quiz

1. How do you add an image resource to an iPad project?

2. Is there a facility in Xcode for easily tracking multiple versions of your project?

3. Can the iPhone Simulator be used to test your application on older versions of the iPhone OS?

Answers

1. You can add resources, including images, to an iPad project by dragging from the Finder into the project's Resources group.

2. Yes. Using the snapshot feature you can create different copies of your project at specific points in time and even compare the changes.

3. Yes. The Hardware, Versions menu can be used to choose earlier versions of the iPhone OS for testing.

Activities

1. Practice creating projects and navigating the Xcode editor. Try out some of the common editor features that were not covered in this lesson, such as Find and Replace. Test the use of pragma marks for creating helpful jump-to points within your source code.

2. Return to the Apple iPhone Dev Center and download a sample application. Using the techniques described in this hour's lesson, build and test the application in the iPhone Simulator.

HOUR 3

Discovering Objective-C: The Language of Apple Platforms

What You'll Learn in This Hour:

▶ How Objective-C will be used in your projects
▶ The basics of object-oriented programming
▶ Simple Objective-C syntax
▶ Common data types
▶ How to manage memory

This hour's lesson marks the midpoint in our exploration of the Apple iPhone OS development platform. It will give us a chance to sit back, catch our breath, and get a better idea of what it means to "code" for the iPad. Both the Macintosh and the iPad share a common development environment and, with them, a common development language: Objective-C.

Objective-C provides the syntax and structure for creating applications on Apple platforms. For many, learning Objective-C can be daunting, but with patience, it may quickly become the favorite choice for any development project. This hour takes you through the steps you need to know to be comfortable with Objective-C and starts you down the path to mastering this unique and powerful language.

Object-Oriented Programming and Objective-C

To better understand the scope of this hour, take a few minutes to search for Objective-C or object-oriented programming in your favorite online bookstore. You will find quite a few books—lengthy books—on these topics. In this book, we have roughly 20 pages to cover what these books teach in hundreds. While it's not possible to fully cover Objective-C and object-oriented development in this single hour, we can make sure that you understand enough to develop fairly complex apps.

To provide you with the information you need to be successful in iPad development, we concentrate on fundamentals—the core concepts that will be used repeatedly throughout the examples and tutorials in this book. Our approach in this hour's lesson is to introduce you to a programming topic in general terms—then look at how it will be performed when you sit down to write your application. Before we begin, let's learn a bit more about Objective-C and object-oriented programming.

What Is Object-Oriented Programming?

Most people have an idea of what programming is and have even written a simple program. Everything from setting your TiVo to record a show to configuring a cooking cycle for your microwave is a type of programming. You use data (such as times) and instructions (like "record") to tell your devices to complete a specific task. This certainly is a long way from developing for the iPad, but in a way the biggest difference is in the amount of data you can provide and manipulate and the number of different instructions available to you.

Imperative Development

There are two primary development paradigms. First, imperative programming (sometimes called procedural programming) implements a sequence of commands that should be performed. The application follows the sequence and carries out activities as directed. Although there may be branches in the sequence or movement back and forth between some of the steps, the flow is from a starting condition to an ending condition with all the logic to make things "work" sitting in the middle.

The problem with imperative programming is that it lends itself to growing, without structure, into an amorphous blob. Applications gain features when developers tack on bits of code here and there. Frequently, instructions that implement a piece of functionality are repeated over and over wherever something needs to take place. On the other hand, imperative development is something that many people can pick up and do with very little planning.

The Object-Oriented Approach

The other development approach, and what we use in this book, is object-oriented programming (OOP). OOP uses the same types of instructions as imperative development, but structures them in a way that makes your applications easy to maintain and promotes code reuse whenever possible. In OOP, you will create objects that hold the data that describes something along with the instructions to manipulate that data. Perhaps an example is in order.

Consider a program that enables you to track reminders. With each reminder, you want to store information about the event that will be taking place—a name, a time to sound an alarm, a location, and any additional miscellaneous notes that you may want to store. In addition, you need to be able to reschedule a reminder's alarm time, or completely cancel an alarm.

In the imperative approach, you have to write the steps necessary to track all the reminders, all the data in the reminders, check every reminder to see whether an alarm should sound, and so on. It's certainly possible, but just trying to wrap your mind around everything that the application needs to do could cause some serious headaches. An object-oriented approach brings some sanity to the situation.

In an object-oriented model, you could implement a reminder as a single object. The reminder object would know how to store the properties such as the name, location, and so on. It would implement just enough functionality to sound its own alarm and reschedule or cancel its alarm. Writing the code, in fact, would be very similar to writing an imperative program that only has to manage a single reminder. By encapsulating this functionality into an object, however, we can then create multiple copies of the object within an application and have them each fully capable of handling separate reminders. No fuss and no messy code!

> Most of the tutorials in this book make use of one or two objects, so don't worry about being overwhelmed with OOP. You'll see enough to get accustomed to the idea—but we're not going to go overboard!

By the Way

Another important facet of OOP is inheritance. Suppose you want to create a special type of reminder for birthdays that includes a list of birthday presents that a person has requested. Rather than tacking this onto the reminder object, you could create an entirely new "birthday reminder" that inherits all of the features and properties of a reminder, and then adds in the list of presents and anything else specific to birthdays.

The Terminology of Object-Oriented Development

OOP brings with it a whole range of terminology that you need to get accustomed to seeing in this book (and in Apple's documentation). The more familiar you are with these terms, the easier it will be to look for solutions to problems and interact with other iPad developers. Let's establish some basic vocabulary now:

Class: The code, usually consisting of a header and implementation file, which defines an object and what it can do.

Subclass: A class that builds upon another class, adding additional features. Almost everything you use in iPad development will be a subclass of something else, inheriting all of the properties and capabilities of its parent class.

Superclass/parent class: The class that another class inherits from.

Singleton: A class that is only instantiated once during the lifetime of a program. For example, a class to read your iPad's orientation is implemented as a singleton because there is only one sensor that returns tilt information.

Object/instance: A class that has been invoked and is active in your code. Classes are the code that makes an object work, while an object is the actual class "in action." This is also known as an "instance" of a class.

Instantiation: The process of creating an active object from a class.

Instance method: A basic piece of functionality, implemented in a class. For the reminder class, this might be something like `setAlarm` to set the alarm for a given reminder.

Class method: Similar to an instance method, but applicable to all the objects created from a class. The reminder class, for example, might implement a method called `countReminders` that provides a count of all the reminder objects that have been created.

Message: When you want to use a method in an object, you send the object a message (the name of the method). This process is also referred to as "calling the method."

Instance variable: A storage place for a piece of information specific to a class. The name of a reminder, for example, might be stored in an instance variable. All variables in Objective-C have a specific "type" that describes the contents of what they will be holding.

Variable: A storage location for a piece of information. Unlike instance variables, a "normal" variable is only accessible in the method where it is defined.

Parameter: A piece of information that is provided to a method when it is messaged. If you were to send a reminder object the "set alarm" method, you would presumably need to include the time to set. The time, in this case, would be a parameter used with the `setAlarm` method.

Property: An instance variable that has been configured using special directives to provide easy access from your code.

You may be wondering, if almost everything in iPad development is a subclass of something else, is there some sort of master class that "starts" this tree of inheritance? The answer is yes—the NSObject class serves as the starting point for most of the classes you'll be using on the iPad. This isn't something you'll really need to worry about in the book—just a piece of trivia to think about.

It's important to know that when you develop on the iPad, you're going to be taking advantage of hundreds of classes that Apple has already written for you! Everything from creating onscreen buttons to manipulating dates and writing files is covered by prebuilt classes. You'll occasionally want to customize some of the functionality in those classes, but you'll be starting out with a toolbar that is already overflowing with functionality.

Confused? Don't worry! We introduce these concepts slowly, and you'll quickly get a feel for how they apply to your projects as we work through several tutorials in the upcoming hours.

What Is Objective-C?

A few years ago, I would have answered this question with "one of the strangest looking languages I've ever seen." Today, I love it (and so will you!). Objective-C was created in the 1980s and is an extension of the C language. It adds many additional features to C and, most important, an OOP structure. Objective-C is primarily used for developing Mac and iPad applications, and has attracted a devoted group of followers who appreciate its capabilities and syntax.

Objective-C statements are easier to read than other programming languages and often can be deciphered just by looking at them. For example, consider the following line that compares whether the contents of a variable called myName is equal to John:

```
[myName isEqualToString:@"John"]
```

It doesn't take a very large mental leap to see what is going on in the code snippet. In traditional C, this might be written as follows:

```
strcmp(myName,"John")
```

The C statement is a bit shorter, but does little to convey what the code is actually doing.

Because Objective-C is implemented as a layer on top of C, it is still fully compatible with code that is written entirely in C. For the most part, this isn't something that you should concern yourself with, but unfortunately, Apple has left a bit of "cruft" in their iPhone OS SDK that relies on C-language syntax. You'll encounter this infrequently and it isn't difficult to code with when it occurs, but it does take away from the elegance of Objective-C just a little.

Now that you have an idea of what OOP and Objective-C are, let's take a look at how you'll be using them over the course of this book.

Exploring the Objective-C File Structure

In the last hour, you learned how to use Xcode to create projects and navigate their files. As we mentioned then, the vast majority of your time will be spent in the Classes folder of Xcode, shown in Figure 3.1. You'll be adding methods to class files that Xcode creates for you when you start a project, or occasionally, creating your own class files to implement entirely new functionality in your application.

FIGURE 3.1
Most of your coding will occur within the files in the Classes folder.

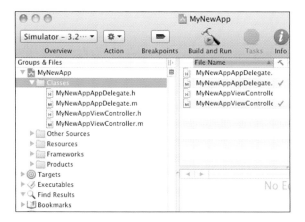

Okay, sounds simple enough, but where will the coding take place? If you create a project and look in the Classes folder, you'll see quite a few different files staring back at you.

Header/Interface Files

Creating a class creates two different files: an interface (or header) file (.h) and an implementation file (.m). The interface file is used to define a list of all of the methods and properties that your class will be using. This is useful for other pieces of code, including Interface Builder (which you'll learn about in Hour 5, "Exploring Interface Builder"), to determine how to access information and features in your class.

The implementation file, on the other hand, is where you'll go to write the code that makes everything defined in the header file work. Let's review the structure of the very short, and entirely made-up, interface file in Listing 3.1.

LISTING 3.1

```
 1: #import <UIKit/UIKit.h>
 2:
 3: @interface myClass : myParent <myProtocol> {
 4:     NSString *myString;
 5:     IBOutlet UILabel *myLabel;
 6: }
 7:
 8: +(NSString)myClassMethod:(NSString)aString;
 9:
10: -(NSDate)myInstanceMethod:(NSString)aString anotherParameter:(NSURL)aURL;
11:
12: @property (nonatomic, retain) UILabel *myLabel;
13:
14: @end
```

The #import Directive

```
 1: #import <UIKit/UIKit.h>
```

First, in line 1, the interface file uses the #import directive to include any other interface files that our application will need to access. The string <UIKit/UIKit.h> designates the specific file (in this case, UIKit, which gives us access to a vast majority of the classes). If we need to import a file, we'll be explaining how and why in the text. The UIKit example will be included by default when Xcode sets up your classes and covers most of what you'll need for this book's examples.

Wait a Sec, What's a "Directive"?

Directives are commands that are added to your files that help Xcode and its associated tools build your application. They don't implement the logic that makes your app work, but they are necessary for providing information on how your applications are structured so that Xcode knows how to deal with them.

The @interface Directive and Instance Variables

Line 3 uses the @interface directive to begin a set of lines (enclosed in {} braces) to describe all the instance variables that your class will be providing:

```
3: @interface myClass : myParent <myProtocol> {
4:   NSString *myString;
5:   IBOutlet UILabel *myLabel;
6: }
```

In this example, a variable that contains an object of type NSString named myString is declared, along with an object of type UILabel that will be referenced by the variable myLabel. An additional keyword IBOutlet is added to the front of the UILabel declaration to indicate that this is an object that will be defined in Interface Builder. You'll learn more about IBOutlet in Hour 5.

> All instance variables, method declaration lines, and property declarations must end with a semicolon (;).

Notice that line 3 includes a few additional items after the @interface directive: myClass : myParent <myProtocol>. The first of these is the name that we're giving the class that we're working on. Here, we've decided the class will be called myClass. The class name is then followed by a colon (:) and a list of the classes that this class is inheriting from (that is, the "parent" classes). Finally, the parent classes are followed by a list of "protocols" enclosed within angle brackets, <>.

> The implementation and interface files for a class will usually share the name of the class. Here, the interface file would be named myClass.h and the implementation file myClass.m.

Protocols? What's a Protocol?

Protocols are a unique feature of Objective-C that sound complicated, but really aren't. Sometimes you will come across features that require you to write methods to support their use—such as providing a list of items to be displayed in a table. The methods that you need to write are grouped together under a common name—this is known as a "protocol."

Some protocol methods are required, others are optional—it just depends on the features you need. A class that implements a protocol is said to "conform" to that protocol.

Defining Methods

Lines 8 and 10 declare two methods that need to be implemented in the class:

```
8: +(NSString)myClassMethod:(NSString)aString;
9:
10: -(NSDate)myInstanceMethod:(NSString)aString anotherParameter:(NSURL)aURL;
```

Method declarations follow a simple structure. They begin with a + or -; the + denotes a class method, while - indicates an instance method. Next, the type of information the method returns is provided in parenthesis, followed by the name of the method itself. If the method takes a parameter, the name is followed by a colon, the type of information the method is expecting, and the variable name that the method will use to refer to that information. If multiple parameters are needed, a short descriptive label is added, followed by another colon, data type, and variable name. This pattern can repeat for as many parameters as needed.

In the example file, line 8 defines a class method named myClassMethod that returns an NSString object and accepts an NSString object as a parameter. The input parameter is made available in a variable called aString.

Line 10 defines an instance method named myInstanceMethod that returns an NSDate object, also takes an NSString as a parameter, and includes a second parameter of the type NSURL that will be available to the method via the variable aURL.

> You'll learn more about NSString, NSDate, and NSURL in Hour 4, "Inside Cocoa Touch," but as you might guess, these are objects for storing and manipulating strings, dates, and URLs, respectively.

By the Way

> Very frequently you will see methods that accept or return objects of the type id. This is a special type in Objective-C that can reference any kind of object and is useful if you don't know exactly what you'll be passing to a method, or if you want to be able to return different types of objects from a single method.
>
> Another popular return type for methods is void. When you see void used, it means that the method returns *nothing*.

Did you Know?

The @property Directive

The final functional piece of the interface file is the addition of @property directives, demonstrated in line 12:

```
12: @property (nonatomic, retain) UILabel *myLabel;
```

The @property directive is used in conjunction with another command called synthesize in the implementation file to simplify how you interact with the instance variables that you've defined in your interface.

Traditionally, to interact with the objects in your instance variables, you have to use methods called *getters* and *setters* (or accessors and mutators, if you want to sound a bit more exotic). These methods, as their names suggest, get and set values in your instance variable objects. For example, a `UILabel` object, like what we're referencing with the `myLabel` instance variable in line 12, represents an onscreen text label that a user can see. The object, internally, has a variety of instance variables itself, such as color, font, and the text that is displayed. To set the text, you might write something like this:

```
[myLabel setText:@"Hello World"];
```

And to retrieve the text currently displayed, you'd use the following:

```
theCurrentLabel=[myLabel getText];
```

Not too tough, but it's not as easy as it could be. If we use `@property` and `synthesize` to define these as properties, we can simplify the code so that it looks like this:

```
myLabel.text=@"Hello World";
theCurrentLabel=myLabel.text;
```

We'll make use of this feature nearly everywhere that we need easy access to instance variables. After we've given this treatment to an instance variable, we can refer to it as a property. Because of this, you'll typically see things referred to as "properties" rather than instance variables.

Technically, you can use `@property` and `synthesize` to create a property that references an instance variable via another name. This is hardly ever used in practice and has little real value beyond serving as a point of confusion.

The attributes (`nonatomic`, `retain`) that are provided to the `@property` directive tell Xcode how to treat the property it creates. The first, `nonatomic`, informs the system that it doesn't need to worry about different parts of the application using the property at the same time, while `retain` makes sure that the object the property refers to will be kept around. These are the attributes you should use in nearly all circumstances, so get used to typing them!

Ending the Interface File

To end the interface file, add `@end` on its own line. This can be seen on line 14 of our example file:

```
14: @end
```

That's it for the interface! Although that might seem like quite a bit to digest, it covers almost everything you'll see in an interface/header file. Now let's look at the file where the actual work gets done: the implementation file.

Implementation Files

After you've defined your instance variables (or properties!) and methods in your interface file, you need to do the work of writing code to implement the logic of your application. The implementation file (.m) holds all of the "stuff" that makes your class work. Let's take a look at Listing 3.2 - a sample skeleton file myClass.m that corresponds to the interface file we've been reviewing.

Listing 3.2

```
 1: #import "myClass.h"
 2:
 3: @implementation myClass
 4:
 5: @synthesize myLabel;
 6:
 7: +(NSString)myClassMethod:(NSString)aString {
 8:     // Implement the Class Method Here!
 9: }
10:
11: -(NSString)myInstanceMethod:(NSString)aString anotherParameter:(NSURL)aURL {
12:     // Implement the Instance Method Here!
13: }
14:
15: @end
```

The #import Directive

The #import directive kicks things off in line 1 by importing the interface file associated with the class:

```
1: #import "myClass.h"
```

When you create your projects and classes in Xcode, this will automatically be added to the code for you. If any additional interface files need to be imported, you should add them to the top of your interface file rather than here.

The @implementation Directive

The implementation directive, shown in line 3, tells Xcode what class the file is going to be implementing. In this case, the file should contain the code to implement myClass:

```
3: @implementation myClass
```

The @synthesize Directive

In line 5, we use the @synthesize directive to, behind the scenes, generate the code for the getters and setters of an instance variable:

```
5: @synthesize myLabel;
```

Used along with the @property directive, this ensures that we have a straightforward way to access and modify the contents of our instance variables as described earlier.

Method Implementation

To provide an area to write your code, the implementation file must restate the method definitions, but, rather than ending them with a semicolon (;), a set of curly braces, {}, is added at the end, as shown in lines 7–9 and 11–13. All the magic of your programming will take place between these braces:

```
 7: +(NSString)myClassMethod:(NSString)aString {
 8:    // Implement the Class Method Here!
 9: }
10:
11: -(NSString)myInstanceMethod:(NSString)aString anotherParameter:(NSURL)aURL {
12:    // Implement the Instance Method Here!
13: }
```

> You can add a text comment on any line within your class files by prefixing the line with the // characters. If you'd like to create a comment that spans multiple lines, you can begin the comment with the characters /* and end with */.

Ending the Interface File

To end the implementation file, add @end on its own line just like the interface file. This can be seen on line 15 of our example:

```
15: @end
```

Structure for Free

Even though we've just spent quite a bit of time going through the structure of the interface and implementation files, you're rarely (if ever) going to need to type it all out by hand. Whenever you add a new class to your Xcode project, the structure of the file will be set up for you. Of course, you'll still need to define your variables and methods, but the @interface and @implementation directives and overall file structure will be in place before you write a single line of code.

Objective-C Programming Basics

We've explored the notion of classes, methods, and instance variables, but we still don't have a real idea of how to go about making a program do something. In this section of our lesson, we'll review several key programming tasks that you'll be using to implement your methods:

▶ Declaring variables

▶ Allocating and initializing objects

▶ Using an object's instance methods

▶ Making decisions with expressions

▶ Branching and looping

Declaring Variables

Earlier we documented what instance variables in your interface file will look like, but we didn't really get into the process of *how* you declare (or "define") them (or use them!). Instance variables are also only a small subset of the variables you'll use in your projects. Instance variables store information that is available across all the methods in your class—but they're not really appropriate for small temporary storage tasks, such as formatting a line of text to output to a user. Most commonly, you'll be declaring several variables at the start of your methods, using them for various calculations, then getting rid of them when you're done with them.

Whatever the purpose, you'll declare your variables using this syntax:

```
<Type> <Variable Name>;
```

The type is either a primitive data type, or the name of a class that you want to instantiate and use.

Primitive Data Types

Primitive data types are defined in the C language and are used to hold very basic values. Common types you'll encounter include the following:

int	Integers (whole numbers such as 1, 0, and -99)
float	Floating-point numbers (numbers with decimal points in them)
double	Highly precise floating-point numbers that can handle a large number of digits

For example, to declare an integer variable that will hold a user's age, you might enter the following:

```
int userAge;
```

After a primitive data type is declared, the variable can be used for assignments and mathematical operations. The following code, for example, declares two variables, `userAge` and `userAgeInDays`, and then assigns a value to one and calculates the other:

```
int userAge;
int userAgeInDays;
userAge=30;
userAgeInDays=userAge*365;
```

Pretty easy, don't you think? Primitive data types, however, will make up only a very small number of the variables types that you use. Most variables you declare will be used to store objects.

Object Data Types and Pointers

Just about everything that you'll be working with in your iPad applications will be an object. Text strings, for example, will be instances of the class `NSString`. Buttons that you display on the iPad screen are objects of the class `UIButton`. You'll learn about several of the common data types in the next hour's lesson. Apple has literally provided hundreds of different classes that you can use to store and manipulate data.

Unfortunately for us, for a computer to work with an object, it can't just store it like a primitive data type. Objects have associated instance variables and methods, making them far more complex. To declare a variable as an object of a specific class, we must declare the variable as a *pointer* to an object. A pointer references the place in memory where the object is stored, rather than a value. To declare a variable as a pointer, prefix the name of the variable with an asterisk. For example, to declare a variable of type `NSString` with the intention of holding a user's name, we might type this:

```
NSString *userName;
```

Once declared, you can use the variable without the asterisk. It is only used in the declaration to identify the variable as a pointer to the object.

When a variable is a pointer to an object, it is said to *reference* or *point to* the object. This is in contrast to a variable of a primitive data type, which is said to *store* the data.

Even after a variable has been declared as a pointer to an object, it still isn't ready to be used. Xcode, at this point, only knows what object you intend the variable to reference. Before the object actually exists, you must manually prepare the memory it will use and perform any initial setup required. This is handled via the processes of allocation and initialization—which we review next.

Allocating, Initializing, and Releasing Objects

Before an object can be used, memory must be allocated and the contents of the object initialized. This is handled by sending an `alloc` message to the class that you're going to be using, followed by an `init` message to what is returned by `alloc`. The syntax you'll use is this:

```
[[<class name> alloc] init];
```

For example, to declare and create a new instance of `UILabel` class, you could use the following code:

```
UILabel *myLabel;
myLabel=[[UILabel alloc] init];
```

Once allocated and initialized, the object is ready to use.

> We haven't covered the method messaging syntax in Objective-C, but we'll be doing so shortly. For now, it's just important to know the pattern for creating objects.

By the Way

Convenience Methods

When we initialized the `UILabel` instance, we *did* create a *usable* object, but it doesn't yet have any of the additional information that makes it *useful*. Properties such as what the label should say, or where it should be shown on the screen, have yet to be set. We would need to use several of the object's other methods to really make use of the object.

Sometimes, these configuration steps are a necessary evil, but Apple's classes often provide a special initialization method called a *convenience method*. These methods can be invoked to set up an object with a basic set of properties so that it can be used almost immediately.

For example, the `NSURL` class, which you'll be using later on to work with web addresses, defines a convenience method called `initWithString`.

To declare and initialize an NSURL object that points to the website http://www.teachyourselfipad.com, we might type the following:

```
NSURL *iPadURL;
iPadURL=[[NSURL alloc] initWithString:@"http://www.teachyourselfipad.com/"];
```

Without any additional work, we've allocated and initialized a URL with an actual web address in a single line of code.

Did you Know?

> In this example, we actually created *another* object, too: an `NSString`. By typing the `@` symbol followed by characters in quotes, you allocate and initialize a string. This feature exists because strings are so commonly used that having to allocate and initialize them each time you need one would make development quite cumbersome.

Using Methods and Messaging

You've already seen the methods used to allocate and initialize objects, but this is only a tiny picture of the methods you'll be using in your apps. Let's start by reviewing the syntax of methods and messaging.

Messaging Syntax

To send an object a message, give the name of the variable that is referencing the object followed by the name of the method—all within square brackets. If you're using a class method, just provide the name of the class rather than a variable name:

```
[<object variable or class name> <method name>];
```

Things start to look a little more complicated when the method has parameters. A single parameter method call looks like this:

```
[<object variable> <method name>:<parameter value>];
```

Multiple parameters look even more bizarre:

```
[<object variable> <method name>:<parameter value>
additionalParameter:<parameter value>];
```

An actual example of using a multiple parameter method looks like this:

```
[userName compare:@"John" options:NSCaseInsensitive];
```

Here an object `userName` (presumably an `NSString`) uses the `compare:options` method to compare itself to the string `"John"` in a non-case-sensitive manner. The result of this particular method is a Boolean value (true or false), which could be used as part of an expression to make a decision in your application. (We'll review expressions and decision making next!)

Throughout the lessons, we refer to methods by name. If the name includes a colon (:), this indicates a required parameter. This is a convention that Apple has used in their documentation and that we've adopted for this book.

A useful predefined value in Objective-C is nil. The nil value indicates a *lack* of any value at all. You'll use nil in some methods that call for a parameter that you don't have available. A method that receives nil in place of an object can actually pass messages to nil without creating an error—nil simply returns another nil as the result.

We'll use this a few times later in the book, which should give you a better clearer picture of why this behavior is something we'd actually *want* to happen!

Nested Messaging

Something that you'll see when looking at Objective-C code is that the result of a method is sometimes used directly as a parameter within another method. In some cases, if the result of a method is an object, a developer will send a message directly to that result.

In both of these cases, using the results directly avoids the need to create a variable to hold the results. Want an example that puts all of this together? We've got one for you!

Assume you have two NSString variables, userFirstName and userLastName, that you want to capitalize and concatenate, storing the results in another NSString called finalString. The NSString instance method capitalizedString returns a capitalized string, while stringByAppendingString takes a second string as a parameter and concatenates it onto the string invoking the message. Putting this together (disregarding the variable declarations), the code looks like this:

```
tempCapitalizedFirstName=[userFirstName capitalizedString];
tempCapitalizedSecondName=[userLastName capitalizedString];
finalString=[tempCapitalizedFirstName
    stringByAppendingString:tempCapitalizedSecondName];
```

Instead of using these temporary variables, however, you could just substitute the method calls into a single combined line:

```
finalString=[[userFirstName capitalizedString]
stringByAppendingString:[userLastName capitalizedString]];
```

This can be a very powerful means of structuring your code, but can also lead to long and rather confusing statements. Do what makes you comfortable—both approaches are equally valid and have the same outcome.

> A confession. I have a difficult time referring to using a method as sending a "message to an object." Although this is the preferred terminology for OOP, all we're really doing is executing an object's method by providing the name of the object and the name of the method.

Expressions and Decision Making

For an application to react to user input and process information, it must be capable of making decisions. Every decision in an app boils down to a "yes" or "no" result based on evaluating a set of tests. These can be as simple as comparing two values, to something as complex as checking the results of a complicated mathematical calculation. The combination of tests used to make a decision is called an *expression*.

Using Expressions

If you recall your high-school algebra, you'll be right at home with expressions. An expression can combine arithmetic, comparison, and logical operations.

A simple numeric comparison checking to see whether a variable userAge is greater than 30 could be written as follows:

```
userAge>30
```

When working with objects, we need to use properties within the object and values returned from methods to create expressions. To check to see whether a string stored in an object userName is equal to "John", we could use this:

```
[userName compare:@"John"]
```

Expressions aren't limited to the evaluation of a single condition. We could easily combine the previous two expressions to find a user who is over 30 and named John:

```
userAge>30 && [userName compare:@"John"]
```

> ### Common Expression Syntax
>
> ( )   Groups expressions together, forcing evaluation of the innermost group first
>
> ==   Tests to see whether two values are equal (e.g., userAge==30)
>
> !=   Tests to see if two values are not equal (e.g., userAge!=30)
>
> &&   Implements a logical AND condition (e.g., userAge>30 && userAge<40)
>
> || Implements a logical OR condition (e.g., userAge>30 || userAge<10)

> ! Negates the result of an expression, returning the opposite of the original
> result (e.g., !(userAge==30) is the same as userAge!=30)
>
> For a complete list of C expression syntax, you may want to refer to
> http://www.cs.drexel.edu/~rweaver/COURSES/ISTC-2/TOPICS/expr.html.

As we've said repeatedly, you're going to be spending lots of time working with complex objects and using the methods within the objects. You can't make direct comparisons or between objects as you can with simple primitive data types. To successfully create expressions for the myriad objects you'll be using, you'll need to review each object's methods and properties.

Making Decisions with if-then-else and switch Statements

Typically, depending on the outcome of the evaluated expression, different code statements are executed. The most common way of defining these different execution paths is with an if-then-else statement:

```
if (<expression>) {
  // do this, the expression is true.
} else {
  // the expression isn't true, do this instead!
}
```

For example, consider the comparison we used earlier to check a userName NSString variable to see whether its contents were set to a specific name. If we want to react to that comparison, we might write the following:

```
If ([userName compare:@"John"]) {
  userMessage=@"I like your name";
} else {
  userMessage=@"Your name isn't John, but I still like it!";
}
```

Another approach to implementing different code paths when there are potentially many different outcomes to an expression is to use a switch statement. A switch statement checks a variable for a value, and then executes different blocks of code depending on the value that is found:

```
switch (<numeric value>) {
  case <numeric option 1>:
    // The value matches this option
    break;
  case <numeric option 2>:
    // The value matches this option
    break;
  default:
    // None of the options match the number.
}
```

Applying this to a situation where we might want to check a user's age (stored in userAge) for some key milestones and then set an appropriate userMessage string if they are found, the result might look like this:

```
switch (userAge) {
  case 18:
    userMessage=@"Congratulations, you're an adult!";
    break;
  case 21:
    userMessage=@"Congratulations, you can drink champagne!";
    break;
  case 50:
    userMessage=@"You're half a century old!";
    break;
  default:
    userMessage=@"Sorry, there's nothing special about your age.";
}
```

Repetition with Loops

Sometimes you'll have a situation where you need to repeat several instructions over and over in your code. Instead of typing the lines repeatedly, you can, instead, *loop* over them. A loop defines the start and end of several lines of code. As long as the loop is running, the program executes the lines from top to bottom, and then restarts again from the top. The loops you'll use are of two types: count based and condition based.

In a count-based loop, the statements are repeated a certain number of times. In a condition-based loop, an expression determines whether a loop should occur.

The count-based loop you'll be using is called a for loop, with this syntax:

```
for (<initialization>;<test condition>;<count update>) {
  // Do this, over and over!
}
```

The three "unknowns" in the for statement syntax are a statement to initialize a counter to track the number of times the loop has executed, a condition to check to see if the loop should continue, and finally, an increment for the counter. An example of a loop that uses the integer variable count to loop 50 times could be written as follows:

```
int count;
for (count=0;count<50;count=count+1) {
  // Do this, 50 times!
}
```

The for loop starts by setting the count variable to 0. The loop then starts and continues as long as the condition of count<50 remains true. When the loop hits the bottom curly brace (}) and starts over, the increment operation is carried out and count is increased by 1.

> In C and Objective-C, integers are usually incremented by using ++ at the end of the variable name. In other words, rather than using count=count+1, most frequently you'll encounter count++, which does the same thing. Decrementing works the same way, but with --.

Did you Know?

In a condition-based loop, the loop continues either while an expression remains true. There are two variables of this loop type that you'll encounter, while and do-while:

```
while (<expression>) {
    // Do this, over and over, while the expression is true!
}
```

and

```
do {
    // Do this, over and over, while the expression is true!
} while (<expression>);
```

The only difference between these two loops is when the expression is evaluated. In a standard while loop, the check is done at the beginning of the loop. In the do-while loop, however, the expression is evaluated at the end of every loop.

For example, suppose you are asking users to input their name and you want to keep prompting them until they type John, you might format a do-while loop like this:

```
do {
    // Get the user's input in this part of the loop
} while (![userName compare:@"John"]);
```

The assumption is that the name is stored in a string object called userName. Because you wouldn't have requested the user's input when the loop first starts, you would use a do-while loop to put the test condition at the end. Also, the value returned by the string compare method has to been negated with the ! operator, because you want to continue looping as long as the comparison of the userName to John *isn't* true.

Loops are a very useful part of programming, and, along with the decision statements, will form the basis for structuring the code within your object methods. They allow code to branch and extend beyond a linear flow.

Although we can't paint an all-encompassing picture of programming, this should give you some sense of what to expect in the rest of the book. We'll close out the hour with a topic that causes quite a bit of confusion for beginning developers: memory management.

Memory Management

In the first hour of this book, you learned a bit about the limitations of the iPad as a platform. One of the biggies, unfortunately, is the amount of memory that your programs have available to them. Because of this, you must be extremely judicious in how you manage memory.

The iPad doesn't clean up memory for you. Instead, you must keep track of your memory usage manually. This is such an important notion, in fact, that we've broken it out into its own section.

Releasing Objects

Each time you allocate memory for an object, you're using up memory on the iPad. If you allocate too many objects, you run out of memory and your application crashes or is forced to quit. To avoid a memory problem, you should only keep objects around long enough to use them, and then get rid of them. When you are finished using an object, you can send the `release` message (or "call the `release` method" if you prefer that semantic), like this:

```
[<variable> release];
```

Consider the earlier example of allocating an instance of NSURL:

```
NSURL *iPadURL;
iPadURL=[[NSURL alloc] initWithString:@"http://www.teachyourselfipad.com/"];
```

Suppose that after you allocate and initialize the URL, you use it to load a web page. Once the page is loaded, there's no sense in having the URL sitting around taking up memory. To tell Xcode that you no longer have a need for it, you can use the following:

```
[iPadURL release];
```

Using the `autorelease` Method

In some instances, you may allocate an object, and then have to pass that object off to another method to use as it pleases. In a case like this, you can't directly release the object, because you are no longer in control of it. If you find yourself in a position where an object is "out of your hands," so to speak, you can still indicate that you are done with it and absolve yourself of the responsibility of releasing it. To do this, use the `autorelease` method:

```
[<variable> autorelease];
```

The `autorelease` method shouldn't be used unless `release` can't be. Objects that are autoreleased are added to a pool of objects that are *occasionally* automatically released by the iPad system. This isn't nearly as efficient as taking care of it yourself.

By the Way

Retaining Objects

On some occasions, you may not be directly responsible for creating an object. (It may be returned from another method, for example.) Depending on the situation, you may actually need to be worried about it being released before you're done using it. To tell the system that an object is still needed, you can use its `retain` method:

```
[<variable> retain];
```

Again, you'll want to release the object when you've completed using it.

Retain and Release, Behind the Scenes

Behind the scenes, the iPad maintains a "retain" count to determine when it can get rid of an object. For example, when an object is first allocated, the "retain" count is incremented. Any use of the `retain` message on the object also increases the count.

The `release` message, on the other hand, decrements the count. As long as the retain count remains above zero, the object will not be removed from memory. When the count reaches zero, the object is considered unused and is removed.

By the Way

Releasing Instance Methods in `dealloc`

Instance variables are unique in that they usually stick around for as long as an object exists—so, when do they get released? To release instance variables, you add the appropriate release lines to a method called `dealloc` that will exist in each of your classes. By default, this method has a single line that calls its parent class's `dealloc` method. You should add your release messages prior to this. An implementation of `dealloc` that releases an instance variable called `myLabel` would read as follows:

```
- (void)dealloc {
  [myLabel release];
  [super dealloc];
}
```

Because managing memory is such a critical piece of creating an efficient and usable iPad application, we make a point of indicating when you should release objects throughout the text—both for variables you use in your methods and instance variables that are defined for your classes.

Rules for Releasing

If you find yourself looking at your code wondering what you should release and what you shouldn't, there are a few simple rules that can help:

▶ Variables that hold primitive data types do not need to be released.

▶ If you allocate an object, you are responsible for releasing it.

▶ If you use `retain` to keep an object around, you need to send a `release` when you're done with it.

▶ If you use a method that allocates and returns an object on its own, you are not responsible for releasing it.

▶ You are not responsible for releasing strings that are created with the `@"text string"` syntax.

As with everything, practice makes perfect and you'll have plenty of opportunities for applying what you've learned in the book's tutorials.

Keep in mind that a typical book would spend multiple chapters on these topics, so our goal has been to give you a starting point that future hours will build on, not to define everything you'll ever need to know about Objective-C and OOP.

Further Exploration

Although you can be successful in learning iPad programming without spending hours and hours learning more Objective-C, you will find it easier to create complex applications if you become more comfortable with the language. Objective-C, as we've said, is not something that can be described in a single hour. It has a far-reaching feature set that makes it a powerful and elegant development platform.

To learn more about Objective-C, we recommend *Programming in Objective-C 2.0, Second Edition* (Addison-Wesley Professional, 2009), *Mac OS X Advanced Development Techniques* (Sams, 2003), and *Xcode 3 Unleashed* (Sams, 2008).

Of course, Apple has its own Objective-C documentation that you can access directly from within the Xcode documentation tool. (You'll learn more about this in the next hour.) I recommend the following documents provided by Apple:

Learning Objective-C: A Primer

Object-Oriented Programming with Objective-C

The Objective-C 2.0 Programming Language

You can read these within Xcode, or via the online Apple iPhone OS Reference Library at http://developer.apple.com/iphone/library. One quick warning: These documents total several hundred pages in length, so you may want to continue your Objective-C education in parallel with the iPad lessons in this book.

Summary

In this hour, you learned about object-oriented development and the Objective-C language. Objective-C will form the structure of your applications and give you tools to collect and react to user input and other changes. After reading this hour's lesson, you should understand how to make classes, instantiate objects, call methods, and use decision and looping statements to create code that implements more complex logic than a simple top-to-bottom workflow. You should also have an understanding of memory management on the iPad and how to free memory used by objects that you have instantiated.

Much of the functionality that you'll be using in your applications will come from the hundreds of built-in classes that Apple provides within the iPhone OS SDK, which we'll delve into in Hour 4.

Q&A

Q. *Is Objective-C on the iPad the same as on Mac OS X?*

A. For the most part, yes. One of the big differences, however, is that Mac OS X implements automatic garbage collection, meaning that much of the memory management is handled for you, rather than the manual process used on the iPad.

Q. *Can an* `if-then-else` *statement be extended beyond evaluating and acting on a single expression?*

A. Yes. The if-then-else statement can be extended by adding another if statement after the else:

```
if (<expression>) {
    // do this, the expression is true.
} else if (<expression>) {
    // the expression isn't true, do this instead.
} else {
    // Neither of the expressions are true, do this anyway!
}
```

You can continue expanding the statement with as many else-ifs as you need.

Q. *Why are primitive data types used at all? Why aren't there objects for everything?*

A. Primitive data types take up much less memory than objects, and are much easier to manipulate than objects. Implementing a simple integer within an object would add a layer of complexity and inefficiency that just isn't needed.

Q. *Why do I have to release objects that exist for the entire lifetime of my application. Won't they just go away when it quits?*

A. It's good practice. Even if your application is quitting, it is still responsible for cleaning up after itself.

Workshop

Quiz

1. When creating a subclass, do you have to rewrite all the methods in from the parent class?

2. What is the basic syntax for allocating and initializing an object?

3. What does the `release` message do?

Answers

1. No. The subclass inherits all the methods of the parent class.

2. To allocate and initialize an object, use the syntax `[[<class name> alloc] init]`.

3. Sending the `release` message to an object decrements the object's retain count. When the count is zero, the object is removed from memory.

Activities

1. Start Xcode and create a new project using the iPad View-Based Application template. Review the contents of the classes in the Xcode Classes folder. With the information you've read in this hour, you should now be able to read and navigate the structure of these files.

2. Return to the Apple iPhone OS Dev Center (http://developer.apple.com/iphone/library) and begin reviewing the Learning Objective-C: A Primer tutorial.

HOUR 4

Inside Cocoa Touch

What You'll Learn in This Hour:

▶ What is Cocoa Touch and what makes it unique

▶ The technology layers that make up the iPhone OS Platform

▶ A basic iPad application life cycle

▶ Common classes and development techniques you'll be using

▶ How to find help using the Apple developer documentation

When computers first started to appear in households almost 30 years ago, applications rarely shared common interface elements. It took an instruction manual just to figure out the key sequence to exit from a piece of software. Today, user interfaces have been standardized so that moving from application to application doesn't require starting from scratch.

What has made this possible? Not faster processors or better graphics, but frameworks that enforce consistent implementation of the features provided by the device they're running on. In this hour, we'll take a look at the frameworks you'll be using in your iPad applications.

What Is Cocoa Touch?

In the last hour, you learned about the Objective-C language, the basic syntax, and what it looks like. Objective-C will form the functional skeleton of your applications. It will help you structure your applications, make logical decisions during the life cycle of your application, and enable you to control how and when events will take place. What Objective-C doesn't provide, however, is a way to access what makes your iPad the compelling touch-driven platform that it is.

Consider the following "Hello World" application:

```
int main(int argc, char *argv[]) {
    printf("Hello World");
}
```

This code is typical of a beginner "Hello World" application written in C. It will compile and execute on the iPad, but because the iPad relies on Cocoa Touch for creating interfaces and handling user input and output, this version of "Hello World" is quite meaningless. Cocoa Touch is the collection of software frameworks that is used to build iPhone OS applications, and the runtime that those applications are executed within. Cocoa Touch includes hundreds of classes for managing everything from buttons to URLs.

Cocoa Touch is the highest of several "layers" of services in the iPhone OS, and isn't necessarily the only layer that you'll be developing in. That said, there really isn't a need to worry too much about where Cocoa Touch begins and ends—the development will be the same, regardless. We'll give an overview of complete OS service layers later in the hour.

Returning to the "Hello World" example, if we had defined a text label object named iPadOutput within a project, we could set it to read "Hello World" using Objective-C and the appropriate Cocoa Touch class property like this:

```
[iPadOutput.text=@"Hello World"];
```

Seems simple enough, as long as we know that the UILabel object has a text property, right?

Keeping Your Cool in the Face of Overwhelming Functionality

The questions that should be coming to most beginners right about now include "I know there are many different features provided through iPad applications, how in the world will this book document all of them? How will I ever find what I need to use for my own applications?"

These are great questions, and probably some of the biggest concerns that I've heard from individuals who want to program for the platform, but have no idea where to start. The bad news is that we can't document everything. We can cover the fundamentals that you need to start building, but even in a multivolume set of "teach yourself" books, there is so much depth to what is provided by Cocoa Touch that it isn't feasible to document a complete how-to reference.

The good news is that Cocoa Touch and the Apple developer tools encourage exploration. In Hour 6, Model-View-Controller Application Design," you'll start building interfaces visually using the Interface Builder application. As you drag objects (buttons, text fields, and so on) to your interface, you will be creating instances of Cocoa Touch classes. The more you "play," the quicker you will begin to recognize class names and properties and the role they play in development. Even better, Xcode's developer documentation provides a complete reference to Cocoa Touch—allowing you to search across all available classes, methods, properties, and so on. We'll take a look at the documentation tool later this hour.

Young, Yet Mature

One of the most compelling advantages to programming using Cocoa Touch versus platforms such as Android or the Palm Pre is that while the iPhone OS family is a "young" platform for Apple, the Cocoa frameworks are quite mature. Cocoa was borne out of the NeXTSTEP platform—the environment that was used by NeXT computers in the mid-1980s. In the early 90s, NeXTSTEP evolved into the cross-platform OpenStep. Finally, in 1996, Apple purchased NeXT Computer, and over the next decade the NeXTSTEP/OpenStep framework became the de facto standard for Macintosh development and was renamed Cocoa. You'll notice that there are still signs of Cocoa's origins in class names that begin with NS.

What Is the Difference Between Cocoa and Cocoa Touch?   *By the Way*

Cocoa is the development framework used for most native Mac OS X applications. The iPad, although based on many of the foundational technologies of Mac OS X, isn't quite the same. Cocoa Touch is heavily customized for a touch interface and working within the constraints of a handheld system. Desktop application components that would traditionally require extensive screen real estate have been replaced by simpler multiple-view components, mouse clicks with "touch up" and "touch down" events.

The good news is that if you decide to make the transition from iPhone OS developer to Mac developer, you'll follow many of the same development patterns on both platforms—it won't be like starting from scratch.

Exploring the iPhone OS Technology Layers

Apple describes the technologies implemented within the iPhone operating system as a series of layers, with each layer being made up of different frameworks that can be used in your applications. As you might expect, the Cocoa Touch layer is at the top (see Figure 4.1).

FIGURE 4.1
The technology
layers that
make up the
iPhone OS.

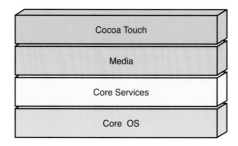

Let's review some of the most important frameworks that make up each of the layers.

> Apple has included three important frameworks in every iPad application template (CoreGraphics, Foundation, and UIKit). These frameworks are all that is needed for simple iPad applications, and will cover most of what you do in this book. When additional frameworks are needed, we describe how to include them in your projects.

The Cocoa Touch Layer

The Cocoa Touch layer is made up of several frameworks that will provide the core functionality for your applications. Of these, UIKit could be described as the "rock star"—delivering much more than the UI in its name implies.

UIKit

UIKit covers a wide range of functionality. It is responsible for application launching and termination, controlling the interface and multitouch events, and providing access to common views of data (including web pages and Word and Excel documents, among others).

UIKit is also responsible for many intra-iPad integration features. Accessing the media library, photo library, and accelerometer is also accomplished using the classes and methods within UIKit.

Map Kit

The Map Kit framework enables developers to add Google Map views to any application, including annotation, location, and event-handling features.

Game Kit

The Game Kit framework adds network-interactivity to iPad applications. Game Kit supplies mechanisms for creating and using peer-to-peer networks, including session discovery, mediation, and voice chat. These features can be added to any application, game or not!

Message UI/Address Book UI

Apple is sensitive to the need for integration between iPad applications. The Message UI and Address Book UI frameworks can be used to enable email composition and contact access from any application you develop.

The Media Layer

When Apple makes a computing device, you'd better believe that they put some thought into the media capabilities. The iPad can create complex graphics, play back audio and video, and even generate real-time three-dimensional graphics. The Media layer's frameworks handle it all.

Audio Toolbox

The Audio Toolbox framework exposes methods for handling the playback and recording of audio on the iPad. It also includes System Sound Services, which can be used for playing alert sounds or generating short vibrations.

OpenGL ES

OpenGL ES is a subset of the popular OpenGL framework for embedded systems (ES). OpenGL ES can be used to create 2D and 3D animation on the iPad. Using OpenGL requires additional development experience beyond Objective-C, but can generate amazing scenes for a handheld device—similar to what is possible on modern game consoles.

Media Player

The Media Player framework provides you, the developer, with an easy way to play back movies with typical onscreen controls. The player can be invoked directly from your application.

Core Graphics

Use the Core Graphics framework to add 2D drawing and compositing features to your applications. Although most of this book will use existing interface classes and images in its applications, you can use core graphics to programmatically manipulate the iPad's view.

Quartz Core

The Quartz Core framework is used to create animations that will take advantage of the hardware capabilities of your iPad. This includes the feature set known as Core Animation.

The Core Services Layer

The Core Services layer is used to access lower-level operating system services, such as file access, networking, and many common data object types. You'll make use of core services frequently by way of the Foundation framework.

Foundation

The Foundation framework provides an Objective-C wrapper around features in Core Foundation. Manipulation of strings, arrays, and dictionaries is handled through the Foundation framework, as are other fundamental application necessities, including managing application preferences, threads, and internationalization.

Core Foundation

Core Foundation provides much of the same functionality of the Foundation framework, but is a procedural C framework, and therefore requires a different development approach that is, arguably, less efficient than Objective-C's OO model. You should probably avoid Core Foundation unless you absolutely need it.

Core Location

The Core Location framework can be used to obtain latitude and longitude information from the iPad 3G's GPS (WiFi-based location service in the WiFi-only version of the device) along with a measurement of precision.

Core Data

The Core Data framework can be used to create the data model of iPad applications. Core Data provides a relational data model based on SQLite, and can be used to bind data to interface objects to eliminate the need for complex data manipulations in code.

Store Kit

The Store Kit framework enables developers to create in-application transactions for purchasing content without exiting the software. All interactions take place through the App Store, so no financial data is requested or transmitted through the Store Kit methods.

System Configuration

Use the System Configuration framework to determine the current state of the iPad network configuration—what network it is connected to (if any), and what devices are reachable.

The Core OS Layer

The Core OS layer, as you'd expect, is made up of the lowest-level services in the iPhone OS. These features include threads, hardware accessories, network services, and cryptography. You should only need to access these frameworks in rare circumstances.

CFNetwork

The CFNetwork provides access to BSD sockets, HTTP and FTP protocol requests, and Bonjour discovery.

External Accessory

The External Accessory framework is used to develop interfaces to accessories connected via the dock connector or Bluetooth.

Security

The Security framework provides functions for performing cryptographic functions (encrypting/decrypting data). This includes interacting with the iPad keychain to add, delete, and modify items.

System

The System framework gives developers access to a subset of the typical tools they would find in an unrestricted UNIX development environment.

Tracing the iPad Application Life Cycle

To help you get a sense for where your "work" in developing an iPad application fits in, it helps to look at the iPad application life cycle. Apple's simplified diagram of the life cycle is pictured in Figure 4.2.

FIGURE 4.2
The life cycle of a typical iPad application.

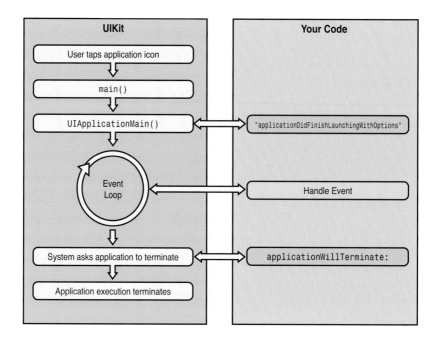

Let's try to put some context around what you're looking at, starting on the left side of the diagram. As you've learned, UIKit is a component of the Cocoa Touch that provides much of the foundation of iPad applications—user interface management, event management, and overall application execution management. When you create an iPad application, UIKit handles the setup of the application object via the main and UIApplicationMain functions—neither of which you should need to touch.

Once the application is started, an event loop begins. This loop receives the events such as screen touches, and then hands them off to your own methods. The loop continues until the application is asked to terminate (usually through the user pushing the iPad's Home button).

Your code comes into play on the right side of the diagram. Xcode will automatically set up your iPad projects to include an application delegate class. This class can implement the methods application:didFinishLaunchingWithOptions and application:willTerminate (among others) so that your program can execute its own custom code once the application launches and when it is exiting.

After an application finishes launching, the delegate object typically creates a view controller object and view, and adds them to the iPad "window." We'll learn more about these concepts in the next hour, but for now, think of a view as what is being displayed on the iPad screen, and the view controller as an object that can be programmed to respond when it receives an event notification (such as touching a button) from the event loop.

The majority of your work will take place within the view controller. You'll receive events from the Cocoa Touch interface and react to them by writing Objective-C code that manipulates other objects within the view. Of course, things can get a bit more complex than a single view and a single view controller, but the same basic approach can be applied in most cases.

Now that we have a better picture of the iPhone OS service layers and application life cycle, let's take a look at some of the classes that you'll be seeing throughout this book.

Cocoa Fundamentals

Hundreds of classes are available in the iPhone SDK, but most of your applications will be using a small set of classes to implement 90% of their features. To get you familiarized with the classes and their purposes, let's review some of the names you're going to be seeing very, very frequently over the next few hours. Before we begin, there are a few key points to keep in mind:

▶ Apple sets up much of the structure of your application for you in Xcode. This means that even though you need some of these classes, you won't have to lift a finger to use them. Just create a new Xcode project and they're added for you.

▶ You'll be adding instances of many of these objects to your projects just by dragging icons in the Interface Builder application. Again, no coding needed!

▶ When a class is used, we'll tell you why it is needed, what it does, and how it is used in the project. We don't want you to have to jump around digging for references in the book, so focus on the concepts, not memorization.

▶ In the next section of this hour's lesson, you'll learn about the Apple documentation tools. These helpful utilities will enable you to find all the class, property, and method information that you could ever hope for. If it's gritty details you want, you'll have them at your fingertips!

Core Application Classes

When you create a new application with even the most basic user interaction, you'll be taking advantage of a collection of common core classes. Many of these you won't be touching, but they still perform an important role. Let's review several of these classes now.

The Root Class (NSObject)

As you learned in Hour 3, "Discovering Objective-C: The Language of Apple Platforms," the power of object-oriented programming is that when you create a subclass of an object, you inherit that object's functionality. The root class, from which almost all Objective-C classes inherit, is NSObject. This object defines methods common to all classes, such as alloc, dealloc, and init. You will not need to create NSObject instances manually in this book, but you will use methods inherited from this class to create and manage new objects.

The Application Object (UIApplication)

Every application on the iPad implements a subclass of UIApplication. This class handles events, such as notification of when an application has finished loading, as well as application configuration, such as controlling the status bar and setting badges (the little red numbers that can appear on application icons). Like NSObject, you won't need to create this yourself; just be aware it exists.

Window Objects (UIWindow)

The UIWindow class provides a container for the management and display of views. In iPad-speak, a view is more like a typical desktop application "window," whereas an instance of UIWindow is just a container that holds the view. You will be using only a single UIWindow instance in this book, and it will be created automatically in the project templates that Xcode provides for us.

Views (UIView)

The UIView class defines a rectangular area and manages all the onscreen display within that region—what we will refer to as a view. Most of your applications will start by adding a view to an instance of UIWindow.

Views can be nested to form a hierarchy; they rarely exist as a single object. A top-level view, for example, may contain a button and field. These controls would be referred to as subviews and the containing view as the superview. Multiple levels of views can be nested, creating a complex hierarchy of subviews and superviews. You'll be creating almost all of your views visually in Interface Builder, so don't worry: Complex doesn't mean difficult!

Where Are My Windows?

You might be getting the impression that the iPad doesn't have "windows"—and you're mostly right. Windows don't translate well into an application on a touch platform. Imagine trying to access the standard close, minimize, and expand buttons on the iPad (and trying to manage a complex set of application windows like in Photoshop). You should quickly see the problem with traditional "window" interfaces.

To get around the use of windows, Apple has provided a number of different tools to hide and show information within a view. Popovers and modal dialogs, for example, can appear over existing content (much like a window) and present the user with choices or tasks. Thinking outside the desktop metaphor can take time, but when you start playing with these interface elements later in the book, you'll see that the iPad approach leads to user and touch-friendly applications.

Responders (UIResponder)

The UIResponder class provides a means for classes that inherit from it to respond to the touch events produced by the iPad. UIControl, the superclass for virtually all onscreen controls, inherits from UIView, and subsequently, UIResponder. An instance of UIResponder is just called a responder.

Because there can be multiple objects that could potentially respond to an event, the iPad will pass events up what is referred to as a chain of responders. The responder instance that can handle the event is given the designation first responder. When you're editing a field, for example, the field has first responder status because it is actively handling user input. When you leave the field, it "resigns" first responder status. For most of your iPad development work, you won't be directly managing responders in code.

Onscreen Controls (UIControl)

The UIControl class inherits from UIView and is used as the superclass for almost all onscreen controls, such as buttons, fields, popovers, and sliders. This class is responsible for handling the triggering of actions based on touch events, such as "pressing" a button.

As you'll learn in the next hour, a button defines a handful of events that you can respond to; Interface Builder gives you a means of tying those events to actions that you've coded. UIControl is responsible for implementing this behavior behind the scenes.

View Controllers (`UIViewController`)

You'll be using the `UIViewController` class in almost all the application projects throughout this book to manage the contents of your views. You'll use a `UIViewController` subclass, for example, to determine what to do when a user taps a button. Make a sound? Display an image? However you choose to react, the code you use to carry out your action will be implemented as part of a view controller instance. You'll learn much more about view controllers over the next 2 hours.

Data Type Classes

An object can potentially hold data. In fact, most of the classes we'll be using contain a number of properties that store information about an object. There are, however, a set of Foundation classes that you'll be using throughout this book for the sole purpose of storing and manipulating information.

> If you've used C/C++ before, you may find that these data type objects are similar to data types already defined outside of Apple's frameworks. By using the Foundation framework implementations, you gain access to a wide range of methods and features that go well beyond the C/C++ data types. You will also be able to work with the objects in Objective-C using the same development patterns as any other object.

Strings (`NSString/NSMutableString`)

Strings are collections of characters—numbers, letters, and symbols. You'll be using strings to collect user input and to create and format user output frequently throughout the book.

As with many of the data type objects you'll be using, there are two string classes: `NSString` and `NSMutableString`. The difference, as the name describes, is that one of the classes can be used to create strings that can be changed (mutable). An `NSString` instance remains static once it is initialized, whereas an `NSMutableString` can be changed (lengthened, shortened, replaced, and so on).

Strings are used so frequently in Cocoa Touch applications that you can create and initialize an `NSString` using the notation `@"<my string value>"`. For example, if you needed to set the `text` property of an object called `myLabel` to a new string that reads `"Hello World!"`, you could use the following:

```
myLabel.text=@"Hello World!"
```

Strings can also be initialized with the values of other variables, such as integers, floating-point numbers, and so on.

Arrays (NSArray/NSMutableArray)

A useful category of data type is a collection. Collections enable your applications to store multiple pieces of information in a single object. An NSArray is an example of a collection data type that can hold multiple objects, accessed by a numeric index.

You might, for instance, create an array that contains all the user feedback strings you want to display in an application:

```
myMessages = [[NSArray alloc] initWithObjects: @"Good Job!",@"Bad job!",nil]
```

A nil value is always used to end the list of objects when initializing an array. To access the strings, you use the index value. This is the number that represents its position in the list, starting with 0. To return the "Bad job!" message, we would use the objectAtIndex method:

```
[myMessages objectAtIndex: 1]
```

As with strings, there is a mutable NSMutableArray class that creates an array capable of being changed after it has been created.

Dictionaries (NSDictionary/NSMutableDictionary)

Like arrays, dictionaries are another collection data type, but with an important difference. Whereas the objects in an array are accessed by a numeric index, dictionaries store information as object/key pairs. The key is an arbitrary string, whereas the object can be anything you want, such as a string. If the previous array were to be created as an NSDictionary instead, it might look like this:

```
myMessages = [[NSDictionary alloc] initwithObjectsAndKeys:@"Good
Job!",@"positive",@"Bad Job!",@"negative",nil];
```

Now, instead of accessing the strings by a numeric index, they can be accessed by the keys "positive" and "negative" with the objectForKey method, as follows:

```
[myMessages objectForKey:@"negative"]
```

Dictionaries are useful because they let you store and access data in abstract ways rather than in a strict numeric order. Once again, the mutable form of the dictionaries, NSMutableDictionary, can be modified after it has been created.

Numbers (NSNumber/NSDecimalNumber)

We can store strings and collections of objects, but what about numbers? Working with numbers is a bit different. In general, if you need to work with an integer, you'll use the C data type int, and for floating-point numbers, float. You won't need to worry about classes and methods and object-oriented programming at all.

So, what about the classes that refer to numbers? The purpose of the `NSNumber` class is to take a numeric C data type and store it as an `NSNumber` object. The following line creates a number object with the value 100:

```
myNumberObject = [NSNumber alloc]numberWithInt: 100]
```

You can then work with the number as an object—adding it to arrays, dictionaries, and so on. `NSDecimalNumber`, a subclass of `NSNumber`, can be used to perform decimal arithmetic on very large numbers, but will only be needed in special cases.

Dates (`NSDate`)

If you've ever tried to work with a date manually (interpreting a date string in a program, or even just doing date arithmetic by hand), you know it can be a great cause of headaches. How many days were there in September? Was this a leap year? And so on. The `NSDate` class provides a convenient way to work with dates as an object.

For example, assume you have a user-provided date (`userDate`) and you want to use it for a calculation, but only if it is earlier than the current date, in which case, you want to use *that* date. Typically, this would be a bunch of nasty comparisons and assignments. With `NSDate`, you would create a date object with the current date in it (provided automatically by the `init` method):

```
myDate=[NSDate alloc] init]
```

And then grab the earlier of the two dates using the `earlierDate` method:

```
[myDate earlierDate: userDate]
```

Obviously, you can perform many other operations, but you can avoid much of the ugliness of data and time manipulation using `NSDate` objects.

URLs (`NSURL`)

URLs are certainly a different type of data from what we're accustomed to thinking about, but on an Internet-connected device like the iPad, you'll find that the ability to manipulate URLs comes in very handy. The `NSURL` class will enable you to manage URLs with ease. For example, suppose you have the URL http://www.floraphotographs.com/index.html and want to get just the machine name out of the string? You could create an `NSURL` object:

```
MyURL=[[NSURL alloc] initWithString:
@"http://www.floraphotographs.com/index.html"]
```

Then use the host method to automatically parse the URL and grab the text www.floraphotographs.com:

```
[MyURL host]
```

This will come in very handy as you start to create Internet-enabled applications. Of course, many more data type objects are available, and as we mentioned earlier, some objects store their own data, so you won't, for example, need to maintain a separate string object to correspond to the text in labels that you have onscreen.

Speaking of labels, let's round out our introduction to common classes with a quick look at some of the UI elements that you'll be adding to your applications.

Interface Classes

Part of what makes the iPad such a fun device to use are the onscreen touch interfaces that you can create. As we explore Interface Builder in the next hour, you'll get your first hands-on experience with some of these interface classes. Something to keep in the back of your head as you read through this section is that many UI objects can take on very different visual appearance based on how they are configured—so there is quite a bit of flexibility in your presentation

Labels (UILabel)

You'll be adding labels to your applications both to present static text onscreen (as a typical label) and as a controllable block of text that can be changed as needed by your program (see Figure 4.3).

A Label (UILabel)

FIGURE 4.3
Labels add text to your application views.

Buttons (UIButton)

Buttons are one of the simplest user input methods that you'll be using. Buttons can respond to a variety of touch events and give your users an easy way to make onscreen choices (see Figure 4.4).

A Button (UIButton)

FIGURE 4.4
Buttons provide a simple form of user input/ interaction.

Switches (`UISwitch`)

A switch object can be used to collect "on" and "off" responses from a user. It is displayed as a simple toggle and is frequently used to activate or deactivate application features (see Figure 4.5).

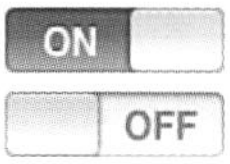

FIGURE 4.5
A switch moves
between on and
off states.

Segmented Control (`UISegmentedControl`)

A segmented control creates an elongated touchable bar with multiple named selections (Category 1, Category 2, and so on). Touching a selection will activate it and can trigger your application to perform an action, such as updating the screen to hide or show other controls (see Figure 4.6).

FIGURE 4.6
Segmented con-
trols can be
used to choose
one item out of
a set and react
accordingly.

Sliders (`UISlider`)

A slider provides the user with a draggable bobble for the purpose of choosing a value from across a range. Sliders, for example, are used to control volume, screen brightness, and other inputs that should be presented in an "analog" fashion (see Figure 4.7).

FIGURE 4.7
Sliders offer a
visual means of
entering a value
within a range.

Text Fields (`UITextField`/`UITextView`)

Text fields are used to collect user input through the iPad's onscreen keyboard. The `UITextField` is a single-line field, similar to what you'd see on a web page order form. The `UITextView` class, on the other hand, creates a larger multiline text entry block for more lengthy compositions (see Figure 4.8).

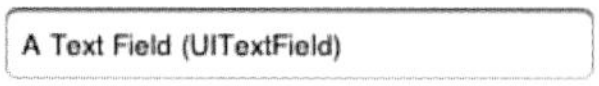

FIGURE 4.8
Collect user
input through
text fields.

Pickers (`UIDatePicker/UIPicker`)

A picker is an interesting interface element that resembles a slot machine display. By letting the user change each segment on the wheel, it can be used to enter a combination of several different values. Apple has implemented one complete picker for you: the `UIDatePicker` class. With this object, a user can quickly enter dates and times. You can also implement your own arbitrary pickers with the `UIPicker` class (see Figure 4.9).

FIGURE 4.9
Pickers enable users to choose a combination of several options.

Popovers (`UIPopoverController`)

Unique to the iPad, popovers are both a UI element and a means of displaying *other* UI elements. They allow you to display a view on top of any other view for the purpose of making a choice. The iPad's Safari browser, for example, uses a popover to present the user with a list of bookmarks to choose from, as seen in Figure 4.10.

FIGURE 4.10
Popovers present a user interface on top of an existing view.

Popovers will become very handy as you start to create applications that use the full screen real-estate of the iPad.

These are only a sample of the classes that you can use in your applications. We'll be exploring these and many others in the hours to come.

Exploring the iPhone OS Frameworks with Xcode

So far in this hour, you've learned about dozens of frameworks and classes. Each framework could be made up of dozens of classes, and each class with hundreds of methods, and so on—in other words, there's a ridiculous amount of information available about the iPhone OS frameworks.

One of the most efficient ways to learn more is to pick an object or framework you're interested in and then turn to the Xcode documentation system. Xcode provides an interface to the immense Apple development library in both a searchable browser-like interface as well as a context-sensitive Research Assistant. Let's take a look at both of these features now so that you can start using them immediately.

Xcode Documentation

To open the Xcode documentation application, choose Help, Developer Documentation from the menu bar. The help system will launch, as shown in Figure 4.11.

FIGURE 4.11
Search through the documentation to find tutorial articles and programming information.

Find information by typing into the search field. You can enter specific class, method, or property names, or just type in a concept that you're interested in. As you type, Xcode will start returning results.

Navigating Content

The documentation window is divided into two parts. The left column contains the information that matches your search—divided into groups based on whether the results were found in the API (programming) documentation, tutorial files, and so on. On the right, the content of the selected is displayed, as seen in Figure 4.12.

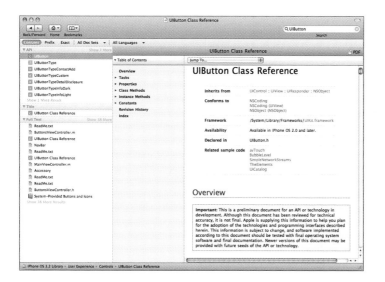

FIGURE 4.12
Navigate through the available documentation using the web-like search, results, and navigation features.

When you've arrived at a document that you're interested in, you can read and navigate within the document using the blue links—just like a web page. It's so much like a web page, in fact, that you can add and jump-to bookmarks to the current document by clicking the Bookmarks button in the toolbar. You can also navigate forward and backward using the arrow buttons, and access a history of documents you've visited using the Home button to the right of the arrows. Within individual documents, you may also see a Jump To menu; this enables you to quickly move to different topics of interest within that file.

Limiting the Search

If you know exactly what you want to find, you can limit the search results using the button bar that appears directly underneath the toolbar. If you want only exact matches, for example, you can click the Exact button. You can also use the Languages button in the toolbar to limit your search to a specific implementation language, such as Objective-C or C, and the Doc Sets drop-down menu to focus on specific types of documentation.

Managing Document Sets

Document sets are broad categories of documents that cover development for specific Mac OS X versions, Xcode itself, and the iPhone OS releases. To download and automatically receive updates to a documentation set, open the Xcode preferences (Xcode, Preferences) and click the Documentation icon in the preference pane list.

In the Documentation pane, click the Check For and Install Updates Automatically check box. Xcode will connect to Apple's servers and automatically update your local documentation. You'll also notice that additional documentation sets may be listed. Click the Get button beside any of the listed items to download and automatically include it in any future updates.

Did you Know?

You can force a manual update of the documentation using the Check and Install Now button.

Quick Help

One of the easiest and fastest ways to get help while coding is through the Xcode Quick Help assistant. To open the assistant, hold down Option and double-click a symbol in Xcode (for example, a class name or method name) or choose Help, Quick Help. A small window opens with basic information about the symbol, as well as links to other documentation resources.

Using Quick Help

Consider the following line that allocates and initializes a string with the contents of an integer variable:

```
myString=[[NSString alloc] initWithFormat:@"%d",myValue]
```

In this sample, there is a class (NSString), and two methods (alloc and initWithFormat). To get information about the initWithFormat: method, hold down Option, and then double-click initWithFormat:. Quick Help window appears, as shown in Figure 4.13.

FIGURE 4.13
Quick Help updates as you type.

To open the full Xcode documentation for the symbol, click the "book" icon in the upper-right corner. You can also click any of the hyperlinks in Quick Help results to jump to a specific piece of documentation or code.

By default, Quick Help will close itself when you click off of the selected symbol. To keep Quick Help open, just drag the assistant window outside of the Xcode window. While open, its contents will automatically update as you click on other symbols in your code. It will even update as you *type* new symbols, providing documentation on-the-fly!

Quick Help will remain open until you click the X close box in the upper-left corner.

Interpreting Quick Help Results

Quick Help displays context-sensitive information related to your code in up to eight different sections. What you see depends on the type of symbol (code) you have selected. A class property, for example, doesn't have a return type—but a class method does:

Abstract: A description of the feature that the class, method, or other symbol provides

Declaration: The structure of a method or definition of a data type

Parameters: The required or option information that can be provided to a method

Return Value: What information will be returned by a method when it completes

Sample Code: Sample code files that include examples of class/method/ property use

Related Documents: Additional documentation that references the selected symbol

Related API: Other methods within the same class as your selected method

Availability: The versions of the operating system where the feature is available

Quick Help simplifies the process of finding the right method to use with an object. Instead of trying to memorize dozens of instance methods, you can learn the basics and let Quick Help act as an on-demand reference of all an object's exposed methods.

Summary

In this hour, you explored the layers that make up the iPhone OS: Cocoa Touch, Media, Core Services, and Core OS. You learned the structure of a basic application—what objects it uses, and how the iPad manages its application life cycle. We also reviewed the common classes that you'll encounter as you begin to work with Cocoa, including data types and UI controls.

To give you the tools you need to find class and method references on your own, we introduced you to two features in Xcode. The first, the Xcode documentation window, offers a browser-like interface to the complete iPhone OS documentation. The second, Quick Help, finds help for the class or method you are working with, automatically, as you type. Ultimately, it will be these tools that help you dive deeper into the Apple development environment.

Q&A

Q. *Why are the operating system services layered? Doesn't that add complexity?*

A. Using the upper-level frameworks reduces the complexity of your code. By providing multiple levels of abstraction, Apple has given developers the tools they need to easily use iPad features as well as the flexibility to highly customize their application's behavior by using lower-level services more closely tied to the OS.

Q. *What do I do if I can't find an interface object I want?*

A. Chances are, if you're writing a "normal" iPad application, Apple has provided a UI class to fill your need. If you find that you'd like to do things differently, you can always subclass an existing control and modify its behavior as you see fit—or create a completely new control!

Workshop

Quiz

1. How many layers are there in the simplified Apple iPhone OS architecture?

2. How frequently will you be manually creating the `UIApplication` object in your applications?

3. What helpful feature can watch your typing and show relevant help articles?

Answers

1. Four. Cocoa Touch, Media, Core Services, and Core OS.

2. If you're building using Apple's iPad application templates, the initial setup of the UIApplication object is automatic. You don't need to do a thing!

3. Quick Help offers interactive help as you code.

Activities

1. Using the Apple Xcode Documentation utility, explore the NSString class and instance methods. Identify the methods you'd use to compare strings, create a string from a number, and change a string to upper- and lowercase.

2. Open Xcode and create a new window-based application on your desktop. Expand the Classes folder and click the file that ends in AppDelegate.m. When the contents of the file appear, open Quick Help by holding Option and double-clicking inside the class name UIApplication. Review the results. Try clicking other symbols in the Xcode class file and see what happens!

HOUR 5

Exploring Interface Builder

What You'll Learn in This Hour:

▶ What Interface Builder does, and what makes it special
▶ How to create user interfaces using the Library
▶ Common attributes that can be used to customize your interface
▶ Ways to make your interface accessible to the visually impaired
▶ How to connect interfaces to code with outlets and actions

Over the past few hours, you've become familiar with the core iPhone OS technologies and the Xcode and iPhone Simulator applications. While these are certainly important skills for becoming a successful developer, there's nothing quite like building your first iPad application interface and seeing it come alive on the screen.

In this hour, we introduce the third (and flashiest) component of the Apple Developer Suite: Interface Builder. Interface Builder provides a visual approach to application interface design, but, behind the scenes, does much, much more.

Understanding Interface Builder

Let's get it out of the way up front: Yes, Interface Builder (or IB for short) does help you create interfaces for your iPad applications, but it isn't a just a drawing tool for GUIs; it helps you symbolically build application functionality without writing code. This translates to fewer bugs, less development time, and easier-to-maintain projects!

Although IB is a standalone application, it is dependent on Xcode and, to some extent, the iPhone Simulator. In this hour, we focus on navigating through Interface Builder, but will return in Hour 6, "Model-View-Controller Application Design," to combine all three pieces of the Apple Developer Suite for the first time.

The Interface Builder Approach

Using Xcode and the Cocoa toolset, you can program iPad interfaces by hand—instantiating interface objects, defining where they appear on the screen, setting any attributes for the object, and, finally, making them visible. For example, in Hour 2, "Introduction to Xcode and the iPhone Simulator," you entered this listing into Xcode to make your iPad display the text Hello Xcode in the middle of the screen:

```
UILabel *myMessage;
UILabel *myUnusedMessage;
myMessage=[[UILabel alloc] initWithFrame:CGRectMake(190,300,500,75)];
myMessage.text=@"Hello Xcode";
[window addSubview:myMessage];
```

Imagine how long it would take to build interfaces with text, buttons, images, and dozens of other controls—and think of all the code you'd need to wade through just to make small changes!

Over the years, there have been many different approaches to graphical interface builders. One of the most common implementations is to enable the user to "draw" an interface, but, behind the scenes, create the code that generates that interface. Any tweaks require the code to be edited by hand—hardly an acceptable situation.

Another tactic is to maintain the interface definition symbolically, but to attach the code that implements functionality directly to interface elements. This, unfortunately, means that if you want to change your interface, or swap functionality from one UI element to another, you have to move the code as well.

Interface Builder works differently. Rather than autogenerating interface code or tying source listings directly to interface elements, IB builds live objects that connect to your application code through simple links called *connections*. Want to change how a feature of your app is triggered? Just change the connection. As you'll learn a bit later, changing how your application works with the objects you create in Interface Builder is, quite literally, a matter of connecting or reconnecting the dots as you see fit.

The Anatomy of an Interface Builder XIB File

Your work in Interface Builder results in an XML file called an XIB or (for legacy reasons) NIB file, containing a hierarchy of objects. The objects could be interface elements—buttons, toggle switches, and so forth—but might also be other noninterface objects that you need to use in your app. When the XIB file is loaded by your application, the objects described in it are instantiated and can be accessed by your code.

By the Way

Instantiation, just as a quick refresher, is the process of creating an instance of an object that you can work with in your program. An instantiated object gains all the functionality described by its class. Buttons, for example, automatically highlight when clicked, content views scroll, and so on.

The Document Window

What do XIB files look like in IB? Open the Hour 5 Projects folder and double-click the file EmptyView.xib to open Interface Builder and display a barebones XIB file. The contents of the file are shown in the IB "document" window (see Figure 5.1).

FIGURE 5.1
An XIB file's objects are represented by icons.

By the Way

If you do not see a window with icons when opening the XIB file, choose Window, Document to ensure that the document window is active and visible on your screen.

In this sample file, there are three icons initially visible: File's Owner, First Responder, and View. The first two are special icons used to represent unique objects in our application; these will be present in all XIB files that you work with:

File's Owner: The File's Owner icon denotes the object that loads the XIB file in your running application. This is the object that effectively instantiates all the other objects described in the XIB file. For example, you may have an interface defined in myInterface.xib, which is loaded by an object you've written called `myInterfaceController`. In this case, the File's Owner would represent the `myInterfaceController` object. You'll learn more about the relationship between interfaces and code in Hour 6.

First Responder: The first responder icon stands for the object that the user is currently interacting with. When a user works with an iPad application, there are multiple objects that could potentially respond to the various gestures or keystrokes that the user creates. The first responder is the object currently in control and interacting with the user. A text field that the user is typing into, for example, would be the first responder until the user moves to another field or control.

View: The view icon is an instance of the object UIView and represents the visual layout that will be loaded and displayed on the iPad's screen. You can double-click view icons to open and edit them with the IB tools, as shown in Figure 5.2.

FIGURE 5.2
Double-click the view icon to open and edit the iPad application GUI.

Views are hierarchical in nature. This means that as you add controls to your interface, they will be contained *within* the view. You can even add views within views to cluster controls or create visual elements that can be shown or hidden as a group. Because a view can contain many other objects, we recommend using the list or column view of the document window to make sure that you can view the full hierarchy of objects you've created in an XIB file. To change the document view, click the view mode icon in the document window toolbar (see Figure 5.3).

FIGURE 5.3
Using the list view mode ensures that you can see all of the objects in your XIB files. Here an XIB with a full interface and view hierarchy is displayed.

At its most basic level, a view (UIView) is a rectangular region that can contain content and respond to user events (touches and so forth). All the controls (buttons, fields, and so on) that you'll add to a view are, in fact, subclasses of UIView. This isn't necessarily something you need to be worried about, except that you'll be encountering documentation that refers to buttons and other interface elements referred to as subviews and the views that contain them as superviews.

Just keep in the back of your mind that pretty much everything you see on the iPad screen can be considered a "view" and the terminology will seem a little less alien.

Did you Know?

Working with the Document Icons

The document window shows icons for objects in your application, but what good are they? Aside from presenting a nice list, do the document window icons provide any functionality?

Absolutely! These icons give you a visual means of referring to the objects they represent. You will interact with the icons by dragging to and from them to create the connections that drive your application's features.

Consider an onscreen control, such as a button, that needs to be able to trigger an action in your code. By dragging from the button to the File's Owner icon, you can create a connection from the GUI element you've drawn to a method you've written in the object that loaded the XIB file.

We'll go through a hands-on example later this hour so that you can get a feel for how this works. Before we do that, however, let's take a look at how you go about turning a blank view into an interface masterpiece.

Creating User Interfaces

In Figures 5.2 and 5.3, you've seen an empty view and a fully fleshed-out iPad interface—but how do we get from one to the other? In this section, we explore how interfaces are created with Interface Builder. In other words, it's time for the fun stuff!

If you haven't already, open the EmptyView.xib file included in this hour's Projects folder. Use the document window to open the empty view and prepare for adding content.

The Objects Library

Everything that you add to a view comes from the IB Objects Library, shown in Figure 5.4. The Library can be opened from the menu bar by choosing Tools, Library (Command+Shift+L). After the Library palette opens, click the Objects button at the top of the window to focus on interface objects. When you click an element in the Library, the bottom of the window refreshes to show a description of how it can be used in the interface.

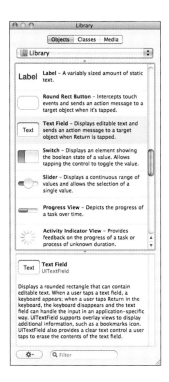

FIGURE 5.4
The Library provides a palette of objects that can be added to your views.

Using the action (gear) menu at the bottom of the Library, you can change the Library to show just the icons, icons and names, or icons and full descriptions for each object. You can even group items based on their purpose. If you know the name of an object but can't locate it in the list, use the search field to quickly find it.

The button bar and drop-down menu at the top of the Library can be used to focus on specific parts of the Library, or change how the information is organized. When starting out, however, using the default settings should give you everything you need for most application and interface design.

Did you Know?

To add a object to the view, just click and drag from the Library to the view. For example, find the label object (UILabel) in the Library and drag it into the center of the view window. The label should appear in your view and read Label. Double-click the label and type **Hello**. The text will update, as shown in Figure 5.5, just as you would expect.

With that simple action, you've almost entirely replicated the functionality implemented by the code fragment earlier in the lesson. Try dragging other objects from the Library into the view—buttons, text fields, and so on. With few exceptions, the objects should appear and behave just the way you'd expect.

FIGURE 5.5
If an object con-
tains text, in
many cases,
just double-click
to edit it.

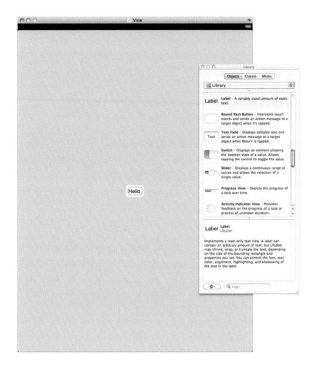

To remove an object from the view, click to select it, then press the Delete key. You
may also use the options under the edit menu to copy and paste between views, or
duplicate an element several times within a view.

Layout Tools

Instead of relying on your visual acuity to position objects in a view, Apple has
included some useful tools for fine-tuning your layout. If you've ever used a drawing
program like OmniGraffle or Adobe Illustrator, many of these will be familiar.

Guides

As you drag objects in a view, you'll notice guides (shown in Figure 5.6) appearing
to help with the layout. These blue dotted lines will be displayed to align objects
along the margins of the view, to the centers of other objects in the view, and to the
baseline of the fonts used in the labels and object titles.

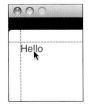

FIGURE 5.6
Guides help position your objects within a view.

As an added bonus, guides will automatically appear to indicate the approximate spacing requirements of Apple's interface guidelines. If you're not sure why it's showing you a particular margin guide, it's likely that your object is in a position that Interface Builder considers "appropriate" for something of that type and size.

You can manually add your own guides by choosing Layout, Add Horizontal Guide or by choosing Layout, Add Vertical Guide.

Did you Know?

Selection Handles

In addition to the layout guides, most objects include selection handles to stretch an object either horizontally, vertically, or both. Using the small boxes that appear alongside an object when it is selected, just click and drag to change its size, as demonstrated using a button in Figure 5.7.

FIGURE 5.7
Use the resize handles around the perimeter of an object to change its size.

Note that some objects will constrain how you can resize them; this preserves a level of consistency within iPad application interfaces.

Alignment

To quickly align several objects within a view, select them by clicking and dragging a selection rectangle around them or by holding down the Shift key, and then choose Layout, Alignment and an appropriate alignment type from the menu.

For example, try dragging several buttons into your view, placing them in a variety of different positions. To align them based on their horizontal center (a line that runs vertically through each button's center), select the buttons, and then choose Layout, Alignment, Align Horizontal Centers. Figure 5.8 shows the before and after results.

FIGURE 5.8
Use the
Alignment menu
to quickly align
a group of items
to an edge or
center.

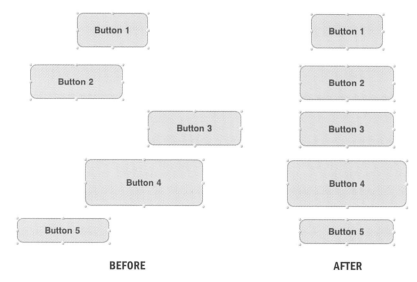

BEFORE   AFTER

Did you
Know?

To fine-tune an object's position within a view, select it, and then use the arrow
keys to position it left, right, up, or down, one pixel at a time.

The Size Inspector

Another tool that you may want to use for controlling your layout is the Size
Inspector. Interface Builder has a number of "inspectors" for examining the attributes of an object. As the name implies, the Size Inspector provides information
about sizes, but also position and alignment. To open the Size Inspector, first select
the object (or objects) that you want to work with, and then press Command+3 or
choose Tools, Size Inspector (see Figure 5.9).

Using the fields at the top of the inspector, you can view or change the size and
position of the object by changing the coordinates in the H/W and X/Y fields. You
can also view the coordinates of a specific portion of an object by clicking one of the
black dots in the size and grid to indicate where the reading should come from.

By the
Way

Within the Size and Position settings, you'll notice a drop-down menu where you
can choose between Frame and Layout. These two settings will usually be very
similar, but there is a slight difference. The frame values represent the exact area
an object occupies onscreen, whereas the layout values take into account spacing
around the object.

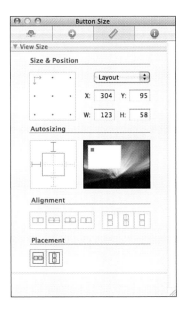

FIGURE 5.9
The Size
Inspector
enables you to
adjust the size
and position of
one or more
objects.

The Autosizing settings of the Size Inspector determine how controls resize/reposition themselves when the iPad changes orientation. You'll learn more about these in Hour 17, "Building Rotatable and Resizable User Interfaces."

Finally, the same controls found under Layout, Alignment can be accessed as clickable icons at the bottom of the inspector. Choose your objects, and then click one of the icons to align according to the red line.

Customizing Interface Appearance

How your interface appears to the end user isn't just a combination of control sizes and positions. For many kinds of objects, there are literally dozens of different attributes that can be adjusted. While you could certainly configure things such as colors and fonts in your code, it's easier to just use the tools included in Interface Builder.

Using the Attributes Inspector

The most common place you'll tweak the way your interface objects appear is through the Attributes Inspector, available by choosing Tools, Attributes Inspector or by pressing Command+1. Let's run through a quick example to see how this works.

Make sure that the EmptyView.xib file is still open and that you've added a text label to the view. Select the label, and then press Command+1 to open the Attributes Inspector, shown in Figure 5.10.

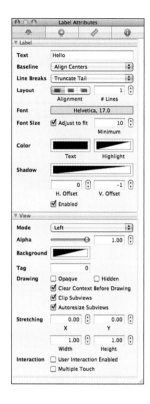

The top portion of the Attributes Inspector will contain attributes for the specific object. In the case of the text object, this includes settings such as font, size, color, and alignment—everything you'd expect to find for editing text.

In the lower portion of the inspector are additional inherited attributes. Remember that onscreen elements are a subclass of a view? This means that all the standard view attributes are also available for the object and for your tinkering enjoyment. In many cases, you'll want to leave these alone, but settings such as background and transparency can come in handy.

> Don't get hung up on trying to memorize every attribute for every control now—we'll cover interesting and important attributes when they are needed throughout the book.

Feel free to explore the many different options available in the Attributes Inspector, and to see what can be configured for different types of objects. There is a surprising amount of flexibility to be found within the tool.

The attributes you change in Interface Builder are simply properties of the objects themselves. To help identify what an attribute does, use the documentation tool in Xcode to look up the object's class and review the descriptions of its properties.

Setting Accessibility Attributes

For many years, the "appearance" of an interface meant just how it looks visually. Today, the technology is available for an interface to vocally describe itself to the visually impaired. The iPad includes Apple's screen reader technology: Voiceover. Voiceover combines speech synthesis with a customized interface to aid users in navigating applications.

Using Voiceover, a user can touch interface elements and hear a short description of what they do and how they can be used. While you gain much of this functionality "for free" (the iPad Voiceover software will read button labels, for example), you can provide additional assistance by configuring the accessibility attributes in Interface Builder.

To access the Accessibility settings, you'll need to open the Identity Inspector by choosing Tools, Identity Inspector or pressing Command+4. The Accessibility options have their own section within the Identity Inspector, as shown in Figure 5.11.

There are four sets of attributes that you can configure within this area:

Accessibility: If enabled, the object is considered accessible. If you create any custom controls that must be seen to be used, this setting should be disabled.

Label: A simple word or two that serves as the label for an item. A text field that collects the user's name might use "your name," for example.

Hint: A short description, if needed, on how to use the control. This is needed only if the label doesn't provide enough information on its own.

Traits: This set of check boxes is used to describe the features of the object—what it does, and what its current state is.

FIGURE 5.11
Use the Accessibility section in the Identity Inspector to configure how the Voiceover interacts with your application.

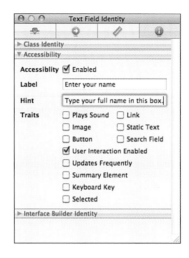

For an application to be available to the largest possible audience, you should take advantage of accessibility tools whenever possible. Even objects like the text labels you've used in this lesson should have their traits configured to indicate that they are static text. This helps a potential user know that he or she can't interact with them.

Simulating the Interface

At any point in time during the construction of your iPad interface, you can test the controls in the iPhone Simulator. To test the interface, choose File, Simulate Interface (Command+R). After a few seconds, the iPhone Simulator will start and display your interface design. You can use all of the same gestures and controls that you learned about in Hour 2.

Watch Out!

When you use the Simulate Interface command, only the interface code is being run. Nothing that you may have written in Xcode is included. This means that you can simulate interfaces even if you haven't written a single line of supporting code or if your code has errors. However, it also means that if your code modifies the display in any way, you won't see those changes onscreen.

To compile and run your code along with the interface, switch to Xcode and click Build and Run, or, as a shortcut, choose File, Build and Go in Xcode from the IB menu (Command+Shift+R).

Enabling the Accessibility Inspector

If you are building accessible interfaces, you may want to enable the Accessibility Inspector in the iPhone Simulator. To do this, start the simulator and click the Home button to return to the home iPad screen. Start the Settings application and navigate to General, Accessibility, and then use the toggle button to turn the Accessibility Inspector on, as shown in Figure 5.12.

By the Way

By the Way

FIGURE 5.12
Toggle the Accessibility Inspector on.

The Accessibility Inspector adds an overlay to the simulator workspace that displays the label, hints, and traits that you've configured for your interface elements. Note that navigating the iPad interface is *very* different when operating in accessibility mode.

Using the X button in the upper-left corner of the inspector, you can toggle it on and off. When off, the inspector collapses to a small bar, and the iPhone simulator will behave normally. Clicking the X button again turns it back on. To disable the Accessibility Inspector altogether, just revisit the Accessibility setting in the Settings application.

Connecting to Code

You know how to make an interface, but how do you make it *do* something? Throughout this hour, we've been alluding to the idea that connecting an interface to the code you write is just a matter of "connecting the dots." In this last part of the hour, we'll do just that: take an interface and connect it to the code that makes it into a functional application.

Launching Interface Builder from Xcode

To get started, we'll use the project Disconnected contained within this hour's Projects folder. Open the folder and double-click the Disconnected.xcodeproj file. This will open the project in Xcode, as shown in Figure 5.13. Almost all of your work in Interface Builder will start from inside of Xcode, so we might as well get used to using it as our launching point for IB.

FIGURE 5.13
Almost all of your work in Interface Builder will start in Xcode.

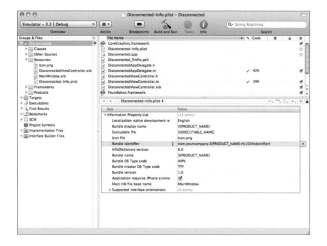

Once the project is loaded, expand the Resources file group, and double-click the DisconnectedViewController.xib file. This XIB file contains the view that this application displays as its interface. After a few seconds, IB will launch and display the interface document window as well as the view, as shown in Figure 5.14.

FIGURE 5.14
After launching, Interface Builder will show the document window and view from the XIB file.

Implementation Overview

The interface contains four interactive elements: a button bar (called a segmented control), a push button, an output label, and a web view (an integrated web browser component). Together, these controls will interface with application code to enable a user to pick a flower color, click the Get Flower button, and then display the chosen color in a text label along with a matching flower photo fetched from the website www.floraphotographs.com. The final result is demonstrated in Figure 5.15.

Unfortunately, right now the application does nothing. The interface isn't connected to any application code, so it is hardly more than a pretty picture. To make it work, we'll be creating connections to outlets and actions that have been defined in Xcode.

FIGURE 5.15
The finished
application will
enable a user to
choose a color
and have a
flower image
returned that
matches that
color.

FIGURE 5.15
The finished
application will
enable a user to
choose a color
and have a
flower image
returned that
matches that
color.

Outlets and Actions

An outlet is nothing more than a variable by which an object can be referenced. For example, if you had created a field in Interface Builder intending that it would be used to collect a user's name, you might want to create an outlet for it in your code called userName. Using this outlet, you could then access or change the contents of the field.

An action, on the other hand, is a method within your code that is called when an event takes place. Certain objects, such as buttons and switches, can trigger actions when a user interacts with them through an event—such as touching the screen. By defining actions in your code, Interface Builder can make them available to the onscreen objects.

Joining an element in Interface Builder to an outlet or action creates what is generically termed a *connection*.

For the Disconnected app to function, we need to create connections to these outlets and actions:

> ColorChoice—An outlet created for the button bar to access the color the user has selected
>
> GetFlower—An action that retrieves a flower from the web, displays it, and updates the label with the chosen color
>
> ChosenColor—An outlet for the label that will be updated by getFlower to show the name of the chosen color
>
> FlowerView—An outlet for the web view that will be updated by getFlower to show the image

Let's make the connections now.

Creating Connections to Outlets

To create a connection from an interface item to an outlet, Control-drag from the File's Owner icon either to the visual representation of the object in the view or to its icon in the document window of Interface Builder.

Try this with the button bar (segmented control). Pressing Control, click and drag from the File's Owner icon in the document window to either the onscreen image of the bar or its icon in the document window. A line will appear as you drag, enabling you to easily point to the object that you want to use for the connect. When you release the mouse button, the available connections will be shown in a pop-up menu (see Figure 5.16).

FIGURE 5.16
Choose from
the outlets that
are available for
that object.

Interface Builder knows what type of object is allowed to connect to a given outlet,
so it will only display the outlets that are appropriate for the connection you're trying to make.

Repeat this process for the label with the text "Your Color", connecting it to the
chosenColor outlet, and the web view, connecting to flowerView.

Creating Connections to Actions

Connecting to actions is a bit different; an object's events trigger actions (methods)
in your code. So, the connection direction reverses; you connect from the object to
the File's Owner icon. Although it is possible to Control-drag and create a connection in the same manner you did with outlets, this isn't recommended because you
don't get to specify which event triggers it. Does the user have to touch the button?
Release their finger from a button?

Actions can be triggered by *many* different events, so you need to make sure that you're picking exactly the right one, instead of leaving it up to Interface Builder. To do this, select the object that will be connecting to the action and open the Connections Inspector by choosing Tools, Connections Inspector (or by pressing Command+2).

The Connections Inspector, in Figure 5.17, shows a list of the events that the object supports—in this case, a button. Beside each event is an open circle. To connect an event to an action in your code, click and drag from one of these circles to the File's Owner icon.

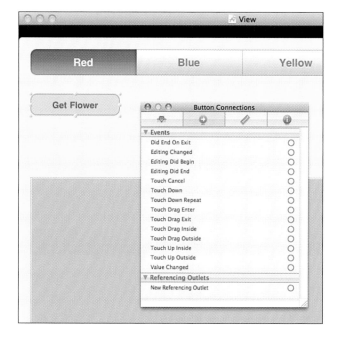

FIGURE 5.17
The Connections Inspector shows all the connections you've made to and from an object.

For example, to connect the Get Flower button to the `getFlower` method, select the button, and then open the Connections Inspector (Command+2). Drag from the circle beside the Touch Up Inside event to the File's Owner icon and release, as demonstrated in Figure 5.18. When prompted, choose the `getFlower` action.

FIGURE 5.18
Drag from the
event to the
File's Owner
Icon, and then
choose the
action you want
to use.

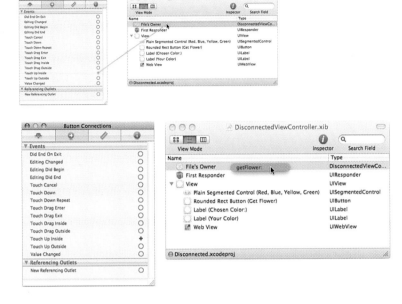

After a connection has been made, the inspector will update to show the event and
the action that it calls, as shown in Figure 5.19. If you click other objects, you'll
notice that the Connections Inspector shows connections to outlets as well as
actions.

FIGURE 5.19
The
Connections
Inspector
updates to
show the
actions and out-
lets that an
object refer-
ences.

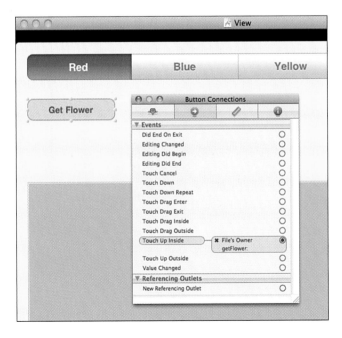

Connections Without Code!

Although most of your connections in Interface Builder will be between objects and outlets and actions you've defined in your code, there are actually some built-in actions that certain objects implement without you writing a single line of code.

The web view, for example, implements actions, including goForward and goBack. Using these actions, you could add basic navigation functionality to a web view by dragging from a button's Touch Up Inside event directly to the web view object (rather than the File's Owner). As described previously, you'll be prompted for the action to connect to, but this time, it isn't an action you had to code yourself!

Well done! You've just linked an interface to the code that supports it. Switch to Xcode and choose Build and Run to run and test the application in the iPhone Simulator.

Object Identity

As we finish up our introduction to Interface Builder, we'd be remiss if we didn't introduce one more feature: the Identity Inspector. You've already accessed this tool to view the accessibility attributes for interface objects, but there is another reason why we'll need to use the inspector in the future—setting class identities.

As you drag objects into the interface, you're creating instances of classes that already exist (buttons, labels, and so on). Throughout this book, however, we're going to be building custom subclasses that we'll also need to be able to reference in Interface Builder. In these cases, we'll need help Interface Builder out by identifying the subclass it should use.

For example, suppose we created a subclass of the standard button class (UIButton) that we named ourFancyButtonClass. We might drag a button into Interface Builder to represent our fancy button, but when the XIB file loads, it would just create the same old UIButton.

To fix the problem, we select the button we've added to the view, open the Identity Inspector by choosing Tools, Identity Inspector (Command+4), and then use the drop-down menu/field to enter the class that we really want instantiated at runtime (see Figure 5.20).

FIGURE 5.20
If you're using a
custom class,
you'll need to
manually set
the identity of
your objects in
Interface
Builder.

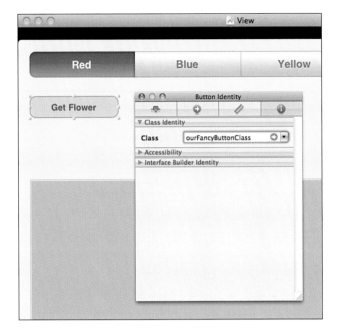

This is something we'll cover on an as-needed basis, so if it seems confusing, don't worry. We'll come back to it later in the book.

Further Exploration

Interface Builder gives you the opportunity to experiment with many of the different GUI objects you've seen in iPad applications and read about in the previous hours. In the next hour, Xcode and Interface Builder will finally come together for your first full project, from start to finish.

To learn even more about what you can do in Interface Builder, I suggest reading through the following three Apple publications:

> **Interface Builder User Guide**: Accessed by choosing Help, Interface Builder Help from the IB menu, this is more than a simple help document. Apple's user guide walks you through all of the intricacies of IB and covers some advanced topics that will be important as your development experience increases.

> **iPad Human Interface Guidelines**: Accessible through the Xcode documentation system, the Apple iPad HIG document provides a clear set of rules for building usable interfaces on the iPad. This document describes when you should use controls and how they should be displayed, helping you to create more polished, professional-quality applications.

Accessibility Programming Guide for iPhone OS (accessible through the Xcode documentation system): If you're serious about creating accessible apps, this is a mandatory read. The Accessibility Programming Guide describes the accessibility features mentioned in this hour's lesson as well as ways to improve accessibility programmatically and methods of testing accessibility beyond the tips given in this hour.

As a general note, from here on, you'll be doing quite a bit of coding in each lesson, so now would be a great time to review the previous hours if you have any questions.

Summary

In this hour, you explored Interface Builder and the tools it provides for building rich graphical interfaces for your iPad applications. You learned how to navigate the IB document window and access the GUI elements from the Objects Library. Using the various inspector tools within Interface Builder, you customized the look and feel of the onscreen controls and how they can be made accessible to the visually impaired.

More than just a pretty picture, an IB-created interface uses simple outlets and actions to connect to functionality in your code. You used Interface Builder's connection tools to turn a nonfunctioning interface into a complete application. By maintaining a separation between the code you write and what is displayed to the user, you can revise your interface to look however you want, without breaking your application. In Hour 6, you'll examine how to create outlets and actions from scratch in Xcode (and thus gain a full toolset to get started developing).

Q&A

Q. *Why do I keep seeing things referred to as NIB files?*

A. The origins of Interface Builder trace back to the NeXT Computer, which made use of NIB files. These files, in fact, still bore the same name when Mac OS X was released. In recent years, however, Apple has renamed the files to have the XIB extension—unfortunately, documentation hasn't quite caught up yet.

Q. *Some of the objects in the Interface Builder Library can't be added to my view. What gives?*

A. Not all of the Library objects are interface objects. Some represent objects that provide functionality to your application. In the next hour, we'll look at the first object that does this (a view controller).

Q. *I've seen controls in applications that aren't available here. Where are they?*

A. Keep in mind that the iPad isn't an iPhone—not all user interface features work or look the same. In addition, some developers choose to make their own UI classes or subclasses that can vary tremendously from the stock UI appearance.

Workshop

Quiz

1. Simulating an interface from IB also compiles the project's code in Xcode. True or false?

2. What tool can you use within the iPhone Simulator to help review accessibility of objects in your apps?

3. How is Interface Builder typically launched?

Answers

1. False. Simulating the interface does not use the project code at all. As a result, the interface will not perform any actions that may be assigned.

2. The Accessibility Inspector makes it possible to view the accessibility attributes configured within Interface Builder.

3. Although Interface Builder is a standalone application, it is typically launched by opening an XIB file from within Xcode.

Activities

1. Practice using the interface layout tools on the EmptyView.xib file. Add each available interface object to your view, and then review the Attributes Inspector for that object. If an attribute doesn't make sense, remember that you can review documentation for the class to identify the role of each of its properties.

2. Revise the Disconnected project with an accessible interface. Review the finished design using the Accessibility Inspector in the iPhone Simulator.

HOUR 6

Model-View-Controller Application Design

What You'll Learn in This Hour:

▶ What the Model-View-Controller design pattern means
▶ Ways in which the Apple Developer Suite implements MVC
▶ Design of a basic view
▶ Implementation of a corresponding view controller

You've come a long way in the past few hours—you've provisioned a developer profile for your phone, learned the basics of the Objective-C language, explored Cocoa Touch, and gotten a feel for Xcode and Interface Builder. Although you've already used a few prebuilt projects, you have yet to build one from scratch. That's about to change!

In this hour, you will learn about the application design pattern known as Model-View-Controller and create an iPad application from start to finish.

Understanding the Model-View-Controller Paradigm

When you start programming, you'll quickly come to the conclusion that there is more than one "correct" way to do just about everything. Part of the joy of programming is that it is a creative process that allows you to be as clever as your imagination allows. This doesn't mean, however, that adding structure to the development process is a bad idea. Having a defined and documented structure means that other developers will be able to work with your code, projects large and small will be easy to navigate, and you'll be able to reuse your best work in multiple applications.

The application design approach that you'll be using on the iPad is known as Model-View-Controller (MVC), and will guide you in creating clean, efficient applications.

> In Hour 3, "Discovering Objective-C," you learned about object-oriented (OO) programming and the reusability that it can provide. OO programs, however, can still be poorly structured—thus the need to define an overall application architecture that can guide the object-oriented implementation.

Making Spaghetti

Before we get into MVC, let's first talk about the development practice that we want to avoid, and why. When creating an application that interacts with a user, several things must be taken into account. First, the user interface. You must present *something* that the user interacts with: buttons, fields, and so on. Second, handling and reacting to the user input. Finally, the application must store the information necessary to correctly react to the user—frequently in the form of a database.

One approach to incorporating all of these pieces is to combine them into a single class. The code that displays the interface is mixed with the code that implements the logic and the code that handles data. This can be a very straightforward development methodology, but it limits the developer in several ways:

▶ When code is mixed together, it is difficult for multiple developers to work together because there is no clear division between any of the functional units.

▶ The interface, application logic, and data are unlikely to be reusable in other applications because the combination of the three is too specific to the current project to be useful elsewhere.

▶ The application is difficult to extend. Adding features requires working around existing code. The developer must work around the existing code to include new features, even if they are unrelated.

In short, mixing code, logic, and data leads to a mess! This is known as "spaghetti code" and is the exact opposite of what we want for our iPad applications. Model-View-Controller to the rescue!

Structured Application Design with MVC

MVC defines a clean separation between the critical components of our apps. As implied by the name, MVC defines three parts of an application:

▶ A *model* provides the underlying data and methods that provide information to the rest of the application. The model does not define how the application will look or how it will act.

▶ One or more *views* make up the user interface. A view consists of the different onscreen widgets (buttons, fields, switches, and so forth) that a user can interact with.

▶ A *controller* is typically paired with a view. The controller is responsible for receiving the user's input and acting accordingly. Controllers may access and update a view using information from the model and update the model using the results of user interactions in the view. In short, it bridges the MVC components.

The logical isolation created between the functional parts of an application, illustrated in Figure 6.1, means the code becomes more easily maintainable, reusable, and extendable—the exact opposite of spaghetti code.

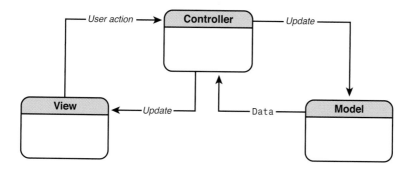

FIGURE 6.1
MVC design isolates the functional components of an app.

Unfortunately, MVC comes as an afterthought in many application development environments. A frequent question that I am asked when suggesting MVC design is, "How do I do that?" This isn't indicative of a misunderstanding of what MVC is or how it works, but a lack of a clear means of implementing it.

In the Apple Development Suite, MVC design is natural. As you create new projects and start coding, you'll be guided into using MVC design patterns automatically. It actually becomes more difficult to program poorly than it does to build a well-structured app.

How Xcode and Interface Builder Implement MVC

Over the past few hours, you've learned about Xcode and Interface Builder and have gotten a sense for what the two applications do. In Hour 5, "Exploring Interface Builder," you even connected XIB file objects to the corresponding code in an application. Although we didn't go into the nitty-gritty details at the time, what you were doing was binding a view to a controller.

Views

Views, although possible to create programmatically, will most frequently be designed visually in Interface Builder. Views can consist of many different interface elements—the most common of which we covered in Hour 5 and Hour 4, "Inside Cocoa Touch." When loaded at runtime, views create any number of objects that can implement a basic level of interactivity on their own (such as a text field opening a keyboard when touched). Even so, a view is entirely independent of any application logic. This clear separation is one of the core principles of the MVC design approach.

For the objects in a view to interact with application logic, they require a connection point to be defined. These connections come in two varieties: outlets and actions. An outlet defines a path between the code and the view that can be used to read and write values. Second, an action defines a method in your application that can be triggered via an event within a view, such as a touch or swipe.

So, how do outlets and actions connect to code? In the preceding hour, you learned to control-drag in Interface Builder to create a connection, but Interface Builder "knew" what connections were valid. It certainly can't "guess" where in your code you want to create a connection; instead, you must define the outlets and actions in the code that implement the view's logic (that is, the controller).

View Controllers

A controller, known in Xcode as a view controller, handles the interactions with a view, and establishes the connection points for outlets and actions. To accomplish this, two special directives, IBAction and IBOutlet, will be added to your project's code. Specifically, you add these directives to the header files of your view controller. IBAction and IBOutlet are markers that Interface Builder recognizes; they serve no other purpose within Objective-C.

> View controllers can hold application logic, but we don't mean to imply that all your code should be within a view controller. Although this is largely the convention for the tutorials in this book, as you create your own apps, you can certainly define additional classes to abstract your application logic as you see fit.

By the Way

Using `IBOutlet`

An `IBOutlet` is used to enable your code to talk to objects within views. For example, consider a text label (`UILabel`) that you've added to a view. If you want to access the label under the name `myLabel` within your view controller, you would declare it like this in the header file:

```
IBOutlet UILabel *myLabel;
```

Once declared, Interface Builder enables you to visually connect the view's label object to the `myLabel` variable. Your code can then fully interact with the label object—changing its properties, calling its methods, and so on.

> **Easy Access with** property **and** synthesize
>
> In Hour 3, you learned about the Objective-C @property and @synthesize directives, but you're about to start seeing them frequently, so we think a refresher is in order.
>
> The @property directive declares elements in a class that should be exposed via "getters" and "setters" (or accessors and mutators, if you prefer). Properties are defined with a series of attributes, most frequently nonatomic and retain during iPad development.
>
> The @synthesize directive creates simplified getters and setters, making retrieving and setting values of an object very simple.
>
> Returning to the example of a UILabel instance called myLabel, I would initially declare it as a property in the header file of my view controller:
>
> ```
> @property (retain, nonatomic) NSString *myLabel;
> ```
>
> And then use @synthesize in the implementation file to create simplified getters and setters:
>
> ```
> @synthesize myLabel;
> ```
>
> Once those lines are added, the current myLabel value could be retrieved from UILabel's text property using theCurrentLabel=myLabel.text (the getter) or set to something new with myLabel.text=@"My New Label" (the setter).

By the Way

Using IBAction

An IBAction is used to "advertise" a method in your code that should be called when a certain event takes place. For instance, if a button is pushed, or a field updated, you will probably want your application to take action and react appropriately. When you've written a method that implements your event-driven logic, you can declare it with IBAction in the header file, which subsequently will expose it to Interface Builder.

For instance, a method doCalculation might be declared like this:

```
-(IBAction)doCalculation:(id)sender;
```

Notice that the declaration includes a sender parameter with the type of id. This is a generic type that can be used when you don't know (or need to know) the type of object you'll be working with. By using id, you can write code that doesn't tie itself to a specific class, making it easier to adapt to different situations.

When creating a method that will be used as an action (like our doCalculation example), you can identify and interact with the object that invoked the action through the sender variable (or whatever you decide to call it in your code). This will be handy if you decide to design a method that handles multiple different events, such as button presses from several different buttons.

Data Models

Let me get this out of the way upfront: For many of the exercises we'll be doing in this book, a separate data model is not needed; the data requirements are handled within the controller. This is one of the trade-offs of small projects like the one you'll be working through in a few minutes. Although it would be ideal to represent a complete MVC application architecture, sometimes it just isn't possible in the space and time available. In your own projects, you'll need to decide whether to implement a standalone model. In the case of small utility apps, you may find that you rarely need to consider a data model beyond the logic you code into the controller.

As you grow more experienced with the iPhone OS Software Development Kit (SDK) and start building data-rich applications, you'll want to begin exploring Core Data. Core Data abstracts the interactions between your application and an underlying datastore. It also includes a modeling tool, like Interface Builder, that helps you design your application, but rather than visually laying out interfaces, you can use it to visually map a data structure, as shown in Figure 6.2.

For our beginning tutorials, using Core Data would be like using a sledgehammer to drive a thumbtack. Right now, let's get started building your first app with a view and a view controller!

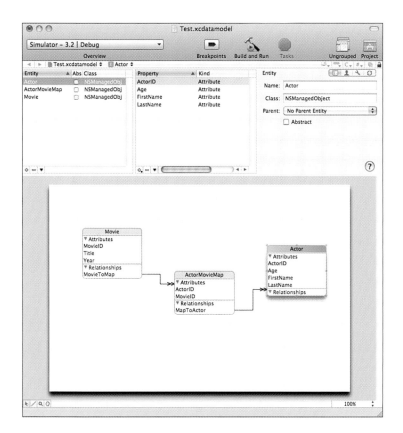

FIGURE 6.2
Once you become more familiar with iPad development, you may want to explore the Core Data tools for managing your data model.

Using the View-Based Application Template

The easiest way to see how Xcode and Interface Builder manage to separate logic from display is to build an application that follows this approach. Apple has included a useful application template in Xcode that quickly sets up an empty view and an associated view controller. This View-Based Application template will be the starting point for many of your projects, so we'll spend the rest of this chapter getting accustomed to using it.

Implementation Overview

The project we'll be building is simple: Instead of just writing the typical "Hello World" app, we want to be a bit more flexible. The program will present the user with a field (UITextField) for typing and a button (UIButton). When the user types into the field and presses the button, the display will update an onscreen label

(UILabel) so that "Hello" is seen, followed by the user's input. The completed HelloNoun, as we've chosen to call this project, is shown in Figure 6.3.

FIGURE 6.3
The app will
accept input
and update the
display based
on what the
user types.

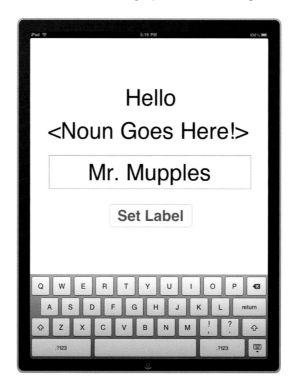

Although this won't be a masterpiece of development, it does contain almost all the different elements we discuss in this hour: a view, a controller, outlets, and actions. Because this is the first full development cycle that we've worked through, we'll pay close attention to how all the pieces come together and why things work the way they do.

Setting Up the Project

First we want to create the project, which we'll call HelloNoun, in Xcode:

1. Launch Xcode from the Developer/Applications folder.

2. Choose File, New Project.

3. You'll be prompted to choose a project type and a template. On the left side of the New Project window, make sure that Application is selected under the iPhone OS project type. Next find and select the View-Based Application

option from the list on the right, be sure that iPad is selected, as shown in Figure 6.4, and then click Choose.

4. Choose a save location and type **HelloNoun** when prompted for a file name. Click Save to generate the project.

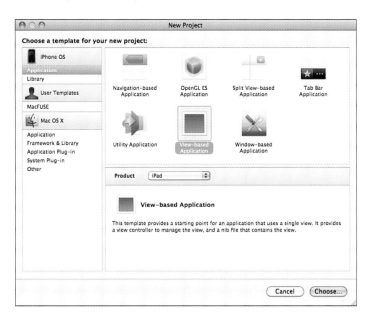

FIGURE 6.4
Choose the iPad View-Based Application template.

This will create a simple application structure consisting of an application delegate, a window, a view, and a view controller. After a few seconds, your project window will open (see Figure 6.5).

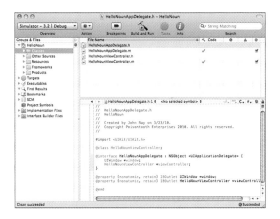

FIGURE 6.5
Your new project is open and ready for coding.

Classes

Click the Classes folder and review the contents. You should see four files (visible in Figure 6.5). The HelloNounAppDelegate.h and HelloNounAppDelegate.m files make up the delegate for the instance of UIApplication that our project will create. In other words, these files can be edited to include methods that govern how the application behaves when it is running. By default, the delegate will be responsible for one thing: adding a view to a window and making that window visible. This occurs in the aptly named application:DidFinishLaunchingWithOptions method in HelloNounAppDelegate.m, shown in Listing 6.1.

LISTING 6.1

```
- (BOOL)application:(UIApplication *)application
    didFinishLaunchingWithOptions:(NSDictionary *)launchOptions {

    // Override point for customization after app launch
    [window addSubview:viewController.view];
    [window makeKeyAndVisible];

    return YES;
}
```

You won't need to edit anything in the application delegate, but keep in mind the role that it plays in the overall application life cycle.

The second set of files, HelloNounViewController.h and HelloNounViewController.m, will implement the class that contains the logic for controlling our view—a view controller (UIViewController). These files are largely empty to begin, with just a basic structure in place to ensure that we can build and run the project from the outset. In fact, feel free to click the Build and Run button at the top of the window. The application will compile and launch, but there won't be anything to do!

Notice that when we create a project, Xcode automatically names the classes and resources based on the project name.

To impart some functionality to our app, we need to work on the two areas we discussed previously: the view and the view controller.

XIB Files

After looking through the classes, click the Resources folder to show the XIB files that are part of the template. You should see MainWindow.xib and HelloNounViewController.xib files. Recall that these files are used to hold instances of objects that we can add visually to a project. These objects are automatically instantiated when the XIB loads. Open the MainWindow.xib file by double-clicking it in Xcode. Interface Builder should launch and load the file. Within Interface Builder, choose Window, Document to show the components of the file.

The MainWindow XIB, shown in Figure 6.6, contains icons for the File's Owner (UIApplication), the First Responder (an instance of UIResponder), the HelloNoun App Delegate (HelloNounAppDelegate), the Hello Noun View Controller (HelloNounViewController), and our application's Window (UIWindow).

As a result, when the application launches, MainWindow XIB is loaded, a window is created, along with an instance of the HelloNounViewController class. In turn, the HelloNounViewController defines its view within the second XIB file, HelloNounViewController.xib—this is where we'll visually build our interface.

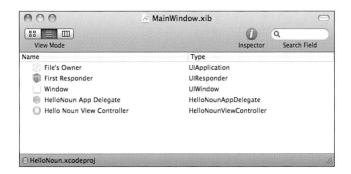

FIGURE 6.6
The MainWindow.xib file handles creating the application's window and instantiating our view controller.

Any reasonable person is probably scratching his head right now wondering a few things. First, why does MainWindow.xib get loaded at all? Where is the code to tell the application to do this?

The MainWindow.xib file is defined in the HelloNoun-Info.plist file as the property value for the key "Main nib file base name". You can see this yourself by clicking the Resources folder and then clicking the plist file to show the contents (see Figure 6.7).

FIGURE 6.7
The project's plist file defines the XIB loaded when the application starts.

Second, what about the HelloNounViewController.xib tells the application that it contains the view we want to use for our user interface? The answer lies in the MainWindow XIB file. Return to the MainWindow.xib document window in Interface Builder.

Click once on Hello Noun View Controller to select it in the list, and then press Command+1 or choose Attributes Inspector from the Tools menu. A small window will appear, as shown in Figure 6.8. Expand the View Controller section and you should see that the NIB Name field is set to `HelloNounViewController`. This means that the view controller loads its view from that XIB file.

FIGURE 6.8
After the MainWindow.xib instantiates the view controller, it loads its view from HelloNounView Controller.xib.

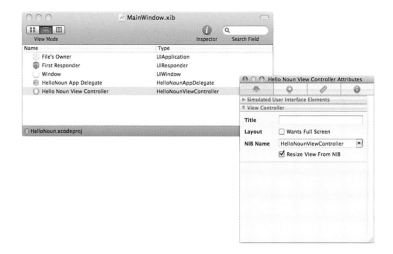

In short, the application is configured to load MainWindow.xib, which creates an instance of our view controller class (`HelloNounViewController`), which subsequently loads its view from the HelloNounViewController.xib. If that still doesn't make sense, don't fret; we'll guide you through this every step of the way.

Preparing the View Controller Outlets and Actions

A view is connected to its view controller class through outlets and actions. These must be present in our code files before Interface Builder will have a clue where to connect our user interface elements, so let's work through adding those connection points now.

For this simple project, we're going to need to interact with three different objects:

▶ A text field (`UITextField`)

▶ A label (`UILabel`)

▶ A button (`UIButton`)

The first two provide input (the field) and output (the label) for the user. The third (the button) triggers an action in our code to set the contents of the label to the contents of the text field. Based on what we now know, we can define the following outlets:

```
IBOutlet UILabel *userOutput;
IBOutlet UITextField *userInput;
```

And this action:

```
-(IBAction)setOutput:(id)sender;
```

Open the HelloNounViewController.h file in Xcode and add the IBOutlet and IBAction lines. Remember that the outlet directives fall inside the @interface block, and the action should be added immediately following it. Your header file should now resemble this:

```
#import <UIKit/UIKit.h>

@interface HelloNounViewController : UIViewController {
    IBOutlet UILabel *userOutput;
    IBOutlet UITextField *userInput;
}

-(IBAction)setOutput:(id)sender;

@end
```

Congratulations! You've just built the connection points that you'll need for Interface Builder to connect to your code. Save the file and get ready to create a user interface!

Creating the View

Interface Builder makes designing a user interface (UI) as much fun as playing around in your favorite graphics application. That said, our emphasis will be on the fundamentals of the development process and the objects we have at our disposal. Where it isn't critical, we move quickly through the interface creation.

Adding the Objects

The interface for the HelloNoun application is quite simple—it must provide a space for output, a field for input, and a button to set the output to the same thing as the input. Follow these steps to create the UI:

1. Open HelloNounViewController.xib by double-clicking it within the Xcode project's Resources folder.

2. If it isn't already running, Interface Builder will launch and open the XIB file, displaying the document window for the XIB file (see Figure 6.9). If you don't see the window, choose Window, Document from the menu.

FIGURE 6.9
The
HelloNounView
Controller.xib
file's view will
contain all the
UI objects for
the application.

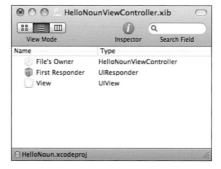

3. Double-click the icon for the instance of the view (UIView). The view itself, currently empty, will display. Open the Library by choosing Tools, Library. Make sure that the Objects button is selected within the Library—this displays all the components that we can drag into the view. Your workspace should now resemble Figure 6.10.

FIGURE 6.10
Open the view
and the object
Library to begin
creating the
interface.

4. Add two labels to the view by clicking and dragging the label (`UILabel`) object from the Library into the view.

5. The first label will simply be static text that says Hello. Double-click the default text that reads Label to edit it and change the content to read **Hello**. Position the second label underneath it; this will act as the output area.

For this example, I changed the text of the second label to read "<Noun Goes Here!>". This will serve as a default value until the user provides a new string. You may need to expand the text labels by clicking and dragging their handles to create enough room for them to display.

I also chose to set my labels to align their text in the center and increase the font size to 72. If you want to do the same, select the label within the view by clicking it, and then press Command+1 or choose Tools, Attributes Inspector from the menu. This opens the Attributes Inspector for the label, as demonstrated in Figure 6.11.

FIGURE 6.11
Use the Attributes Inspector to set the label to center itself and to increase the font size.

You may also explore the other attributes to see the effect on the text, such as style, color, and so on. Your view should now resemble Figure 6.12.

6. When you're happy with the results, it's time to add the elements that the user will be interacting with: the text field and button. Find the Text Field object (UITextField) within the Library and click and drag to position it under your two labels. Using the handles on the field, stretch it so that it matches the length of your output label.

7. Open the Attributes Inspector again (Command+1) and set the text size to match the labels you added earlier. You'll notice that the field itself doesn't get any bigger. This is because the default field type on the iPad has a set height. To change the height, click the square-shadowed "border" button in the inspector. The field will then allow you to resize its height freely.

8. Finally, click-drag a Round Rect button (UIButton) from the Library into the view, positioning it right below the text field. Double-click in the center of the button to add a title to the button, such as Set Label. Resize the button to fit the label appropriately. You may also want to again use the attributes inspector to increase the font size.

Figure 6.13 shows our version of this view.

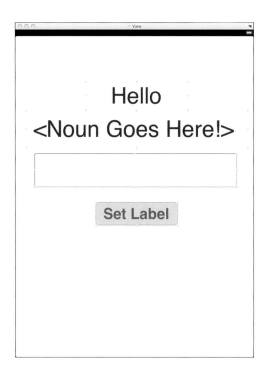

FIGURE 6.13
Your interface
should include
two labels, a
field, and
button—just
like this!

Connecting Outlets and Actions

Our work in Interface Builder is almost complete. The last remaining step is to connect the view to the view controller. Because we already created the outlet and action connection points in the HelloNounViewController.h file, this will be a piece of cake!

Make sure that you can see both the document window and the view you just created. You're going to be dragging from the objects in the view to the File's Owner icon in the document window. Why File's Owner? Because, as you learned earlier, the XIB is "owned" by the HelloNounViewController object, which is responsible for loading it.

1. Control-drag from the File's Owner icon to the label that you've established for output (titled <Noun Goes Here!> in the example), and then release the mouse button. You can use either the visual representation of the label in the view or the listing of the label object within the document window.

2. When you release the mouse button, you'll be prompted to choose the appropriate outlet. Pick userOutput from the list that appears (see Figure 6.14).

FIGURE 6.14
Connect the
label that will
display output
to the
userOutput
outlet.

3. Repeat the process for the text field, this time choosing userInput as the outlet. The link between the input and output view objects and the view controller is now established.

4. To finish the view, we still need to connect the button to the setOutput action. Although you *could* do this by Control-dragging, it isn't recommended. Objects may have dozens of different events that can be used as a trigger. To make sure that you're using the right event, you must select the object in the view, and then press Command+3 or choose Tools, Connections Inspector. This opens the Connections Inspector, which shows all the possible events for the object. For a button object, the event that you're most likely to want to use is Touch Up Inside, meaning that the user had a finger on the button, and then released the finger while it was still inside the button.

5. Make sure the button is selected, and then drag from the circle beside Touch Up Inside in the Connections Inspector to the File's Owner icon. When prompted for an action, choose setOutput (it should be the only option). The Connections Inspector should update to show the completed connection, as shown in Figure 6.15.

FIGURE 6.15
Use the
Connections
Inspector to cre-
ate a link from
the event to the
action it should
trigger.

Your view is now complete! You can safely exit Interface Builder, saving your changes.

Implementing the View Controller Logic

With the view complete and the connection to the view controller in place, the only task left is to fill in the view controller logic. Let's turn our attention back toward the HelloNounViewController.h and HelloNounViewController.m files. Why do we need to revisit the interface file (.h)? Because we'll need to easily access the `userOutput` and `userInput` variables, and to do that, we'll have to define these as properties, like this:

```
@property (retain, nonatomic) UITextField *userInput;
@property (retain, nonatomic) UILabel *userOutput;
```

Edit HelloNounViewController.h to include these lines after the `@interface` block. The finished file is shown in Listing 6.2:

LISTING 6.2

```
#import <UIKit/UIKit.h>

@interface HelloNounViewController : UIViewController {
    IBOutlet UILabel *userOutput;
    IBOutlet UITextField *userInput;
}

@property (retain, nonatomic) UITextField *userInput;
@property (retain, nonatomic) UILabel *userOutput;

-(IBAction)setOutput:(id)sender;

@end
```

To access these properties conveniently, we must use `@synthesize` to create the getters/settings for each. Open the HelloNounViewController.m implementation file and add these lines immediately following the `@implementation` directive:

```
@synthesize userInput;
@synthesize userOutput;
```

This leaves us with the implementation of `setOutput`. The purpose of this method is to set the output label to the contents of the field that the user edited. How do we get/set these values? Simple! Both `UILabel` and `UITextField` have a property called `text` that contains their contents. By reading and writing to these properties, we can set `userInput` to `userOutput` in one easy step.

Edit HelloNounViewController.m to include this method definition, following the `@synthesize` directives:

```
-(IBAction) setOutput:(id)sender {
    userOutput.text=userInput.text;
}
```

It all boils down to a single line! Thanks to our getters and setters, this single assignment statement does everything we need.

Had we not used @synthesize to create the accessors, we could have implemented the setOutput logic like this:

```
[userOutput setText: [userInput text]];
```

Either way is fine technically, but you should always code for readability and ease of maintenance.

Freeing Up Memory

Whenever we've used an object and are done with it, we need to release it so that the memory can be freed and reused. Even though this application needs the label and text field objects (userOutput and userInput), as long as it is running, it is still good practice to release them in the dealloc method of the view controller. The release method is called like this:

```
[<my Object> release]
```

Edit the HelloNounViewController.m file's dealloc method to release both userOutput and userInput. The result should look like this:

```
- (void)dealloc {
    [userInput release];
    [userOutput release];
    [super dealloc];
}
```

Well done! You've written your first iPad application!

Building the Application

The app is ready to build and test. If you'd like to deploy to your iPad, be sure it is connected and ready to go, and then choose iPhone Device from the drop-down menu in the upper left of the Xcode window. Otherwise, choose Simulator. Click Build and Run.

After a few seconds, the application will start on your iPad or within the simulator window, as shown in Figure 6.16.

FIGURE 6.16
Your finished application makes use of a view to handle the UI, and a view controller to implement the functional logic.

Further Exploration

Before moving on to subsequent hours, you may want to learn more about how Apple has implemented the MVC design versus other development environments that you may have used. An excellent document, titled "Cocoa Design Patterns," provides an in-depth discussion of MVC as applied to Cocoa. You can find and read this introduction by searching for the title in the Xcode documentation system, which we discussed in Hour 4.

You may also want to take a breather and use the finished HelloNoun application as a playground for experimentation. We discussed only a few of the different Interface Builder attributes that can be set for labels, but there are dozens more that can customize the way that fields and buttons are displayed. The flexibility of the view creation in Interface Builder goes well beyond what can fit in one book, so exploration *will* be necessary to take full advantage of the tools. This is an excellent opportunity to play around in the tools and see the results—before we move into more complex (and easy to break!) applications.

Summary

In this hour, you learned about the MVC design pattern and how it separates the display (view), logic (controller), and data (model) components of an application. You also explored how Apple implements this design within Xcode through the use Core Data, views, and view controllers. This approach will guide your applications through much of this book and in your own real-world application design, so learning the basics now will pay off later.

To reinforce the lesson, we worked through a simple application using the View-Based Application template. This included creating outlets and actions that linked a view and view controller via Xcode and Interface Builder. While not the most complex app you'll write, it included the elements of a fully interactive user experience: input, output, and (very simple) logic.

Q&A

Q. *Is it possible to have multiple views or view controllers?*

A. Yes, absolutely. In Hours 11–14, you'll create several applications with multiple view controllers.

Q. *Why do I drag from the File's Owner to the Object in Interface Builder, rather than the other way around?*

A. Think of the File's Owner as the code that you're going to be writing. Your code needs to reference the Interface Builder object (through an outlet), not the other way around.

Workshop

Quiz

1. What event do you use to detect a button tap?

2. What purpose does the @synthesize directive accomplish?

3. Which Apple project template creates a simple view/view controller application?

Answers

1. The Touch Up Inside event is most commonly used to trigger actions based on a button press.

2. The @synthesize directive creates the simplified getters and setters for a property. In the case of the label and field we used in the tutorial, it enabled us to access the text property by using <variable name>.text.

3. The View-Based Application template sets up a view and a view controller.

Activities

1. Explore the attributes of the interface objects that you added to the tutorial project in Interface Builder. Try setting different fonts, colors, and layouts. Use these tools to customize the view beyond the simple layout created this hour.

2. Review the Apple Xcode documentation for the Core Data features of Cocoa. Although you won't be using this technology in this book's tutorials, it is an important tool that you'll ultimately want to become more familiar with for advanced data-driven applications.

HOUR 7

Working with Text, Keyboards, and Buttons

What You'll Learn in This Hour:

- ▶ How to use text fields
- ▶ Input and output in scrollable text views
- ▶ How to enable data detectors
- ▶ A way to spruce up the standard iPad buttons

In the last hour, you explored views and view controllers and created a simple application that accepted user input and generated output when a button was pushed. These are the basic building blocks that we expand on in this hour. We'll be creating an application that uses multiple different input and output techniques. You'll learn how to implement and use editable text fields, text views, graphical buttons, and how to configure the onscreen keyboard.

This is quite a bit of material to be covering in an hour, but the concepts are very similar, and you'll quickly get the hang of these new elements.

Basic User Input and Output

The iPad gives us many different ways of displaying information to a user and collecting feedback. There are so many ways, in fact, that we're going to be spending the next several hours working through the tools that the iPhone OS SDK provides for interacting with your users—starting with the basics.

Buttons

One of the most common interactions you'll have with your users is detecting and reacting to the touch of a button (UIButton). Buttons, as you may recall, are elements of a view that respond to an event that the user can trigger in the interface, usually a "Touch Up Inside" event to indicate that the user's finger was on a button and then released it. When an event is detected, it can trigger an action (IBAction) within a corresponding view controller.

Buttons are used for everything from providing preset answers to questions to triggering motions within a game. Although we've used only a single Rounded Rect button up to this point, they can take on many different forms through the use of images. Figure 7.1 shows an example of a fancy button.

FIGURE 7.1
Buttons can be simple, fancy (like this one), or set to any arbitrary image.

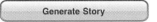

Generate Story

Text Fields and Views

Another common input mechanism is a text field. Text fields (UITextField) give users space to enter any information they'd like into a single line in the application—these are similar to the form fields in a web form. When users enter data into a field, you can constrain their input to numbers or text by using different iPad keyboards, something we'll do later this hour. Text fields, like buttons, can respond to events, but frequently are implemented as passive interface elements, meaning that their contents (provided through the text property) can be read at any time by the view controller.

Similar to the text field is the text view (UITextView). The difference is a text view can present a scrollable and editable block of text for the user to either read or modify. These should be used when more than a few words of input are required. Figure 7.2 shows examples of a text field and text view.

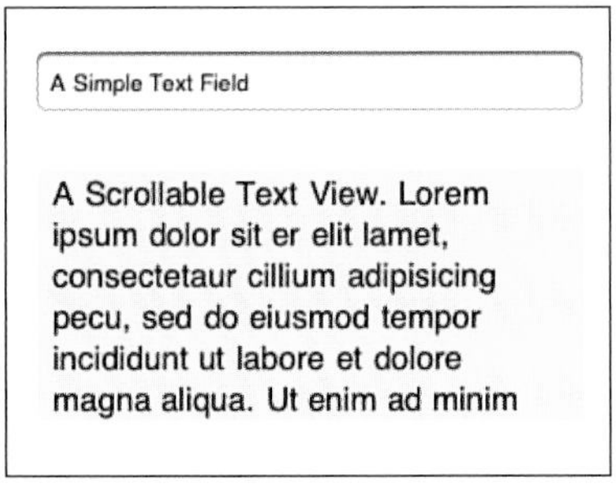

FIGURE 7.2
Text fields and text views provide a means for entering text using the iPad's virtual keyboard.

A Simple Text Field

A Scrollable Text View. Lorem ipsum dolor sit er elit lamet, consectetaur cillium adipisicing pecu, sed do eiusmod tempor incididunt ut labore et dolore magna aliqua. Ut enim ad minim

Labels

The final interface feature that we're going to be using here and throughout this book is the label (`UILabel`). Labels are used to display strings within a view by setting their `text` property.

The text within a label can be controlled via a wide range of label attributes, such as font and text size, alignment, and color. As you'll see, labels prove useful both for static text in a view and for presenting dynamic output that you generate in your code.

Now that you have basic insight into the input and output tools we'll be using in this hour, let's go ahead and get started with our project: a simple substitution-style story generator.

Using Text Fields, Text Views, and Buttons

Despite what some people might think, I enjoy entering text on a touch-screen keyboard. The iPad's virtual keyboard is responsive and simple to navigate, and big enough to type on comfortably. What's more, the input process can be altered to constrain the user's input to only numbers, only letters, or other variations. You can even have the iPad automatically correct simple misspellings or capitalize letters. This project reviews many aspects of the text input process.

Implementation Overview

In this project, we'll be creating a Mad Libs–style story creator. The user will enter a noun (place), verb, and number through three text fields (`UITextField`). The user may also enter or modify a template that contains the outline of the story to be generated. Because the template can be several lines long, we'll use a text view (`UITextView`) to present this information. A button press (`UIButton`) will trigger an action that generates the story and outputs the finished text in another text view, as demonstrated in Figure 7.3.

FIGURE 7.3
The tutorial app
this hour uses
two types of
text input
objects.

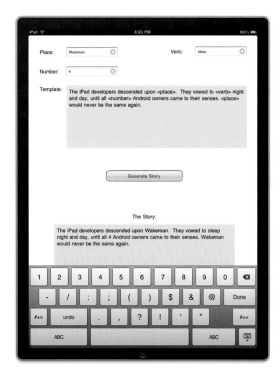

Although not directly part of the input or output process, we'll also investigate how to implement the now-expected "touch the background to make the keyboard disappear" interface standard, along with a few other important points. In other words, pay attention!

> Unlike the iPhone, the iPad includes a virtual key to hide the keyboard. Implementing the ability to touch the background to hide the keyboard *isn't* a requirement, but it *is* an interface convention that users will be expecting.

We'll be naming this tutorial project FieldButtonFun. You may certainly use something more creative if you'd like.

Setting Up the Project

This project will use the same View-Based Application template as the preceding hour. If it isn't already running, launch Xcode (Developer/Applications), and then choose File, New Project.

Select the iPhone OS Application project type, and then find and select the iPad version of the View-Based Application in the Template list. Click Choose to continue, and then enter the project name, **FieldButtonFun**, and save the new project.

Xcode will set up a skeleton project for you. As before, we'll be focusing on the view, which has been created in FieldButtonFunViewController.xib, and the view controller class `FieldButtonFunViewController`.

Preparing the Outlets and Actions

This project contains a total of six input areas: Three text fields will be used to collect the place, verb, and number values. We'll be calling these `thePlace`, `theVerb`, and `theNumber`, respectively. The project also requires two text views: one to hold the editable story template, `theTemplate`; and the other to contain the output, `theStory`. Finally, a single button is used to trigger a method, `createStory`, which will create the story text.

> Yes, we'll be using a text view for output as well as input. Text views provide a built-in scrolling behavior and can be set to read-only, making them convenient for both collecting and displaying information. They do not, however, allow for rich text input or output. A single font style is all you get!

By the Way

Start by preparing the outlets and actions in the view controller's header file, FieldButtonFunViewController.h. Edit the file to contain the code shown in Listing 7.1.

LISTING 7.1

```
 1: #import <UIKit/UIKit.h>
 2:
 3: @interface FieldButtonFunViewController : UIViewController {
 4:     IBOutlet UITextField *thePlace;
 5:     IBOutlet UITextField *theVerb;
 6:     IBOutlet UITextField *theNumber;
 7:     IBOutlet UITextView *theStory;
 8:     IBOutlet UITextView *theTemplate;
 9:     IBOutlet UIButton *generateStory;
10: }
11:
12: @property (retain,nonatomic) UITextField *thePlace;
13: @property (retain,nonatomic) UITextField *theVerb;
14: @property (retain,nonatomic) UITextField *theNumber;
15: @property (retain,nonatomic) UITextView *theStory;
16: @property (retain,nonatomic) UITextView *theTemplate;
17: @property (retain,nonatomic) UIButton *generateStory;
18:
19: -(IBAction)createStory:(id)sender;
20:
21: @end
```

Lines 4–9 create the outlets for each of the input elements, while lines 12–17 establish them as properties so that we can easily manipulate their contents. Line 19 declares a `createStory` method where we'll eventually implement the logic behind the application.

> If you're paying close attention, you may notice that we've declared an outlet and a property for the view's button, generateButton. As mentioned earlier, typically buttons are used to trigger a method when a certain event takes place, so we don't usually need an outlet or property to manipulate them.
>
> In this example, however, we're going to programmatically alter the visual appearance of the button, so we need to be able to access the object, not just receive messages from it.

After you've set up the outlets and actions, save the header file and open FieldButtonViewController.m. As you've learned, properties usually have corresponding @synthesize directives so that they can easily be accessed in code. Add the appropriate statements for all the properties defined in the header. Your additions should fall after the @implementation directive and look like this:

```
@synthesize thePlace;
@synthesize theVerb;
@synthesize theNumber;
@synthesize theStory;
@synthesize theTemplate;
@synthesize generateStory;
```

That should be all the setup we need for now. Let's turn our attention to creating the user interface.

In the preceding hour, you learned that the MainWindow.xib is loaded when the application launches and that it will instantiate the view controller, which subsequently loads its view from the second XIB file in the project (in this case, FieldButtonFunViewController.xib). Locate the file in the project's Resources folder, and then double-click it to launch Interface Builder.

When Interface Builder has started, open the XIB file's document window (Window, Document), and then double-click the view icon to open the blank view for editing.

Adding Text Fields

Begin creating the user interface by adding three text fields to the top of the view. To add a field, open the Objects Library by choosing Tools, Library, and then locate the Text Field object (`UITextField`) and drag it into the view. Repeat this two more times for the other two fields.

Arrange the fields at the top of the view, taking full advantage of the iPad's screen width. (We went with two side by side, and one below.) To help the user differentiate between the three fields, you'll want to add labels to the view as well. Click and drag the Label (UILabel) object from the Library into the view. Align three labels directly across from the three fields. Double-click the label within the view to set its text. I've labeled my fields Place, Verb, and Number, as shown in Figure 7.4.

FIGURE 7.4
Add text fields and labels to differentiate between them.

Editing Text Field Attributes

The fields that you've created are technically fine as is, but you can adjust their appearance and behavior to create a better user experience. To view the field attributes, click a field, and then press Command+1 (Tools, Attributes Inspector) to open the Attributes Inspector (see Figure 7.5).

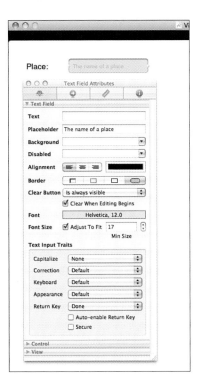

FIGURE 7.5
Editing a field's attributes can help create a better UI.

For example, you can use the Placeholder Text field to enter text that will appear in the background of the field until the user begins editing. This can be a helpful tip or an additional explanation of what the user should be entering.

You may also choose to activate the Clear button. The Clear button is a small X icon added to a field that the user can touch to quickly erase the contents. To add the Clear button, simply choose one of the visibility options from the Clear button pop-up menu; the functionality is added for free to your application! Note that you may also choose to automatically clear the field when the user taps into it to start editing. Just enable the Clear When Editing Begins check box.

Add these features to the three fields within the view. Figure 7.6 shows how they will appear in the application.

Placeholder text also helps identify which field is which within the Interface Builder document window. It can make creating your connections much easier down the road!

In addition to these changes, attributes can adjust the text alignment, font and size, and other visual options. Part of the fun of working in Interface Builder is that you can explore the tools and make tweaks (and undo them) without having to edit your code.

Customizing the Keyboard Display with Text Input Traits

Probably the most important attributes that you can set for an input field are the "text input traits," or simply, how the keyboard is going to be shown onscreen. Seven different traits are currently available:

Capitalize: Controls whether the iPad will automatically capitalize words, sentences, or all the characters entered into a field.

Correction: If explicitly set to on or off, the input field will correct (on) or ignore (off) common spelling errors. If left to the defaults, it will inherit the behavior of the OS settings.

Keyboard: Sets a predefined keyboard for providing input. By default, the input keyboard lets you type letters, numbers, and symbols. Choosing the option Number Pad will only allow numbers to be entered. Similarly, using Email Address constrains the input to strings that look like email addresses. Seven different keyboard styles are available.

Appearance: Changes the appearance of the keyboard to look more like an alert view (which you'll learn about in a later hour).

Return Key: If the keyboard has a Return key, it is set to this label. Values include Done, Search, Next, Go, and so on.

Auto-Enable Return Key: Disables the Return key on the keyboard unless the user has entered at least a single character of input into the field.

Secure: Treats the field as a password, hiding each character as it is typed.

Of the three fields that we've added to the view, the Number field can definitely benefit from setting an input trait. With the Attributes Inspector still open, select the Number field in the view, and then choose the Number Pad option within the Keyboard pop-up menu (see Figure 7.7).

FIGURE 7.7
Choosing a keyboard type can help constrain a user's input.

You may also want to alter the capitalization and correction options on the other two fields and set the Return key to Done. Again, all of this functionality is gained "for free." So, you can return to Interface Builder to experiment all you want later on.

Connecting to the Outlets

The first three fields of the view are now finished and ready to be connected to their variables back in Xcode. To connect to the outlets defined earlier, Control-drag from the File's Owner icon in the document window to the first field (Place) either in the view window, or within the document window's view hierarchy. When prompted, choose `thePlace` from the pop-up list of outlets, as shown in Figure 7.8.

FIGURE 7.8
Connect each
field to its corre-
sponding outlet.

Repeat the process for the Verb and Number fields, connecting them to the theVerb and theNumber instance variable outlets. The primary input fields are connected.

Now we're ready to move on to the next element of the user interface: text views.

By the Way

Copy and Paste

Your text entry areas will automatically gain copy and paste without needing to change anything in your code. For advanced applications, you can override the protocol methods defined in UIResponderStandardEditActions to customize the copy, paste, and selection process.

Adding Text Views

Now that you know the ins and outs of text fields, let's move on to the two text views (UITextView) present in this project. Text views, for the most part, can be used just like text fields. You can access their contents the same way, and they support many of the same attributes as text fields, including text input traits.

To add a text view, find the Text View object (UITextView) and drag it into the view. This will add a block to the view, complete with Greeked text (*Lorem ipsum...*) that represents the input area. Using the resizing handles on the sizes of the block, you can shrink or expand the object to best fit the view. Because this project calls for two text views, drag two into the view and size them to fit underneath the existing three text fields.

As with the text fields, the views themselves don't convey much information about their purpose to the user. To clarify their use, add two text labels for each of the views, **Template** for the first, and **The Story** for the second. Your view should now resemble Figure 7.9.

FIGURE 7.9
Add two text views with corresponding labels to the view.

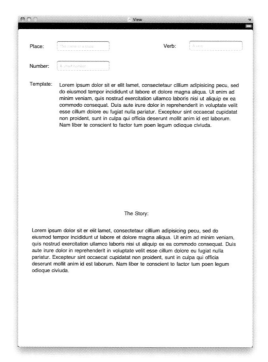

Editing Text View Attributes

Text view attributes provide many of the same visual controls as text fields. Select a view, and then open the Attributes Inspector (Command+1) to see the available options, as shown in Figure 7.10.

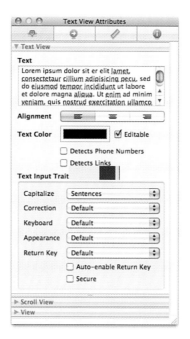

FIGURE 7.10
Edit the attributes of each text view to prepare them for input and output.

To start, we need to update the Text attribute to remove the initial Greeked text and provide our own content. For the top field, which will act as the template, select the content within the Text attribute of the Attributes Inspector, and then clear it. Enter the following text, which will be available within the application as the default:

```
The iPad developers descended upon <place>.  They vowed to <verb> night and day,
until all <number> Android owners came to their senses. <place> would never be
the same again.
```

When we implement the logic behind this interface, the placeholders (<place>, <verb>, <number>) will be replaced with the user's input.

Next, select the "story" text view, and then again use the Attributes Inspector to clear the contents entirely. Because the contents of this text view will be generated automatically, we can leave the Text attribute blank. This view will also be a read-only view, so uncheck the Editable attribute.

In this example, to help provide some additional contrast between these two areas, I've set the background color of the template to a light red and the story to a light green. To do this in your copy, simply select the text view to stylize, and then click the Attributes Inspector's View background attribute to open a color chooser. Figure 7.11 shows our final text views.

FIGURE 7.11
When complet-
ed, the text
views should
differ in color,
editability, and
content.

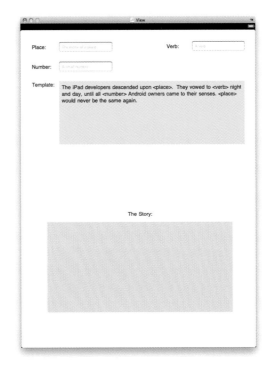

Setting Scrolling Options

When editing the text view attributes, you'll notice that a range of options exist that are specifically related to its ability to scroll, as shown in Figure 7.12.

FIGURE 7.12
Scrolling regions
have a number
of attributes
that can change
their behavior.

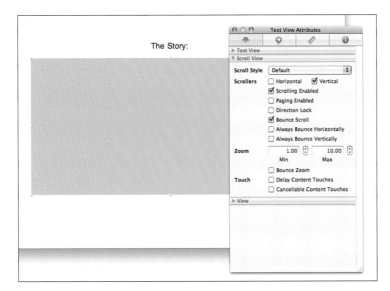

Using these features, you can set the color of the scroll indicator (black or white), choose whether both horizontal and vertical scrolling are enabled, and even whether the scrolling area should have the rubber-band "bounce" effect when it reaches the ends of the scrollable content.

Using Data Detectors

By the Way

Data detectors automatically analyze the content within onscreen controls and provide helpful links based on what they find. Phone numbers, for example, can be touched to dial the phone; detected web addresses can be set to launch Safari when tapped by the user. All of this occurs without your application having to do a thing. No need to parse out strings that look like URLs or phone numbers. In fact, all you need to do is click a button.

To enable data detectors on a text view, select the view and return to the Attributes Inspector (Command+1). Within the Text View Attributes area, click the check boxes for Detects Phone Numbers to identify any sequence of numbers that looks like a phone number, or Detects Links to provide a clickable link for web and email addresses.

Watch Out!

Data detectors are a great convenience for users, but *can* be overused. If you enable data detectors in your projects, be sure they make sense. For example, if you are calculating numbers and outputting them to the user, chances are you *don't* want the digits to be recognized as telephone numbers.

Connecting to the Outlets

Connect the text views to the theStory and theTemplate outlets you defined earlier. Control-drag from the File's Owner icon in the document window to the text view that contains the template. When prompted, choose theTemplate from the pop-up list of outlets (see Figure 7.13).

FIGURE 7.13
Connect each
view to its corre-
sponding outlet.

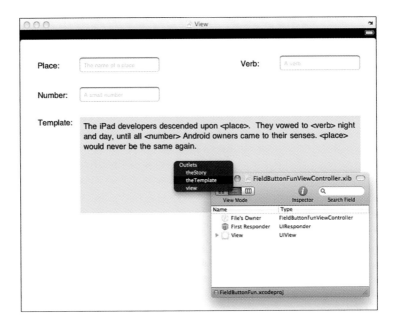

Repeat this for the second text view, this time choosing theStory for the outlet. You've just completed the text input and output features of the application. All that remains is a button!

Creating Customized Buttons

In Hour 6, "Model-View-Controller Application Design," you created a button (UIButton) and connected it to the implementation of an action (IBAction) within a view controller. Nothing to it, right? Working with buttons is relatively straightforward, but what you may have noticed is that, by default, the buttons you create in Interface Builder are, well, kind of boring.

We need a single button in this project, so drag an instance of the Rounded Rect button (UIButton) from the Objects Library to the bottom of the view. Title the button **Generate Story**. The final view, with a default button, can be seen in Figure 7.14.

While you're certainly welcome to use the standard buttons, you may want to explore what visual changes you can make in Interface Builder, and ultimately through code changes.

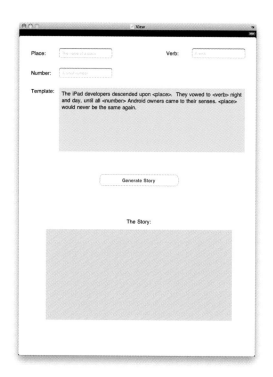

FIGURE 7.14
The default button styles are less than appealing.

Editing Button Attributes

To edit a button's appearance, your first stop is, once again, the Attributes Inspector (Command+1). Using the Attributes Inspector, you can dramatically change the appearance of the button. Use the Type drop-down menu, shown in Figure 7.15, to choose common button types:

Rounded Rect: The default button style.

Detail Disclosure: An arrow button used to indicate additional information is available.

Info Light: An *i* icon, typically used to display additional information about an application or item. The "Light" version is intended for dark backgrounds.

Info Dark: The dark (light background) version of the Info Light button.

Add Contact: A + button, frequently used to indicate the addition of a contact to the address book.

Custom: A button that has no default appearance. Usually used with button images.

FIGURE 7.15
The Attributes
Inspector gives
several options
for common
button types,
as well as a
custom option.

In addition to choosing a button type, you can make the button interact with user touches, a concept known as changing state. For instance, by "default," a button is displayed unhighlighted within the view. When a user touches a button, it changes to a highlighted "on" state, showing that it has been touched.

Using the Attributes Inspector, you can use the State Configuration menu to change the button's title, background color, or even add a graphic image.

Setting Custom Button Images

To create custom iPad buttons, you'll need to make custom images, including versions for the highlighted on state and the default off state. These can be any shape or size, but PNG format is recommended.

Once you've added these to the project through Xcode, you'll be able to select the image from the Image or Background drop-down menus in Interface Builder's button attributes. Using the Image menu sets an image that appears inside the button alongside the button title. This option allows you to decorate a button with an icon.

Using the Background menu sets an image that will be stretched to fill the entire background of the button. The option lets you create a custom image as the entire button, but you'll need to size your button exactly to match the image. If you don't, the image will be stretched and pixilated in your interface.

Another way to use custom button images that will correctly size to your text is through the code. We'll apply this technique to our project now.

Remember how we created an outlet for a button earlier in the project? We need the outlet so that we can manipulate the button in Xcode. Control-drag from the File's Owner icon in the document window in Interface Builder to the Generate Story button. Pick the generateStory outlet when prompted, as demonstrated in Figure 7.16.

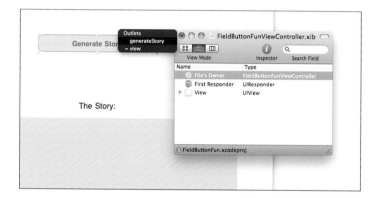

FIGURE 7.16
We need to access the button properties from our application to manipulate its images.

Now, switch your attention to Xcode. Inside the FieldButtonFun directory is an Images folder with two Apple-created button templates: whiteButton.png and blueButton.png. Drag these image files into the Resources folder in Xcode, choosing to copy the resources, if necessary, as shown in Figure 7.17.

Within Xcode, open the FieldButtonFunViewController.m file and search for the method viewDidLoad, uncomment it by removing the /* */ comment markers that surround it.

FIGURE 7.17
To use custom buttons, drag them into the Resources folder in Xcode, and choose to copy the resources if needed.

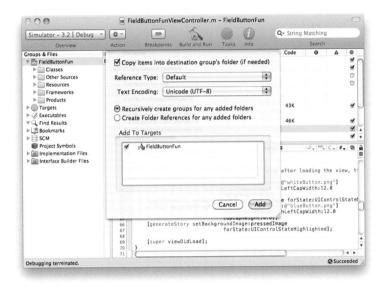

Implement the `viewDidLoad` method using the code in Listing 7.2:

LISTING 7.2

```
 1: -(void)viewDidLoad {
 2:    UIImage *normalImage = [[UIImage imageNamed:@"whiteButton.png"]
 3:                         stretchableImageWithLeftCapWidth:12.0
 4:                         topCapHeight:0.0];
 5:[generateStory setBackgroundImage:normalImage forState:UIControlStateNormal];
 6:    UIImage *pressedImage = [[UIImage imageNamed:@"blueButton.png"]
 7:                         stretchableImageWithLeftCapWidth:12.0
 8:                         topCapHeight:0.0];
 9:    [generateStory setBackgroundImage:pressedImage
10:                         forState:UIControlStateHighlighted];
11:
12:    [super viewDidLoad];
13: }
```

In this code block, we're accomplishing several different things, all focused on providing the button instance (`generateStory`) with a reference to an image object (`UIImage`) that "knows" how it can be stretched.

Why are we implementing this code in the `viewDidLoad` method? Because it is automatically invoked after the view is successfully instantiated from the XIB file. This gives us a convenient hook for making changes (in this case, adding button graphics) right as the view is being displayed onscreen.

In lines 2–4 and 6–8, we first return an instance of an image from the image files that we added to the project resources. Then we define that image as being "stretchable." Let's break this down into the individual statements:

To create an instance of an image based on a named resource, we use the `UIImage` *class method* `imagenamed`, along with a string that contains the filename of the image resource. For example, this code fragment creates an instance of the whiteButton.png image:

```
[UIImage imageNamed:@"whiteButton.png"]
```

Next, we use the *instance method* `stretchableImageWithLeftCapWidth:topCapHeight` to return another new instance of the image, but this time with properties that define how it can be stretched. These properties are the left cap width and top cap width, which describe how many pixels in from the left or down from the top of the image should be ignored before reaching a 1-pixel-wide strip that can be stretched. For instance, if the left cap is set to 12, a vertical column 12 pixels wide is ignored during stretching, and then the 13th column is repeated however many times is necessary to stretch to the requested length. The top cap works the same way, but repeats a horizontal row to grow the image to the correct size vertically, as illustrated in Figure 7.18. If the left cap is set to zero, the image can't be stretched horizontally; similarly, if the top cap is zero, the image can't be stretched vertically.

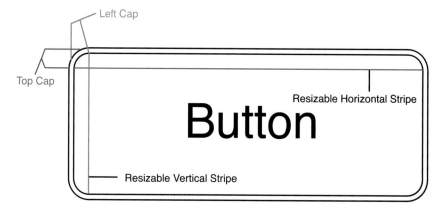

FIGURE 7.18
The caps define where, within an image, stretching can occur.

In this example, we use `stretchableImageWithLeftCapWidth:12.0 topCapHeight:0.0` to force horizontal stretching to occur at the 13th vertical column of pixels in, and to disable any vertical stretching. The `UIImage` instance returned is then assigned to the `normalImage` and `pressedImage` variables, corresponding to the default and highlighted button states.

Lines 5 and 9–10 use the `setBackgroundImage:forState` instance method of our `UIButton` object (`generateStory`) to set the stretchable images `normalImage` and `pressedImage` as the backgrounds for the predefined button states of `UIControlStateNormal` (default) and `UIControlStateHighlighted` (highlighted).

This might seem a bit confusing, and I empathize. Apple has not provided these same features directly in Interface Builder, despite their usefulness in almost any application with buttons. The good news is that there is no reason that you can't reuse this same code repeatedly in your applications.

Within Xcode, click Build and Run to compile and run your application. The Generate Story button should take on a new appearance (see Figure 7.19).

FIGURE 7.19
The end result is a shiny new button in the application.

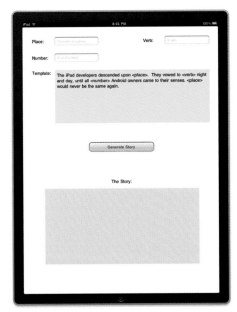

Remember that despite all of our efforts to make a pretty button, we still haven't connected it to an action. Switch back to Interface Builder to make the connection.

Connecting to the Action

To connect the button to the previously declared `createStory` action method, select the button object and open the Connections Inspector (Command+3) or choose Tools, Connections Inspector. Drag from the circle beside Touch Up Inside to the File's Owner icon in the Interface Builder document window.

When prompted for a method, choose `createStory`. The Connections Inspector should update, showing both the outlet that references the button (`generateStory`) and the `createStory` method, similar to Figure 7.20.

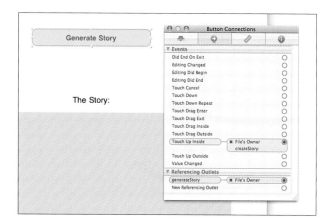

FIGURE 7.20
The button should now be connected to an outlet and an action.

At long last, our button is done!

Hiding the Keyboard

Before completing the application by implementing the view controller logic to construct the story, we need to look at a "problem" that is inherent to applications with character entry: keyboards that won't go away! To see what we mean, switch back into Xcode and use Build and Run to launch the FieldButtonFun application in the iPhone Simulator.

With your app up and running, click into any field. The keyboard appears. Now what? Click into another field, the keyboard changes to match the text input traits you set up, but it remains onscreen. Touch the word Done. Nothing happens! Right now, the only way to hide the keyboard is to use the dedicated keyboard-hiding button on the virtual keyboard. Isn't that enough? Yes and no. It works, but users of the iPhone OS platform have come to expect that tapping outside of a field will hide the keyboard.

Hour 4, "Inside Cocoa Touch," described "responders" as objects that process input. The "first responder" is the first object that has a shot at handling user input. In the case of a text field or text view, when it gains first responder status, the keyboard is shown and will remain onscreen until the field gives up or "resigns" first responder status. What does this look like in code? For the field `thePlace`, we could resign first responder status and get rid of the keyboard with this line of code:

```
[thePlace resignFirstResponder]
```

Calling the `resignFirstResponder` method tells the input object to "give up" its claim to the input; as a result, the keyboard disappears.

Hiding with the Done Button

The most common trigger for hiding the keyboard in applications is through the Did End on Exit event of the field. This event occurs when the Done (or similar) keyboard button is pressed.

To add keyboard hiding to the FieldButtonFun application, switch to Xcode, and create the action declaration for a method `hideKeyboard` in FieldButtonViewController.h by adding the following line after the `createStory` action:

`-(IBAction)hideKeyboard:(id)sender;`

Next, implement the `hideKeyboard` method within the FieldButtonFunViewController.m file by adding the method in Listing 7.3, immediately following the `@synthesize` directives.

LISTING 7.3

```
-(IBAction) hideKeyboard:(id)sender {
    [thePlace resignFirstResponder];
    [theVerb resignFirstResponder];
    [theNumber resignFirstResponder];
    [theTemplate resignFirstResponder];
}
```

By the
Way

> You might be asking yourself, isn't the sender variable the field that is generating the event? Couldn't we just resign the responder status of the sender? Yes! Absolutely! This would work just fine, but we're going to also need the hideKeyboard method to work when sender isn't necessarily the field. You'll learn more about this in a few minutes.

To connect fields to `hideKeyboard`, open the FieldButtonFunViewController.xib file in Interface Builder, and then open the view window so that the current interface is visible. Select the Place field, and open the Connections Inspector (Command+3). Drag from the circle beside the Did End on Exit event to the File's Owner icon in the document window. Choose the `hideKeyboard` action when prompted, as shown in Figure 7.21.

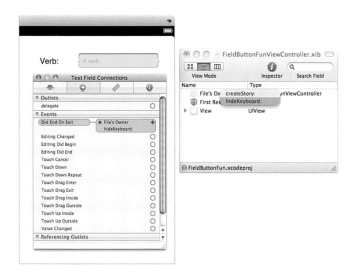

FIGURE 7.21
Connect each
field to the
hideKeyboard
method.

Repeat this process for the Verb and Number fields. Now when you press the Done button, it has the same effect as using the hide keyboard key.

Hiding with a Background Touch

A popular iPhone OS platform interface convention is that if a keyboard is open and you touch the background (outside of a field), the keyboard disappears. This will be the approach we need to take for the number-input text field and the text view—and functionality that we need to add to all of the other fields to keep things consistent.

Wondering how we detect an event outside of a field? Nothing special: All we do is create a big invisible button that sits behind all of the other controls, and then attach it to the hideKeyboard method already written.

Note that in this case we won't know exactly *which* field is going to be the first responder when hideKeyboard is called, therefore the implementation that asks each possible input area to resign first responder status. If it isn't the first responder, it has no effect.

Within Interface Builder, access the Library (Tools, Library) and drag a new button (UIButton) from the Library into the view.

Because this button needs to be invisible, make sure it is selected, and then open the Attributes Inspector (Command+1) and set the type to Custom. Use the resizing handles to size the button to fill the entire view. With the button selected, choose Layout, Send to Back to position the button in the back of the interface.

To connect the button to the hideKeyboard method, it's easiest to use the Interface Builder document window. Expand the view hierarchy, select the custom button you created (it should be at the top of the view hierarchy list), then Control-drag from the button to the File's Owner icon. When prompted, choose the hideKeyboard method.

Save your work in Interface Builder and Xcode, and then use Build and Run to try running the application again. This time, when you click outside of a field or the text view, or use the Done button, the keyboard disappears!

Implementing the View Controller Logic

To finish off FieldButtonFun, we need to add the createStory method within the view controller (FieldButtonFunViewController). This method will search the template text for the <place>, <verb>, and <number> placeholders, and then replace them with the user's input, storing the results in the text view. We'll make use of the NSString instance method stringByReplacingOccurrencesOfString:WithString to do the heavy lifting. This method performs a search and replace on a given string.

For example, if the variable myString contains Hello town and you wanted to replace *town* with *world*, you might use the following:

```
myNewString=[myString stringByReplacingOccurrencesOfString:@"town"
WithString:@"world"];
```

In this case, our strings are the text properties of the text fields and text views (thePlace.text, theVerb.text, theNumber.text, theTemplate.text, and theStory.text).

Add the final method implementation, shown in Listing 7.4 to FieldButtonFunViewController.m after the @synthesize directives.

LISTING 7.4

```
 1: -(IBAction) createStory:(id)sender {
 2:     theStory.text=[theTemplate.text
 3:                    stringByReplacingOccurrencesOfString:@"<place>"
 4:                    withString:thePlace.text];
 5:     theStory.text=[theStory.text
 6:                    stringByReplacingOccurrencesOfString:@"<verb>"
 7:                    withString:theVerb.text];
 8:     theStory.text=[theStory.text
 9:                    stringByReplacingOccurrencesOfString:@"<number>"
10:                    withString:theNumber.text];
11: }
```

Lines 2–4 replace the <place> placeholder in the template with the contents of the thePlace field, storing the results in the story text view. Lines 5–7 then update the story text view by replacing the <verb> placeholder with the appropriate user input. This is repeated again in lines 8–10 for the <number> placeholder. The end result is a completed story, output in the theStory text view.

Releasing the Objects

When you're done using an object in your applications, you should always release it to free up memory. This is good practice even if the application is about to exit. In this application, we've retained six objects—each of the interface elements—that need to be released. Edit the dealloc method to release these now:

```
- (void)dealloc {
    [thePlace release];
    [theVerb release];
    [theNumber release];
    [theStory release];
    [theTemplate release];
    [generateStory release];
    [super dealloc];
}
```

Our application is finally complete!

Building the Application

To view and test FieldButtonFun, click Build and Run in Xcode. Your finished app should look very similar to Figure 7.22, fancy button and all!

FIGURE 7.22
The finished application includes scrolling views, text editing, and a pretty button! What more could we want?

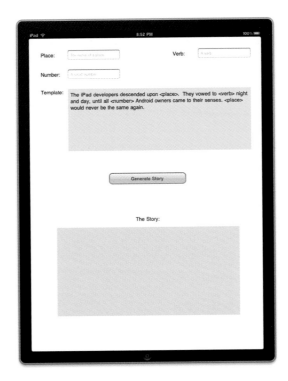

This project provided a starting point for looking through the different properties and attributes that can alter how objects look and behave within the iPad interface. The take-away message: Don't assume anything about an object until you've reviewed how it can be configured.

Further Exploration

Throughout the next few hours, you'll be exploring a large number of user interface objects, so your next steps should be to concentrate on the features you've learned in this hour—specifically, the object properties, methods, and events that they respond to.

For text fields and text views, the base object mostly provides for customization of appearance. However, you may also implement a delegate (UITextFieldDelegate, UITextViewDelegate) that responds to changes in editing status, such as starting or ending editing. You'll learn more about implementing delegates in Hour 10, "Getting the User's Attention," but you can start looking ahead to the additional functionality that can be provided in your applications through the use of a delegate.

It's also important to keep in mind that although there are plenty of properties to explore for these objects, there are additional properties and methods that are inherited from their superclasses. All UI elements, for example, inherit from `UIControl`, `UIView`, and `UIResponder`, which bring additional features to the table, such as properties for manipulating size and location of the object's onscreen display, as well as customizing the copy and paste process (through the `UIResponderStandardEditActions` protocol). By accessing these lower-level methods, you can customize the object beyond what might be immediately obvious.

Apple Tutorials

Apple has provided a sample project that includes examples of almost all the available iPhone OS user interface controls: UICatalog (accessible via the Xcode documentation). This project also includes a wide variety of graphic samples, such as the button images used in this hour's tutorial. It's an excellent playground for experimenting with the iPhone OS UI.

Summary

This hour described the use of common input features and a few important output options. You learned that text fields and text views both enable the user to enter arbitrary input constrained by a variety of different virtual keyboards. Unlike text fields, however, text views can handle multiline input as well as scrolling, making them the choice for working with large amounts of text. We also covered the use of buttons and button states, including how buttons can be manipulated through code.

We'll continue to use the same techniques you used in this hour throughout the rest of the book, so don't be surprised when you see these elements again!

Q&A

Q. *Why can't I use a* `UILabel` *in place of a* `UITextView` *for multiline output?*

A. You certainly can! The text view, however, provides scrolling functionality "for free," whereas the label will display only the amount of text that fits within its bounds.

Q. *Why doesn't Apple just handle hiding text input keyboards for us?*

A. Although I can imagine some circumstances where it would be nice if this were an automatic action, it isn't difficult to implement a method to hide the keyboard. This gives you total control over the application interface—something you'll grow to appreciate.

Q. *Are text views (*`UITextView`*) the only way to implement scrolling content on the iPad?*

A. No. You'll learn about implementing general scrolling behavior in Hour 9, "Using Advanced Interface Objects and Views."

Workshop

Quiz

1. What properties are needed to configure a stretchable image?

2. How do you get rid of an onscreen keyboard?

3. Are text views used for text input, or output?

Answers

1. The left cap and top cap values define what portion of an image can be stretched.

2. To clear the onscreen keyboard, you must send the `resignFirstResponder` message to the object that currently controls the keyboard (such as a text field).

3. Text views (`UITextView`) can be implemented as scrollable output areas or multi-line input fields. It's entirely up to you!

Activities

1. Expand the story creator with additional placeholders and word types. Use the same string manipulation functions described in this lesson to add the new functionality.

2. Modify the story creator to use a graphical button of your design. Either use an entirely graphical button, or the stretchable image approach described in this hour's tutorial.

HOUR 8

Handling Images, Animation, and Sliders

What You'll Learn in This Hour:

▶ The use of Sliders for user input
▶ Configuring and manipulating the slider input range
▶ How to add Image Views to your projects
▶ Ways of creating and controlling simple animations

The text input and output that you learned about in the last hour is certainly important, but the iPad has gorgeous graphics and a "touchable" UI. In this hour, we expand our interface toolkit to include images, animation, and the very touchable slider control.

We'll be implementing an application to combine these new features along with simple logic to manipulate input data in a unique way. These new capabilities will help you build more interesting and interactive applications—and, of course, there's more to come in the next hour as well!

User Input and Output

When I first started developing for the iPhone OS platform, I was anxious to explore all that the interface had to offer. While application logic is always the most important part of an application, the way the interface works plays a big part in how well it will be received. The SDK's interface options give you the tools to express your application's functionality in fun and unique ways.

This hour introduces two very visual interface features—sliders for input, and image views for output.

Sliders

The first new interface component that we'll be using this hour is a slider (UISlider). Sliders are a convenient touch control that is used to visually set a point within a range of values. Huh? What?

Imagine that you want your user to be able to speed something up or slow it down. Asking the user to input timing values is unreasonable. Instead, you can present a slider, as seen in Figure 8.1, where they can touch and drag an indicator back and forth on a line. Behind the scenes, a value property is being set that your application can access and use to set the speed. No need for users to understand the behind-the-scene details or do anything more than drag with their finger.

FIGURE 8.1
Use a slider to collect a value from a range of numbers without requiring the user to type.

Sliders, like buttons, can react to events, or can be read passively like a text field. If you want the user's changes to a slider to immediately have an effect on your application, you'll need to have it trigger an action.

Image Views

Image views (UIImageView) are precisely what you'd think—they display images! They can be added to your application views and used to present information to the user. An instance of UIImageView can even be used to create a simple frame-based animation with controls for starting, stopping, and even setting the speed at which the animation is shown.

Creating and Managing Image Animations and Sliders

There's something about interface components that *move* that make users take notice. They're visually interesting, attract and keep attention, and, on the iPad's touch screen, are fun to play with. In this hour's project, we take advantage of both of our new UI elements (and some old friends!) to create a user-controlled animation.

Implementation Overview

As mentioned earlier, image views can be used to display image file resources and show simple animations, whereas sliders provide a visual way to choose a value from a range. We'll combine these in an application we're calling ImageHop.

In ImageHop, we'll be creating a looping animation using a series of images and an image view instance (UIImageView). We'll allow the user to set the speed of the animation using a slider (UISlider). What will we be using as an animation? A field of hopping bunnies. What will the user control? Hops per second for the "lead" bunny, of course! The "hops" value set by the slider will be displayed in a label (UILabel). The user will also be able to stop or start the animation using a button (UIButton).

Figure 8.2 shows the completed application at rest.

FIGURE 8.2
ImageHop uses an image view and a slider to create and control a set of simple animations.

We should discuss two aspects of this project before getting too far into the implementation:

▶ First, image view animations are created using a series of images. We've provided a 20-frame animation with this project, but you're welcome to use your own images if you prefer.

▶ Second, although sliders enable users to visually enter a value from a range, there isn't much control over how that is accomplished. For example, the minimum value must be smaller than the maximum, and you can't control which dragging direction of the slider increases or decreases the result value. These limitations aren't show-stoppers; they just mean that there may be a bit of math (or experimentation) involved to get the behavior you want.

Setting Up the Project

Begin this project in the same way as the last. Launch Xcode (Developer/Applications), and then choose File, New Project.

Select the iPhone OS Application project type, and then find and select the iPad View-Based Application option in the Template list on the right. Click Choose to continue, enter the project name **ImageHop**, and save the new project.

Adding the Animation Resources

This project makes use of 20 frames of animation stored as PNG files as well as a JPG background. The frames and background are included in the Images folder within the ImageHop project folder.

Because we know up front that we'll need these images, drag them into the Xcode project's Resources folder, being sure to choose the option to copy the resources if needed.

Preparing the Outlets and Actions

In this application, we need to provide outlets and actions for several objects.

For outlets, first we need five image views (UIImageView), which will contain five copies of our bunny animation. We'll reference these the variables imageView, imageView2, imageView3, imageView4, imageView5. The slider control (UISlider) will set the speed of the "lead" image view animations (imageView) and will be connected via animationSpeed, while the speed value itself will be output in a label named hopsPerSecond (UILabel). The remaining four animations will start out at the same speed, but be sent to a randomized percentage of the speed of imageView when the speed is changed. Finally, a button (UIButton) will toggle the animation on and off and will be connected to an outlet toggleButton.

Why do we need an outlet for the button? Shouldn't it just be triggering an action to toggle the animation? Yes, the button could be implemented without an outlet, but by including an outlet for it, we have a convenient way of setting the button's title in the code. We can use this to change the button to read "Stop" when the image is animating, or "Start" when the animation has stopped.

By the Way

For actions, we need only two: `setSpeed` will be the method called when the slider value has changed and the animation speed needs to be reset, and `toggleAnimation` will be used to start and stop the animation sequence.

Go ahead and define these outlets and actions within ImageHopViewController.h. You'll also want to declare the eight outlet variables as properties so that we can easily access them in the view controller code. The resulting header file is shown in Listing 8.1.

LISTING 8.1

```
#import <UIKit/UIKit.h>

@interface ImageHopViewController : UIViewController {
    IBOutlet UIImageView *imageView;
    IBOutlet UIImageView *imageView2;
    IBOutlet UIImageView *imageView3;
    IBOutlet UIImageView *imageView4;
    IBOutlet UIImageView *imageView5;
    IBOutlet UIButton *toggleButton;
    IBOutlet UISlider *animationSpeed;
    IBOutlet UILabel *hopsPerSecond;
}

@property (retain,nonatomic) UIImageView *imageView;
@property (retain,nonatomic) UIImageView *imageView2;
@property (retain,nonatomic) UIImageView *imageView3;
@property (retain,nonatomic) UIImageView *imageView4;
@property (retain,nonatomic) UIImageView *imageView5;
@property (retain,nonatomic) UIButton *toggleButton;
@property (retain,nonatomic) UISlider *animationSpeed;
@property (retain,nonatomic) UILabel *hopsPerSecond;

-(IBAction)toggleAnimation:(id)sender;
-(IBAction)setSpeed:(id)sender;

@end
```

For all the properties you've defined in the header file, add a `@synthesize` directive in the ImageHopViewController.m implementation file. Your additions should fall after the `@implementation` line and look like this:

```
@synthesize toggleButton;
@synthesize imageView;
@synthesize imageView2;
@synthesize imageView3;
@synthesize imageView4;
@synthesize imageView5;
@synthesize animationSpeed;
@synthesize hopsPerSecond;
```

Make sure that both the `ImageHopViewController` interface (header) and implementation files have been saved, and then launch Interface Builder by double-clicking the ImageHopViewController.xib file within the project's Resources folder.

After it has loaded, switch to the document window (Window, Document), and double-click the view icon to open it and begin editing.

Adding an Image View

In this exercise, our view creation will begin with the most important object of the project: the image view (`UIImageView`). Open the Interface Builder Objects Library and drag an image view into the view window.

Because the view has no images assigned, it will be represented by a light-colored rectangle. Use the resize handles on the rectangle to size it to fit in the upper center of the interface, as shown in Figure 8.3.

FIGURE 8.3
Set the image view to fill the upper two-thirds of the iPad interface.

Setting the Default Image

There are few attributes for configuring the functionality of an image view. In fact, there is only one: the image that is going to be displayed. Select the image view and press Command+1 to open the Attributes Inspector, demonstrated in Figure 8.4.

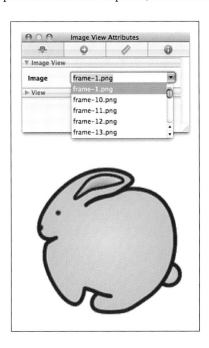

FIGURE 8.4
Set the image that will be shown in the view.

Using the Image drop-down menu, choose one of the image resources available. This will be the image that is shown before the animation runs, so using the first frame (frame-1.png) is a good choice.

By the Way

What about the animation? Isn't this just a frame? Yes, if we don't do anything else, the image view will show a single static image. To display an animation, we need to create an array with all of the frames and supply it programmatically to the image view object. We're going to be doing this in a few minutes, so just hang in there!

The image view will update in Interface Builder to show the image resource that you've chosen.

Making Copies

After you've added the image, create four additional copies by selecting the image view and choosing Edit, Duplicate (Command+D) from the menu. Scale and position the copies around the first image view. For my implementation, I also used the Attributes Inspector (Command+1) to set an alpha of .75 and .50 on some of the image views to make them partially transparent.

You've just created your field of bunnies! Your display should now resemble Figure 8.5.

FIGURE 8.5
Create your own field of bunnies.

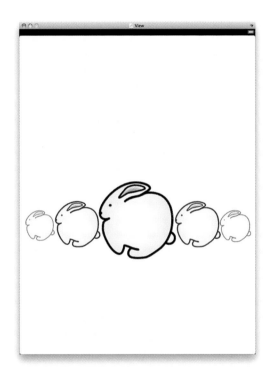

Connecting to the Outlets

To display an animation in our image views, we need to access them from the ImageHop view controller. Let's connect all five image views to the outlets that we created earlier.

Starting with the "lead" bunny, Control-drag from the File's Owner icon to the image view icon in the document window, or to the graphical representation in the view window. When prompted for the outlet, choose imageView, as shown in Figure 8.6.

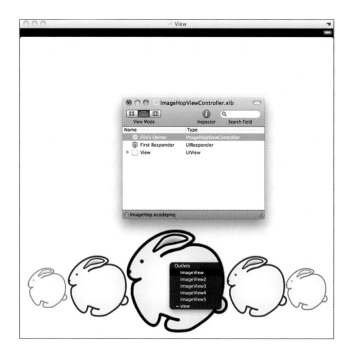

FIGURE 8.6
Connect the
image view to
an outlet so it
can be easily
accessed from
code.

Repeat the process, connecting the remaining four bunnies to `imageView2`, `imageView3`, and so on. The order and position is unimportant.

Now that the image views are in place, let's look at the code we need to add to change from a static image to an animation.

Animating the Image View

To truly customize an image view, we need to write some code. Animating images requires us to build an array of image objects (`UIImage`) and pass them to the image view. Where should we do this? As with the last project, the `ViewDidLoad` method of our view controller provides a convenient location for doing additional setup for the view, so that's what we'll use.

Switch back into Xcode, and open the view controller implementation file, ImageHopViewController.m. Find the `ViewDidLoad` method and uncomment it, and then add the following code to the method. Note that in Listing 8.2, we've removed lines 7–20 to save space (they follow the same pattern as lines 4–6 and 21–23):

LISTING 8.2

```
 1: - (void)viewDidLoad {
 2:     NSArray *hopAnimation;
 3:     hopAnimation=[[NSArray alloc] initWithObjects:
 4:                     [UIImage imageNamed:@"frame-1.png"],
 5:                     [UIImage imageNamed:@"frame-2.png"],
 6:                     [UIImage imageNamed:@"frame-3.png"],
...
21:                     [UIImage imageNamed:@"frame-18.png"],
22:                     [UIImage imageNamed:@"frame-19.png"],
23:                     [UIImage imageNamed:@"frame-20.png"],
24:                     nil
25:                 ];
26:     imageView.animationImages=hopAnimation;
27:     imageView2.animationImages=hopAnimation;
28:     imageView3.animationImages=hopAnimation;
29:     imageView4.animationImages=hopAnimation;
30:     imageView5.animationImages=hopAnimation;
31:     imageView.animationDuration=1;
32:     imageView2.animationDuration=1;
33:     imageView3.animationDuration=1;
34:     imageView4.animationDuration=1;
35:     imageView5.animationDuration=1;
36:     [hopAnimation release];
37:     [super viewDidLoad];
38: }
```

To configure the image view for animation, first an array (NSArray) variable is declared (line 2) called hopAnimation. Next, in line 3, the array is allocated and initialized via the NSArray instance method initWithObjects. This method takes a comma-separated list of objects, ending with nil, and returns an array.

The image objects (UIImage) are initialized and added to the array in lines 4–24. Remember that you'll need to fill in lines 7–20 on your own; otherwise, several frames will be missing from the animation!

Once an array is populated with image objects, it can be used to set up the animation of an image view. To do this, set the animationImages property of each image view (imageView, imageView2, imageView3, imageView4, imageView5) to the array. Lines 26–30 accomplish this for our example project.

Another image view property that we want to set right away is the animationDuration. This is the number of seconds it takes for a single cycle animationDurationof the animation to be played. If the duration is *not* set, the playback rate will be 30 frames per second. To start, all of our animations will be set to play all the frames in 1 second, so lines 31–35 set the `animationDuration` to 1 for the image views.

Finally, in line 36, we're finished with the `hopAnimation` array, so it can be released.

Starting and Stopping the Animation

A little later in this tutorial, we'll be adding controls to change the animation speed and to start/stop the animation loops. You've just learned how the `animationDuration` property can change the animation speed, but we'll need three more properties/methods to accomplish everything we want:

> `isAnimating`—This property returns true if the image view is currently animating its contents.
>
> `startAnimating`—Starts the animation.
>
> `stopAnimating`—Stops the animation, if it is running.

If you run the application now, it will work, but only static images will displayed. The image views do not start animating until the `startAnimating` method is called. We'll take care of that when implementing the view controller logic.

Adding a Slider

The next piece that our interface needs is the slider that will control the speed. Return to Interface Builder and the view, and then navigate to the Objects Library and drag the slider (`UISlider`) into the view, just under the image views. Using the resize handles on the slider, click and drag to size it to about two-thirds of view width. This leaves just enough room for a label to the left of the slider.

Because a slider has no visual indication of its purpose, it's a good idea to always label sliders so that your users will understand what they do. Drag a label object (`UILabel`) from the Library into your view. Double-click the text and set it to read **Speed:**. Position it so that it is aligned with the slider and they are both centered under the image views, as shown in Figure 8.7.

FIGURE 8.7
Add the slider
and a corre-
sponding label
to the view.

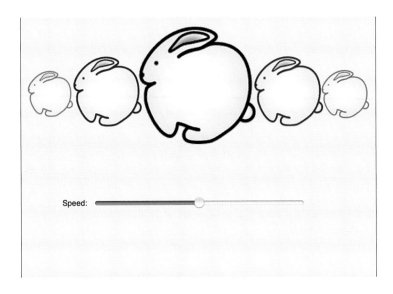

Setting the Slider Range Attributes

Sliders make their current setting available through a `value` property that we'll be accessing in the view controller. To change the range of values that can be returned, we'll need to edit the slider attributes. Click to select the slider in the view, and then open the Attributes Inspector (Command+1), as shown in Figure 8.8.

FIGURE 8.8
Edit the slider's
attributes to
control the
range of values
it returns.

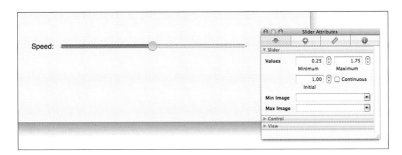

The Minimum, Maximum, and Initial fields should be changed to contain the smallest, largest, and starting values for the slider. For this project, use .25, 1.75, and 1.0, respectively.

Where Did These Min, Max, and Initial Values Come From?

This is a great question, and one that doesn't have a clearly defined answer. In this application, the slider represents the speed of the animation, which, as we've discussed, is set through the `animationDuration` property of the image view as the number of seconds it takes to show a full cycle of an animation. Unfortunately, this means the *faster* animations would use smaller numbers and *slower* animations use larger numbers, which is the exact opposite of traditional user interfaces where "slow" is on the left and "fast" is on the right. Because of this, we need to reverse the scale. In other words, we want the big number (1.75) to appear when the slider is on the left side and the small number (.25) on the right.

To reverse the scale, we'll take the combined total of the minimum and maximum (1.75+0.25), and subtract the value returned by the slider from that total. For example, when the slider returns 1.75 at the top of the scale, we'll calculate a duration of 2 – 1.75, or 0.25. At the bottom of the scale, the calculation will be 2 – 0.25, or 1.75.

Our initial value will be 1.0, which falls directly in the middle of the scale.

Make sure the Continuous check box isn't checked. This option, when enabled, will have the control to generate a series of events as the user drags back and forth on the slider. When it isn't enabled, events are generated only when the user lifts his or her finger from the screen. For our application, this makes the most sense and is certainly the least resource-intensive option.

The slider can also be configured with images at the minimum and maximum sliders of the control. Use the Min Image and Max Image drop-downs to select a project image resource if you'd like to use this feature. (We're not using it in this project.)

Connecting to the Outlet

For convenient access to the slider, we created an outlet, `animationSpeed`, that we'll be using in the view controller. To connect the slider to the outlet, Control-drag from the File's Owner icon to the slider object in the view, or the slider icon in the document window. When prompted, choose the `animationSpeed` outlet.

In case you're wondering, it's certainly possible to implement this application without an outlet for the slider. When the slider triggers an action, we could use the sender variable to reference the slider `value` property. That said, this approach will allow us to access the slider properties anywhere in the view controller, not just when the slider triggers an action.

Connecting to the Action

When the user drags the slider and releases their finger, the application should trigger the action method `setSpeed`. Create this connection by selecting the slider and then opening the Connections Inspector (Command+2).

Drag from the circle beside Value Changed to the File's Owner icon in the document window. When prompted, choose to connect to the `setSpeed` action. Once complete, Connections Inspector should reflect this change, and show both the `setSpeed` and `animationSpeed` connections, as demonstrated in Figure 8.9.

FIGURE 8.9
When the user drags and releases the slider, the setSpeed method is called.

That completes the major parts of the UI, but there's still some cleanup work to do.

Finishing the Interface

The remaining components of the ImageHop application are interface features that you've used before, so we've saved them for last. We'll finish things up by adding a button to start and stop the animation, a readout of the speed of the animated lead rabbit in "hops per second," and a background for the bunnies to hop on.

Adding Labels

Start by dragging two labels (`UILabel`) to the view. The first label should be set to read **Maximum Hops Per Second:** and be located at the very top of the view. Add the second label, which will be used as output of the actual speed value, to the right of the first label.

Change the output label to read **1.00 hps** (the speed that the animation will be starting out at). Using the Attributes Inspector (Command+1), set the text of the output label to align right; this will keep the text from jumping around as the user changes the speed.

Finally, Control-drag from the File's Owner icon to the output label, and choose the hopsPerSecond outlet, as shown in Figure 8.10.

FIGURE 8.10
Connect the label that will be used to display the speed.

Adding the Hop Button

The last part of the ImageHop interface is the button (UIButton) that starts and stops the animation. Drag a new button from the Objects Library to the view, positioning it at the bottom center of the UI. Double-click the button to edit the title, and set it to **Hop!**

Like the slider, the hop button needs to be connected to an outlet (toggleButton) and an action (toggleAnimation). Control-drag from File's Owner icon in the document window to the button and choose the toggleButton outlet when prompted.

Next, select the button and open the Connection Inspector (Command+2). Within the inspector, click and drag from the circle beside the Touch Up Inside event to the File's Owner icon in the document window. Connect to the toggleAnimation action. Figure 8.11 shows the completed button connections.

FIGURE 8.11
Connect the
button to its
outlet and
action.

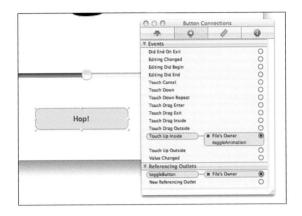

Setting a Background Graphic and Color

For fun, we can spruce up the application a bit by toning down the blinding white screen that the iPad views use by default. To do this, select the View icon in the Document window and open the Attributes Inspector (Command+1). Use the Background attribute to set a green background for the application, as seen in Figure 8.12.

FIGURE 8.12
Set a green
color for the
background of
the application.

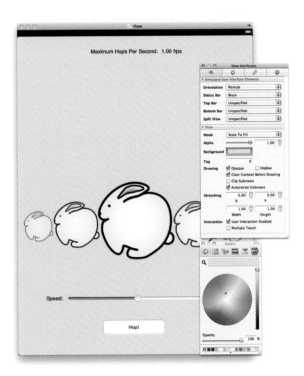

In addition to the color, it would be great if the bunnies could be hopping in grass, wouldn't it? (Bunnies like grass). To add a background image, drag another instance of UIImageView to the view. Resize it to cover the image views that contain the bunny animations, then use Layout, Send to Back to place the background image view behind the animation image views.

Finally, with the background image view selected, open the Attributes Inspector (Command+1), and set the Image value to the background.jpg file that you added earlier this hour, as shown in Figure 8.13.

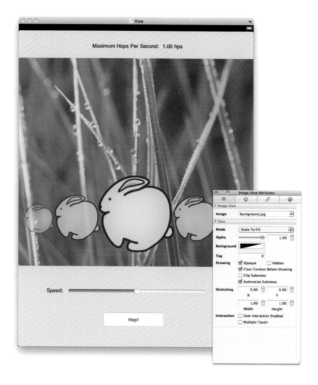

FIGURE 8.13
Use another UIImageView to create a background for the application.

The application interface is finished. In the next section, we'll complete the application by writing the code for starting and stopping the animation and setting the speed.

Implementing the View Controller Logic

The ImageHopViewController still needs a bit of work before we can call ImageHop done and finally view the animation. Two actions, toggleAnimation and setSpeed, need to be written. These methods will handle the user's interaction with the ImageHop application through the button and slider, respectively.

Starting and Stopping the Animation

When the user touches the Hop! button, the `toggleAnimation` method is called. This method should use the `isAnimating` property of the image view (`imageView`) to check to see whether an animation is running. If it isn't, the animation should start; otherwise, it should stop. To make sure the user interface makes sense, the button itself (`toggleButton`) should be altered to show the title Sit Still! if the animation is running, and Hop! when it isn't.

Add the code in Listing 8.3 to the `ImageHopViewController` implementation file, after the `@synthesize` directives.

LISTING 8.3

```
 1: -(IBAction) toggleAnimation:(id)sender {
 2:     if (imageView.isAnimating) {
 3:         [imageView stopAnimating];
 4:         [imageView2 stopAnimating];
 5:         [imageView3 stopAnimating];
 6:         [imageView4 stopAnimating];
 7:         [imageView5 stopAnimating];
 8:         [toggleButton setTitle:@"Hop!" forState:UIControlStateNormal];
 9:     } else {
10:         [imageView startAnimating];
11:         [imageView2 startAnimating];
12:         [imageView3 startAnimating];
13:         [imageView4 startAnimating];
14:         [imageView5 startAnimating];
15:         [toggleButton setTitle:@"Sit Still!" forState:UIControlStateNormal];
16:     }
```

Lines 2 and 9 provide the two different conditions that we need to work with. Lines 3–8 are executed if the animation is running, while lines 10-15 are executed if it isn't. In lines 3–7 and lines 10–14, the `stopAnimating` and `startAnimating` methods are called for the image views to start and stop the animation, respectively.

Lines 8 and 15 use the `UIButton` instance method `setTitle:forState` to set the button title to the string `"Hop!"` or `"Sit Still!"`. These titles are set for the button state of `UIControlStateNormal`. As you learned earlier this hour, the "normal" state for a button is its default state, prior to any user event taking place.

Setting the Animation Speed

The slider triggers the `setSpeed` action after the user adjusts the slider control. This action must translate into several changes in the actual application: First, the speed of the animation (`animationDuration`) should change. Second, the animation should be started if it isn't already running. Third, the button (`toggleButton`) title should be updated to show the animation is running. Lastly, the speed should be displayed in the hopsPerSecond label.

Add the code in Listing 8.4 to the view controller, and then let's review how it works.

LISTING 8.4

```
 1: -(IBAction) setSpeed:(id)sender {
 2:     NSString *hopRateString;
 3:     imageView.animationDuration=2-animationSpeed.value;
 4:     imageView2.animationDuration=
 5:             imageView.animationDuration+((float)(rand()%11+1)/10);
 6:     imageView3.animationDuration=
 7:             imageView.animationDuration+((float)(rand()%11+1)/10);
 8:     imageView4.animationDuration=
 9:             imageView.animationDuration+((float)(rand()%11+1)/10);
10:     imageView5.animationDuration=
11:             imageView.animationDuration+((float)(rand()%11+1)/10);
12:
13:     [imageView startAnimating];
14:     [imageView2 startAnimating];
15:     [imageView3 startAnimating];
16:     [imageView4 startAnimating];
17:     [imageView5 startAnimating];
18:     [toggleButton setTitle:@"Sit Still!"
19:                 forState:UIControlStateNormal];
20:     hopRateString=[[NSString alloc]
21:             initWithFormat:@"%1.2f hps",1/(2-animationSpeed.value)];
22:     hopsPerSecond.text=hopRateString;
23:     [hopRateString release];
24: }
```

Because we'll need to format a string to display the speed, we kick things off by declaring an NSString reference, hopRateString, in line 2. In line 3, the image view's (imageView) animationDuration property is set to 2 minus the value of the slider (animationSpeed.value)—this sets the speed of our "lead" bunny animation. This, if you recall, is necessary to reverse the scale so that faster is on the right and slower is on the left.

Lines 4–11 set the remaining image animations to the same speed as the "lead" animation (imageView.animationDuration) plus a fraction of a second. How do we get this fraction of a second? Through the magic of this randomization function: ((float)(rand()%11+1)/10), rand()%11+1 returns a random number between 1 and 10. We divide this by 10 to give us a fraction (1/10, 2/10, and so on). Using float ensures that we get a floating-point result rather than an integer.

Lines 13–17 use the startAnimating method to start the animations running. Note that it is safe to use this method if the animation is already started, so we don't really need to check the state of the image view. Lines 18–19 set the button title to the string "Sit Still!" to reflect the animated state.

Lines 20–21 allocate and initialize the `hopRateString` instance that we declared in line 2. The string is initialized with a format of `"1.2f"`, based on the calculation of 1 / (2 – `animationSpeed.value`). Let's break that down a bit further.

Recall that the speed of the animation is measured in seconds. The fastest speed we can set is 0.25 (a quarter of a second), meaning that the animation plays four times in 1 second (or "4 hops per second"). To calculate this in the application, we just divide 1 by the chosen animation duration, or 1 / (2 – `animationSpeed.value`). Because this doesn't necessarily return a whole number, we use the `initWithFormat` method to create a string that holds a nicely formatted version of the result. The `initWithFormat` parameter string `"1.2f hps"` is shorthand for saying the number being formatted as a string is a floating-point value (`f`), and that there should always be one digit on the left of the decimal, and two digits on the right (`1.2`). The hps portion of the format is just the "hops per second" unit that we want to append to the end of the string. For example, if the equation returns a value of .5 (half a hop a second), the string stored in `hopRateString` is set to `"0.50 hps"`.

In line 22, the output label (`UILabel`) in the interface is set to the `hopRateString`. Once finished with the string, line 23 releases it, freeing up the memory it was using.

By the Way

> Don't worry if the math here is a bit befuddling. This is not critical to understanding Cocoa or iPhone OS development, it's just an annoying manipulation we needed to perform to get the values the way we wanted them. I strongly urge you to play with the slider values and calculations as much as you'd like so that you can get a better sense of what is happening here and what steps you might need to take to make the best use of slider ranges in your own applications.

Releasing the Objects

Our development efforts have resulted in eight objects that should be released when we're finished: `toggleButton`, `imageView`, `imageView2`, `imageView3`, `imageView4`, `imageView5`, `hopsPerSecond`, and `animationSpeed`. Edit the `dealloc` method to release these now:

```
- (void)dealloc {
    [toggleButton release];
    [imageView release];
    [imageView2 release];
    [imageView3 release];
    [imageView4 release];
    [imageView5 release];
    [animationSpeed release];
    [hopsPerSecond release];
    [super dealloc];
}
```

Well done! You've just completed the app!

Building the Application

To try your hand at controlling our out-of-control bunnies, click Build and Run in Xcode. After a few seconds, the finished ImageHop application will start, as shown in Figure 8.14.

Although ImageHop isn't an application that you're likely to keep on your iPad (for long), it did provide you with new techniques for your application toolkit. The UIImageView class can easily add dynamic images to your programs, while UISlider offers a uniquely touchable input solution.

Further Exploration

Although many hours in this book focus on adding features to the user interface, it is important to start thinking about the application logic that will bring your user interface to life. As we experienced with our sample application, sometimes creativity is required to make things work the way we want.

Review the properties and methods for `UISlider` class and consider how you might use a slider in your own apps. Can you think of any situations where the slider values couldn't be used directly in your software? How might you apply application logic to map slider values to usable input? Programming is very much about problem solving—you'll rarely write something that doesn't have at least a few "gotchas" that need solved.

In addition to `UISlider`, you may want to review the documentation for `UIImage`. While we focused on `UIImageView` for displaying our image animation, the images themselves were objects of type `UIImage`. Image objects will come in handy for future interfaces that integrate graphics into the user controls themselves.

Apple Tutorials

`UIImageView`, `UIImage`, `UISlider`: UICatalog (accessible via the Xcode documentation). Once again, this project is a great place for exploring any and everything (including images, image views, and sliders) related to the iPhone OS interface.

Summary

Users of highly visual devices demand highly visual interfaces. In this hour's lesson, you learned about the use of two visual elements that we can begin adding to our applications: image views and sliders. Image views provide a quick means of displaying images that you've added to your project—even using a sequence of images to create animation. Sliders can be used to collect user input from a continuous range of values. These new input/output methods start our exploration of iPad interfaces that go beyond simple text and buttons.

The information you learned today, although not complex, will help pave the way for mega-rich touch-centric user interfaces.

Q&A

Q. *Is the* `UIImageView` *the only means of displaying animated movies?*

A. No. The iPhone OS SDK includes a wide range of options for playing back video and even drawing onscreen. The `UIImageView` is not meant to be used as a video playback mechanism.

Q. *Is there a vertical version of the slider control* (UISlider)?

A. Unfortunately, no. Only the horizontal slider is currently available in the SDK. If you want to use a vertical slider control, you'll need to implement your own.

Workshop

Quiz

1. What is one of the limitations of the slider control (UISlider)?

2. What is the default playback rate for an animation, prior to the animationDuration property being set?

3. What is the value of the isAnimating property in an instance of UIImageView?

Answers

1. The slider is limited in that the values must increase from left to right. This can be overcome, but not without programmatically manipulating the numbers.

2. By default, animation frames are shown at a rate of 30 frames per second.

3. The isAnimating property is set to true when the UIImageView instance is displaying an animation. When the animation is stopped (or not configured), the property is false.

Activities

1. Increase the range of speed options for the ImageHop animation example. Be sure to set the default location for the slider to rest in the middle.

2. Provide an alternative means of editing the speed by enabling the user to manually enter a number in addition to using the slider. The placeholder text of the field should default to the current slider value.

HOUR 9

Using Advanced Interface Objects and Views

What You'll Learn This Hour:

▶ How to use segmented controls (a.k.a. button bars)
▶ Ways of inputting Boolean values via switches
▶ How to include web content within your application
▶ The use of scrolling views to expand screen area

After the previous few hours' lessons, you now have a good understanding of the basic iPad interface elements, but we've only just scratched the surface. There are additional user input features to help a user quickly choose between several predefined options. After all, there's no point in typing when a touch will suffice! This hour's lesson picks up where the last left off, providing you with hands-on experience with a new set of user input options that go beyond fields, buttons, and sliders.

In addition, we'll look at two new ways that you can present data to the user: via web and scrolling views. These features will make it possible to create applications that can extend beyond the physical boundaries of the iPad screen and include content from remote web servers.

User Input and Output (Continued)

What makes the iPad different from a laptop? They're both portable and provide a computing and entertainment platform, yet using an iPad captures the imagination far more than sitting in front of a laptop. The difference? The interface; touching your technology is fun!

The interface options are what makes the iPad so enjoyable to use, and what gives you, the developer, a truly rich canvas to work with. You'll still need to come up with ideas for what your application will *do*, but the interface can be the deciding factor in whether your vision "clicks" with its intended audience.

In the last two hours, you learned about fields, sliders, labels, and images as input and output options. In this lesson, you'll be exploring two new input options for handling discrete values, along with two new view types that extend the information you can display to web pages and beyond.

Switches

In most traditional desktop applications, the choice between something being "active" or "inactive" is made by checking or unchecking a check box, or by choosing between radio buttons. On the iPad, Apple has chosen to abandon these options in favor of switches and segmented controls. Switches (UISwitch) present a simple on/off UI element that resembles a traditional physical toggle switch, as seen in Figure 9.1. Switches have few configurable options and should be used for handling Boolean values.

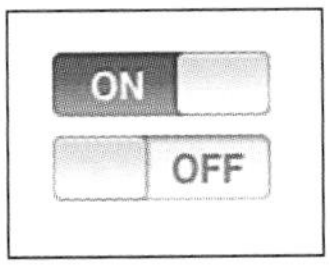

FIGURE 9.1
Use switches to provide on/off input options to your user.

By the Way

Check boxes and radio buttons, although not part of the iPhone OS UI Library, can be created with the UIButton class using the button states and custom button images. Apple provides the flexibility to customize to your heart's content—but sticking with what a user expects to see on the iPad screen is recommended.

To work with the switch, we'll make use of its Value Changed event to detect a toggle of the switch, and then read its current value via the on property or the isOn instance method.

The value returned when checking a switch is a Boolean, meaning that we can compare it to TRUE or FALSE (or YES/NO) to determine its state, or evaluate the result directly in a conditional statement.

For example, to check if a switch mySwitch is turned on, we can use code similar to this:

```
if ([mySwitch isOn]) { <switch is on> } else { <switch is off> }
```

Segmented Controls

When user input needs to extend beyond just a Boolean value, a segmented control (UISegmentedControl) can be used. Segmented controls present a linear line of buttons (sometimes referred to as a button bar) where a single button can be active within the bar, as demonstrated in Figure 9.2.

FIGURE 9.2
Segmented controls combine multiple buttons into a single control.

Segmented controls, when used according to Apple's guidelines, result in a change in what the user is seeing onscreen. They are frequently used to choose between categories of information or to switch between the display of application screens, such as configuration and results screens. For simply choosing from a list of values where no immediate visual change takes place, the Picker object should be used instead. We'll be looking at this feature in Hour 12, "Implementing Multi-Value Interfaces with Pickers and Action Sheets."

Apple recommends using segmented controls to update the information visible in a view. If the change, however, means altering *everything* onscreen then you are probably better off switching between multiple independent views. We'll start looking at the multiview approach in Hour 1, "Implementing Multiple Views with Toolbars and Tab Bars."

By the Way

Handling interactions with a segmented control will be very similar to the toggle button. We'll be watching for the Value Changed event, and determining the currently selected button through the selectedSegmentIndex, which returns the number of the button chosen (starting with 0, from left to right).

We can combine the index with the object's instance method titleForSegmentAtIndex to work directly with the titles assigned to each segment. To retrieve the name of the currently selected button in a segmented control called mySegment, we could use the code fragment:

```
[mySegment titleForSegmentAtIndex: mySegment.selectedSegmentIndex]
```

We'll make use of this technique later in the lesson.

Web Views

In the previous iPad applications that you've built, you've used the typical view: an instance of UIView to hold your controls, content, and images. This is the view you'll use most frequently in your apps, but it isn't the only view supported in the iPhone OS SDK. A web view, or UIWebView, provides advanced features that open up a whole new range of possibilities in your apps.

Think of a web view as a borderless Safari window that you can add to your applications and control programmatically. You can present HTML, load web pages, and offer pinching and zooming gestures all "for free" using this class.

Supported Content Types

Web views can also be used to display a wide range of files, without needing to know anything about the file formats:

> HTML and CSS
>
> Word documents (.doc)
>
> Excel spreadsheets (.xls)
>
> Keynote presentations (.key.zip)
>
> Numbers spreadsheets (.numbers.zip)
>
> Pages documents (.pages.zip)
>
> PDF files (.pdf)
>
> PowerPoint presentations (.ppt)

You can add these files as resources to your project and display them within a web view, access them on remote servers, or read them from the iPad sandbox file storage (which you'll learn about in Hour 16, "Reading and Writing Application Data").

Loading Remote Content with NSURL, NSURLRequest, and requestWithURL

Web views implement a method called requestWithURL that you can use to load an arbitrary URL, but, unfortunately, you can't just pass it a string and expect it to work.

To load content into a web view, you'll frequently use NSURL and NSURLRequest. These two classes provide the ability to manipulate URLs and prepare them to be used as a request for a remote resource. You will first create an instance of an NSURL object, most frequently from a string. For example, to create an NSURL that stores the address for Apple, you could use the following:

```
NSURL *appleURL;
appleURL=[[NSURL alloc] initWithString:@"http://www.apple.com/"];
```

Once the NSURL object is created, you will need to create an NSURLRequest object that can be passed to a web view and loaded. To return an NSURLRequest from an NSURL object, we can use the NSURLRequest class method requestWithURL that, given an NSURL, returns the corresponding request object:

```
[NSURLRequest requestWithURL: appleURL]
```

Finally, this value would be passed to the requestWithURL method of the web view, which then takes over and handles loading the process. Putting all the pieces together, loading Apple's website into a web view called appleView would look like this:

```
NSURL *appleURL;
appleURL=[[NSURL alloc] initWithString:@"http://www.apple.com/"];
[appleView loadRequest:[NSURLRequest requestWithURL: appleURL]];
```

We'll be implementing web views in this hour's first project, so you'll have a chance to put this to use shortly.

> Another way that you get content into your application is by loading HTML directly into a web view. For example, if you generate HTML content in a string called myHTML, you can use the loadHTMLString:baseURL method of a web view to load the HTML content and display it. Assuming a web view called htmlView, this might be written as follows:
>
> ```
> [htmlView loadHTMLString:myHTML baseURL:nil]
> ```

Did you Know?

Scrolling Views

The iPad has a large screen, but compared to a desktop (with screens up to three or four times larger), it's not *that* big. To get around screen space limitations, you can build applications that scroll. Scrolling views, implemented through UIScrollView, provide scrolling features and can display more than a single screen's worth of information.

Unfortunately, Apple has gone about halfway toward making scrolling views something that you can add to your projects in Interface Builder. You can add the view, but until you add a line of code to your application, it won't scroll! We'll close out this hour's lesson with a very quick example (a single line of code!) that will enable UIScrollView instances that you create in Interface Builder to scroll your content.

Using Switches, Segmented Controls, and Web Views

As you've probably noticed by now, we prefer to work on examples that do something. It's one thing to show a few lines of code in a chapter and say "this will do <blah>," but it's another to take a collection of features and combine them in a way that results in a working application. In some cases, the former approach is unavoidable, but this isn't one of them. Our first hands on example will make use of web views, a segmented control, and a toggle switch.

Implementation Overview

In this project, we'll be creating an application that displays flower photographs and flower information from the website FloraPhotographs.com. The application will enable a user to touch a flower color within a segmented control (UISegmentedControl), resulting in a flower of that color being fetched and displayed from the FloraPhotographs site in a web view (UIWebView). The user can then use a toggle switch (UISwitch) to show and hide a second web view that contains details about the flower being displayed. Finally, a standard button (UIButton) will enable the user to fetch another flower photo of the currently selected color from the site. The result should look very much like Figure 9.3.

FIGURE 9.3
The finished application will make use of a segmented control, a switch, and two web views.

Setting Up the Project

This project will, once again, use the View-Based Application template we're starting to love. If it isn't already running, launch Xcode (Developer/Applications), and then create a new project called **FlowerWeb**.

You should now be accustomed to what happens next. Xcode sets up the project and creates the default view in FlowerWebViewController.xib and a view controller class in `FlowerWebViewController`. We'll start with setting up the outlets and actions we need in the view controller.

Preparing the Outlets and Actions

To create the web-based image viewer, we'll need three outlets and two actions. The segmented control will be connecting to an outlet called `colorChoice`, because we'll be using it to choose which color is displayed. The web view that contains the flower will be connected to `flowerView`, and the associated details web view to `flowerDetailView`.

For the actions, the application must do two things: get and display a flower image, which we'll define as the action method `getFlower`; and toggle the flower details on and off, something we'll handle with a `toggleFlowerDetail` action.

Why Don't We Need an Outlet for the Switch?

We don't need to include an outlet for the switch because we will be connecting its Value Changed event to the `toggleFlowerDetail` method. When the method is called, the `sender` parameter sent to the method will reference the switch, so we can just use `sender` to determine whether the switch is on or off.

Did you Know?

If we have more than one control using `toggleFlowerDetail`, it would be helpful to define outlets to differentiate between them, but in this case, sender will suffice.

By the Way

Open the flowerWebViewController.h file in Xcode and create the IBOutlets for `colorChoice`, `flowerView`, and `flowerDetailView`. Then add the IBActions for `getFlower` and `toggleFlowerDetail`. Finally, add @property directives for the segmented control and both web views so that we can easily manipulate them in our code.

The completed header file should look similar to Listing 9.1.

LISTING 9.1

```
#import <UIKit/UIKit.h>

@interface FlowerWebViewController : UIViewController {
              IBOutlet UISegmentedControl *colorChoice;
              IBOutlet UIWebView *flowerView;
              IBOutlet UIWebView *flowerDetailView;
}

-(IBAction)getFlower:(id)sender;
-(IBAction)toggleFlowerDetail:(id)sender;

@property (nonatomic, retain) UISegmentedControl *colorChoice;
@property (nonatomic, retain) UIWebView *flowerView;
@property (nonatomic, retain) UIWebView *flowerDetailView;

@end
```

Save the header file and open the view controller implementation file
(flowerWebViewController.m). Add matching @synthesize directives for each of the
properties you declared in the header. These, as always, should be added after the
@implementation directive:

```
@synthesize colorChoice;
@synthesize flowerDetailView;
@synthesize flowerView;
```

Now, let's build the user interface. Open the FlowerWebViewController.xib file in
Interface Builder, and make sure that the view is open and visible. We'll begin by
adding the segmented control.

Adding a Segmented Control

Add a segmented control to the user interface, by opening the Library (Tools,
Library), finding the Segmented Control (UISegmentedControl) object, and dragging it into the view. Position the control near the top of the view, in the center.
Because this control will ultimately be used to choose colors, click and drag a label
(UILabel) into the view as well, position it above the segmented control, and
change it to read **Choose a Flower Color:**. Your view should now resemble Figure
9.4.

By default, the segmented control will have two segments, titled First and Second.
You can double-click these titles and edit them directly in the view, but that won't
quite get us what we need.

For this project, we need a control that has six segments, each labeled with a color:
Red, Blue, Yellow, Green, Violet, and Magenta. These are the colors that we can

request from the FloraPhotographs website for displaying. Obviously, we need to add a few more segments to the control before all of the choices can be represented.

FIGURE 9.4
The default segmented control has two buttons, First and Second.

Adding and Configuring Segments

The number of segments displayed in the segmented control is configurable in the Attributes Inspector for the object. Select the control that you've added to the view, then press Command+1 to open the Attributes Inspector, demonstrated in Figure 9.5.

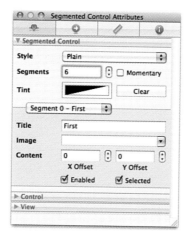

FIGURE 9.5
Use the Attributes Inspector for the segmented control to increase the number of segments displayed.

Using the Segments field, increase the number from 2 to 6. You should immediately see the new segments displayed. Notice that directly below where you set the number of segments in the inspector is a drop-down with entries for each segment you've added. You can choose a segment in this drop-down, and then specify its title in the Title field. You can even add images resources and have them displayed within each segment.

> Note that the first segment is segment 0, the next is segment 1, and so on. It's important to keep this in mind when you're checking to see which segment is selected. The first segment is *not* segment 1, as you might assume.

By the Way

Update the four segments in the control so that the colors Red, Blue, Yellow, Green, Violet, and Magenta are represented.

Sizing the Control

Chances are, the control you've set up doesn't quite look right in the view. To size the control to aesthetically pleasing dimensions, use the selection handles on the sides of the control to stretch and shrink it appropriately. You can even optimize the size of individual segments using the Segmented Control Size options in the Size Inspector (Command+3), as shown in Figure 9.6.

FIGURE 9.6
You can use the Size Inspector to size each segment individually, if desired.

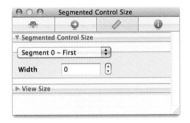

Choosing a Segment Control Appearance

In addition to the usual color options and controls available in Attributes Inspector, there are three variations of how the segmented control can be presented. Use the Style drop-down menu (visible in Figure 9.5) to choose between Plain, Bordered, and Bar. Figure 9.7 shows each of these.

FIGURE 9.7
You can choose between three different presentation styles for your segmented control.

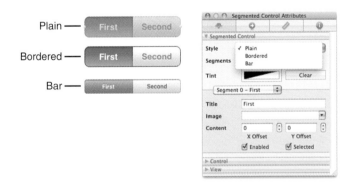

For this project, stick with Plain or Bordered. The segmented control should now have titles for all the colors and a corresponding label to help the user understand its purpose.

To finish things up for the segmented control, we need to connect it to the outlet we defined earlier (`colorChoice`) and make sure that it triggers the `getFlower` action method when a user switches between colors.

Connecting to the Outlet

To connect the segmented control to the `colorChoice` outlet, make sure the document window is visible, and then Control-drag from the File's Owner icon to either the visual representation of the control in the view, or to its icon in the document window, then release the mouse button. When prompted, choose the `colorChoice` outlet to finish the connection, as shown in Figure 9.8.

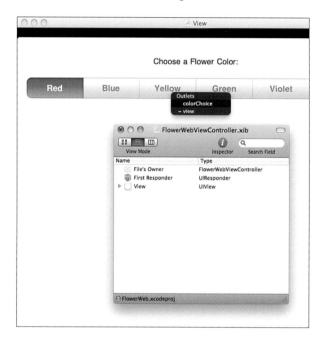

FIGURE 9.8
Connect the segmented control to the `colorChoice` outlet so that we can easily access the selected color from within our application.

Connecting to the Action

Like other UI elements, the segmented control can react to *many* different touch events. Most frequently, however, you'll want to carry out an action when the user clicks a segment and switches to a new value (such as choosing a new color in this app). Thankfully, Apple has implemented a Value Changed event that does exactly what we want!

In our application, we want to load a new flower if the user switches colors. To do this, we need to create a connection from the Value Changed event to the `getFlower` action. Open the Connections Inspector by selecting the segmented control and then pressing Command+2. Drag from the circle beside Value Changed to the File's Owner icon in the document window, and release your mouse button. When prompted, choose the `getFlower` action method, as shown in Figure 9.9.

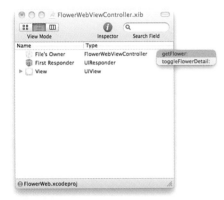

The segmented control is now wired into the interface and ready to go. Let's add our
other interface objects, and then write the code to pull it together.

Adding a Switch

The switch that we'll use in our application has one role: to toggle a web view that
displays details about the flower (flowerDetailView) on and off. Add the switch to
the view by dragging the switch (UISwitch) object from the Library into the view.
Position it just under the segmented control.

As with the segmented control, providing some basic user instruction through an
onscreen label can be helpful. Drag a label (UILabel) into the view and place it to
the left of the switch. Change the text to read **Show Photo Details:**. Your view
should now resemble Figure 9.10, but your switch will likely show up as "on."

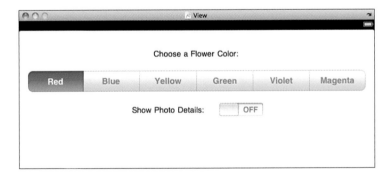

Setting the Default State

I know you're getting used to many of the different configuration options for the controls we use, but in this case, the switch has only a single option: whether the default state is on or off. The switch that you added to the view is set to "on"; we want to change it so that it is "off" by default.

To change the default state, select the switch and open the Attributes Inspector (Command+1). Using the State pop-up menu, change the default state to off. That covers just about everything for switches! We just need to connect it to an action and we can move on to the next element.

Connecting to the Action

The only time we're really interested in the switch is when its value changes, so, like the segmented control, we need to take advantage of the event Value Changed and connect that to the toggleFlowerDetail action method.

With the document window visible, select the switch, and then open the Connections Inspector (Command+2). Drag from the circle beside the Value Changed event to the File's Owner icon in the document window. When you release your mouse button, choose the toggleFlowerDetail action to complete the connection, as shown in Figure 9.11.

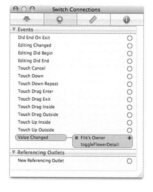

FIGURE 9.11
Connect the Value Changed event to the toggleFlower Detail action.

We're cruising now! Let's wrap this up by adding the web views that will show the flower and flower details, then the button that will let us load a new image whenever we want.

Adding the Web Views

The application that we're building relies on two different web views. One will display the flower image itself, while the other view (which can be toggled on and off) shows details about the image. The details view will be overlaid on top of the image itself, so let's start by adding the main view, `flowerView`.

To add a web view (`UIWebView`) to your application, locate it in the Library, and then simply drag it into your view. The web view will display a resizable rectangle that you can drag and position anywhere you'd like. Because this is the view that the flower image will be shown in, position it to fall about one-third of the way down the iPad screen, and then resize it so that it is the same width as the screen and so that it covers the lower portion of the view entirely.

Repeat this to add a second web view for the flower details (`flowerDetailView`). This time, size the view so that it is about 25% the height of the flower view, and locate it at the very bottom of the screen, over top of the flower view, as shown in Figure 9.12.

FIGURE 9.12
Add two web views (`UIWebView`) to your screen, and then position them as shown here.

Setting the Web View Attributes

Web views, surprisingly, have very few attributes that you can configure in Interface Builder, but what is available can be very important! To access the web view attributes, select one of the views you added, and then press Command+1 to open the Attributes Inspector (see Figure 9.13).

FIGURE 9.13
Configure how
the web view
will behave.

There are three options you can select: Scales Page to Fit, Detect Phone Numbers, and Detect Links. If Scales Page to Fit is selected, large pages will be scaled to fit in the size of the area you've defined. If the Detect options are used, the iPad's data detectors go to work and will underline items that it has decided are phone numbers or additional web links.

For the main flower view, we absolutely want the images to be scaled to fit within the view. Select the web view, and then use the Properties Inspector to choose the Scales Page to Fit option.

For the second view, we do *not* want this to be set, so select the web view where the application will be showing the flower details and use the Attributes Inspector to ensure that no scaling will take place. You might also want to change the view attributes for the detail view to have an alpha value of around 0.65. This will create a nice translucency effect when the details are displayed on top of the photograph.

> Scaling doesn't necessarily do what you'd expect for "small" web pages. If you display a page with only the text Hello World on it in a scaled web view, you might expect the text to be shown to fill the web view. Instead, the text will be *tiny*. The web view assumes that the text is part of a larger page, and scales it down rather than making it appear bigger.

Watch Out!

Connecting to the Outlets

To prepare the two web views so that we can use them to display content, we need to connect them to the `flowerView` and `flowerDetailView` outlets created at the start of the project. To do this, Control-drag from the File's Owner icon in the document window to the web view in your view, or its icon in the document window. Release your mouse button, then, when prompted, choose the appropriate outlet.

For the larger view, connect to flowerView, as demonstrated in Figure 9.14. Repeat the process, connecting the smaller view to flowerDetailView.

FIGURE 9.14
Connect each
web view to its
corresponding
outlet.

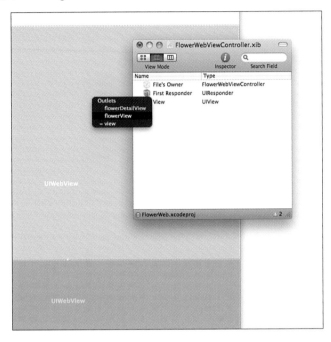

With the tough stuff out of the way, we just have one more finishing touch to put on the interface, then we're ready to code.

Finishing the Interface

The only functional piece that is missing from our interface is a button (UIButton) that we can use to manually trigger the getFlower method anytime we want. Without the button, we'd have to switch between colors using the segmented control if we wanted to see a new flower image. This button does nothing more than trigger an action (getFlower), something you've done repeatedly in the past few hours, so this should be a walk in the park for you by now.

Drag a button into the view, positioning it in the center of the screen, above the web views. Edit the button title to read **Get New Photo**.

Finally, select the button and open the Connections Inspector (Command+2). Drag from the Touch Up Inside event to the File's Owner icon in the document window. When prompted choose the getFlower action, as shown in Figure 9.15.

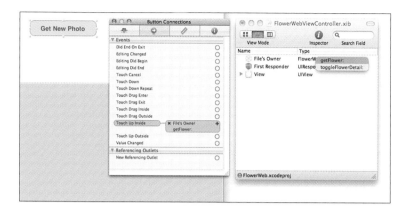

FIGURE 9.15
Connect the Get New Photo button's Touch Up Inside event to the getFlower action.

Although your interface might be functionally complete, you might want to select the view itself and set a background color. I find the harsh white background a bit "too much" on the iPad screen. Keep your applications from blinding your users!

Did you know?

The interface, shown in Figure 9.16, is complete! Switch back to Xcode and let's get to coding!

FIGURE 9.16
The finished interface of the FlowerWeb application.

Implementing the View Controller Logic

There are two pieces of functionality that our view controller needs to implement via two action methods. The first `toggleFlowerDetail` will show and hide the `flowerDetailView` web view depending on whether the switch has been flipped on (show) or off (hide). The second method, `getFlower`, will load a flower image into the `flowerView` web view and details on that photograph into the `flowerDetailView` web view. We'll start with the easier of the two, `toggleFlowerDetail`.

Hiding and Showing the Detail Web View

A useful property of any object that inherits from `UIView` is that you can easily hide (or show) it within your application interfaces. Because almost everything you see onscreen inherits from this class, this means you can hide and show labels, buttons, fields, images, and yes, other views. To hide an object, all we need to do is set its Boolean property `hidden` to TRUE or YES (both have the same meaning). So, to hide the `flowerDetailView`, we'd write:

```
flowerDetailView.hidden=YES;
```

To show it again, we just reverse the process, setting the `hidden` property to FALSE or NO:

```
flowerDetailView.hidden=NO;
```

To implement the logic for the `toggleFlowerDetail:` method, we need to figure out what value the switch is currently set to. As mentioned earlier in the lesson, we can check the state of a toggle switch through the `isOn` method that returns a Boolean value of TRUE/YES if the switch is set to on, or FALSE/NO if it is off.

Because we don't have an outlet specifically set aside for the switch, we'll use the `sender` variable to access it in our method. When the `toggleFlowerDetail` action method is called, this variable is set to reference the object that invoked the action (in other words, the switch). So, to check to see whether the switch is on, we can write the following:

```
If ([sender isOn]) { <switch is on> } else { <switch is off> }
```

Now, here's where we can get clever (you're feeling clever, right?). We want to hide and show the `flowerDetailView` using a Boolean value and we *get* a Boolean value from the switch's `isOn` method. This maps to two conditions:

▶ When [sender isOn] is YES, the view should *not* be hidden
(flowerDetailView.hidden=NO).

▶ When [sender isOn] is NO, the view *should* be hidden
(flowerDetailView.hidden=YES).

In other words, the state of the switch is the exact opposite of what we need to
assign to the hidden property of the view. In C (and therefore Objective-C), to get
the opposite of a Boolean value, we just put an exclamation mark in front (!). So all
we need to do to hide or show flowerDetailView is to set the hidden property to
![sender isOn]. That's it! A single line of code!

Implement toggleFlowerDetail: in FlowerWeb right after the @synthesize directives. The full method should look a lot like this:

```
-(IBAction)toggleFlowerDetail:(id)sender{
    flowerDetailView.hidden=![sender isOn];
}
```

Loading and Displaying the Flower Image and Details

To fetch our flower images, we'll be making use of a feature provided by the Flora
Photographs website for specifically this purpose. We'll complete four steps to interact with the website:

1. We'll get the chosen color from the segmented control.

2. We will generate a random number called a session ID so that florapho-
tographs.com can track our request.

3. We will request the URL http://www.floraphotographs.com/
showrandomipad.php?color=<color>&session=<session ID>, where
<color> is the chosen color and <session ID> is the random number. This
URL will return a flower photo.

4. We will request the URL
http://www.floraphotographs.com/detailipad.php?session=<session
ID>, where <session ID> is the same random number. This URL will return
the details for the previously requested flower photo.

Let's go ahead and see what this looks like in code, and then discuss details behind
the implementation. Add the getFlower code block, shown in Listing 9.2, following
the toggleFlowerDetail method that you implemented.

LISTING 9.2

```
 1: -(IBAction)getFlower:(id)sender {
 2:     NSURL *imageURL;
 3:     NSURL *detailURL;
 4:     NSString *imageURLString;
 5:     NSString *detailURLString;
 6:     NSString *color;
 7:     int sessionID;
 8:
 9:     color=[colorChoice titleForSegmentAtIndex:
10:            colorChoice.selectedSegmentIndex];
11:     sessionID=random()%10000;
12:
13:     imageURLString=[[NSString alloc] initWithFormat:
14: @"http://www.floraphotographs.com/showrandomipad.php?color=%@&session=%d"
15:                     ,color,sessionID];
16:     detailURLString=[[NSString alloc] initWithFormat:
17:     @"http://www.floraphotographs.com/detailipad.php?session=%d"
18:                     ,sessionID];
19:
20:     imageURL=[[NSURL alloc] initWithString:imageURLString];
21:     detailURL=[[NSURL alloc] initWithString:detailURLString];
22:
23:     [flowerView loadRequest:[NSURLRequest requestWithURL:imageURL]];
24:     [flowerDetailView loadRequest:[NSURLRequest requestWithURL:detailURL]];
25:
26:     flowerDetailView.backgroundColor=[UIColor clearColor];
27:
28:     [imageURLString release];
29:     [detailURLString release];
30:     [imageURL release];
31:     [detailURL release];
32: }
```

This is the most complicated code that you've written to date, but it's broken down into the individual pieces, so it's not difficult to understand:

Lines 2–7 declare the variables that we need to prepare our requests to the website. The first variables, imageURL and detailURL, are instances of NSURL that will contain the URLs that will be loaded into the flowerView and flowerDetailView web views. To create the NSURL objects, we'll need two strings, imageURLString and detailURLString, which we'll format with the special URLs that we presented earlier, including the color and sessionID values.

In lines 9–10, we retrieve the title of the selected segment in our instance of the segmented control: colorChoice. To do this, we use the object's instance method titleForSegmentAtIndex along with the object's selectedSegmentIndex property. The result, [colorChoice titleForSegmentAtIndex: colorChoice.selectedSegmentIndex], is stored in the string color and is ready to be used in the web request.

Line 11 generates a random number between 0 and 9999 and stores it in the integer sessionID.

Lines 13–18 prepare imageURLString and detailURLString with the URLs that we will be requesting. The strings are allocated, and then the initWithFormat method is used to store the website address along with the color and session ID. The color and session ID are substituted into the string using the formatting placeholders %@ and %d for strings and integers, respectively.

Lines 20–21 allocate and create the imageURL and detailURL NSURL objects using the initWithString class method and the two strings imageURLString and detailURLString.

Lines 23–24 use the loadRequest method of the flowerView and flowerDetailView web views to load the NSURLs imageURL and detailURL, respectively. When these lines are executed, the display updates the contents of the two views.

Remember that UIWebView's loadRequest method doesn't handle NSURL objects directly; it expects an NSURLRequest object instead. To work around this, we create and return NSURLRequest objects using the NSURLRequest class method requestWithURL and the imageURL and detailURL objects as parameters.

Line 26 is an extra nicety that we've thrown in. This sets the background of the flowerDetailView web view to a special color called clearColor. This, combined with the alpha channel value that you set earlier, will give the appearance of a nice translucent overlay of the details over the main image. You can comment out or remove this line to see the difference it creates.

To create web views that blend with the rest of your interface, keep clearColor in mind. By setting this color, you can make the background of your web pages translucent, meaning that the content displayed on the page will overlay any other content that you've added to your view.

Finally, lines 28–31 release all the objects that we've allocated in the method. Because getFlower will potentially be called over and over, it's important that we release any memory that we might be using!

Fixing Up the Interface When the App Loads

Now that the getFlower method is implemented, you can run the application and everything should work—except that when the application starts, the two web views will be empty and the detail view will be visible, even though the toggle switch is set to off.

To fix this, we can start loading an image as soon as the app is up and running and set flowerDetailView.hidden to YES. Uncomment the viewDidLoad method and implement it as follows:

```
- (void)viewDidLoad {
    flowerDetailView.hidden=YES;
    [self getFlower:nil];
    [super viewDidLoad];
}
```

As expected, flowerDetailView.hidden=YES will hide the detail view. Using [self getFlower:nil], we can call the getFlower: method from within our instance of the view control (referenced as self) and start the process of loading a flower in the web view. The method getFlower: expects a parameter, so we pass it nil. (This value is never used in getFlower:, however, so there is no problem with providing nil.)

Releasing the Objects

As always, we need to finish things up by releasing the objects that we've kept around. Edit the dealloc method to release the segmented control and two web views now:

```
- (void)dealloc {
    [colorChoice release];
    [flowerDetailView release];
    [flowerView release];
    [super dealloc];
}
```

Building the Application

Test out the final version of the FlowerWeb application by clicking Build and Run in Xcode.

Notice that you can zoom in and out of the web view, and use your fingers to scroll around. These are all features that you get without any implementation cost when using the UIWebView class.

Congratulations! Another app under your belt!

Using Scrolling Views

With so many interface elements at your fingertips, you can fill up your iPad's screen pretty quickly.

One possible solution, as you learned earlier this hour, is to use the hidden property of UI objects to hide and show them in your applications. Unfortunately, when you're juggling a few dozen controls, this is pretty impractical. Another approach is to use multiple different views, something that you'll start learning about in Hour 14.

There is, however, a third way that we can fit more into a single view—by making it scroll. Using an instance of the UIScrollView class, you can add controls and interface elements out beyond the physical boundaries of the iPad's screen. Unfortunately, Apple provides access to this object in Interface Builder, but leaves out the ability to actually make it *work*.

Before closing out this hour, we want to show you how to start using very simple scrolling views in a mini-project.

Implementation Overview

This project will consist of a scroll view (UIScrollView) with content added in Interface Builder that extends beyond the physical screen, as shown in Figure 9.17.

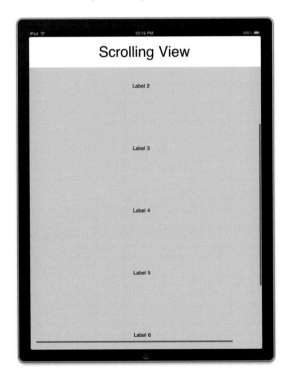

FIGURE 9.17
We're going to make a view that will scroll.

To enable scrolling in the view, we need to define a property called contentSize, which describes how large the content is that needs to be scrolled. That's it.

Setting Up the Project

Begin by creating another View-Based Application. Name the new project **Scroller**. For this example, we're going to be adding the scroll view (UIScrollView) as a subview to the existing view (UIView) in ScrollerViewController.xib. This is a perfectly acceptable approach, but as you get more experienced with the tools, you may want to just replace the default view entirely.

Preparing the Outlet

There's only one thing we need to do programmatically in this project: set a property on the scroll view object. To access the object, we need to create an outlet for it. Open ScrollerViewController.h and add an outlet for a UIScrollView instance called theScroller, and then declare it as a property. The finished header is shown in Listing 9.3.

LISTING 9.3

```
#import <UIKit/UIKit.h>
@interface ScrollerViewController : UIViewController {
    IBOutlet UIScrollView *theScroller;
}
@property (nonatomic, retain) UIScrollView *theScroller;
@end
```

Update the ScrollerViewController implementation file (ScrollerViewController.m) with the corresponding @synthesize directive added after the @implementation directive:

```
@synthesize theScroller;
```

Now that we'll be able to easily access the scroll view, let's go ahead and add it in Interface Builder.

Adding a Scroll View

Open the ScrollerViewController.xib file in Interface Builder, making sure that the document window is open (Window, Document) and the view is visible. Using the object Library (Tools, Library) drag an instance of a Scroll View into your view. Position the view however you'd like it to appear and place a label above it that reads Scrolling View (just in case you forget what we're building).

The Text View (UITextView) you used in Hour 7, "Working with Text, Keyboards, and Buttons," is a specialized instance of a scrolling view. The same scrolling attributes that you can set for the text view can be applied for the scroll view, so you may want to refer to the previous hour for more configuration possibilities. Or just press Command+1 to bring up the Attributes Inspector and explore!

Adding Objects to the Scroll View

Now that your scroll view is included in the XIB file, you need to populate it with something! Frequently, objects are placed in scroll views by writing code that calculates their position. In Interface Builder, Apple *could* add the ability to visually position objects in a larger virtual scroll view canvas, but they haven't.

So, how do we get our buttons and other widgets onscreen? First, start by dragging everything that you want to present into the scroll view object. For this example, I've added six labels. You can use buttons, images, or anything else that you'd normally add to a view.

Once the objects are in the view, you have two options. First, you can select the object, then use the arrow keys to position the objects outside of the visible area of the view to "guesstimate" a position, or you can select each object in turn and use the Size Inspector (Command+3) to set their X and Y coordinates manually, as shown in Figure 9.18.

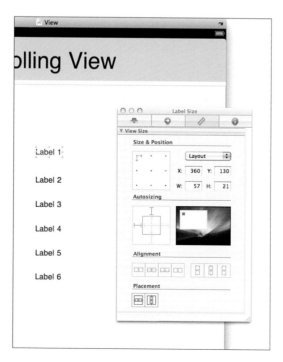

FIGURE 9.18
Use the Size Inspector to set the X and Y coordinates for each object.

By the
Way

The coordinates of objects are relative to the view they are in. In this example, left corner of our scrolling view defines 0,0 (called the "origin point") for everything we add to it.

To help you out, these are the X,Y coordinates' left centers of my six labels:

Label 1   360,130

Label 2   360,330

Label 3   360,530

Label 4   360,730

Label 5   360,930

Label 6   360,1130

As you can see from my final view, shown in Figure 9.19, the fifth and sixth label aren't visible, so we'll certainly need some scrolling if we're going to be able to view them!

FIGURE 9.19
The final scrolling view, with a title, scrolling view, and labels for content.

Connecting to the Outlet

To connect the scrolling view to theScroller outlet defined earlier, control drag from the File's Owner icon in the document window to the scroll view rectangle. When prompted, choose theScroller as your outlet, as shown in Figure 9.20.

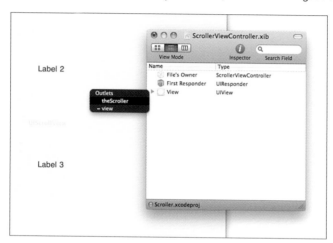

FIGURE 9.20
We'll need to access the scroll view so we can set its contentSize attribute. Create the connection to the theScroller outlet.

That finishes up our work in Interface Builder. Be sure to save the XIB file, and then switch back into Xcode.

Implementing Scrolling Behavior

For fun, try using Build and Run to run the application as it stands. It will compile and launch, but it doesn't scroll. In fact, it behaves just like we'd expect a typical *nonscrolling* view to behave. The reason for this is because we need to tell it the horizontal and vertical sizes of the region it is going to scroll. To do this, we need to set the contentSize attribute to a CGSize value. CGSize is just a simple C data structure that contains a height and a width, and we can easily make one using the CGSizeMake(<width>,<height>) function. For example, to tell our scroll view (theScroller) that it can scroll up to 900 pixels horizontally and 1,500 pixels vertically, we could type the following:

```
theScroller.contentSize=CGSizeMake(900,1500);
```

Guess what? That isn't just what we could do; it's what we will do! Edit the ScrollerViewController.m file's viewDidLoad method to read as follows:

```
- (void)viewDidLoad {
    theScroller.contentSize=CGSizeMake(900,1500);
    [super viewDidLoad];
}
```

> ### Where Did You Get the Width and Height Values?
> The width we used in this example is just the width of the scroll view itself. Why? Because we don't have any reason to scroll horizontally. The height is just a nice number we chose to illustrate that, yes, the view is scrolling. In other words, these are pretty arbitrary! You'll need to choose them to fit your own content in the way that works best for your application.

Releasing the Object

Edit the `dealloc` method to release the scroll view, and we're done:

```
- (void)dealloc {
    [theScroller release];
    [super dealloc];
}
```

Building the Application

The moment of truth has arrived. Does the single line of code make magic? Choose Build and Run, and then try scrolling around the view you created. Everything should work like a charm.

Yes, this was a quick and dirty project, but there seems to be a lack of information on getting started with `UIScrollView` and we thought it was important to run through a short tutorial. We hope this gives you new ideas on what you can do to create more feature-rich interfaces.

Further Exploration

Although useful, the segmented control (`UISegmentedControl`) and switch (`UISwitch`) classes are quite easy to get the hang of. The best place to focus your attention for additional exploration is on the feature set provided by the `UIWebView` and `UIScrollView` classes.

As described at the start of this hour, `UIWebView` can handle a large variety of content beyond what might be inferred by the "web" portion of its name. By learning more about `NSURL`, such as the `initFileURLWithPath:isDirectory` method, you can load files directly from your project resources. You can also take advantage of the web view's built-in actions, such as `goForward` and `goBack`, to add navigation functionality without a single line of code. One might even use a collection of html files to create a self-contained website within an iPad application. In short, web views extend the traditional interface features of your applications by bringing in HTML markup, JavaScript, and CSS—creating a very potent combination.

The `UIScrollView` class, on the other hand, gives us an important capability that expands our usable interface area: touch scrolling. We briefly demonstrated this at the end of the hour, but there are additional features, such as pinching and zooming, that can be enabled by implementing the `UIScrollViewDelegate` protocol. We'll have our first look at building a class that conforms to a protocol in the next hour, so keep this in mind as you get more comfortable with the concepts.

Apple Tutorials

Segmented Controls, Switches, and Web Views — UICatalog (accessible via the Xcode developer documentation). Mentioned in the last hour's lesson, UICatalog shows virtually all the interface concepts in clearly defined examples.

Scrolling—ScrollViewSuite (accessible via the Xcode developer documentation). The ScrollViewSuite provides examples of just about everything you could ever want to do in a scroll view.

Summary

In this hour, you learned how to use two controls that enable applications to respond to user input beyond just a simple button press or a text field. The switch and segmented control, while limited in the options they can present, give a user a touch-friendly way of making decisions within your applications.

You also explored how to use web views to bring web content directly into your projects and how to tweak it so that it integrates into the overall iPad user experience. This powerful class will quickly become one of your most trusted tools for displaying content.

Because we've reached a point in our development where things are starting to get a bit cramped, we closed out the hour with a quick introduction to the scroll view. You learned how, despite appearances, scroll views can be very easily added to apps.

Q&A

Q. *Why can't I visually lay out my scroll view in Interface Builder?*

A. Apple has been making steady improvements to Interface Builder to accommodate iPhone OS development, and while I hope they add this feature in the future, it just isn't currently available.

Q. *You mentioned the UIWebView includes actions? What does that mean and how do I use them?*

A. This means that the object you drag into your view in Interface Builder is already capable of responding to actions (such as navigation actions) on its own—no code required. To use these, you would connect from the UI event that should trigger the action to your instance of the web view (as opposed to the File's Owner icon), and then choose the appropriate action from the pop-up window that appears.

Workshop

Quiz

1. What properties need to be set before a scroll view (`UIScrollView`) will scroll?

2. How do you get the opposite of a Boolean value?

3. What type of object does a web view expect as a parameter when loading a remote URL?

Answers

1. The `contentSize` property must be set for a scroll view before it will allow scrolling.

2. To negate a Boolean value, just prefix it with an exclamation point. `!TRUE`, for example, is the same as `FALSE`.

3. You typically use an `NSURLRequest` object to initiate a web request within a web view.

Activities

1. Create your own "mini" web browser by combining a text field, buttons, and a segmented control with a web view. Use the text field for URL entry, buttons for navigation, and hard-code some shortcuts for your favorite sites into the segmented control. To make the best use of space, you may want to overlay the controls on the web view, and then add a switch that hides or shows the controls when toggled.

2. Practice laying out a user interface within a scrollable view. Use graph paper to sketch the view and determine coordinates before laying it out in Interface Builder.

HOUR 10

Getting the User's Attention

What You'll Learn in This Hour:

▶ Different types of user notifications
▶ How to create alert views
▶ Methods for collecting input from alerts
▶ How to implement short system sounds

The iPad presents developers with many opportunities for creating unique user interfaces, but certain elements must be consistent across all applications. When users need to be notified of an application event or make a critical decision, it is important that they be presented with interface elements that immediately make sense. In this hour, we look at a few of the different ways an application can notify a user that *something* has happened. It's up to you to determine what that "something" is, but these are the tools you'll need to keep users of your apps "in the know."

Exploring User Alert Methods

Applications on the iPad are user centered, which means they typically don't perform utility functions in the background or operate without an interface. They enable users to work with data, play games, communicate, or carry out dozens of other activities. Despite the variation in activities, when an application needs to show a warning, provide feedback, or ask the user to make a decision, the iPad does so in a common way. Cocoa Touch leverages a variety of objects and methods to gain your attention, including UIAlertView and System Sound Services.

This hour explains how you can implement these notification features into your application.

Prepping the Notification Project Files

To practice using these alert classes and methods, we need to create a new project
with buttons for activating the different styles of notifications. Open Xcode and create a new project based on the View-based Application iPad template. Name the
project **GettingAttention**.

Within Xcode, open the GettingAttentionViewController.h file and add the following
outlets and actions, shown in Listing 10.1.

LISTING 10.1

```
#import <UIKit/UIKit.h>

@interface GettingAttentionViewController : UIViewController {
    IBOutlet UILabel *userOutput;
}

@property (retain, nonatomic) IBOutlet UILabel *userOutput;

- (IBAction)doAlert:(id)sender;
- (IBAction)doMultiButtonAlert:(id)sender;
- (IBAction)doAlertInput:(id)sender;
- (IBAction)doSound:(id)sender;

@end
```

The first outlet, userOutput, will be implemented as a text label for providing simple feedback within the application. The three actions are methods that correspond
to the different notification methods we'll be writing throughout the hour.

Next, edit the start of the GettingAttentionViewController.m file and add the following code after the existing @implementation line:

```
@synthesize userOutput;

-(IBAction)doAlert:(id)sender {
}
-(IBAction)doMultiButtonAlert:(id)sender {
}
-(IBAction)doAlertInput:(id)sender {
}
-(IBAction)doSound:(id)sender {
}
```

The @synthesize directive is used to create the getter/setter for the userOutput text
label. Next, five stub methods are defined for our actions. Finally, be sure to edit the
dealloc method to release the userOutput object:

```
- (void)dealloc {
    [userOutput release];
    [super dealloc];
}
```

That completes the code skeleton that we'll be using throughout this hour. Now let's create the interface in Interface Builder and connect the outlets and actions.

Creating the Notification Project Interface

Open the GettingAttentionViewController XIB file in Interface Builder. We need to add two buttons and a text label to the empty view. You should be getting quite familiar with this process by now. Just follow these steps:

1. Double-click the View icon in the Documents window. This will open the empty view.

2. Add a button to the view by opening the library (Tools, Library), and dragging a Round Rect Button (IUButton) to the View window.

3. Add three more buttons, spaced out evenly below the first. Make sure you leave room at the bottom for a label.

4. Change the button labels to correspond to the different notification types that we'll be using. Specifically, name the buttons (top to bottom) **Alert Me!**, **Alert with Buttons!**, **I Need Input!**, and **Play Sound**.

5. Drag a label (UILabel) from the library to the bottom of the view. Remove the default label text and increase the font size, if desired. The interface should resemble Figure 10.1.

Connecting the Outlets and Actions

The interface itself is finished, but we still need to make the connection to our properties and method stubs, as follows:

1. Click to select the first button (Alert Me!), and then press Command+2 to open the Connection Inspector.

FIGURE 10.1
Create an inter-
face with four
buttons and a
label at the
bottom.

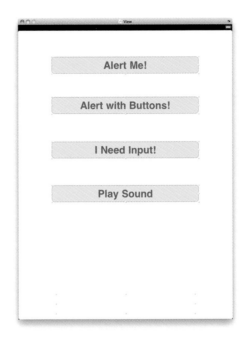

2. From the Touch Up Inside connection point, click and drag to the File's Owner icon in the Document window.

3. When prompted, choose the doAlert method from the list (see Figure 10.2).

FIGURE 10.2
Connect the
buttons to the
method stubs.

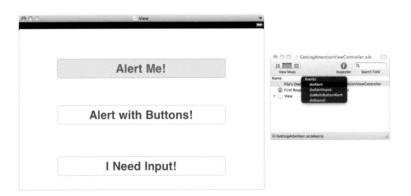

4. Repeat this pattern for the other two buttons. Alert with Buttons! connects to doMultiButtonAlert, I Need Input! should connect to the doAlertInput method, and Play Sound to doSound.

5. To connect the label, Control-drag from the File's Owner icon in the Document window to the label (either in the View window, or the View hierarchy in the Document window). Choose the userOutput outlet to make the final connection, as demonstrated in Figure 10.3.

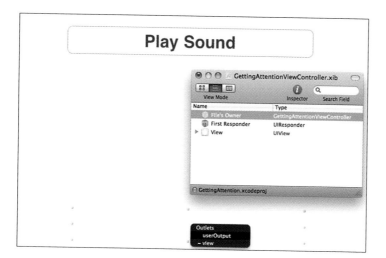

FIGURE 10.3
Connect the userOutput outlet to the label in the view.

The framework for our test of notification is ready. We'll start by implementing a simple alert view.

Generating Alerts

Sometimes users need to be informed of changes when an application is running. More than just a change in the current view is required when an internal error event occurs (such as low-memory condition or a dropped network connection), for example, or upon completion of a long-running activity. Enter the UIAlertView class.

The UIAlertView class creates a simple modal alert window that presents a user with a message and a few option buttons (see Figure 10.4).

What Does *Modal* Mean?

Modal UI elements require the user to interact with them (usually push a button) before the user can do anything else. They are typically layered on top of other windows and block all other interface actions while visible. In Hour 13, "Focusing on Tasks with Modal Views," you'll learn how create entire modal views.

Displaying a Simple Alert

In the preceding section, you created a simple project (GettingAttention) with several buttons that we'll use to activate the different notification events. The first button, Alert Me!, should be connected to a method stub called doAlert in GettingAttentionViewController.m. In this first exercise, we write an implementation of doAlert that displays an alert message with a single button that the user can push to dismiss the dialog.

Edit GettingAttentionViewController.m and enter the code shown in Listing 10.2 for doAlert.

LISTING 10.2

```
 1: -(IBAction)doAlert:(id)sender {
 2:     UIAlertView *alertDialog;
 3:     alertDialog = [[UIAlertView alloc]
 4:                     initWithTitle: @"Alert Button Selected"
 5:                     message:@"I need your attention NOW!"
 6:                     delegate: nil
 7:                     cancelButtonTitle: @"Ok"
 8:                     otherButtonTitles: nil];
 9:     [alertDialog show];
10:     [alertDialog release];
11: }
```

In lines 2 and 3, we declare and instantiate our instance of UIAlertView with a variable called alertDialog. As you can see, the convenient initialization method of the alert view does almost all the work for us. Let's review the parameters:

`initWithTitle:` — Initializes the view and sets the title that will appear at the top of the alert dialog box.

`message:` — Sets the string that will appear in the content area of the dialog box.

`delegate:` — Contains the object that will serve as the delegate to the alert. Initially, we don't need any actions to be performed after the user dismisses the alert, so we can set this to `nil`.

`cancelButtonTitle:` — Sets the string shown in the default button for the alert.

`otherButtonTitles:` — Adds an additional button to the alert. We're starting with a single-button alert, so this is set to `nil`.

After `alertDialog` has been initialized, the next step is to show it by using (surprise!) the `show` method, as shown in line 9. Finally, as soon as we're done with the alert, we can release it, as shown in line 10.

> If you prefer to set the alert message and buttons independently of the initialization, the `UIAlertView` class includes properties for setting the text labels (`message`, `title`) individually and methods for adding buttons (`addButtonWithTitle`).

By the Way

Figure 10.5 shows the outcome of these settings.

FIGURE 10.5
In its simplest form, an alert view displays a message and button to dismiss it.

> An alert doesn't have to be a single-use object. If you're going to be using an alert repeatedly, create an instance when your view is loaded and show it as needed—but remember to release the object when you've finished using it!

Creating Multi-Option Alerts

An alert with a single button is easy to implement because there is no additional logic to program. The user taps the button, the alert is dismissed, and execution continues as normal. If you need to add additional buttons, however, your application needs to be able to identify the button pressed and react appropriately.

In additional to the single-button alert that you just created, you need to learn two additional configurations. The difference between them is how many buttons you're asking the alert to display. A two-button alert places buttons side by side. When more than two buttons are added, the buttons are stacked, as you'll soon see.

Adding Buttons

Creating an alert with multiple buttons is simple: We just take advantage of the `otherButtonTitles` parameter of the initialization convenience method. Instead of setting to `nil`, we provide a list of strings terminated by `nil` that should be used as the additional button names. The "cancel" button will always be displayed on the left in a two-button scenario or at the bottom of a longer button list.

> At most, an alert view can display five buttons (including the button designated as the "cancel" button) simultaneously. Attempting to add more may result in some very unusual onscreen effects, such as display of clipped/partial buttons. This limitation, for whatever reason, appears to have carried over to the iPad from the iPhone, despite the much larger screen size.

For example, to expand the previous example to include two new buttons, the initialization can be changed as follows:

```
alertDialog = [[UIAlertView alloc]
              initWithTitle: @"Alert Button Selected"
              message:@"I need your attention NOW!"
              delegate: nil
              cancelButtonTitle: @"Ok"
              otherButtonTitles: @"Maybe Later", @"Never", nil];
```

Write an updated version of the `doAlert` method within the `doMultiButtonAlert` method stub created earlier. Listing 10.3 shows the final code.

LISTING 10.3

```
-(IBAction)doMultiButtonAlert:(id)sender {
     UIAlertView *alertDialog;

     alertDialog = [[UIAlertView alloc]
               initWithTitle: @"Alert Button Selected"
               message:@"I need your attention NOW!"
               delegate: nil
               cancelButtonTitle: @"Ok"
               otherButtonTitles: @"Maybe Later", @"Never", nil];

     [alertDialog show];
     [alertDialog release];
}
```

Pressing the Alert with Buttons! button should now open the alert view displayed in
Figure 10.6.

Try pushing one of the buttons. The alert view is dismissed. Push another? The same
thing happens. All the buttons do exactly the same thing: absolutely nothing.
Although this behavior was fine with a single button, it's not going to be very useful
with our current configuration.

FIGURE 10.6
Add additional
buttons during
initialization of
the alert view.

Responding to a Button Press with the Alert View Delegate Protocol

When I first started using Objective-C, I found the terminology painful. It seemed that no matter how easy a concept was to understand, it was surrounded with language that made it appear harder than it was. A protocol, in my opinion, is one of these things.

Protocols define a collection of methods that perform a task. To provide advanced functionality, some classes, such as UIAlertView, require you to implement methods defined in a related protocol. Some methods are required, others are optional; it just depends on the features you need.

To make the full use of an alert view, an additional protocol method must added to one of our classes. We'll be using our main application's view controller class for this purpose, but in larger projects it may be a completely separate class—the choice is entirely up to you. A class that implements a protocol is said to "conform" to that protocol.

To identify the button that was pressed in a multi-option alert, for example, our GettingAttentionViewController should conform to the UIAlertViewDelegate protocol and implement the alertView:clickedButtonAtIndex: method.

Edit the GettingAttentionViewController.h interface file to declare that the class will be conforming to the necessary protocol by modifying the @interface line as follows:

```
@interface GettingAttentionViewController : UIViewController
➥<UIAlertViewDelegate> {
```

Next, update the initialization code of the alert view in doMultiButtonAlert so that the delegate is pointed to the object that implements the UIAlertViewDelegate. Because this is the same object (the view controller) that is creating the alert, we can just use self:

```
alertDialog = [[UIAlertView alloc]
            initWithTitle: @"Alert Button Selected"
            message:@"I need your attention NOW!"
            delegate: self
            cancelButtonTitle: @"Ok"
            otherButtonTitles: @"Maybe Later", @"Never", nil];
```

The alertView:clickedButtonAtIndex method that we write next will receive the index of the button that was pushed and give us the opportunity to act on it. To make this easier, we can take advantage of the UIAlertView instance method buttonTitleAtIndex. This method will return the string title of a button from its index, eliminating the need to keep track of which index value corresponds to which button.

Add the code in Listing 10.4 to GettingAttentionViewController.m to display a message when a button is pressed.

LISTING 10.4

```
 1: - (void)alertView:(UIAlertView *)alertView
 2:     clickedButtonAtIndex:(NSInteger)buttonIndex {
 3:     NSString *buttonTitle=[alertView buttonTitleAtIndex:buttonIndex];
 4:     if ([buttonTitle isEqualToString:@"Maybe Later"]) {
 5:         userOutput.text=@"Clicked 'Maybe Later'";
 6:     } else if ([buttonTitle isEqualToString:@"Never"]) {
 7:         userOutput.text=@"Clicked 'Never'";
 8:     } else {
 9:         userOutput.text=@"Clicked 'Ok'";
10:     }
11: }
```

To start, in line 3, buttonTitle is set to the title of the button that was clicked. Lines 4 through 10 test the value of buttonTitle against the names of the buttons that we initialized when creating the alert view. If a match is found, the userOutput label in the view is updated to something appropriate.

This is just one way to implement the button handler for your alert. In some cases (such as dynamically generated button labels), it may be more appropriate to work directly with the button index values. You may also want to consider defining constants for button labels.

Don't assume that application processing stops when the alert window is on the screen! Your code will continue to execute after you show the alert. You may even want to take advantage of this by using the UIAlertView instance method dismissWithClickedButtonIndex: to remove the alert from the screen if the user does not respond within a certain length of time.

Adding Fields to Alerts

Although buttons can be used to generate user input from an alert, you may have noticed that some applications actually present text fields within an alert box. The App Store, for example, prompts for your iTunes password before it starts downloading a new app.

To add fields to your alert dialogs, you'll need to be a bit "sneaky." There isn't a simple "add text field" option, but you can take advantage of the method addSubView which is common to all subclasses of a UIView (which includes alert views and text fields). In short, we need to manually create a field and position it within the alert view. Because the alert view doesn't "know" it's going to be there, we can the alert view's message text to create space to contain the field. Sound bizarre? It is—but it isn't difficult.

Let's start by providing a place to store and reference the field.

Adding the Text Field Instance Variable

We don't have Interface Builder around to drag a field into an alert view, so we need to declare, allocate, and initialize it manually. Open the GettingAttentionViewController.h file and modify it to include a UITextField named userInput. Be sure to include a @property directive for it, too, as shown in Listing 10.5.

LISTING 10.5

```
#import <UIKit/UIKit.h>

@interface GettingAttentionViewController :
UIViewController <UIAlertViewDelegate> {
    IBOutlet UILabel *userOutput;
    UITextField *userInput;
}

@property (retain, nonatomic) IBOutlet UILabel *userOutput;
@property (retain, nonatomic) UITextField *userInput;

- (IBAction)doAlert:(id)sender;
- (IBAction)doMultiButtonAlert:(id)sender;
- (IBAction)doAlertInput:(id)sender;
- (IBAction)doSound:(id)sender;

@end
```

Next, open the implementation file (GettingAttentionViewController.m) and add a @synthesize line for userInput immediately following the userOutput @synthesize line:

```
@synthesize userInput;
```

Finally, update the dealloc method to release userInput when the application is completed:

```
- (void)dealloc {
    [userInput release];
    [userOutput release];
    [super dealloc];
}
```

Now we're ready to build the doAlertInput method.

Adding a Text Field Subview

The steps that we take to add a field to an alert may seem unusually convoluted, but, broken down, they're easy to understand. First, we initialize the alert, making sure that it includes enough space in the view (by adding a message) so that we can add a field over top of it. Next, we allocate and initialize a new text field (userInput), and set its color to white so we can see it on top of the alert view. Finally, we add the text field to the alert using the addSubView method to position it over top of where the alert's message line would appear.

Enter the doAlertInput method in GettingAttentionViewController.m using the code in Listing 10.6.

LISTING 10.6

```
 1: -(IBAction)doAlertInput:(id)sender {
 2:     UIAlertView *alertDialog;
 3:
 4:     alertDialog = [[UIAlertView alloc]
 5:                     initWithTitle: @"Please Enter Your Email Address!"
 6:                     message:@"You won't see me"
 7:                     delegate: self
 8:                     cancelButtonTitle: @"Ok"
 9:                     otherButtonTitles: nil];
10:
11:     userInput=[[UITextField alloc] initWithFrame:
12:             CGRectMake(12.0, 70.0, 260.0, 25.0)];
13:
14:     [userInput setBackgroundColor:[UIColor whiteColor]];
15:
16:     [alertDialog addSubview:userInput];
17:     [alertDialog show];
18:     [alertDialog release];
19: }
```

The beginning and end of this method should look familiar. (It's identical to doAlert, with the exception of the delegate being set to self—more on that a little later.) The differences are in lines 11–16.

Line 11 and 12 allocate, initialize, and assign a new UITextField instance to the userInput field. The initWithFrame method initializes the object with a rectangle returned by the CGRectMake() function. The values of 12.0, 70.0, 260.0, and 25.0 indicate that the field with be located 12.0 pixels from the left side of the view it is placed within and 70.0 pixels from the top. It will be 260.0 pixels wide and 25.0 pixels tall. Where did these values come from? Experimentation! These are the values that will correctly position the field over top of the message "You won't see me."

Line 14 sets the background of the text field to white.

Line 16 adds the field to the alert view using the addSubView method.

You should now be able to Build and Run the GettingAttention application, tap the I Need Input! button, and see an alert with an input field, as demonstrated in Figure 10.7.

FIGURE 10.7
Add fields to
your alert views
using the
addSubView
method.

All that remains is being able to do something with the contents of the field—and that part is easy!

Accessing the Text Field

To access the input the user provided in the alert view, we just need to read the text property of userInput. Where do we do this? In the alert view's delegate method alertView:clickedButtonAtIndex.

Ah ha! You say, "But didn't we already use that method to handle the alert view from doMultiButtonAlert? Yes we did, but if we're clever, we can tell the difference between which alert is calling that method and react appropriately.

Because we have access to the view object itself within the alertView:clickedButtonAtIndex method, why don't we just check the title of the view and, if it is equal to the title of our input alert (Please Enter Your Email Address!), we can set userOutput to the text the user entered in userInput. This is easily accomplished by a simple string comparison using the `title` property of the alert view object passed to `alertView:clickedButtonAtIndex`.

Add the following code snippet to the end of the `alertView:clickedButtonAtIndex` method:

```
if ([alertView.title
        isEqualToString: @"Please Enter Your Email Address!"]) {
        userOutput.text=userInput.text;
}
```

Build and Run the application with these changes in place. Now, when the alert view with the text field is dismissed, the delegate method is called, and the user output label is properly set to the text the user entered.

Using these techniques, you can expand the capabilities of alert views beyond the simple implementation provided in the base iPhone OS SDK.

Using Alert Sounds

Visual notifications are great for providing feedback to a user and getting critical input. Other senses, however, can be just as useful for getting a user's attention. Sounds, for example, play an important role on nearly every computer system (regardless of platform or purpose). They tell us when an error has occurred or an action has been completed. Sounds free a user's visual focus and still provide feedback about what an application is doing.

The best news of all? iPad alert sounds are handled through very simple code, so you'll be able to implement with relative ease in your applications.

System Sound Services

To enable sound playback, we will take advantage of the System Sound Services C-style interface. System Sound Services provides an interface for playing back sounds that are 30 seconds or less in length. It supports a limited number of file formats (specifically CAF, AIF, and WAV files). The functions provide no manipulation of the sound, nor control of the volume, so you won't want to use System Sound Services to create the soundtrack for your latest and greatest iPad game. In Hour 20, "Working with Rich Media," you'll explore additional media playback features of the iPhone OS.

Unlike most of the other development functionality we've discussed in this book, the System Sound Services functionality is not implemented as a class. Instead, you will be using more traditional C-style function calls to trigger playback.

The iPhone OS supports three different notifications using this API:

Sound: A simple sound file is played back immediately. If the device is muted, the user will hear nothing.

Alert: Again, a sound file is played, but if the device is muted and set to vibrate, the user is alerted through vibration.

Vibrate: The device is vibrated, regardless of any other settings.

Because the iPad does not support vibration, we'll only need the Sound notification type.

Playing Sounds

To play a sound file, you first need to make the file available as a resource to your iPad application. Let's continue to expand the GettingAttention project to include sound playback:

1. With your project open in Xcode, return to the Finder and navigate to the "sounds" directory within this hour's project folder.

2. Drag the soundeffect.wav file into your Xcode project's Resources folder.

You should see the file listed as a resource (see Figure 10.8).

FIGURE 10.8
Add the sound files as resources to your project.

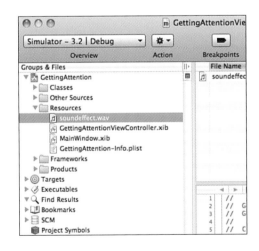

Adding the AudioToolbox Framework

The AudioToolbox framework must be added to our project before we can use any of the playback functions. To add this framework, complete the following steps:

1. Right-click the Frameworks group in Xcode and choose Add Existing Framework.

2. Navigate to AudioToolbox.framework and Click Add.

3. Open the GettingAttentionViewController.h file and import the interface file necessary to access the sound functions (AudioToolbox/AudioToolbox.h). This edit should fall directly after the existing import line:

   ```
   #import <AudioToolbox/AudioToolbox.h>
   ```

Creating and Playing System Sounds

With the prep work out of the way, we're ready to add some sounds to our project. The two functions that we'll need to use are AudioServicesCreateSystemSoundID and AudioServicesPlaySystemSound. We'll also need to declare a variable of the type SystemSoundID. This will represent the sound file that we are working with.

Edit GettingAttentionViewController.m and add the implementation for the doSound method shown in Listing 10.7.

LISTING 10.7

```
 1: -(IBAction)doSound:(id)sender {
 2:     SystemSoundID soundID;
 3:     NSString *soundFile = [[NSBundle mainBundle]
 4:                         pathForResource:@"soundeffect" ofType:@"wav"];
 5:
 6:     AudioServicesCreateSystemSoundID((CFURLRef)
 7:                              [NSURL fileURLWithPath:soundFile]
 8:                              , &soundID);
 9:     AudioServicesPlaySystemSound(soundID);
10: }
```

The code to play a system sound might look a bit alien after all the Objective-C we've been using. Let's take a look at the functional pieces.

Line 2 starts things off by declaring a variable, soundID, that we will use to refer to the sound file. (Note that this is *not* declared as a pointer, as pointers begin with a *!) Next, in line 3, we declare and assign a string (soundFile) to the path of the sound file soundeffect.wav. This works by first using the NSBundle class method mainBundle to return an NSBundle object that corresponds to the directory containing the current application's executable binary. The NSBundle object's `pathForResource:ofType:` method is then used to identify the specific sound file by name and extension.

Once a path has been identified for the sound file, we must use the `AudioServicesCreateSystemSoundID` function to create a `SystemSoundID` that will represent this file for the functions that will actually play the sound. This function takes two parameters: a `CFURLRef` object that points to the location of the file, and a pointer to the `SystemSoundID` variable that we want to be set. For the first parameter, we use the `NSURL fileURLWithPath` class method to return an `NSURL` object from the sound file path. We preface this with `(CFURLRef)` to cast the `NSURL` object to the `CFURLRef` type expected by the system. The second parameter is satisfied by passing `&soundID` to the function.

> Recall that `&<variable>` returns a reference (pointer) to the named variable. This is rarely needed when working with the Objective-C classes, because nearly everything is already a pointer!

After `soundID` has been properly set up, all that remains is playing it. Pass the `soundID` variable to the `AudioServicesPlaySystemSound` function, as shown in line 9, and we're in business.

Build and test the application. Pressing the Play Sound button should now play back the sound effect WAV file.

That's all there is to it. You've now built three different ways of getting a user's attention. These are techniques that you can use in any application to make sure that your user is aware of changes and can respond if needed.

Further Exploration

Your next step in making use of the notification methods discussed in this hour is to use them. These simple, but important, UI elements will help facilitate many of your critical user interactions. One topic that is beyond the scope of this book is the ability for a developer to push notifications to the iPad.

Even without push notifications, you might want to add numeric badges to your applications. These badges are visible when the application isn't running and can display any integer you'd like—most frequently, a count of items identified as "new" within the application (such as new news items, messages, events, and so on). To create application badges, look at the `UIApplication` class property `applicationIconBadgeNumber`. Setting this property to anything other than zero will create and display the badge.

Another area that you might like to explore is how to work with rich media (Hour 20). The audio playback functions discussed in this hour are intended for alert-type sounds only. If you're looking for more complete multimedia features, you'll need to tap into the AVFoundation framework, which gives you complete control over recording and playback features of the iPad.

Summary

In this hour, you learned about alert dialogs that can be used to communicate information to an application user, as well as enable users to provide input at critical points in time. Unlike many of the UI components we've used in this book, alerts cannot be instantiated with a simple drag and drop in Interface Builder.

We also explored a nonvisual means of communicating with a user: sounds. Using the System Sound Services (by way of the AudioToolbox framework), you can easily add short sound effects to your applications. Again, these have to be implemented in code, but in fewer than five lines, you can have your applications making noises that will completely baffle your pets.

Q&A

Q. *I found an addTextField method for alert views mentioned online. This looks like an easy way to add text fields to alerts, why aren't you using it?*

A. The `addTextField` method is a private API call. Even though it works (and works well), your application will be rejected by Apple if you use it.

Q. *Can sounds be used in conjunction with alert views?*

A. Yes. Because alerts are frequently displayed without warning, there is no guarantee that the user is looking at the screen. Using an alert sound provides the best chance for getting the user's attention.

Workshop

Quiz

1. Alert views are tied to a specific UI element. True or false?

2. Adding a text field to an alert automatically shifts the content of the alert view to make room for it. True or false?

3. System Sound Services supports playing back a wide variety of sound file formats, including MP3s. True or false?

Answers

1. False. Alert views are displayed outside the context of a view and are not tied to any other UI element.

2. False. The text field lies on top of existing alert view content. Adding a message to the alert view is an easy way to make room for the field.

3. False. System Sound Services supports only AIF, WAV, and CAF formats.

Activities

1. Rewrite either the alert view handler to determine button presses using the button index values rather than the titles. This will help you prepare for projects where buttons may be generated and added to the view/sheet dynamically rather than during initialization.

2. Return to one or more of your earlier projects and add audio cues to the interface actions. Make switches click, buttons ding, and so on. Keep your sounds short, clear, and complementary to the actions that the users are performing.

HOUR 11

Presenting Options with Popovers and Toolbars

What You'll Learn in This Hour:

▶ How to add toolbars and toolbar buttons to your projects

▶ The role of popovers in the iPhone OS

▶ How to generate custom popover views in your projects

▶ Tricks for checking to see whether a popover is already displayed

On the iPhone, what you see is typically what you get. The user interface elements either show the options that are available to you, offer the ability to scroll to additional options, or swap out the current screen for another view that displays more information. The multiple-window model used in Mac OS X is gone. Although you might encounter an occasional alert dialog, windowing is not a standard in iPhone interfaces. On the iPad, things have changed. Apple has introduced the popover: a user interface element that can present views on top of other views.

In this hour, we explore how to prepare views for use in popovers, including adding toolbars and toolbar buttons (the most frequent UI element used to invoke a popover). You'll also configure the different display attributes associated with popovers, and communicate information between popover views and your main application view. Popovers are such a prevalent and important UI element that we'll be focusing on them for the next few hours, so be sure to work through this lesson carefully.

Understanding Popovers and Toolbars

Popovers are everywhere in the iPad interface, from Mail to Safari, as demonstrated in Figure 11.1. Using a popover enables you to display new information to your users without leaving the screen you are on, and to hide the information when the user is done with it. There are few desktop counterparts to popovers, but they are roughly analogous to tool palettes, inspector panels, and configuration dialogs. In other words, they provide user interfaces for interacting with content on the iPad screen, but without eating up permanent space in your UI.

FIGURE 11.1
Popovers are unique to the iPad UI.

Popovers, although capable of being displayed when a user interacts with any onscreen object, are most often shown when the user presses a toolbar button (UIBarButton) from within a toolbar object (UIToolbar). This is exactly the scenario shown in Figure 11.1. Because of this relationship, we will be presenting both of these objects within this hour's lesson. Let's quickly review what we need for each before we get started coding.

Popovers

Unlike other UI elements, popovers aren't something you just drag into a view from the Interface Builder Library. They are, in fact, entirely independent views, designed just like your main application view. The display of the views is governed by a popover controller (UIPopoverController). The controller displays the popover when a user event is triggered, such as touching a toolbar button. When the user is done with the popover, touching outside of its visible rectangle automatically closes the view.

To create a popover, we'll need to cover three different requirements. First, we need to make a view and view controller specially designed for the popover's contents. Second, when the proper event occurs in the user interface, we need to allocate and initialize an instance of popover controller. Third, when the user is done with the popover, we want to make sure that any changes made in the popover are reflected in the main application.

Popover Views

You've been developing views and view controllers for the past several hours, so you'll feel right at home working with a popover view. It uses the same `UIViewController` that we've been using all along, but with the addition of one unique property: `contentSizeForViewInPopover`.

This property should be set to the width and height of the popover to be displayed. Apple allows popovers up to 600 pixels wide and the height of the iPad screen, but recommends that they be kept to 320 pixels wide, or less. For example, to set the content size of 320 pixels by 200 pixels for a view controller that will be displaying a popover, we might add the following to the `viewDidLoad` method:

```
self.contentSizeForViewInPopover=CGSizeMake(320.0,200.0);
```

In fact, that's exactly what we're going to be doing in the tutorial shortly.

Popover Controller

Like views need view controllers, popovers need popover controllers (`UIPopoverController`). Popover controllers take care of all the hard work of rendering popovers on the screen in the right place. We'll focus on two methods of the popover controller:

> `initWithContentViewController`—Initializes the popover with the contents of a view controller. When the popover is displayed, whatever the view controller's view is, is displayed.

> `presentPopoverFromBarButtonItem:permittedArrowDirections:animated` —Invokes the display of the popover so that it appears to emerge from (and point to) a toolbar button. The parameters for this method allow fine-tuning of the arrow from the popover to the UI element it is appearing from, and whether its display is animated.

The popover controller will also need the `delegate` property set to an object that will take care of all the "cleanup" when the popover is dismissed by the user. This includes releasing the popover controller and updating the contents of the main application to reflect the user's actions in the popover. This leads us to the final popover requirement: the `UIPopoverControllerDelegate` protocol.

Popover Controller Delegate Protocol

To make the full use of a popover, we'll need an additional protocol method added to one of our classes. In our sample application, we'll be using our main application's view controller class for this purpose. This means we need to add a line to our main view controller's interface (.h) file to state that we're conforming to the `UIPopoverControllerDelegate` protocol. Second, we'll be adding the protocol method `popoverControllerDidDismissPopover` to our application's view controller implementation file. That's it.

When the popover is dismissed by the user touching outside of its display, the `popoverControllerDidDismissPopover` method is invoked and we can react appropriately.

Toolbars

Toolbars (`UIToolbar`) are, comparatively speaking, one of the simpler UI elements that you have at your disposal. A toolbar is implemented as a solid bar, either at the top or bottom of the display, with buttons (`UIBarButtonItem`) that correspond to actions that can be performed in the current view. The buttons provide a single selector action, which works nearly identically to the typical Touch Up Inside event that you've encountered before.

Toolbars, as their name implies, are used for providing a set of static choices to the user—interface options that should be visible regardless of whether the application's primary content is changing. As you'll see, they can be implemented almost entirely visually and are the de facto standard for triggering the display of a popover on the iPad.

Although implementing popovers might be sounding a bit convoluted at this point, hang in there. After you've created one, the process will seem incredibly simple, and you'll want to use them everywhere!

Using Popovers with Toolbars

Popovers are used to display interface elements that configure how your application behaves but that don't need to be visible all the time. Our sample implementation will display a toolbar, complete with a Configure button, that invokes a popover. The popover will display configuration four switches (`UISwitch`) for a hypothetical time-based application: Weekends, Weekdays, AM, and PM.

The user will be able to update these switches in the popover, and then touch outside the popover to dismiss it. Upon dismissal, four labels in the main application view will be update to show the user's selections. The final application will resemble Figure 11.2.

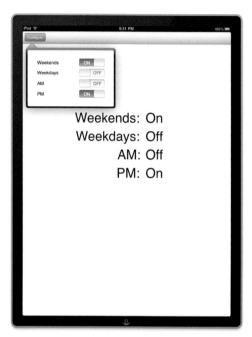

FIGURE 11.2
This application will display a popover and update the main application view to reflect a user's actions in the popover.

Implementation Overview

The implementation of this project is simpler than it may seem at the onset. You'll be creating a View-based iPad application that includes a toolbar with the Configure button and four labels that will display what a user has chosen in the popover. The popover will require its own view controller and view. We'll add these to the main project, but they'll be set up almost entirely independently from the main application view.

Building the connection between the main view and the popover will require surprisingly few lines of code. We need to be careful that touching the Configure button doesn't continue to add popovers to the display if one is already shown, but you'll learn a trick that keeps it all under control.

Setting Up the Project

This project will start with the View-Based Application template; we'll be adding in another view and view controller to handle the popover. Let's begin. Launch Xcode

(Developer/Applications), and then create a new View-based iPad project called
PopoverConfig.

Xcode will create the basics structure for your project, including the
`PopoverConfigViewController` classes. We'll refer to this as the *main application
view controller* (the class the implements the view that the user sees when the application runs). For the popover content itself, we need to add a new view controller
and XIB file to the PopoverConfig project.

Adding an Additional View Controller Class

With the Classes group selected in your Xcode project, choose File, New File, from
the menu bar. Within the New File dialog box, choose the Cocoa Touch Class within
the iPhone OS category, and then the `UIViewController` subclass icon, as shown in
Figure 11.3.

Be sure that Targeted for iPad and With XIB for user interface are selected, and then
choose Next. When prompted, name the new class **PopoverContentViewController**
and click Finish.

The `PopoverContentViewController` implementation and interface files are added
to the Classes group.

> Depending on your version of Xcode, the XIB file may also be added to the folder you had selected when creating the class files. If this is the case, drag it to the Resources group.

Did you Know?

Preparing the Popover Content

This hour's project is unique in that most of your interface work takes place in a view that is only onscreen occasionally when the application is running—the popover's content view. The view will have four switches (UISwitch), which we'll need to account for.

We only need to be able to read values from the popup view, not invoke any actions, so we'll just add four IBOutlets.

Adding Outlets

Open the PopoverContentViewController.h interface file and add outlets for four UISwitch elements: weekendSwitch, weekdaySwitch, amSwitch, pmSwitch. Be sure to also at @property directives for each switch. The resulting interface file is shown in Listing 11.1.

LISTING 11.1

```
#import <UIKit/UIKit.h>

@interface PopoverContentViewController : UIViewController {
    IBOutlet UISwitch *weekendSwitch;
    IBOutlet UISwitch *weekdaySwitch;
    IBOutlet UISwitch *amSwitch;
    IBOutlet UISwitch *pmSwitch;
}

@property (nonatomic,retain) UISwitch *weekendSwitch;
@property (nonatomic,retain) UISwitch *weekdaySwitch;
@property (nonatomic,retain) UISwitch *amSwitch;
@property (nonatomic,retain) UISwitch *pmSwitch;

@end
```

For each of the properties we've declared, we need to add a @synthesize directive in the implementation (popoverContentViewController.m) file. Open this file and make your additions following the @implementation line:

```
@synthesize weekdaySwitch;
@synthesize weekendSwitch;
@synthesize amSwitch;
@synthesize pmSwitch;
```

Setting the Popover Content Size

Our next step is easy to overlook, but amazingly important to the final application. For an application to present an appropriately sized popover, you must manually define the popover's content size. The easiest (and most logical) place to do this is within the popover's view controller.

Continue editing the popoverContentViewController.m file to uncomment its viewDidLoad method and add a size definition:

```
- (void)viewDidLoad {
    self.contentSizeForViewInPopover=CGSizeMake(320.0,200.0);
    [super viewDidLoad];
}
```

For this tutorial project, our popover will be 320 pixels wide and 200 pixels tall. Remember that Apple supports values up to 600 pixels wide and a height as tall as the iPad's screen area allows.

Releasing Objects

Even though this view controller sits outside of our main application, we still need to clean up memory properly. Finish up the implementation of the popoverContentViewController class by releasing the four switch instance variables in the dealloc method:

```
- (void)dealloc {
    [weekdaySwitch release];
    [weekendSwitch release];
    [amSwitch release];
    [pmSwitch release];
    [super dealloc];
}
```

That finishes the popoverContentViewController logic! Although we still have a little bit of work to do in Interface Builder, the rest of the programming efforts will take place in the main popoverConfig view controller class.

Preparing the View

Building a popover's view is *identical* to building any other view with one small difference: You can only use the portion of the view that fits within the size of the popover you're creating. Open the popoverContentViewController XIB file in Interface Builder and add four labels (Weekends, Weekdays, AM, and PM) and four corresponding switches (UISwitch) from the library.

Position these in the upper-left corner of the view to fit within the 320x200 dimensions we've defined, as shown in Figure 11.4.

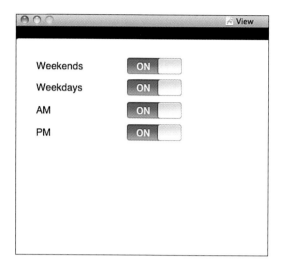

FIGURE 11.4
Add four config-
uration switches
and correspon-
ding labels to
the popover
content view.

Connecting the Outlets

After creating the view, connect the switches to the IBOutlets. Control-drag from
the File's Owner icon in the Document window to the first switch in the view (the
Weekends switch in my implementation) and choose the weekendSwitch outlet
when prompted, as shown in Figure 11.5.

FIGURE 11.5
Connect the
switches to
their outlets.

Repeat these steps for the other three switches, connecting them to the
weekdaySwitch, amSwitch, and pmSwitch outlets.

The popover content is now complete. Let's move to the main application.

Preparing the Application View

With the popover content under control, we'll build out the main application view/view controller. There are only a few "gotchas" here, such as declaring that we're going to conform to the `UIPopoverControllerDelegate` protocol, and making sure that we create an instance of the popover content view.

Conforming to a Protocol

To conform to the popover controller delegate, open the popoverConfigViewController.h interface file, and modify the `@interface` line to include the name of the protocol, enclosed in <>. The line should read as follows:

```
@interface PopoverConfigViewController : UIViewController
<UIPopoverControllerDelegate> {
```

We still need to implement a method for the protocol within the view controller, but more on that a bit later.

Adding Outlets, Actions, and Instance Variables

We need to keep track of quite a few things within the main application's view controller. We're going to need an instance variable for the popover's controller (`popoverController`). This will be used to display the popover, and to check whether the popover is already onscreen. We'll also need an `IBAction` defined (`showPopover`) for displaying the popover.

In addition, five `IBOutlets` are required—four for `UILabels` that will display the values the user enters in the popover (`weekdayOutput`, `weekendOutput`, `amOutput`, `pmOutput`), and the last for the popover's view controller (`popoverContent`).

Sound like enough? Not quite! Because we're going to be using the `popoverContentViewController` class within the main application, we need to import its interface file, too.

What About the Configure Button?
If you're following closely, you might wonder whether we need an instance variable for the Configure button. When we initialize the popover controller, we need to tell it what onscreen object it should point to (that is, the Configure button). Thankfully, the button passes a reference of itself to the action it calls when pressed, so we can use that reference rather than keeping track of the button separately.

Edit the interface file so that it matches Listing 11.2.

LISTING 11.2

```
#import <UIKit/UIKit.h>
#import "PopoverContentViewController.h"

@interface PopoverConfigViewController : UIViewController
            <UIPopoverControllerDelegate> {
    UIPopoverController *popoverController;
    IBOutlet    UILabel *weekdayOutput;
    IBOutlet    UILabel *weekendOutput;
    IBOutlet    UILabel *amOutput;
    IBOutlet    UILabel *pmOutput;
    IBOutlet    popoverContentViewController *popoverContent;
}

@property (retain,nonatomic) UILabel *weekdayOutput;
@property (retain,nonatomic) UILabel *weekendOutput;
@property (retain,nonatomic) UILabel *amOutput;
@property (retain,nonatomic) UILabel *pmOutput;
@property (retain,nonatomic) PopoverContentViewController *popoverContent;

-(IBAction)showPopover:(id)sender;

@end
```

For each @property directive, there needs to be a corresponding @synthesize in the popoverConfigViewController.m file. Edit the file now, adding these lines following the @implementation line:

```
@synthesize popoverContent;
@synthesize weekdayOutput;
@synthesize weekendOutput;
@synthesize amOutput;
@synthesize pmOutput;
```

This gives us everything we need to build and connect the main application interface elements, but before we do, let's make sure that everything we're added here is properly released.

Releasing Objects

Edit popoverConfigViewController.m's dealloc method to release the UILabels, and the instance of the popover content view controller (popoverContent):

```
- (void)dealloc {
    [weekdayOutput release];
    [weekendOutput release];
    [amOutput release];
    [pmOutput release];
    [popoverContent release];
    [super dealloc];
}
```

Nicely done! All that's left now is to edit the popoverConfigViewController XIB file to create the main application interface and write the methods for showing and handling the subsequent dismissal of the popover.

Creating the View

Open the popoverConfigViewController XIB file in Interface Builder. We need to add a toolbar, a toolbar button, and some labels to display our application's output. Let's start with the labels, because we've got plenty of experience with them. Drag a total of eight UILabel objects to the screen. Four will hold the application's output, and four will just be labels (fancy that!).

Arrange the labels near the center of the screen, forming a column with Weekends:, Weekdays:, AM:, and PM: on the left, and On, On, On, On aligned with them on the right. The On labels are the labels that will map to the IBOutlet output variables; they've been set to a default value of On because the switches in the popover content view default to the On position.

If desired, use the Attributes Inspector (Command+1) to resize the labels to something a bit larger than the default. I've used a 48pt font in my interface, as shown in Figure 11.6.

FIGURE 11.6
Add a total of
eight labels to
the view.

Adding a Toolbar and Toolbar Button

Using the Interface Builder Library, drag an instance of a toolbar (`UIToolbar`) to top of the view. The toolbar object includes, by default, a single button called Item. Double-click the button to change its title to Configure; the button will automatically resize itself to fit the label.

In this application, the single button is all that is needed. If your project needs more, you can drag Bar Button Items from the library into the toolbar. The buttons are shown as subviews of the toolbar within the Interface Builder Document window.

Figure 11.7 shows the final interface and the Document window showing the interface hierarchy.

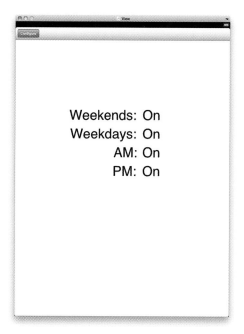

FIGURE 11.7
Labels, and toolbar, and a toolbar button complete the interface.

Connecting the Outlets and Actions

It's time to connect the interface we've built to the outlets and actions we defined in the view controller. Control-drag from the File's Owner icon in the IB Document window to the first On label, connecting to the `weekendOutput` outlet, as shown in Figure 11.8. Repeat for the other three labels, connecting to `weekdayOutput`, `amOutput`, and `pmOutput`.

FIGURE 11.8.
Connect each
output label to
its outlet.

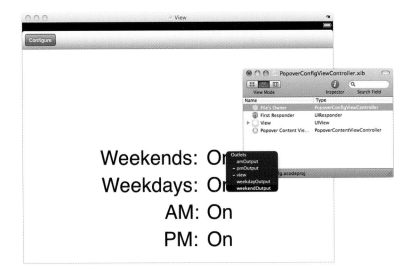

Next, Control-drag from the Configure toolbar button to the File's owner icon. Choose showPopover when prompted, as shown in Figure 11.9. Note that we didn't have to worry about connecting from a Touch Up Inside event because toolbar buttons have only one event that can be used.

FIGURE 11.9
Connect the
configure button
to the
showPopover
action.

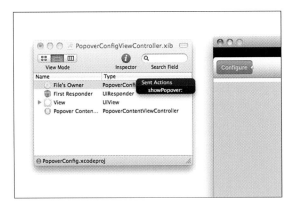

Only one step remains to be completed in interface builder: instantiating the popover content view controller.

Instantiating the Popover Content View Controller

Earlier in the tutorial, we developed the popover content view controller and view (popoverContentViewController). What we haven't done, however, is actually use it anywhere. We can take two approaches to creating an instance of the controller so that we can use it in the application:

1. The content view controller is instantiated whenever the popover is invoked, and released when the popover is dismissed.

2. The content view controller is instantiated when main application view loads and is released when the application is finished.

I've chosen to go with approach number 2. By instantiating the popover's view controller when the main application view loads, we can use it repeatedly without reloading the view. This means that if the user displays the popover and updates the switches, those changes will be visible no matter how many times the user dismisses or opens the popover.

> If you are creating an application with *many* popovers, go with method 1; otherwise, all the views will be kept in memory simultaneously.

Did you
Know?

Without adding any code, we can instantiate popoverContentViewController when the popoverConfigViewController.xib file is loaded:

1. Open the popoverConfigViewController.xib file's document window in Interface Builder.

2. Drag a View Controller object from the Library into the document window.

3. Select the view controller in the Document window, and press Command+4 to open the Identity Inspector.

4. Set the class to the popoverContentViewController rather than the generic UIViewController class set by default. This can be seen in Figure 11.10.

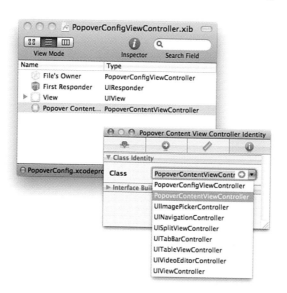

FIGURE 11.10
Set the object to be an instance of popoverContent ViewController.

5. Switch to the Attributes Inspector (Command+1) and set the NIB name field to **popoverContentViewController** so that the view controller knows where its view is stored.

6. Close the Inspector window.

7. Control drag from the File's Owner icon to the popover content view controller icon within the Document window. Choose popoverContent when prompted, as shown in Figure 11.11.

8. Save the XIB file.

FIGURE 11.11
Connect the popover content view controller to the popoverContent outlet.

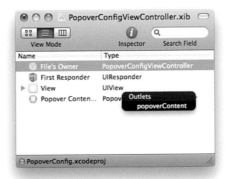

Our views and view controllers are completed. All that remains is writing the code that handles the application logic.

Implementing the Application Logic

We need to implement two methods to complete this tutorial. First, we need to implement showPopover to display the popover and allow the user to interact with it. Second, the popover controller delegate method popoverControllerDidDismissPopover must be built to take care of cleaning up the popover when the user is done with it, and to update the application's view with any changes the user made within the popover.

Displaying the Popover

Open the popoverConfigViewController.m file and add the showPopover method, shown in Listing 11.3, immediately following the @synthesize directives.

LISTING 11.3

```
1: -(IBAction)showPopover:(id)sender {
2:     if (popoverController==nil) {
3:         popoverController=[[UIPopoverController alloc]
4:             initWithContentViewController:popoverContent];
5:         [popoverController presentPopoverFromBarButtonItem:sender
6:          permittedArrowDirections:UIPopoverArrowDirectionAny animated:YES];
7:         popoverController.delegate=self;
8:     }
9: }
```

There are three steps to displaying and configuring the popover.

First, in lines 3–4, the popover controller, popoverController, is allocated and initialized with the popover's content view, popoverContent.

Second, lines 5 and 6 display the popover using the (very verbose) method presentPopoverFromBarButtonItem:permittedArrowDirections:animated. The bar button item (our toolbar button) can be referenced through the sender variable, which is passed to showPopover when the button is pressed. The permittedArrowDirections parameter is passed the constant UIPopoverArrowDirectionAny, meaning the popover can be drawn with an arrow that points in any direction (as long as it points to the specified interface element). The animated parameter gives the iPad the go-ahead to animate the appearance of the popover (currently a nice fade-in effect).

Third, line 7 sets the popover controller's delegate to the same object that is executing the code (self)—in other words, the popoverConfigViewController. By doing this, the popover controller will automatically call the method popoverControllerDidDismissPopover within popoverConfigViewController.m when the user is done with it.

Nothing too scary, right? Right. But what about lines 2 and 8? The entire display of the popover is wrapped in an if-then statement. The reason for this can be easily demonstrated by removing the if-then and running the application. Without the conditional, multiple copies of the popover will be displayed (one on top of the other) each time the Configure button is pressed. This is a large memory leak and would make the application behave very strangely for the user. To get around the problem, we perform a simple comparison: popoverController==nil. When the popover controller hasn't been initialized, it will have a value of nil (that is, no value at all). In this case, the statements to initialize the controller and show the popover are executed. Once the popover is displayed, however, the popoverController has a value and will no longer equal nil, keeping any further instances of it from being displayed.

Of course, we want the user to be able to dismiss and redisplay the popover, so we need to release the popoverController and set it back to nil when we hide the popover again. Let's look at that implementation now.

Did you
Know?

What Constants Can I Provide for a Popover's Arrow Direction?

You can force the popover's arrow (and subsequent onscreen positioning) by using one of five different constants:

UIPopoverArrowDirectionUp—The popover points up toward the interface element.

UIPopoverArrowDirectionDown—The popover points down toward the interface element.

UIPopoverArrowDirectionLeft—The popover points left toward the interface element.

UIPopoverArrowDirectionRight—The popover points right toward the interface element.

UIPopoverArrowDirectionAny—The popover can be oriented in whatever position the iPhone OS finds most appropriate.

Apple recommends using the "Any" option whenever possible in your applications.

Reacting to the Popover Dismissal

When the user gets rid of the popover by touching outside of its content area, we want our application to react and display any changes the user made within the popover view. We also want to prepare the popover's controller to show the popover again. Enter the popover controller delegate method popoverControllerDidDismissPopover as shown in Listing 11.4.

LISTING 11.4

```
 1: -(void)popoverControllerDidDismissPopover:
 2:               (UIPopoverController *)controller {
 3:     weekdayOutput.text=@"On";
 4:     weekendOutput.text=@"On";
 5:     amOutput.text=@"On";
 6:     pmOutput.text=@"On";
 7:
 8:     if (!popoverContent.weekdaySwitch.on) {
 9:         weekdayOutput.text=@"Off";
10:     }
11:     if (!popoverContent.weekendSwitch.on) {
12:         weekendOutput.text=@"Off";
13:     }
14:     if (!popoverContent.amSwitch.on) {
15:         amOutput.text=@"Off";
16:     }
```

```
17:      if (!popoverContent.pmSwitch.on) {
18:          pmOutput.text=@"Off";
19:      }
20:      [popoverController release];
21:      popoverController=nil;
22: }
```

Most of the display logic used in this method should be familiar to you by now. Lines 3–6 set the four output labels to On, because this is the default state of our switches. Lines 8–19 are simple if-then statements which check to see whether a switch is *not* set to on, and, if so, sets the corresponding output label to Off.

Because we have an instance variable for the popover's view controller (popoverContent) and have defined the UISwitches as properties, we can access the individual state of a given switches using its on property in a single line: popoverContent.<switch instance variable>.on.

In the final two lines, 20 and 23, the popover controller is released and its instance variable (popoverController) set to nil. This prepares it for the next time the user presses the Configure button.

> It might surprise you to learn that releasing an object does not automatically set its instance variable to nil. In fact, the instance variable is *not* changed at release and will reference a nonexistent object, potentially causing major problems if you attempt to use it.

Did you Know?

> You might be wondering why we didn't just use the controller reference rather than popoverController instance variable. The answer is that we need to be able to set the popoverController variable to nil. If we use controller, we reference the same object as popoverController, but setting controller to nil doesn't change the value of popoverController.

Watch Out!

The application is now complete. Use Build and Run to test the popover's display on your iPad. You've just implemented one of the most important and flexible UI features available on the iPad platform!

Further Exploration

In this hour's sample project, you attached a toolbar to a "bar button" (toolbar button) using the presentPopoverFromBarButtonItem:permittedArrowDirections:animated method. This, granted, is a very popular approach, but you can create popovers anywhere within your view by using the `UIPopoverController` method `presentPopoverFromRect:inView:permittedArrowDirections:animated`. With this method you can present the popover so that it appears from any rectangular areas, within any view. In addition, popover content does not need to be static! If you'd like, your popover's view controller can update its content on-the-fly, and the popover will update dynamically to display the changes. You'll need to manually update the `popoverContentSize` property of the controller so that all of your content fits, but size changes are animated smoothly for the end user.

To learn more about popovers, be sure to review Apple's `UIPopoverController` class reference within the developer documentation to get a complete picture of this important class and UI element.

Summary

Popovers provide a canvas for creating a range of unique interface elements that can be displayed virtually anywhere in your application. The approach that we took in this hour's lesson (creating a popover that is displayed when a toolbar button is pressed) is the most common implementation that you'll encounter.

You've learned not only how a popover is designed and displayed, but how to access data from within its view, and ways of keeping the popover controller from getting out of hand. In the next hour's lesson, you'll learn about several UI elements that Apple will allow *only* if they are displayed from within a popover. So even if you can't think of any uses for them yet, chances are, you will!

Q&A

Q. *Can I have multiple popover's within a single application view?*

A. Yes, you can, but keep in mind that the example here uses a single delegate for handling the dismissal of a popover. There are a number of ways to get around this, including structuring your code so that changes within a popover are immediately reflected in the application, or you can segment your application so that each popover has a different delegate.

Q. *You told me to drag the toolbar to the top of the window. The developer docs say to drag it to the bottom. What gives?*

A. At the time of this writing, Apple has not yet updated all the descriptions of the toolbar UI element to state that it can be used at the top and bottom of the iPad screen.

Workshop

Quiz

1. What class is a toolbar button?

2. How do you set where a popover appears?

3. Why do we need to compare the popover controller to `nil` before initializing it?

Answers

1. A toolbar button is an instance of the bizarrely named class `UIBarButtonItem`.

2. The iPhone OS determines where a popover appears onscreen. Setting the `permittedArrowDirections` parameter when displaying the popover, however, limits where the OS may position the popover so that it can be drawn with an arrow pointing to the UI element invoking it.

3. If the popover controller is *not* `nil`, that means the popover is visible onscreen and a new copy of it should not be created.

Activities

1. Explore the possibilities of popovers outside of toolbars. Implement an additional button (`UIButton`) within the popoverConfig application that displays the same popover, but located in the center of the screen.

2. Implement a second toolbar-based popover within the popoverConfig application. If you choose to use a single delegate for each, you can check to see which popover is being dismissed by comparing each controller instance variable to the controller variable passed to the `popoverControllerDidDismissPopover` method.

HOUR 12

Making Multivalue Choices with Pickers and Action Sheets

What You'll Learn in This Hour:

▶ The types of picker views available in the iPhone OS
▶ How to implement the Date Picker object
▶ How to developer custom picker views with text and images
▶ When action sheets are used in an application
▶ How to display and react to action sheets

This hour is a bit different from the other lessons we've worked through. In this hour, we explore pickers and action sheets—UI elements that present information to the user *and* collect their input. What truly sets these features apart is that they must be used within a popover! Although both pickers and action sheets can be used almost anywhere in an iPhone app, they must be confined to a popover when used on the iPad.

Despite this constraint, pickers and action sheets will play an important role in many of your applications. You'll use pickers to present the user with a simple means of choosing between many different combinations of values. Action sheets will come into play when you want to give the user a list of choices in a popover.

Popover-centric UI Elements

It might initially seem like a limitation that Apple has asked developers to place certain UI elements within popovers, but as you work with these features, you'll begin to understand why. Both pickers and action sheets do not "make sense" within the main iPad display.

On the iPhone, pickers and action sheets take up a large portion of the screen. When visible, they *are* the primary interface that the user has to work with. The iPad has so much screen real estate that they would become lost within the rest of the content. By having developers place certain UI objects within popovers, Apple keeps the interface simple and ensures that the user understands the context of the feature they are interacting with.

Pickers

Pickers are a unique feature of the iPhone OS. They present a series of multivalue options in a clever spinning interface (often compared to a slot machine). Rather than fruit or numbers the segments, known as *components*, display rows of values that the user can choose from. The closest desktop equivalent would be a set of popup menus. Figure 12.1 displays the standard Date Picker (`UIDatePicker`) in the Contacts applications (they're very young).

FIGURE 12.1
The picker offers a unique interface for choosing a sequence of different, but usually related, values.

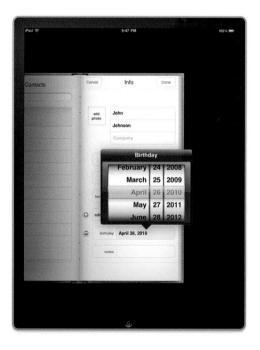

Pickers should be used when a user needs to make a selection between multiple (usually related) values. They are frequently used for setting dates and times, but can be customized to handle just about any selection option that you can come up with.

In Hour 8, "Handling Images, Animation, and Sliders," you learned about the segmented control, which presents the user with multiple options in a single UI element. The segmented control, however, returns a single user selection to your
application. A picker, on the other hand, can return several values from multiple
user selections—all within a single interface.

Apple recognized that pickers are a great option for choosing dates and times, so
they've made them available in two different forms: Date Pickers, which are easy to
implement and dedicated to handling dates and times; and custom picker views
that you can configure to display as many components and rows as you'd like.

Date Pickers

The Date Picker (UIDatePicker) is very similar to the other objects that we've been
using over the past few hours. To use it, we'll add it to a view, wait for the user to
interact with it, and then read its value. Instead of returning a string or integer,
however, the Date Picker returns an NSDate object. The NSDate class is used to store
and manipulate what apple describes as a "single point in time" (in other words, a
date and time).

To access the NSDate represented by a UIDatePicker instance, you'll make use of
the date method. Pretty straightforward, don't you think? In our example project,
we'll implement a Date Picker, retrieve the result, and then perform some date arithmetic and display the results in a custom format.

Pickers Views

Picker views (UIPickerView) are similar in appearance to Date Pickers, but have an
almost entirely different implementation. In a picker view, the only thing that is
defined for you is the overall behavior and general appearance of the control; the
number of components and the content of each component are entirely up to you.
Figure 12.2 demonstrates a picker view that includes two components with images
and text displayed in their rows.

FIGURE 12.2
Picker views can
be configured to
display anything
you'd like.

Unlike other controls, a picker view's appearance is not configured in Interface
Builder's Attributes Inspector or via properties in code. Instead, we need make sure
we have a class that conforms to two protocols: UIPickerViewDelegate and
UIPickerViewDataSource. I know it's been awhile, so let's take a moment for a
quick refresher.

The Picker View Data Source Protocol

There are two protocols required by UIPickerView. The first, the picker view data
source protocol (UIPickerViewDataSource), includes methods that describe how
much information the picker will be displaying:

> numberOfComponentsInPickerView:—Returns the number of components
> (spinning segments) needed in the picker.
>
> pickerView:numberOfRowsInComponent:—Given a specific component, this
> method is required to return the number of rows (different input values) in the
> component.

There's not much to it. As long as we create these two methods and return a meaningful number from each, we'll successfully conform to the picker view data source
protocol. That leaves one protocol, the picker view delegate protocol, between us
and a working picker view.

The Picker View Delegate Protocol

The delegate protocol (`UIPickerViewDelegate`) takes care of the real work in creating and using a picker. It is responsible for passing the appropriate data to the picker for display and for determining when the user has made a choice. We'll use a few protocol methods to make the delegate work the way we want, but, again, only two are required:

> `pickerView:titleForRow:forComponent:`—Given a row number, this method must return the title for the row (that is, the string that should be displayed to the user).

> `pickerView:didSelectRow:inComponent:`—This delegate method will be called when the user makes a selection in the picker view. The method will be passed a row number that corresponds to a user's choice and the component that the user was last touching.

> If you check the documentation for the `UIPickerViewDelegate` protocol, you'll notice that really *all* the delegate methods are optional. Unless we implement at least these two, however, the picker view isn't going to be able to display anything or respond to a user's selection.

By the Way

As you'll recall from earlier hours, implementing protocols isn't something terribly complicated. It just means that we need to implement a handful of methods to help a class, in this case a `UIPickerView`, work the way we want.

Action Sheets

In Hour 10, "Getting the User's Attention," you learned how you can use alert views to display messages that indicate a change in state or a condition within an application that a user should acknowledge. Sometimes, however, a user should be prompted to make a decision based on the result of an action. For example, if you've just chosen an action to share a file, you may want to present options to allow the user to choose between different methods of sharing (email, FTP, and so on). The interface element that provides this is called an *action sheet* and is an instance of the `UIActionSheet` class.

Unlike an alert, an action sheet is directly associated with something the user has done, and, as you already know, should be displayed within a popover. You can see this behavior when adding a location as a contact in the Map application, as shown in Figure 12.3.

FIGURE 12.3
Action sheets
present options
within popovers.

Animated Versus Nonanimated Action Sheets

You can use two types of action sheets: animated and nonanimated. Animated action sheets, which we concentrate on in this hour's lessons, slide into the popover's view when the user triggers an event (such as pressing a button or moving a slider).

Nonanimated action sheets, on the other hand, display immediately when a popover appears. These work much the same was as implementing a popover view that consists of nothing but buttons. The only difference is that with an action sheet, there's a lot less setup work to do and you don't have to track a bunch of different button instance variables!

The Action Sheet Delegate Protocol

To capture what button is pressed in an action sheet, a class must conform to the `UIActionSheetDelegate` protocol. Implementing the `actionSheet:clickedButtonAtIndex` method within that class will give you the ability to react to a choice within the action sheet, and identify (based on a numeric button index value) what the user has chosen.

The PopoverPlayground Project

Now that you know what we're going to be working with in the rest of the lesson, we can get started developing—but we're going to be doing things a bit differently in these tutorials. Because each of our UI objects requires a popover and popovers take a bit of time to set up, we're proving a sample project called PopoverPlayground – Skeleton that will serve as the starting point for each of our three examples. You'll be copying this project folder and renaming the folder (*not the project!*) instead of building a new popover from scratch.

PopoverPlayground – Skeleton is implemented almost identically to the popovers you made in the preceding hour, with two differences. First, instead of using a toolbar and bar button to invoke the popover, we've used a custom image button. Second, because the button isn't a toolbar button, the method used to invoke the popover had to change. This time around, the project uses the following:

```
showPopover:initWithContentViewController:presentPopoverFromRect:inView:
➥permittedArrowDirections:animated
```

The difference is minimal, but this will give you an idea of how to present a popover from *any* object you choose. Be sure to open the PopoverPlaygroundViewController.m file and take a look.

All your work within the PopoverPlayground projects will take place in the `PopoverContentViewController` class and associated XIB files, so no additional setup or coding is needed. Let's begin.

Using Date Pickers

Using the controls you currently know, there are probably half a dozen different ways that you might imagine creating a date entry screen on the iPad. Buttons, segmented controls, text fields—all of these are potential possibilities, but none has the elegance and the inherent usability of a Date Picker. Let's put the picker to use.

Implementation Overview

This project, which we'll be calling PopoverPlayground - DateCalc, will make use of a Date Picker (`UIDatePicker`) that, when set, will trigger an action that shows the difference in days between the chosen date and the current date. This will also make use of an `NSDate` object to store the result returned by the date picker, its instance method `timeIntervalSinceDate:` to perform the calculation, and an `NSDateFormatter` object to format a date so that we can display it in a user-friendly manner via a `UILabel`. The finished application is shown in Figure 12.4.

FIGURE 12.4
The sample application will use a single date picker and a label as its UI.

Keep in mind that, despite its name, the NSDate class also stores the time. The application we create will take into account the time and the date when performing its calculation.

Setting Up the Project

Create a copy of the PopoverPlayground – Skeleton folder named PopoverPlayground – DateCalc. Launch Xcode by opening the project file from the new folder.

Next, open the PopoverContentViewController.h file and add an outlet and property declaration for the label (UILabel) that will display the difference between dates: differenceResult. Next, add an action called showDate:. We'll be calling this when the user changes the value on the Date Picker.

The (very simple) interface file is shown in Listing 12.1.

LISTING 12.1

```
#import <UIKit/UIKit.h>

@interface DateCalcViewController : UIViewController {
    IBOutlet UILabel *differenceResult;
}

@property (nonatomic, retain) UILabel *differenceResult;

-(IBAction)showDate:(id)sender;

@end
```

Switch to the implementation file (PopoverContentViewController.m) and add a corresponding @synthesize directive for differenceResult, located after the @implementation line:

```
@synthesize differenceResult;
```

> Notice that we don't have an outlet or property for the Date Picker itself. To avoid having to manage an instance variable, we'll just use the sender variable to reference the Date Picker within the showDate: action method. Nothing else is calling the method, so we know with certainty that sender will always be the picker.

By the Way

Because we've got a pretty good handle on the project setup and you're probably sick of hearing us go on about it at the end of each project, let's take care of something we've done last, first: make sure we're properly releasing anything we've retained.

For this project, that's one object: differenceResult. Edit PopoverContentViewController.m dealloc method to read as follows:

```
- (void)dealloc {
    [differenceResult release];
    [super dealloc];
}
```

Let's keep up the pace and move on to the UI and our Date Picker. After you've created the outlet and the action, save the file, and open DateCalcViewController.xib in Interface Builder.

Adding a Date Picker

Open the empty view in the PopoverContentViewController.xib file, and then open the Object Library (Tools, Library). Find the Date Picker (UIDatePicker) object and drag it into the upper-left corner of the view. You'll notice immediately that, unlike other UI elements we've used, the Date Picker is pretty "busy" visually and eats up quite a bit of space.

Position the Date Picker as seen in Figure 12.5. We'll be displaying the date calculations below it.

FIGURE 12.5
Add a Date
Picker to the
upper-left side
of the view.

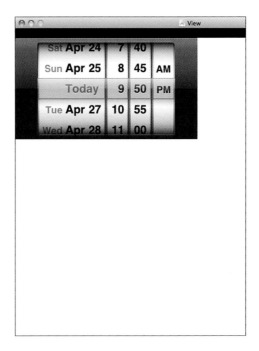

By default, the Date Picker displays a date and time, as demonstrated in our current view. As with other controls, the Attributes Inspector can customize how the Date Picker appears to the user.

Setting the Date Picker Attributes

Choose the Date Picker within the view, and then open the Attributes Inspector (Command+1), shown in Figure 12.6.

FIGURE 12.6
Configure the
appearance of
the Date Picker
in the Attributes
Inspector.

The picker can be configured to display in one of four different modes:

Date & Time: Shows options for choosing both a date and a time

Time: Shows only times

Date: Shows only dates

Timer: Displays a clock-like interface for choosing a duration

You can also set the locale for the picker, which determines the ordering of the different components, set the default date/time that is displayed, and set date/time constraints to help limit the user's choices.

For this project, leave the default settings as they are. We want the user to choose a date and a time that we'll use in our calculations.

> The "Date" attribute is automatically set to the date and time when you add the control to the view.

By the Way

Connecting to the Action

When the user interacts with the Date Picker, we want the showDate: action method to be called. To create this connection, select the picker, and then open the Connections Inspector (Command+2).

Click and drag from the circle beside Value Changed to the File's Owner icon. When you release the mouse button, you'll be prompted for the action. Choose showDate:, as demonstrated in Figure 12.7.

FIGURE 12.7
Connect to the
showDate:
action.

Did you
Know?

We've been making a point of using the Connections Inspector to create connections from objects that support many different events. This is always the safest way to know what connections you're creating, but it isn't the fastest. The picker (along with switches and segmented controls), will default to making connections using the Value Changed event if you Control-drag from the element to the File's Owner icon. You can use this shortcut if you feel comfortable with the process.

Finishing the Interface

Unlike some of our previous projects, the interfaces in this hour are pretty simple. We'll wrap up our work in Interface Builder by adding a label to the view.

Add the Output Label

Use the Library to add a label (UILabel) with the title **Choose a date**, positioned below the picker. This will be used for output in the application. For our implementation, we've used the Attributes Inspector to center the text, make it span four lines, set a font size of 20, and turn on word wrapping. The finished interface and attributes for the label are shown in Figure 12.8.

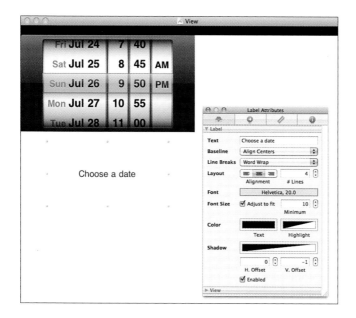

FIGURE 12.8
Finish up the
interface by
adding and
styling a label.

Connecting to the Outlet

Connect the label to the outlet `differenceResult` by control dragging from the File's Owner icon to the `UILabel` within your view or in the Document window. When prompted, choose the `differenceResult` outlet.

The interface is now complete. Save your work, then switch back to Xcode for the implementation.

Implementing the View Controller Logic

As it turns out, the most difficult work that we still have in front of us with the Date Picker implementation is writing the `showDate:` logic. To do what we've set out to (show the difference between today's date and the date in the picker), we need to be able to do several things:

Get today's date

Display a date and time

Calculate the difference between two dates

Before writing `showDate:`, let's look at the different methods and data types that we'll need to complete these tasks.

Getting the Date

To get the current date and store it in an `NSDate` object, all that we need to do is to allocate and initialize a new `NSDate`. When initialized, it automatically stores the current date! This means that a single line takes care of our first hurdle:

```
todaysDate=[[NSDate alloc] init];
```

Displaying a Date and Time

Unfortunately, displaying a date and time is a bit more tricky than *getting* the current date. Because we're going to be displaying the output in a label (`UILabel`), we already know *how* it is going to be shown on the screen, so the question is really, how do we format a string with an `NSDate` object?

Interestingly enough, there's a class to handle this for us! We'll create and initialize an `NSDateFormatter` object. Next, we use the object's `setDateFormat:` to create a custom format using a pattern string. Finally, we apply that format to our date using another method of `NSDateFormatter`, `stringFromDate:`, which, given an `NSDate`, returns a string in the format that we defined.

For example, if we assume that we've already stored an `NSDate` in a variable `todaysDate`, we can output in a format like "`Month Day, Year Hour:Minute:Second(AM or PM)`" with these lines:

```
dateFormat = [[NSDateFormatter alloc] init];
[dateFormat setDateFormat:@"MMMM d, yyyy hh:mm:ssa"];
todaysDateString = [dateFormat stringFromDate:todaysDate];
```

First, the formatter object is allocated and initialized in a new object, `dateFormat`. Then the string `@"MMMM d, YYYY hh:mm:ssa"` is used as a formatting string to set the format internally in the object. Finally, a new string is returned and stored in `todaysDateString` by using the `dateFormat` object's instance method `stringFromDate:`.

Where in the World Did That Date Format String Come From?

The strings that you can use to define date formats are defined by a Unicode standard that you can find at http://unicode.org/reports/tr35/tr35-6.html#Date_Format_Patterns.

For this example, the patterns are interpreted as follows:

MMMM—The full name of the month

d—The day of the month, with no leading zero

YYYY—The full four-digit year

hh—A two-digit hour (with leading zero if needed).

mm—Two digits representing the minute

ss—Two digits representing the second

a—AM or PM

Calculating the Difference Between Two Dates

The last thing that we need to understand is how to compute the difference between two dates. Instead of needing any complicated math, we can just use the `timeIntervalSinceDate:` instance method in an `NSDate` object. This method returns the difference between two dates, in seconds. For example, if we have two `NSDate` objects, `todaysDate` and `futureDate`, we can calculate the time in seconds between them with this:

```
NSTimeInterval difference;
difference = [todaysDate timeIntervalSinceDate:futureDate];
```

Notice that we store the result in a variable of type `NSTimeInterval`. This isn't an object. Internally, it is just a double-precision floating-point number. Typically, this would be declared using the native C data type `double`, but Apple abstracts this from us by using a new type of `NSTimeInterval` so that we know exactly what to expect out of a date difference calculation.

By the Way

Note that if the `timeIntervalSinceDate:` method is given a date *before* the object that is invoking the method (that is, if `futureDate` was *before* `todaysDate` in the example), the difference returned is negative; otherwise, it is positive. To get rid of the negative sign, we'll be using the C function `fabs(<float>)` that, given a floating-point number, returns its absolute value.

Implementing the Date Calculation and Display

Putting together all of these pieces, we should now be able to write the logic for the `showDate:` method. Open the PopoverContentViewController.m file in Xcode and add the implementation for `showDate:` method shown in Listing 12.2.

LISTING 12.2

```
1: -(IBAction)showDate:(id)sender {
2:     NSDate *todaysDate;
3:     NSString *differenceOutput;
4:     NSString *todaysDateString;
5:     NSDateFormatter *dateFormat;
6:     NSTimeInterval difference;
7:
8:
9:     todaysDate=[[NSDate alloc] init];
10:    difference = [todaysDate timeIntervalSinceDate:[sender date]] / 86400;
11:
12:    dateFormat = [[NSDateFormatter alloc] init];
13:    [dateFormat setDateFormat:@"MMMM d, yyyy hh:mm:ssa"];
14:    todaysDateString = [dateFormat stringFromDate:todaysDate];
15:
16:    differenceOutput=[[NSString alloc] initWithFormat:
17:      @"Difference between chosen date and today (%@) in days: %1.2f",
18:            todaysDateString,fabs(difference)];
19:    differenceResult.text=differenceOutput;
20:
21:    [todaysDate release];
22:    [dateFormat release];
23:    [differenceOutput release];
24: }
```

Much of this should look pretty familiar based on the preceding examples, but let's review the logic. First, in lines 2–6, we declare the variables we'll be using: todaysDate will store the current date, differenceOutput will be our final formatted string displayed to the user, todaysDateString will contain the formatted version of the current day's date, dateFormat will be our date formatting object, and difference is the double-precision floating-point number used to store the number of seconds between two dates.

Lines 9 and 10 do most of the work we set out to accomplish! In line 9, we allocate and initialize todaysDate as a new NSDate object. The init automatically stores the current date and time in the object.

In line 10, we use timeIntervalSinceDate: to calculate the time, in seconds, between todaysDate and [sender date]. Remember that sender will be the Date Picker object, and the date method tells an instance of UIDatePicker to return its current date and time in an NSDate object, so this gives our method everything it needs to work with. The result is divided by 86400 and stored in the difference variable. Why 86400? This is the number of seconds in a day, so we will be able to display the number of days between dates, rather than seconds.

In lines 12–14, we create a new date formatter object (NSDateFormatter) and use it to format todaysDate, storing the results in the string todaysDateString.

Lines 16–18 format the final output string by allocating a new string (differenceOutput) and then initializing it with initWithFormat:. The format string provided includes the message to be displayed to the user and the placeholders %@ and %1.2f (representing a string and a floating-point number with a leading zero and two decimal places). These placeholders are replaced with the todaysDateString and the absolute value of the difference between the dates, fabs(difference).

In line 19, the label we added to the view, differenceResult, is updated to display differenceOutput.

The last step is to clean up anything that we allocated in the method, which is accomplished in lines 21–23, where the strings and formatter object are released.

That's it! Use Build and Run to test your application. You've just implemented a Date Picker, learned how to perform some basic date arithmetic, and even formatted dates for output using date formatting strings. What could be better? Creating your own custom picker with your own data, of course!

Implementing a Custom Picker View

In the lead up to this project, we made it pretty clear that implementing your own picker view (UIPickerView) is going to be a bit different from other UI features you've added previously (including the Date Picker you just finished). This doesn't mean it will be *difficult*, just different. Because a picker view starts out empty can contain anything we want, we need to provide it with data to display and describe how it should be displayed.

Implementation Overview

This project, named PopoverPlayground - CustomPicker, will implement an instance of UIPickerView that presents two scrolling wheels of information: animal names and animal sounds. After we have these in place, we'll spruce things up by changing the animal names to actual pictures of the names. The final result that we're aiming for is visible in Figure 12.9.

FIGURE 12.9
We'll use a picker view to create a custom picker with both images and text.

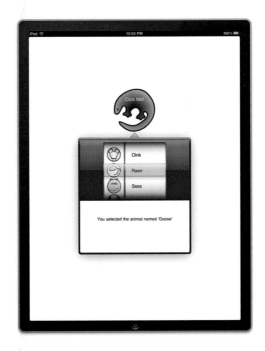

Setting Up the Project

Once again, this project begins with a copy of the PopoverPlayground – Skeleton folder. Create your copy and rename the folder to **PopoverPlayground – CustomPicker**. Double-click the project file within the new folder to launch Xcode.

Conforming to a Protocol

To tell Xcode that one of our classes is going to conform to a protocol (or, in this case, multiple protocols), we need to edit the interface file for the class and include the protocols in the @interface line.

For this project, we want our view controller (PopoverContentViewController) to conform to the UIPickerViewDataSource and UIPickerViewDelegate protocols. Open PopoverContentViewController.h and edit the @interface line to read as follows:

```
@interface MatchPickerViewController : UIViewController <UIPickerViewDataSource,
UIPickerViewDelegate> {
```

Adding a comma-separated list of the name of the protocols we'll be implementing within the angle brackets <> is all we need to do to tell Xcode that we're going to conform to a protocol. The rest of the project setup is pretty standard.

Adding Outlets but Not Actions

This project requires only one outlet, and *no* actions. The outlet is for a single label, `lastAction`, that will display the last action the user performed in the picker.

So, why no action? Because the protocols we're conforming to define a method `pickerView:didSelectRow:inComponent:` that will automatically be called when the user makes a selection. By adding the protocols to the `@interface` line, we've effectively added everything we'll need to connect to inside of Interface Builder.

Edit the `PopoverContentViewController.h` file to include the outlet and property declaration for the `lastAction` label, as seen in Listing 12.3.

LISTING 12.3

```
#import <UIKit/UIKit.h>

@interface MatchPickerViewController : UIViewController
                <UIPickerViewDataSource, UIPickerViewDelegate> {
        IBOutlet UILabel *lastAction;
}

@property (nonatomic, retain) UILabel *lastAction;

@end
```

Next, add the corresponding `@synthesize` line to the implementation file (PopoverContentViewController.m) for the defined property. This should be located after the `@implementation` directive:

```
@synthesize lastAction;
```

Releasing the Objects

Edit the `dealloc` method in PopoverContentViewController.m to release the label we've retained. We'll need to revisit this with a few more edits later on, but, for now, the method should read as follows:

```
- (void)dealloc {
    [lastAction release];
    [super dealloc];
}
```

Make sure you've saved the view controller header and implementation files, and then let's turn our attention to hammering out the picker view interface with Interface Builder.

Adding a Picker View

Because the picker view is controlled mostly by the protocols we'll be implementing, there's surprisingly little to do in Interface Builder. Open the PopoverContentViewController.xib file and make sure the view it contains is open, too.

Using the Object Library (Tools, Library), click and drag an instance of UIPickerView to the view, positioning it at the top left of the iPad interface. That's really all there is to it. If you open up the Attributes Inspector (Command+1), you'll notice that there is only a single attribute for the picker view, whether or not the selection indicator is present. You can turn this on or off, depending on how you feel it works with the aesthetics of your application. Figure 12.10 shows the picker added to the view, along with its available attributes.

FIGURE 12.10
There's not much more to do be done with a picker view in Interface Builder beyond adding it to your view.

When you add a UIPickerView to your view, it will display with a list of cities as the default contents. This won't change! Because the actual contents of the picker are determined by the code you write, you're not going to see the final result until you run the application.

Connecting to the Data Source and Delegate Protocol Outlets

Remember that we didn't add any actions or outlets for the picker view to connect to, but we did declare that the PopoverContentViewController class we're writing will conform to the UIPickerViewDataSource and UIPickerViewDelegate protocols. Behind the scenes, this created the necessary outlets that the picker will need to connect to.

Control-drag from either the visual representation of the picker within your view or
its icon in the document window to the File's Owner icon. When you release your
mouse button, you'll be prompted to connect to either the Delegate or Data Source
outlets, as shown in Figure 12.11. Choose the Delegate option to create the first
connection.

FIGURE 12.11
Even though we
didn't explicitly
create any out-
lets, the view
controller con-
forms to the
picker's dele-
gate and data
source proto-
cols and pro-
vides the appro-
priate connec-
tion points.

After the delegate connection is made, repeat the exact same process, only this time
choose Data Source. When both connections are in place, the picker is as "configured" as we can get it in Interface Builder. All the remaining work will have to take
place in code.

Finishing the Interface

To complete the interface for the MatchPicker application, we need to add a label
(UILabel) for providing feedback of what the user just selected. This label will, in
turn, connect to the lastAction outlet.

Adding the Output Labels

Drag a label into the view, just underneath the picker. Change the title of the label
to read **Last Action**. In our example project, we've also chosen to set the attributes
so that the label text is centered.

Connecting the Outlets

Control-drag from the File's Owner icon to the label, and then choose the
lastAction outlet. Figure 12.12 shows the final UI layout and demonstrates the
connection from the Match Feedback label to its matchResult outlet.

FIGURE 12.12
Connect the
label to its out-
let to finish the
UI design.

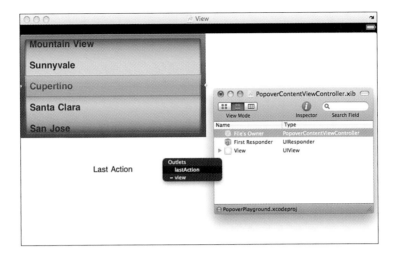

With that simple step, we're done with Interface Builder. All the work of actually customizing the appearance of the picker view must take place in Xcode.

Providing Data to the Picker

A big difference between the UIPickerView we're using now and other controls, such as the UISegmentedControl, is that what the control displays is determined entirely by the code we write. There is no "point and click" to edit the different components and values within Interface Builder. WYSIWYG isn't an option.

So, what information do we need to provide? Remember that the picker displays scrolling wheels called "components." Within each component are any number of "rows" that display the values you want users to select. We'll need to provide the picker with data for each row in each component. For this example, we'll have one component with animal names and another with animal sounds.

Creating the Application Data Structures

Because the picker displays lists of information, it stands to reason that we want to store the data that they display as lists—a perfect job for an array! We'll create two arrays, animalNames and animalSounds, that contain all the information that the picker will display to the user.

We want these arrays to be available to everything in the PopoverContentViewController class, so we first need to add them to the @interface block within the view controller interface file. Edit PopoverContentViewController.h to include two NSArrays, animalNames and animalSounds, as shown in Listing 12.4.

LISTING 12.4

```
#import <UIKit/UIKit.h>

@interface MatchPickerViewController : UIViewController
                    <UIPickerViewDataSource, UIPickerViewDelegate> {
        NSArray *animalNames;
        NSArray *animalSounds;
        IBOutlet UILabel *lastAction;
}

@property (nonatomic, retain) UILabel *lastAction;

@end
```

These two arrays correspond to the components that we'll be displaying in the picker. Components are numbered starting at zero, left to right, so, assuming we want the names of the animals to be on the left and sounds on the right, component 0 will correspond to the animalNames array and component 1 to animalSounds.

Before going any further, take a few seconds to add the appropriate releases for these arrays within the dealloc method. The current version of the method should read as follows:

```
- (void)dealloc {
    [animalNames release];
    [animalSounds release];
    [lastAction release];
    [super dealloc];
}
```

Populating the Data Structures

After the arrays have been declared, they need to be filled with data. The easiest place to do this is in the viewDidLoad method of the view controller (PopoverContentViewController.m). Edit PopoverContentViewController.m by uncommenting the viewDidLoad method and adding the lines, shown in Listing 12.5, to allocate and initialize the arrays with a list of animals and sounds.

LISTING 12.5

```
- (void)viewDidLoad {
    animalNames=[[NSArray alloc]initWithObjects:
      @"Mouse",@"Goose",@"Cat",@"Dog",@"Snake",@"Bear",@"Pig",nil];
    animalSounds=[[NSArray alloc]initWithObjects:
      @"Oink",@"Rawr",@"Ssss",@"Roof",@"Meow",@"Honk",@"Squeak",nil];
}
```

> Warning: nil is needed to denote the end of the array initialization list, so if it's missing, your application will almost certainly crash!

To help simplify the application a bit, it would be nice if we could symbolically refer to "component 0" as the "animalComponent" and "component 1" as the "soundComponent." By defining a few constants at the start of our implementation file, we can do just that! Edit PopoverContentViewController.m and add these lines so that they precede the `#import` line:

```
#define componentCount 2
#define animalComponent 0
#define soundComponent 1
```

The first constant `componentCount` is just the number of components that we want to display in the picker, whereas the other two constants, `animalComponent` and `soundComponent`, can be used to refer to the different components in the picker without resorting to using their actual numbers.

By the
Way

What's Wrong with Referring to Something by Its Number?

Absolutely nothing. The reason that it is helpful to use constants, however, is that if your design changes and you decide to change the order of the components or add another component, you can just change the numbering within the constants rather than each place they're used in the code. This will make a bit more sense in a few minutes as we start implementing the delegate and data source protocol methods.

Our application has everything it requires data-wise. It just needs the methods to get the data into the picker view.

Implementing the Picker Data Source Methods

Despite a promising-sounding name, the picker data source methods (described by the `UIPickerViewDataSource` protocol) really only provide a small amount of information to the picker via these methods:

> `numberOfComponentsInPickerView:`—Returns the number of components the picker should display

> `pickerView:numberOfRowsInComponent:`—Returns the number of rows that the picker will be displaying within a given component

Let's start with component count. Edit PopoverContentViewController.m and add the following method to file:

```
- (NSInteger)numberOfComponentsInPickerView:(UIPickerView *)pickerView {
    return componentCount;
}
```

We already defined a constant, componentCount, with the number of components we want to display (2), so the *entire* implementation of this method is just the line return componentCount.

The second method, pickerView:numberOfRowsInComponent:, is expected to return the number of rows contained within a given component. We'll make use of the NSArray method count to return the number of items within the array that is going to make up the component. For example, to get back the number of names in the animalNames array, we can use the following:

[animalNames count]

Implement it using the code in Listing 12.6.

LISTING 12.6

```
- (NSInteger)pickerView:(UIPickerView *)pickerView
          numberOfRowsInComponent:(NSInteger)component {
    if (component==animalComponent) {
        return [animalNames count];
    } else {
        return [animalSounds count];
    }
}
```

Here, we just compare the component variable provided when the picker calls the method to the animalComponent constant we declared earlier. If they are equal we return a count of the names in animalNames. Otherwise, we return a count of the number of sounds in animalSounds.

Congratulations, you've just completed the methods required for conforming to the UIPickerViewDataSource protocol!

Populating the Picker Display

Where the data source protocol methods were responsible for defining *how many* items will appear in the picker, the UIPickerViewDelegate methods will define *what* items are shown, and how they are displayed. There's only a single method we really *need* before we can start looking at the results of our work: pickerView:titleForRow:forComponent:. This method is called by the picker view to determine what text should be shown in a given component and row.

For example, if component 0 and row 0 are provided to the method as parameters, the method should return Mouse because it is the first element of our animalNames array, which corresponds to component 0 in the picker.

This method requires the ability to retrieve a string from one of our arrays. The NSArray instance method `objectAtIndex:` is exactly what we need. To retrieve row 5 from the `animalSounds` array, we could use the following:

```
[animalSounds objectAtIndex:5]
```

The `pickerView:titleForRow:forComponent:` method provides us with both a row variable and a component variable. Listing 12.7 shows the implementation.

LISTING 12.7

```
- (NSString *)pickerView:(UIPickerView *)pickerView
          titleForRow:(NSInteger)row forComponent:(NSInteger)component {
    if (component==animalComponent) {
        return [animalNames objectAtIndex:row];
    } else {
        return [animalSounds objectAtIndex:row];
    }
}
```

The code first checks to see whether the supplied component variable is equal to the `animalComponent` constant that we configured, and then, if it is, returns the object (a string) from the specified row of the `animalNames` array. If component isn't equal to `animalComponent`, we can assume that we need to be looking at the `animalSounds` array and return a string from it, instead.

By the Way

> Because we have just two components, we're making the assumption that if a method isn't referencing one, it must be referencing the other. If you have more than two components, you need a more complicated if-then-else structure, obviously, or a `switch` statement.

After adding the method to PopoverContentViewController.m, save the file, and then choose Build and Run. The application should launch and show the picker view, complete with the contents of your two arrays, much like Figure 12.13.

Notice that while the picker does work, choosing values has no effect; that's because we need to implement one more delegate method before our efforts will truly pay off.

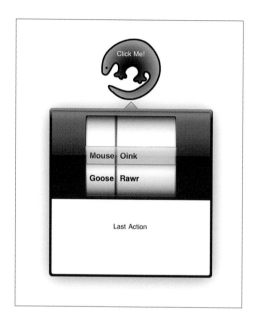

FIGURE 12.13
The application should now run and show the customized picker view.

Reacting to a Picker View Choice

For our application to respond to a user touching and changing the value within one of the picker components, we need to implement another method within the UIPickerViewDelegate protocol: pickerView:didSelectRow:inComponent:. This method is called when the user changes something in the picker view. As part of the parameters, we get back a reference to the picker itself, the row number that was selected, and which component number it was in.

Do you see any problem with that? Although the method certainly tells us when something was picked, and *what* was picked, it only gives us the value for the picker component that the user was changing. In other words, we'll get back the chosen animal name, but not the sound (or vice versa).

To access the value of *any* picker component at any time, we can use the UIPickerView instance method selectedRowInComponent:. This returns the currently selected row in whatever component number we pass to it. If, for example, we have a reference to our picker in pickerView, we could retrieve the selected animal name row like this:

```
[pickerView selectedRowInComponent:animalComponent]
```

I hope it's starting to become obvious why it makes sense to use constants to keep track of the component numbers. Being able to use `animalComponent` or `soundComponent` directly in the code makes it much easier to read, and, long term, easier to maintain.

With all this information in hand, we're ready to write and review the `pickerView:didSelectRow:inComponent:` method. Add the following code in Listing 12.8 into PopoverContentViewController.m.

LISTING 12.8

```
 1: - (void)pickerView:(UIPickerView *)pickerView didSelectRow:(NSInteger)row
 2:        inComponent:(NSInteger)component {
 3:     NSString *actionMessage;
 4:
 5:     if (component==animalComponent) {
 6:         actionMessage=[[NSString alloc]
 7:                     initWithFormat:@"You selected the animal named '%@'",
 8:                     [animalNames objectAtIndex:row]];
 9:     } else {
10:         actionMessage=[[NSString alloc]
11:                     initWithFormat:@"You selected the animal sound '%@'",
12:                     [animalSounds objectAtIndex:row]];
13:     }
14:
15:     lastAction.text=actionMessage;
16:
17:     [actionMessage release];
18: }
```

Line 3 kicks off the implementation by declaring the string `actionMessage`, which will be used to hold the feedback about the user's last choice.

Lines 5–13 allocate and initialize a string, `actionMessage`, which describes what the user has done. If the `component` provided to the method is the `animalComponent`, the string will contain a message stating that they chose an animal. It will also identify the animal via the `row` variable and the `animalNames` array. If they choose a sound, the message and logic will be appropriate to that action instead. We're using the same techniques implemented earlier to populate the picker's display.

Line 15 outputs the `actionMessage` to the user by setting the `text` properties of the `lastAction` label.

Line 17 releases the `actionMessage` string.

Save your updated implementation file and choose Build and Run. Invoke the popover, then scroll through the animals and sounds and make your choices. As you change the selection in the picker view, the program should provide feedback as to what you've chosen, as shown in Figure 12.14.

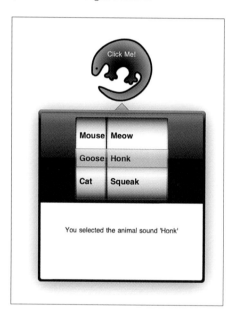

FIGURE 12.14
Your application now reacts to changes in the picker view!

Done? Not just yet! When we started out, I promised that we'd be able to display images in the picker view, and I'm not going to go back on my word!

Tweaking the Picker UI

After you've got a working picker view, you can start using some of the optional `UIPickerViewDelegate` methods to dramatically alter its appearance. To close out this hour, for example, we'll change the picker to display icons of the animals rather than the animal names.

Adding the Image Resources and Data

We've supplied seven animal image PNG files inside the Animals folder within the PopoverPlayground – Skeleton project folder. Start by finding and dragging the image files into the Resources folder of your project in Xcode. When prompted, choose to copy the items if needed, as shown in Figure 12.15.

FIGURE 12.15
Copy the
images to the
project, if
needed.

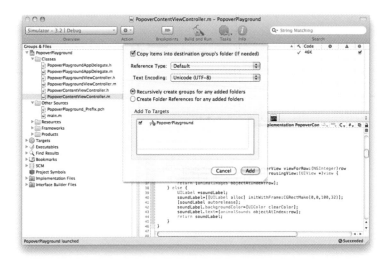

The UIPickerView can display any UIView or subclass of UIView within its components. To display an image, we need to add it to a view and make it available to the
picker. Despite this sounding a bit daunting, we can create a new UIImageView
instance and populate it with an image from our project resources using a single
line:

```
[[UIImageView alloc] initWithImage:[UIImage imageNamed:<image name>]]
```

So, what do we do with these UIImageViews once we create them? The same thing
we did with the animal names and animal sounds: We put them in an array. That
way, we can just pass the appropriate image view to the picker in the exact same
way we were passing strings!

Start by updating the PopoverContentViewController.h file to declare an NSArray
called animalImages. The final (for real!) interface is displayed in Listing 12.9.

LISTING 12.9

```
#import <UIKit/UIKit.h>

@interface MatchPickerViewController : UIViewController
                <UIPickerViewDataSource, UIPickerViewDelegate> {
    NSArray *animalNames;
    NSArray *animalSounds;
    NSArray *animalImages;
    IBOutlet UILabel *lastAction;
}
@property (nonatomic, retain) UILabel *lastAction;

@end
```

Edit the `viewDidLoad` method within PopoverContentViewController.m to include
the code to populate an array with seven image views corresponding to our animal
PNG files. This code should be added following the allocation and initialization of
the `animalSounds` or `animalNames` arrays.

```
animalImages=[[NSArray alloc]initWithObjects:
    [[UIImageView alloc] initWithImage:[UIImage imageNamed:@"mouse.png"]],
    [[UIImageView alloc] initWithImage:[UIImage imageNamed:@"goose.png"]],
    [[UIImageView alloc] initWithImage:[UIImage imageNamed:@"cat.png"]],
    [[UIImageView alloc] initWithImage:[UIImage imageNamed:@"dog.png"]],
    [[UIImageView alloc] initWithImage:[UIImage imageNamed:@"snake.png"]],
    [[UIImageView alloc] initWithImage:[UIImage imageNamed:@"bear.png"]],
    [[UIImageView alloc] initWithImage:[UIImage imageNamed:@"pig.png"]],
    nil
];
```

Next, update the `dealloc` method to release this new array when the application is
finished with it:

```
- (void)dealloc {
    [animalNames release];
    [animalSounds release];
    [animalImages release];
    [lastAction release];
    [super dealloc];
}
```

Using Views (with Images!) in a Picker View

Wouldn't it be great if we could just provide the image view to the picker in place of
the animal name string in `pickerView:titleForRow:forComponent:` and have it
work? Guess what! It won't. Unfortunately, pickers operate in only one of two ways:
either by displaying strings using the aforementioned method, or by displaying custom views using the method
`pickerView:viewForRow:forComponent:reusingView:` (but not a combination).

What this means for us is that if we want to display image views in the picker,
everything else we want to show will also have to be a subclass of `UIView`. The animal sounds are strings, so, to display them, we need to create something that is a
subclass of `UIView` that contains the necessary text. That "something" is a `UILabel`.
By creating `UILabel`s from the strings in the `animalSounds` array, we can successfully populate the picker with both images *and* text.

Begin by commenting out the `pickerView:titleForRow:forComponent:` in
PopoverContentViewController.m, by placing /* before the start, and */ after the
end of the method. Alternatively, you can just delete the entire method, because we
won't really need it again in this project.

Now, enter the implementation of
`pickerView:viewForRow:forComponent:reusingView:` from Listing 12.10.

LISTING 12.10

```
 1: - (UIView *)pickerView:(UIPickerView *)pickerView viewForRow:(NSInteger)row
 2:         forComponent:(NSInteger)component reusingView:(UIView *)view {
 3:     if (component==animalComponent) {
 4:         return [animalImages objectAtIndex:row];
 5:     } else {
 6:         UILabel *soundLabel;
 7:         soundLabel=[[UILabel alloc] initWithFrame:CGRectMake(0,0,100,32)];
 8:         [soundLabel autorelease];
 9:         soundLabel.backgroundColor=[UIColor clearColor];
10:         soundLabel.text=[animalSounds objectAtIndex:row];
11:         return soundLabel;
12:     }
13: }
```

In lines 3–4, we check to see whether the component requested is the animal component, and, if it is, we use the row parameter to return the appropriate UIImageView
stored in the animalImages array. This is nearly identical to how we dealt with the
strings earlier.

If the component parameter isn't referring to the animal component, we need to
return a UILabel with the appropriate referenced row from the animalSounds array.
This is handled in lines 6–11.

In line 6, we declare a UILabel named soundLabel.

Line 7 allocates and initializes soundLabel with a frame using the initWithFrame:
method. Remember from earlier hours that views define a rectangular area for the
content that is displayed on the iPad screen. To create the label, we need to define
the rectangle of its frame. The CGRectMake function takes starting x,y values and
ending x,y values to define the height and width of a rectangle. In this example,
we've defined a rectangle that spans 0–100 pixels horizontally and 0–32 pixels vertically.

Line 8 calls autorelease on the soundLabel object. This is a bit different from what
we've done elsewhere. Why can't we just release soundLabel at the end of the
method like everything else? The answer is that we have to return soundLabel so
the picker can use it, so we can't just get rid of it. By using autorelease, we can
hand off the object to the picker and relieve ourselves of the responsibility of releasing it.

Line 9 sets the background color attribute of the label to be transparent. As you
learned with web views, [UIColor clearColor] returns a color object configured as

transparent. If we leave this line out, the rectangle will not blend in with the background of the picker view.

Line 10 sets the text of the label to the string in of the specified row in animalSounds.

Finally, line 11 returns the UILabel, ready for display.

You can use Build and Run to run the application, but there's still going to be a slight issue; the rows aren't quite the right size to accommodate the images.

Changing Row Sizes

To control the width and height of the rows in the picker components, two additional delegate methods can be implemented:

pickerView:rowHeightForComponent:—Given a component number, this method should return the height, in pixels, of the row being displayed.

pickerView:widthForComponent:—Given a component number, this method returns the width of that component, in pixels.

For this example application, some trial and error led me to determine that the animal component should be 75 pixels wide, while the sound component looks best at around 150 pixels. Both components should use a constant row height of 55 pixels.

Translating this into code, implement pickerView:rowHeightForComponent: as follows:

```
- (CGFloat)pickerView:(UIPickerView *)pickerView
           rowHeightForComponent:(NSInteger)component {
    return 55.0;
}
```

Similarly, pickerView:widthForComponent:, becomes this:

```
- (CGFloat)pickerView:(UIPickerView *)pickerView
           widthForComponent:(NSInteger)component {
    if (component==animalComponent) {
        return 75.0;
    } else {
        return 150.0;
    }
}
```

With those small additions to PopoverContentViewController.m, the UIPickerView project is complete! You should now have a good understanding of how to create and customize pickers and manage a user's interaction with them.

Using Action Sheets

To finish up this hour's examples, we'll implement an action sheet that will appear when a user touches a button inside of a popover. I know your hands are probably getting tired from typing, but we're almost done and almost masters of the popover UI!

Implementation Overview

In this popover variation, which we'll creatively name **PopoverPlayground - ActionSheet**, we'll add a single button (UIButton) and corresponding action to our popover that will present the user with an action sheet (UIActionSheet). Choosing one of the action sheet buttons will set a UILabel to display the name of the button, as demonstrated in Figure 12.16.

FIGURE 12.16
The action sheet will display in response to a button press in the popover.

Setting Up the Project

One last time, create a copy of the PopoverPlayground – Skeleton folder named PopoverPlayground – ActionSheet. Open the project file within the new folder.

Adding Outlets, Actions, and Protocols

When Xcode has launched, open up the PopoverContentViewController.h file and add an action definition, doActionSheet, that will be called when the user presses a button within the popover interface. Next, add an outlet and property declaration for the label (UILabel) that will show what the user picked within the action sheet: statusMessage.

Our PopoverContentViewController will also need to conform to the UIActionSheetDelegate protocol so that we can react to the action sheet buttons.

Putting all this together results in the interface file shown in Listing 12.11.

LISTING 12.11

```
#import <UIKit/UIKit.h>

@interface PopoverContentViewController : UIViewController
        <UIActionSheetDelegate> {
    IBOutlet UILabel *statusMessage;
}

@property (retain, nonatomic) IBOutlet UILabel *statusMessage;

- (IBAction)doActionSheet:(id)sender;
```

Releasing the Objects

Before moving on, update the dealloc method in PopoverContentViewController.m to release the stateMessage label:

```
- (void)dealloc {
    [statusMessage release];
    [super dealloc];
}
```

Creating the Interface

Unlike the pickers we've used, an action sheet doesn't have any representation in the Interface Builder Library; it is entirely built and displayed through code. Even so, we still need to add a button that will make the popup display and a label to show feedback to the user.

Adding the Button and Label

Open the PopoverContentViewController.xib file in Interface Builder. Drag a new button (UIButton) to the top-left side of the view, labeling it **Lights, Camera, Action Sheet!** (or something equally witty of your own choosing). Next, drag a label (UILabel) directly below the button within the view. Expand the label so that it is roughly the same size as the button, and alter its text alignment to center the text it contains. When you are satisfied with the results, remove the default text entirely, so the label is empty.

The finished view should resemble Figure 12.17.

FIGURE 12.17
Add a button and an empty label to the view.

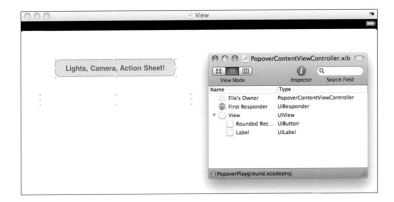

Connecting to the Outlet and Action

Before exiting Interface Builder, remember to connect the UI objects to the corresponding outlet and action! Control-drag from the File's Owner icon to the label. Choose the statusMessage output when prompted.

Next, select the button in the view and open the Connections Inspector (Command+2). Drag from the circle beside the Touch Up Inside event to the File's Owner icon, selecting the doActionSheet method when prompted. Figure 12.18 shows the connected action.

FIGURE 12.18
Connect the button's Touch Up Inside event to the doActionSheet action.

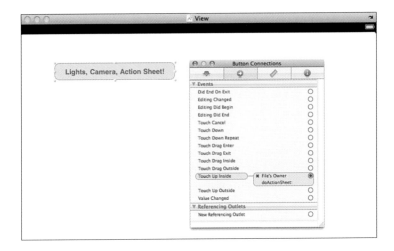

You can now exit Interface Builder. We're ready to finish up by implementing the action sheet itself in PopoverContentViewController.m.

Implementing the View Controller Logic

To create an action sheet, we need to allocate and initialize it and then show it. Add the method doActionSheet, shown in Listing 12.12, to the PopoverContentViewController.m file.

LISTING 12.12

```
1: - (IBAction)doActionSheet:(id)sender {
2:     UIActionSheet *actionSheet;
3:     actionSheet=[[UIActionSheet alloc] initWithTitle:@"Available Actions"
4:                 delegate:self
5:                 cancelButtonTitle:@"Cancel"
6:                 destructiveButtonTitle:@"Destroy"
7:                 otherButtonTitles:@"Negotiate",@"Compromise",nil];
8:     [actionSheet showInView:self.view];
9: }
```

Lines 2–3 declare and instantiate an instance of UIActionSheet called actionSheet. The initialization convenience method takes care of nearly all the setup. The parameters are as follows:

> initWithTitle:—Initializes the sheet with the specified title string.

> delegate:—Contains the object that will serve as the delegate to the sheet. If this is set to nil, the sheet will be displayed, but pressing a button will have no effect beyond dismissing the sheet. We are setting the value to self because we'll be implementing the UIActionSheetDelegate protocol within the PopoverContentViewController.

> cancelButtonTitle:—Set the string shown in the default button for the alert.

> destructiveButtonTitle:—The title of the option that will result in information being lost. This button will be presented in bright red (a sharp contrast to the rest of the choices). If set to nil, no destructive button will be displayed.

> otherButtonTitles:—Adds additional buttons to the sheet. In this example, we will have a total of four buttons: the cancel button, destructive button, and two "other" buttons.

In line 8, the action sheet is displayed in the current view controller's view (self.view) using the UIActionSheet showInView: method.

To add buttons to the action sheet outside of the initialization method, use the addButtonWithTitle: method.

By the Way

Responding to an Action Sheet Button Press

To capture and respond to a touch event on the action sheet, we need to implement the `actionSheet:clickedButtonAtIndex` action sheet delegate method. This provides the button index that was pressed within the action sheet. We can then use this index value and the `buttonTitleAtIndex` method to retrieve the button's title in a string.

Update PopoverContentViewController.m with the method in Listing 12.13.

LISTING 12.13

```
 1: - (void)actionSheet:(UIActionSheet *)actionSheet
 2:     clickedButtonAtIndex:(NSInteger)buttonIndex {
 3:     NSString *buttonTitle=[actionSheet buttonTitleAtIndex:buttonIndex];
 4:     if ([buttonTitle isEqualToString:@"Destroy"]) {
 5:         statusMessage.text=@"You last clicked 'Destroy'";
 6:     } else if ([buttonTitle isEqualToString:@"Negotiate"]) {
 7:         statusMessage.text=@"You last clicked 'Negotiate'";
 8:     } else if ([buttonTitle isEqualToString:@"Compromise"]) {
 9:         statusMessage.text=@"You last clicked 'Compromise'";
10:     } else {
11:         statusMessage.text=@"You last clicked 'Cancel'";
12:     }
13: }
```

Line 3 does the heavily lifting in this method, setting a string, `buttonTitle`, to the title of the button that was touched. Lines 4–12 test for the different button titles and update the view's status message to indicate what was chosen.

An Alternative Approach

In this implementation, we've chosen to match button presses based on the title of the onscreen button. If you're adding buttons dynamically, however, this might not be the best approach. The `addButtonWithTitle` method, for example, adds a button and returns the index of the button that was added. Similarly, the `cancelButtonIndex` and `destructiveButtonIndex` methods provide the indexes for the two specialized action sheet buttons.

By checking against these index values, you can write a version of the `actionSheet:clickedButtonAtIndex:` method that is not dependent on the title strings. The approach you take in your own applications should be based on what creates the most efficient and easy-to-maintain code.

Changing the Action Sheet Appearance and Behavior

Action sheets are more flexible then they may first appear. An action sheet defines three different types of buttons with three different appearances (cancel, destructive, other). Any of the button titles can be set to `nil`, and that button type will not be displayed in the sheet.

You can also change how the sheet is drawn on the screen. In the example we've created, the `showInView:` method is used to animate the opening of the sheet from the current view controller's view. If you have an instance of a toolbar or a tab bar, you could use `showFromToolbar:` or `showFromTabBar:` to make the sheet appear to open from either of these user interface elements.

Perhaps more dramatically, an action sheet can take on different appearances according to how you set the `actionSheetStyle` property. For example, try adding the following line to the `doActionSheet` method:

```
actionSheet.actionSheetStyle=UIBarStyleBlackTranslucent;
```

This code will draw the action sheet in a translucent black style. You can also use `UIActionSheetStyleAutomatic` to inherit the style of the view's toolbar (if any is set), or `UIActionSheetStyleBlackOpaque` for a shiny solid black style.

> **Did you Know?**
>
> Earlier this hour, you learned that an action sheet could be displayed in a "nonanimated" fashion, filling the full popover view when it first appears, rather than waiting for a user to perform an additional action. To do this, you need to show the action sheet with the method `showFromRect:inView:animated` with the "rect" set to the dimensions of the popover, the view set to the popover view controller's view, and `animated` set to `false`. The display of the action sheet would also need to take place when the popover view is first loaded, such as in the `viewDidLoad` method of `PopoverContentViewController`.

Further Exploration

As you learned in this hour, `UIDatePicker` and `UIPickerView` objects are reasonably easy to use and quite flexible in what they can do. There are a few interesting aspects of using these controls that we haven't looked at that you might want to explore on your own. First, both classes implement a means of programmatically selecting a value and animating the picker components so that they "spin" to reach the values you're selecting (`setDate:animated:` and `selectRow:inComponent:animated:`). If you've used applications that implement pickers, chances are, you've seen this in action.

Another popular approach to implementing pickers is creating components that appear to spin continuously (instead of reaching a start or stopping point). You might be surprised to learn that this is really just a programming trick. The most common way to implement this functionality is to use a picker view that just repeats the same component rows over and over (thousands of times). This requires you to write the necessary logic in the delegate and data source protocol methods, but the overall effect is that the component rotates continuously.

Action sheets, while easy to overlook, can play an important role in your application interface. They provide a straightforward way of presenting several options to the user without requiring a separate instance of a UIButton for each. If you find yourself building button after button in a popover, consider whether an action sheet would be a better UI choice.

Summary

In this hour's lesson, you explored two classes, UIDatePicker and UIPickerView, that present the user with a list of choices ranging from dates to images, and the UIActionSheet class which offers a user contextually appropriate choices based on their actions. All these elements are unique in the requirement that they be presented within a popover.

In addition to presenting the UI objects, you also practiced conforming classes to protocols. For the picker view, this included the UIPickerViewDelegate and UIPickerViewDataSource protocols, and UIActionSheetDelegate for action sheets.

You should now have the tools and knowledge to create far more functional popovers and even more powerful user interfaces in your applications.

Q&A

Q. *Why didn't you cover the timer mode of the* **UIDatePicker?**

A. The timer mode doesn't actually implement a timer; it's just a view that can display timer information. To implement a timer, you'll actually need to track the time and update the view accordingly (not something we can easily cover in the span of an hour).

Q. *Where did you get the method names and parameters from for the* `UIPickerView` *protocols?*

A. The protocol methods that we implemented were taken directly from the Apple Xcode documentation for `UIPickerViewDelegate` and `UIPickerViewDataSource`. If you check the documentation, you can simply copy and paste from the method definitions into your code.

Q. *If we had to create a rectangle to define the frame of a* `UILabel`, *why didn't we do the same when creating the* `UIImageView` *objects?*

A. When a `UIImageView` is initialized with an `NSImage`, its frame is set to the dimensions of the image.

Q. *Why can't I just use an alert rather than an action sheet?*

A. You could, but an alert is application-centric and presented without context. An action sheet, on the other hand, is directly tied to an action the user is performing, making it a more user-friendly choice.

Workshop

Quiz

1. An `NSDate` instance stores only a date. True or false?

2. Why doesn't a `UIPickerView` need to have an action defined for it?

3. Picker views can display images using the `pickerView:titleForRow:forComponent:` method. True or false?

4. An action sheet will only display within a popover. True or false?

Answers

1. False. An instance of `NSDate` stores an "instant in time" (meaning a date *and* time).

2. By implementing the `UIPickerViewDelegate` methods and connecting the picker to the delegate, you gain the functionality of an action method automatically.

3. False. The `pickerView:viewForRow:forComponent:reusingView:` method must be implemented to display images within a picker.

4. False. (Trick question!) Action sheets and pickers can be used in views outside of popovers, but Apple declared this a no-no in their human interface guidelines. You can implement it, but don't expect your application to be approved!

Activities

1. Update the PopoverPlayground - dateCalc project so that the program automatically sets the picker to the current date when it is loaded. You'll need to use the `setDate:animated:` method to implement this change.

2. Extend the PopoverPlayground - CustomPicker project to give the appearance of the continuously scrolling/rotating components. You'll need to return a very large number of rows for each component, and then repeat the same rows over and over when they are requested. Rather than adding redundant data to the array, the best approach is to use a single array and map the row requests into the existing data in the array.

3. Implement an action sheet that is displayed immediately after a popover is loaded. Remember that you'll need to use the `showFromRect:inView:animated` method to accomplish this.

Focusing on Tasks with Modal Views

What You'll Learn in This Hour:

▶ The purpose of modal views

▶ How to present modal views

▶ Ways of changing the appearance of modal views

▶ How to dismiss a modal view

In Hour 10, "Getting the User's Attention," you learned about modal views through the iPad alert system. If you recall, a modal view is one that is presented when action is required from the user—they are forced to complete the interaction before proceeding. The alert views that we've used, however, are hardly a replacement for everything we can do with a normal view and view controller.

To give developers more flexibility, the iPhone OS allows almost any view controller to be presented modally. This hour looks at how modal views can be created, displayed, and ultimately, dismissed. You'll also learn how information can be exchanged between your main application views and a modal view.

Modal Views

You've worked with alerts and popovers, both of which present information to the user outside of the main view. These views, however, are very limited in the information that they can present and the situations in which they can be used. Modal views, however, open up the possibilities tremendously.

Modal views, as defined by Apple, should be presented when the user needs to complete a task before moving on. This could be supplying configuration information, filling in a form, sending an email—nearly anything related to a specific task is a candidate for being presented modally. Figure 13.1 shows a common email-composition modal view.

FIGURE 13.1
Email composi-
tion is frequent-
ly presented as
a modal view.

To make things even easier, any view with an accompanying view controller can be presented modally! There are no special requirements for making the view; we just need to use a specific method, `presentModalViewController:animated` within our existing view controller to show it. To hide the modal view, `dismissModalViewControllerAnimated` can be invoked on either the modal view's view controller, or the view controller that displayed the modal view.

Modal View Styles and Transitions

A reasonable question to ask is this: Why don't I just show another view? Why do this modally? The answer is that modal views are presented within the context of the existing view. That might sound like a "high-concept" answer, but it's easy to understand. Assume, for example, you want to provide a button where users can configure a feature in your app. Using a modal view, you can fade out the original view, leaving it visible in the background, then present a modal view in a window overlaying the original information. Replacing the current view can be disorienting to the user. Modal views are presented in a way to show that they are related to the original view, making for a smooth transition.

You can apply several different modal styles to your modal views by setting the modalPresentationStyle property on the corresponding view controller. For example:

UIModalPresentationFormSheet—Sizes the view smaller than the screen (regardless of orientation), showing the original view behind the modal view

UIModalPresentationPageSheet—Sizes the view so that it is presented in a portrait format

UIModalPresentationFullScreen—Sizes the view so that it covers the entire screen

In addition to these styles, there are a handful of transitions that alter how the modal view is revealed to a user. The iPad has a very striking "page curl" effect that you may have seen when using various applications—shown in the Maps application, in Figure 13.2. You can create this effect in your own apps, just by setting a modalTransitionStyle property.

FIGURE 13.2
Apply effects to the modal view's transition, such as the page curl shown in the Maps application.

Currently you can choose from four transitions:

> `UIModalTransitionStyleCoverVertical`—The modal view slides in from the bottom of the screen to cover the existing view.

> `UIModalTransitionStyleFlipHorizontal`—The current view flips horizontally with 3D flair, revealing the modal view as if it were on the back of the original view.

> `UIModalTransitionStyleCrossDissolve`—The existing view fades out while the modal view fades in.

> `UIModalTransitionStylePartialCurl`—The existing view curls up like a notebook page, revealing the modal view underneath.

Watch Out!

Not all styles are compatible with all transitions. A page curl, for example, can't take place on a form sheet that doesn't completely fill the screen. Attempting to use an incompatible combination will result in a crash—so if you've chosen a bad pair, you'll find out pretty quickly (or you could review the documentation for the transition/style you plan to use).

If it sounds straightforward, that's because it is. Modal views do their work without hassle or complicated coding. Despite being roughly equivalent to a "window" on a desktop operating system, our exploration of modal views on the iPad is one of the easier tutorials in the second half of this book.

Using Modal Views

To demonstrate the appearance and use of modal views, our tutorial for this hour presents the user with a button for showing a modal view. It also uses two segmented controls to configure the modal view with any combination of styles and transitions.

Within the modal view, the user will have the option of clicking Yes or No, the results of which will be shown back in the main view. Figure 13.3 shows the finished application.

FIGURE 13.3
This hour's tutorial will give us an opportunity to experiment with configuring and displaying modal views.

Implementation Overview

The majority of development time in this tutorial will be setting up the views. We'll be using the View-based Application template to create the project and adding a second view controller for the modal view. Within the each of the views, we'll use a typical combination of buttons and labels. The button in the main view will invoke an action to configure and show the modal view. The buttons in the modal view will be used to dismiss itself and update the main view with whatever button name the user clicked.

To keep things simple, we'll be instantiating the modal view's controller within the main application view. An alternative, and more memory-friendly approach, is to instantiate the modal view only when you need it, but for most applications, this is just fine.

Setting Up the Project

Begin by creating a new view-based iPad application named **ModalMe.** The default view and view controller will work like any other application that we've built—but, unlike many of our examples, we will be creating a complete second view that will be shown modally.

To create the second view and view controller, choose File, New File from the menu. In the template chooser, pick the Cocoa Touch Class category followed by the `UIViewController` option. Be sure that the Targeted for iPad and With XIB for User Interface check boxes are selected, and then click Next. When prompted, name the new view controller **ContentViewController.m** and be sure that a corresponding interface (.h) file is created.

After creating the new class, drag the interface and implementation files to the Classes folder and the ContentViewController.xib file to the Resources folder to keep things in order.

Preparing the Main View

The main view of the application is far from the most complicated thing that we've built. It is going to have an output label (`outputLabel`), two segmented controls (`presentationStyle` and `transitionStyle`), and a big button that the user can press that calls an instance method `showModal`.

Our view is also going to need to have access to the modal view controller itself. We'll accomplish this by adding a view controller instance to our existing ModalMeViewController.xib file a little later. For now, just know that we need to import the ContentViewController.h interface file, and declare an outlet for and instance of `ContentViewController`, called `modalContent`.

Putting all of this together, edit the ModalMeViewController.h file to include outlets, actions, and properties for all of these items. The final file should resemble Listing 13.1.

Listing 13.1

```
#import <UIKit/UIKit.h>
#import "ContentViewController.h"

@interface ModalMeViewController : UIViewController {
    IBOutlet ContentViewController *modalContent;
    IBOutlet UISegmentedControl *presentationStyle;
    IBOutlet UISegmentedControl *transitionStyle;
    IBOutlet UILabel *outputLabel;
}

-(IBAction) showModal:(id)sender;

@property (nonatomic,retain) ContentViewController *modalContent;
@property (nonatomic,retain) UISegmentedControl *presentationStyle;
@property (nonatomic,retain) UISegmentedControl *transitionStyle;
@property (nonatomic,retain) UILabel *outputLabel;

@end
```

Now, open the ModalMeViewController.m implementation file and add correspon-ding @synthesize directives after the main @implementation line:

```
@synthesize modalContent;
@synthesize presentationStyle;
@synthesize transitionStyle;
@synthesize outputLabel;
```

For good measure (and good practice), release all the objects we've retained by edit-ing the dealloc method:

```
- (void)dealloc {
    [modalContent release];
    [presentationStyle release];
    [transitionStyle release];
    [outputLabel release];
    [super dealloc];
}
```

Building the Interface

To create the main application interface, double-click the ModalMeViewController.xib file to open Interface Builder. Double-click the View icon in the Document window, if it isn't already open.

Start by adding a button (UIButton) to the view. Title the button **Modal Me**, with a nice large font, and center it in the view. Add a label (UILabel) below the button that reads Modal View Result:, and a second label below that that reads Nothing Chosen. This label will be our output label. The modal view will set this label, demonstrating inter-view communication.

Next, add a four segment UISegmentedControl to the top of the view. The segments should read (in order): Cover Vertical, Flip Horizontal, Cross Dissolve, and Partial Curl. If you don't remember how to add segments, take a look at Figure 13.4. Just select the segmented control, open the Attributes Inspector (Command+1), and increase the number of segments.

FIGURE 13.4
Use the Attributes Inspector to set the number of segments.

Add a second segmented control with three segments. These segments should be labeled: **Full Screen**, **Page Sheet**, and **Form Sheet**.

Finish the interface design by adding labels above the segmented controls—**Transition Style** above the first, and **Presentation Style** above the second. Figure 13.5 shows the final design.

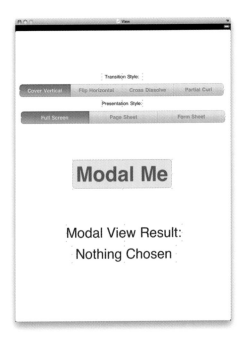

FIGURE 13.5
The completed interface will give us the ability to play around with modal views.

Connecting the Outlets and Actions

Four connections are required for the view. The top (transitions) segmented control will connect to the transitionStyle outlet, the bottom to the presentationStyle outlet. The label with the text Nothing Chosen will connect to outputLabel. Control-drag from the File's Owner icon to each of these objects, either in the interface or in the Document window, and choose the appropriate outlet when prompted.

The last connection is to an action. The Modal Me UIButton will connect to the showModal action. Click to select the button and open the Connections Inspector (Command+2). Drag from the circle beside the Touch Up Inside to the File's Owner icon. Pick showModal when prompted, as shown in Figure 13.6.

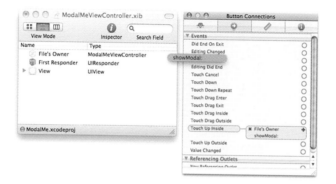

FIGURE 13.6
Connect the UI elements to their outlets, and the button to its action.

Instantiating the Modal View Controller

Before we can close the ModalMeViewController.xib file, we need to make a small addition. The view controller that we created for handling modal content (ContentViewController) needs to be instantiated. We'll do this by adding it to ModalMeViewController.xib.

Search the Library (Tools, Library) for an instance of UIViewController and drag it to the XIB file. This adds a generic view controller—not an instance of ContentViewController. You'll need to set its identity and the view it displays. Select the view controller icon in the Document window, and then open the Identity Inspector (Command+4). Choose ContentViewController from the drop-down list, as shown in Figure 13.7.

FIGURE 13.7
Set
ContentView
Controller as
the class for the
view controller.

Next, switch to the Attributes view. Within the View Controller section, set the NIB file to ContentViewController. This ensures that the ContentViewController.xib file will be providing the view for the view controller.

The last step is to Control-drag from the File's Owner icon to the instance of the ContentViewController, choosing modalContent when prompted. This attaches the instance of the ContentViewController we added to the XIB file to the modalContent instance variable.

The main application interface is complete. Next step: creating the modal view itself.

Preparing the Modal View

Modal views and view controllers are just like any other view and view controller. You can build them out with whatever functionality/features you need. In this case, we'll add two UIButtons along with an action hideModal. We'll call this to dismiss the modal view and to update the main view with the user's choice of buttons.

What's really exciting is that we don't need to keep track of the buttons—so no outlets are required! The only thing that needs to be added to ContentViewController.h is a single line for the action we'll be writing. Insert this line preceding the @end statement:

```
-(IBAction) hideModal:(id)sender;
```

Building the Interface

To build the modal view's interface, open the ContentViewController.xib file by double-clicking it. Again, this is just like any other view, so you can use the same technique for designing it that you'd use anywhere else.

This example is pretty simple—just drag two buttons (UIButton) to the view, one on top of the other. The first button should be named **Yes**, and the second, **No**. Using the Attributes Inspector (Command+1), increase the button's font size, and then drag to resize the buttons accordingly.

To complete the view, add a label above the buttons that reads **Click 'Yes' or 'No'**, as shown in Figure 13.8.

FIGURE 13.8
The completed modal content view has two buttons and a label.

Connecting the Action

We aren't going to be generating any output in this view, so the only connection to be made is from the buttons to the hideModal action. Both buttons will trigger the same method, making life simple.

Select the first button, and then open the Connections Inspector (Command+2). Drag from the circle beside Touch Up Inside to the File's Owner icon. As demonstrated in Figure 13.9, choose hideModal when prompted.

FIGURE 13.9
Both buttons should trigger the hideModal method.

Repeat this for the second button, and then save your work and close the XIB files. All that remains is implementing the logic to tie it all together.

Implementing the Modal View Logic

As you learned earlier this hour, there isn't much to presenting and dismissing modal views. In fact, two methods, coupled with properties for setting the modal presentation style and transition, will do just about everything we need.

Displaying the Modal View

When the user clicks the Modal Me button in the main application view, the showModal method is triggered in ModalMeViewController.m. This method will need to set the modal view's transition and presentation styles and then display the modal view. Implement the method as shown in Listing 13.2.

Listing 13.2

```
 1: -(IBAction) showModal:(id)sender {
 2:     outputLabel.text=@"Nothing Chosen";
 3:     switch (transitionStyle.selectedSegmentIndex) {
 4:         case 0:
 5:             modalContent.modalTransitionStyle=
 6:                     UIModalTransitionStyleCoverVertical;
 7:             break;
 8:         case 1:
 9:             modalContent.modalTransitionStyle=
10:                     UIModalTransitionStyleFlipHorizontal;
11:             break;
12:         case 2:
13:             modalContent.modalTransitionStyle=
14:                     UIModalTransitionStyleCrossDissolve;
15:             break;
16:         default:
17:             modalContent.modalTransitionStyle=
18:                     UIModalTransitionStylePartialCurl;
19:             break;
```

```
20:      }
21:      switch (presentationStyle.selectedSegmentIndex) {
22:          case 0:
23:              modalContent.modalPresentationStyle=
24:                          UIModalPresentationFullScreen;
25:              break;
26:          case 1:
27:              modalContent.modalPresentationStyle=
28:                          UIModalPresentationPageSheet;
29:              break;
30:          default:
31:              modalContent.modalPresentationStyle=
32:                          UIModalPresentationFormSheet;
33:              break;
34:      }
35:      [self presentModalViewController:modalContent animated:YES];
36: }
```

In line 2, we set the outputLabel in the view to read Nothing Chosen—resetting anything the user may have chosen previously.

Next, the bulk of the implementation. In lines 3–34, switch statements evaluate transitionStyle.selectedIndex and presentationStyle.selectedIndex. These two properties contain an integer (0–3 for the transitions, and 0–2 for the presentation styles) that correspond to the transition and style chosen in segmented control. Depending on which number is selected, we configure a different transition and presentation style, assigning them to modalContent.modalTransitionStyle and modalContent.modalPresentationStyle, respectively.

Finally, in line 35, presentModalViewController:animated is used to display the modal view controller, modalContent.

It shouldn't take long to realize that in a real-world application, we wouldn't be giving the user the ability to configure the appearance of the modal view. All that is really necessary to display the view is a maximum of three lines—two for setting up the presentation and transition styles, and one to present the view!

Now let's figure out how to dismiss the modal view.

Dismissing the Modal View

While displaying the modal view took place in the main application view controller, we'll be dismissing the modal view from its own view controller. Depending on your needs, you can use the dismissModalViewControllerAnimated method in either the modal view controller or the controller that invoked the modal view.

Open the ContentViewController.m file and add the hideModal method as follows:

```
-(IBAction) hideModal:(id)sender {
    [[(ModalMeViewController *)self.parentViewController outputLabel]
                             setText:[sender currentTitle]];
    [self dismissModalViewControllerAnimated:YES];
}
```

There are only two statements represented in this method. Let's start with the second: [self dismissModalViewControllerAnimated:YES]. This statement, called from within the modal view itself, dismisses the view, removing it from iPad screen and returning control to the main application interface.

So, what does that first statement do? The key is the property parentViewController that is automatically set to the view controller that invokes a modal view. By using this property, we can grab a reference to the outputLabel instance variable. Next, we can use setText to set the text of the label. Remember that two UIButtons are invoking this method, so the sender variable will refer to one of two buttons, and we can use the construct [sender currentTitle] to grab the text title (label) from whatever button was pressed.

Before we can call things done, there's one problem to resolve. The property parentViewController doesn't "know" what kind of view controller it is—so it doesn't understand, for example, that it has an instance variable called outputLabel. To force self.parentViewController to be a reference to our ModalMeViewController class, add (ModalMeViewController *) before the parent controller property. This is called type-casting.

We also need to import the ModalMeViewController.h interface file at the top of the ContentViewController.m so that our reference to the ModalMeViewController class in this method doesn't confuse Xcode:

```
#import "ModalMeViewController.h"
```

If you don't import the ModalMeViewController.h interface file, and don't type-cast self.parentViewController, the code *will* work. The only problem will be that you see a warning that parentViewController may not have an instance variable called outputLabel. Because it *does*, there won't be any problems once the application starts.

That completes our look at modal views! Build and Run the application, and then use it as a testing area to identify transition and presentation styles that you might want to use in your own creations.

Further Exploration

Modal views can really be just about *any* view that you create. That means that everything you've learned up to this point (and that you'll learn in future hours) applies to modal views. One note of interest that we haven't really touched on is that modal views can spawn other modal views. Each new view stacks on top of the next.

When stacking views, developers typically code to dismiss them from the top down. If you choose to dismiss a modal view located in the middle of the stack, however, it will automatically dismiss any views above it.

Beyond that, there isn't much more to learn. You now have the information needed to implement modal views in any of your applications.

Summary

This hour's lesson introduced you to modal views—not just "alert"-style modal views like you learned about in Hour 10, but full views that you can design directly in Interface Builder. Modal views should be presented when users need to complete a task—it helps them focus on the task, and keeps it within the context of the rest of the application.

Modal views can be customized using presentation and transition style attributes, such as page curls. The end result is an easy-to-implement, and visually impressive way of separating an application's functionality into separate views.

Q&A

Q. Why doesn't the iPad just provide windows?

A. Can you imagine managing windows with just your fingers? The iPad has an interface designed to be touched. It is not meant to model a typical desktop application environment, which was built around the mouse.

Q. Can I use modal views to show different screens of information in an application?

A. Yes and no. If the screens represent different tasks, modal views are perfectly acceptable. If the screens necessary to use the application as a whole, however, they should be implemented using one of the techniques you'll learn about in the next hour.

Workshop

Quiz

1. Modal views can only be displayed as alerts. True or false?

2. How many methods are required to display and dismiss a modal view?

3. All presentation and transition styles are compatible with one another. True or false?

Answers

1. False. While alert views are a modal view, any view controller can be presented modally.

2. Two. The method `presentModalViewController:animated` shows the view, while `dismissModalViewControllerAnimated` dismisses the view.

3. False. Some transitions will not work with some presentation styles. The full guidelines can be found in the developer documentation.

Activities

1. Return to a project in an earlier hour and implement a "configuration" interface by way of a modal view.

2. Use the tutorial you created in this lesson to identify the combinations of presentation and transition styles that you would like to use in your own applications.

Implementing Multiview Applications

What You'll Learn in This Hour:

▶ Why applications use multiple views and view controllers

▶ How to create a multiview application from scratch

▶ How to quickly build a multiview application using a tab bar and tab bar controller

▶ How to enable inter-view communication

Exploring Single Versus Multiview Applications

In the previous hours, the application frameworks that we built have followed the approach of "one app, one view." We've presented a screen with some controls, accepted input, and produced output. These single-view applications use one view and one view controller. Sure, we can use a second or third view / view controller to show a small overlay, or show a task-oriented modal view, but the majority of the user's interactions have been confined to a single visible view. This is perfectly fine if that's all your application needs to do, but the iPad has several interface elements that make it possible to present complex applications across multiple parallel views.

The iPad gives developers the opportunity to segment their applications into multiple different views and view controllers. This keeps the UI clean and not overloaded and helps prevent the creation of "God classes" that attempt to perform every action under the sun. In our previous examples, we dealt with one view and one controller. By introducing multiple-view controllers, we can create the mobile equivalent of a multiwindow desktop application. Information can be organized into logical groupings, and the user can easily switch between them.

In this hour, we explore multiview applications with "parallel" views. This means that the content of one view isn't directly dependent on another—there isn't any set order in which they should be displayed.

Additional functionality usually implies additional complexity, and this isn't an exception. There won't be any real surprises in the code itself, but you'll need to start thinking a bit more about the application architecture and begin considering the additional outlets and connections you'll need to build if your view controllers need to communicate with each other.

Creating a Multiview Application

The first project that we'll build in this chapter creates and manages multiple views from scratch. This will serve as an exercise to familiarize you with an approach to dealing with multiple views and introduce you to some new methods and properties, as well as to the toolbar interface element.

Implementation Overview

Much as a single-view application uses a view controller to direct the interactions of its interface elements, a multiview application needs a controller to help it switch between different views. In this implementation, we'll create a typical view-based application, but will use the default view controller (`UIViewController`) to swap in and out three additional views—each with its own controller. The default controller will need to implement methods for clearing the current view and loading any of the other views—in any order, at any time.

In addition, our default view will be setting up a toolbar. We'll use the toolbar to provide quick access to view switching via a row of buttons at the bottom of the screen, as shown in Figure 14.1.

One interesting challenge that we'll need to overcome with this implementation is that while our main view will include the toolbar, it must be visible in all the other views, too. We need to display the views "under" the toolbar so that the toolbar isn't hidden as new views are shown or removed.

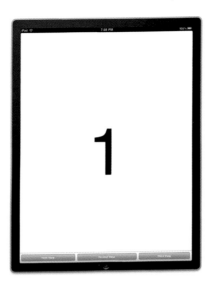

FIGURE 14.1
The final application will switch between views with a toolbar.

Setting Up the Project

To begin, start Xcode and create a new application called **MultipleViews** using the View-based Application template. The layout of this template should be getting very familiar by now. The MainWindow.xib includes a view controller that loads its view from a second XIB file, MultipleViewsViewController.xib. This XIB file will hold the toolbar that serves as our interface for switching between views, as well as instances of three new view controllers that will ultimately manage three new views.

Adding Views and View Controllers

Each of the views that we will be switching between needs its own view controller and XIB file. Create three new UIViewController subclasses (File, New File, Cocoa Touch Class, UIViewController subclass) and name them as follows:

- ▶ FirstViewController
- ▶ SecondViewController
- ▶ ThirdViewController

Be sure to check the Targeted for iPad and With XIB for User Interface check boxes for each of the new classes that you create. When you've created the files, drag the XIB files to the Resources group. Your Xcode Classes and Resources groups should resemble Figure 14.2.

FIGURE 14.2
Our first multi-
view application
will use a total
of four views
and view con-
trollers.

> The goal of this project is to create a simple application that switches between independently controlled views. It is certainly possible that each of the views could share a view controller, but structurally it is a good practice to use separate controllers for views that do not serve the same function.

Prepping the View Content

To make sure that we know (visually) which view is which, in Interface Builder open each of the three XIB files that correspond to the view controller classes. For each view, drag a text label (UILabel) from the Library (Tools, Library) into the view. Change the text of the label to **1** in FirstViewController.xib, **2** in SecondViewController.xib, and **3** in the ThirdViewController.xib file. In the sample files for this project, I've set the font size to 288 points for each label by using the Attributes Inspector (Command+1), as shown in Figure 14.3.

Remember that we're going to be overlaying a toolbar on each of these views, so you don't have the entire screen real estate to work with. Although we can't see the toolbar just yet, we can simulate it for the purposes of laying out the view. To add a simulated toolbar to the view, select the view itself within the Interface Builder Document window, and then press Command+1 to open the View Attributes Inspector. Choose Toolbar from the Bottom Bar Simulated User Interface Elements pop-up menu, shown in Figure 14.4.

FIGURE 14.3
Add labels to each view so they can be easily identified.

FIGURE 14.4
Adding a simulated toolbar to the view can help with layout since the actual toolbar isn't visible.

Instantiating the View Controllers

Your project should now contain content for each of the views and all the view controller classes it needs to function. The classes, however, still need to be instantiated so that we have actual view controllers and view objects to use in the application.

Open the MultipleViewsViewController.xib in Interface Builder. This file contains the parent view that we will be using to for the toolbar interface element, and it is also a logical place to add our other view controller instances.

Using the Library (Tools, Library), drag a view controller (`UIViewController`) into the Document window. We want this view controller to be an instance of our `FirstViewController` class. With the controller selected, press Command+4 to open the Identity Inspector. Use the drop-down menu to choose `FirstViewController`, as shown in Figure 14.5.

FIGURE 14.5
Update the view controllers to point to the classes you created earlier.

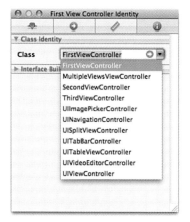

Next, the view controller must be updated to point to the correct XIB file (FileViewController.xib) for its view. Select the controller in the Document window and press Command+1 to open the Attributes Inspector. Within the NIB Name drop-down menu, choose `FirstViewController`, as shown in Figure 14.6.

FIGURE 14.6
Associate every view controller with the appropriate XIB file.

Repeat these steps for the SecondViewController and ThirdViewController class-es; that is, add a new view controller instance, set the class, and associate the view. When finished, your MultipleViewsViewController.xib should look very similar to Figure 14.7.

FIGURE 14.7
Add three view
controller
instances to the
XIB file.

With these changes, our project will build and instantiate the controllers, but there is still no way to display the different views. It's time to add the toolbar controls and code to make that happen!

Adding Toolbar Controls

The MultipleViews application that we're building now requires a single toolbar with buttons for each of the three views that we want to display. The toolbar itself will be added as a subview of the view in the MultipleViewsViewController.xib file.

If you haven't already, open the MultipleViewsViewController.xib file in Interface Builder. The view contained in this XIB file, as you know from previous view-based applications, is what will be added to the application's window when it first launch-es. Instead of providing all the onscreen content, however, we just want this view and its view controller to manage the toolbar and the user's interactions with it.

Open the view and, using the Library objects (Tools, Library), drag an instance of a toolbar (UIToolbar) to the bottom of the view. You should now have an empty view with a single-button toolbar visible.

Adding and Editing Toolbar Buttons

We need three buttons for this project. Drag a bar button item (UIBarButton) from the Library to the toolbar. An insertion point will appear where the button will be added. Repeat this process until there are a total of three buttons (one for each view) in the toolbar.

Double-click the button's title to switch to an editable mode. Edit each button title to correspond to one of the views that needs to be displayed (for example, **First View**, **Second View**, **Third View**).

Did you Know?

If you have difficulty selecting the buttons directly in the layout view, you may also select them using the Document window and edit their titles by accessing the Attributes Inspector (Command+1).

After editing the titles, you might want to resize the buttons to create a uniform appearance in the toolbar. You can use the Size Inspector (Command+3) to adjust the width numerically or just click and drag the resize handle that appears to the right of the currently selected button.

The end result should resemble Figure 14.8.

FIGURE 14.8
The final toolbar should contain three buttons with appropriate titles.

By the Way

Bar button items do not have to be text-labeled buttons. Alternatively, you can set an image file to be used as the button representation in the Attributes Inspector. We will be using this feature of the tab bar UI element in the next project.

Adding Outlets and Actions

Now that all the interface elements are in place for the MultiViews application, we need to connect them to code. The `MultiViewsViewController` object will handle the switching of the views, so we need to edit the class to include outlets for each of the view controllers, as well as actions for each of the toolbar buttons, and a new method `clearView` that we'll use to clear the contents of the view as we switch between them.

Edit MultipleViewsViewController.h to reflect the code in Listing 14.1.

LISTING 14.1

```
 1: #import <UIKit/UIKit.h>
 2:
 3: @class FirstViewController;
 4: @class SecondViewController;
 5: @class ThirdViewController;
 6:
 7: @interface MultipleViewsViewController : UIViewController {
 8:     IBOutlet FirstViewController *firstViewController;
 9:     IBOutlet SecondViewController *secondViewController;
10:     IBOutlet ThirdViewController *thirdViewController;
11: }
12:
13: @property (retain, nonatomic) FirstViewController *firstViewController;
14: @property (retain, nonatomic) SecondViewController *secondViewController;
15: @property (retain, nonatomic) ThirdViewController *thirdViewController;
16:
17: -(IBAction) loadSecondView:(id)sender;
18: -(IBAction) loadThirdView:(id)sender;
19: -(IBAction) loadFirstView:(id)sender;
20:
21: -(void) clearView;
22:
23: @end
```

Let's quickly run through what we've done here. Because this class needs to be aware of our other view controller classes, we first declare the view controller classes in lines 3–5.

Lines 8–10 create `IBOutlets` for each of our view controller instances (`firstViewController`, `secondViewController`, and `thirdViewController`), since we'll need to access them to switch between views.

In lines 13–15, we declare these three instances as properties.

Lines 17–19 declare three methods for switching views and expose them as IBActions for Interface Builder (`loadFirstView`. `loadSecondView`, and `loadFirstView`).

Finally, on line 21, a new method, `clearView`, is declared. It will be used to remove the old content from our view when we switch to a new view.

Connecting Outlets and Actions

Save the changes you've made to MultiViewsViewController.h, and jump back into the MultiViewsViewController.xib file in Interface Builder. We can now make our final connections before writing the view switching code.

From the Document window, Control-drag from the File's Owner icon to the instance of `firstViewController`. When prompted for an outlet, choose `firstViewController`, as shown in Figure 14.9.

FIGURE 14.9
Connect each
view controller
to its outlet
within the
`MultipleViews
ViewController`
class.

Repeat this process for the `secondViewController` and `thirdViewController` instances, choosing the appropriate outlet when prompted.

Next, expand the view and toolbar hierarchy to show the three bar button items that we added earlier. Control-drag from the First View button to the File's Owner icon. When prompted, choose the `loadFirstView` Sent Action.

Do the same for the two other buttons, connecting the Second View button to `loadSecondView`, and the third to `loadThirdView`. The interface connections are now complete, and we can finish up the implementation of the view loading methods.

Implementing the View Switch Methods

To implement the view switching, we'll be making use of a `UIView` instance method called `insertSubview:atIndex:`. This method inserts a view as a subview of another view—just like creating a hierarchy of views within Interface Builder. By inserting a subview at an index of 0 into the view containing our toolbar, we will effectively "float" the toolbar view on top of the subview.

Begin the implementation by opening MultipleViewsViewController.m in Xcode. Import the headers from the three view controller classes so that we can properly access them in the code:

```
#import "MultipleViewsViewController.h"
#import "FirstViewController.h"
#import "SecondViewController.h"
#import "ThirdViewController.h"
```

Next, after the @implementation directive, use @synthesize to create the getters and setters for the view controller instances (firstViewController, secondViewController, thirdViewController):

```
@synthesize firstViewController;
@synthesize secondViewController;
@synthesize thirdViewController;
```

Create the method to load the first view, loadFirstView as follows:

```
-(IBAction) loadFirstView:(id)sender {
        [self.view insertSubview:firstViewController.view atIndex:0];
}
```

This single line of code uses the insertSubview:atIndex: method of the MultiViewsViewController's view instance (which contains our toolbar) to add a subview that will appear below it. That's all there is to it.

Following this pattern, implement the loadSecondView and loadThirdView methods to insert their respective view controller's views as subviews of the toolbar view.

> If you're confused why self.view is the view containing the toolbar, look at the structure of the project and the XIB files. We're adding the loadView methods to the MultiViewsViewController class, so self refers to the instance of that class. The MultiViewsViewController has a single view with a toolbar that we added earlier, so self.view, within this context, is just a reference to that view.

After you've finished the view loading implementation, don't forget to release the view controllers in the dealloc method:

```
- (void)dealloc {
    [firstViewController release];
    [secondViewController release];
    [thirdViewController release];
    [super dealloc];
}
```

Setting a View When the Application Starts

If you try to run the application now, it should work, but it probably won't do quite what you expect. When the application first starts, it loads the initial view containing the toolbar, but nothing else. Until a toolbar button is pressed, none of our three content views are visible. A much more user-friendly approach is to automatically load content as soon as the application starts.

To automatically switch to one of the views, we can just use one of the loadView methods that we just defined.

Editing MultipleViewsViewController.m, implement the viewDidLoad method as follows:

```
- (void)viewDidLoad {
    [self loadFirstView:nil];
    [super viewDidLoad];
}
```

By calling the loadFirstView: method upon successful loading of the view containing the toolbar, we ensure that some initial content is available for the user without them first having to press any buttons.

> Because loadFirstView is defined as requiring a parameter in its implementation, we must pass a parameter when using it here. Since the parameter (sender) is not used in the function, we can safely pass nil with no ill effects.

Clearing the Current View

Try building and executing the application again. This time, an initial view should load, but the application still won't perform correctly. You'll likely see sporadic behavior as you try to navigate between views or the views will overlay on top of one another, creating an onscreen mess. The problem is that while we're adding subviews as the toolbar button is pressed, we're never removing them again! What we need to do to stabilize the application's behavior is to identify and remove the current subview each time the toolbar button is pressed.

When a view is added to another as a subview (its superview), a property called superview is set appropriately. In other words, when firstViewController.view is added as a subview to our toolbar view, its superview property is set to the toolbar view. If a view *hasn't* been added as a subview, the property is nil. So, how can this help us? Easily: By testing to see whether the superview property is set, we can identify which view has been made active, and then remove it when it's time to switch views. To remove a view from its superview, we can use the removeFromSuperview instance method.

Add the following clearView method in MultipleViewsViewController.m as shown in Listing 14.2.

LISTING 14.2

```
-(void) clearView {
    if (firstViewController.view.superview) {
        [firstViewController.view removeFromSuperview];
    } else if (secondViewController.view.superview) {
        [secondViewController.view removeFromSuperview];
    } else {
        [thirdViewController.view removeFromSuperview];
    }
}
```

In this implementation, we test for the existence of the superview property in all of view controller's views, and if we find it, we use removeFromSuperview to remove the view.

All that remains is to add clearView so that it is called before any view is loaded. Listing 14.3 shows a completed version of the loadFirstView method.

LISTING 14.3

```
-(IBAction) loadFirstView:(id)sender {
    [self clearView];
    [self.view insertSubview:firstViewController.view atIndex:0];
}
```

Make the same change to loadSecondView and loadThirdView, and then retest your application. It should now cleanly switch between the different views when the toolbar buttons are touched, as shown in Figure 14.10.

FIGURE 14.10
Switch between
views using the
toolbar buttons.

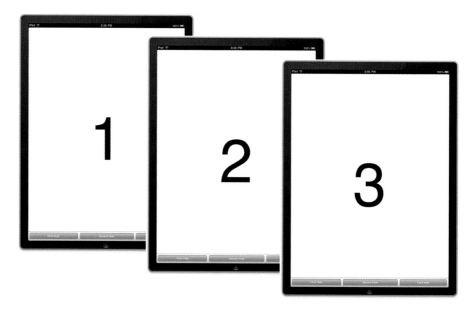

In our next project, we implement multiple views along with another new UI element: the tab bar. In this second application, however, we'll be gaining a lot of "free" functionality that simplifies the process of switching views.

Building a Multiview Tab Bar Application

As you've seen, it isn't difficult to manage multiple-view controllers, but you do need to overcome some peculiarities if you choose to implement the view switching yourself.

Often, a more expeditious approach is to use a tab bar (UITabBar) and tab bar controller (UITabBarController). This combination handles the view-switching process almost entirely on its own. You supply the views and define the interface, and it makes the magic. Tab bars are similar in appearance to toolbars, but are intended solely for switching views rather than executing arbitrary commands.

Implementation Overview

Earlier this hour, we built a simple multiview application that required us to manually insert subviews, clear the view, and deal with other "overhead" activities that would ideally be performed automatically. In this project, we create another application with three views, but this time a tab bar controller will handle switching the views for us. This frees us up to add some *real* functionality.

If you follow along, you'll create an application for calculating areas and volumes. It will also provide a summary view to show how many times the user has performed a calculation. This will help you understand how views, which are implemented largely independently, might exchange data.

The implementation itself requires you to create an instance of a tab bar and tab bar controller and, within that, instances of each of the three view controllers that we will be using for the calculations. You'll also add icons to the tab bar, giving it a professionally designed appearance. The views themselves will be in separate XIB files and will include a number of inputs and outputs. Figure 14.11 shows the application with tab bar that we'll be implementing in this example.

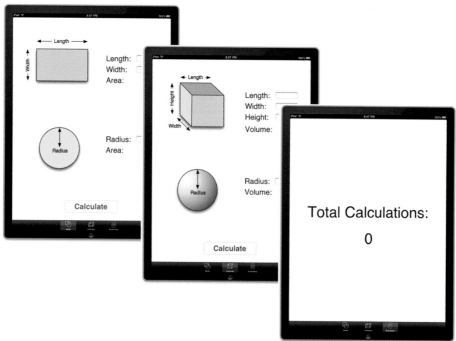

FIGURE 14.11
This application will use a tab bar to enable easy switching between calculations.

Setting Up the Project

As your applications become more complex, you'll want to start using more meaningful names for the classes and XIB files that you use in your projects. In this example, we're implementing a tab bar controller, but we're *not* using Apple's default tab bar template.

Apple's tab bar project template creates a two-view button bar with a view controller class called `FirstViewController`. The first view is contained in the

MainWindow.xib and the second in SecondView.xib. The MainView.xib also contains view controllers instances for both views.

This, frankly, doesn't make much sense. If you're going to separate your content views into multiple XIB files, it should be consistent. This template gives us a tab bar implementation that is scattered and difficult to use. Instead, we're going to start from scratch with a simple Window-based Application template.

Begin by creating a new project and choosing the Window-based iPad Application template. Name the project **TabbedCalculation**.

Adding Additional View Controllers and Views

Our new application will provide three views, each corresponding to a different functional area—calculating area, calculating volume, and displaying a calculation summary. We'll name our view controller classes and corresponding XIB files based on the functions:

- ▶ **AreaViewController/AreaView.xib**

- ▶ **VolumeViewController/VolumeView.xib**

- ▶ **SummaryViewController/SummaryView.xib**

Add the three new view controller classes (`UIViewController`) to the project—make sure that you've chosen to also add the XIB files for the new controllers.

Rename the newly created XIB files that will contain the view layouts to **AreaView**, **VolumeView**, and **SummaryView**. This will finish our initial setup for the view controller classes and XIBs, but we still need a tab bar controller object and instances of the three view controllers that will be managed by the tab bar.

Preparing the Application Delegate for the Tab Bar Controller

Open the TabbedCalculationAppDelegate.h header in Xcode. Within the @interface directive, include an instance variable (`tabBarController`) and IBOutlet for a tab bar controller (`UITabBarController`), as well as a declaration that we will conform to the `UITabBarControllerDelegate` protocol. (All the methods in this protocol are optional—meaning that we can have a fully functional tab bar without doing any additional coding!) Finally, declare `tabBarController` as a property. The final header should resemble Listing 14.4.

LISTING 14.4

```
#import <UIKit/UIKit.h>

@interface TabbedCalculationAppDelegate : NSObject
            <UIApplicationDelegate, UITabBarControllerDelegate> {
    UIWindow *window;
    IBOutlet UITabBarController *tabBarController;
}

@property (nonatomic, retain) IBOutlet UIWindow *window;
@property (nonatomic, retain) IBOutlet UITabBarController *tabBarController;

@end
```

Next, open TabbedCalculationAppDelegate.m, and add the @synthesize directive
for tabBarController to prepare our getters/setters for the property:

```
@synthesize tabBarController;
```

Update the application:DidFinishLaunchingWithOptions method to add the
view of the tabBarViewController instance to the window:

```
- (BOOL)application:(UIApplication *)application
didFinishLaunchingWithOptions:(NSDictionary *)launchOptions {

    // Override point for customization after application launch
    [window addSubview:tabBarController.view];
    [window makeKeyAndVisible];

    return YES;
}
```

Finally, make sure the tab bar controller is released in the dealloc method:

```
- (void)dealloc {
    [tabBarController release];
    [window release];
    [super dealloc];
}
```

This completes all the code additions that we need to make a tab bar controller
function and switch views! Our next step is to instantiate an instance of the controller in the MainWindow.xib file along with the view controllers it will manage.

Adding a Tab Bar Controller

Open the MainWindow.xib file in Interface Builder. Because we started with a window-based application, the file should be looking a bit sparse. We can fix that pretty
quickly. Open the Library (Tools, Library) and drag a tab bar controller
(UITabBarController) into the Document window.

Before doing anything else, Control-drag from the Tabbed Calculation App Delegate icon to the new tab bar controller. Connect the controller instance to the `tabBarController` outlet, as demonstrated in Figure 14.12.

FIGURE 14.12
Connect the controller to its outlet.

Now, double-click the tab bar controller in the Document window to preview what we're creating, and then expand the controller and the objects it contains. As you can see in Figure 14.12, Apple provides us with an initial setup for the tab bar controller. Nested in the controller is the tab bar itself (`UITabBar`), within which are two view controllers (`UIViewController`) and, within them, are tab bar items (`UITabBarItem`). In our project, we need a total of three view controllers—one for the area calculator, another for the volume calculations, and a third for a simple summary. In other words, the default controller is one view short from the three we need.

Adding New View Controllers and Tab Bar Items

We can add a new view controller to the tab bar controller in two ways. We can drag a new view controller into the tab bar instance (this will automatically create the nested tab bar item) or we can use the Attributes Inspector for the tab bar controller object. The Attributes Inspector is my preferred approach, so that's what we'll use here. Select the Tab Bar Controller icon in the Document window, and then press Command+1 to open the Attributes Inspector.

The inspector shows the different view controllers that are controlled by the tab bar, along with the titles of the individual tab bar items. To add a new controller (paired with a tab bar item), click the plus icon below the View Controllers list. This will create the third view controller instance that we need for the project. Now double-click the titles of each of the three view controllers and name them **Area**, **Volume**, and **Summary**, as shown in Figure 14.13.

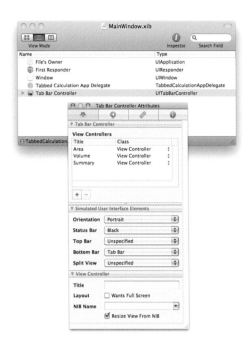

FIGURE 14.13
You can add
additional view
controller
instances along
with tab bar
items in the
Attributes
Inspector.

Adding Tab Bar Item Images

Looking at the preview of the tab bar, you can tell that something is missing—
images. Each tab bar item can have an image that is displayed along with a title.
The images are 32x32 pixels or smaller, and are automatically styled by the iPad to
appear in a monochromatic color scheme (regardless of what you choose). Simple
line drawings turn out the best when creating your interface art.

For this project, three tab bar images are included in the project's Images folder:
Area.png, Volume.png, and Summary.png. Open Xcode and drag these files to the
Resources folder for your project.

Switching back to Interface Builder and MainWindow.xib, use the Document window to drill down to the individual tab bar items. Select the first item, titled Area,
and open the Attributes Inspector (Command+1). Use the Image drop-down to
choose Area.png.

Repeat this step for the last two tab bar items, setting their images to Volume.png
and Summary.png. As the images are set, the preview should update to show the
new interface. If all is going according to plan, your display should resemble
Figure 14.14.

FIGURE 14.14
Your finished
tab bar should
have three but-
tons, complete
with images.

Within the Tab Bar Item Attributes Inspector, there is an Identifier drop-down menu. You can use this menu to configure the tab bar item to one of several different standard types, such as "favorites" or "history." This will automatically set the title and a default image for the item.

Configuring the View Controller Classes

The next step, before we start coding, is to set the view controller instances we've added to the tab bar controller so that they point to the AreaViewController, VolumeViewController, and SummaryViewController classes and their related views (AreaView, VolumeView, and SummaryView).

Select the first view controller icon in the MainWindow.xib (which should contain the Area tab bar item). Open the Identity Inspector (Command+4) and use the Class drop-down to choose AreaViewController. Without closing the inspector, switch to the attributes view (Command+1) and use the NIB Name drop-down to select the AreaView XIB. Set the view controller classes and NIBs for the other two view controller instances in the project.

Implementing the Area View

Although we haven't really written any code specific to switching views or managing view controllers, the TabbedCalculation application can be built and executed and will happily switch views using the tab bar. No need for inserting subviews or clearing views. It just works!

We can now work with our view controller classes just as we would in any other application. The tab bar controller instance will take care of swapping the views when needed. We'll start with the area calculation view.

Adding Outlets and Actions

In the area view, the application will calculate the area of a rectangle given the length and width, and the area of a circle, given the radius. We'll need UITextFields for each of these values, and two UILabel instances for the calculation results.

The view controller will need to access the instance of the SummaryViewController to increment a count of the calculations performed. It will provide calculate and hideKeyboard methods to perform the calculation and hide the input keyboard when the background is tapped, respectively. All told, we'll need six IBOutlets and two IBActions. These are the naming conventions we've used in the sample project:

  rectWidth (UITextField)—Field for entering the width of a rectangle

  rectLength (UITextField)—Field for entering the length of a rectangle

  circleRadius (UITextField)—Field for entering the radius of a circle

  rectResult (UILabel)—The calculated area of the rectangle

  circleResult (UILabel)—The calculated area of the circle

  summaryViewController (SummaryViewController)—The instance of the summary view

  calculate (method)—Performs the area calculation

  hideKeyboard (method)—Hides the onscreen keyboard

Got all that? Good! Within Xcode, open the AreaViewController.h header file and edit the contents to read as shown in Listing 14.5.

LISTING 14.5

```
1: #import <UIKit/UIKit.h>
2: #import "SummaryViewController.h"
3:
4: @interface AreaViewController : UIViewController {
5:     IBOutlet UITextField *rectWidth;
6:     IBOutlet UITextField *rectLength;
```

```
 7:     IBOutlet UITextField *circleRadius;
 8:     IBOutlet UILabel *rectResult;
 9:     IBOutlet UILabel *circleResult;
10:     IBOutlet SummaryViewController *summaryViewController;
11: }
12:
13: @property (retain, nonatomic) UITextField *rectWidth;
14: @property (retain, nonatomic) UITextField *rectLength;
15: @property (retain, nonatomic) UITextField *circleRadius;
16: @property (retain, nonatomic) UILabel *rectResult;
17: @property (retain, nonatomic) UILabel *circleResult;
18:
19: -(IBAction)calculate:(id)sender;
20: -(IBAction)hideKeyboard:(id)sender;
21:
22: @end
```

We'll need to access a method within the SummaryViewController instance, so, in line 2, we import the header for the summary class. Lines 5–10 declare the outlets for the fields, labels, and summary view controller. Lines 13–17 then declare these as properties. Finally, lines 19–20 declare two IBActions that we'll be triggering based on touch up events in the interface.

Creating the View

Based solely on the code, you should be able to get a pretty good sense for what the view is going to need like. Figure 14.15 shows the finished version of our sample AreaView.

FIGURE 14.15
Create inputs, outputs, and a calculate button!

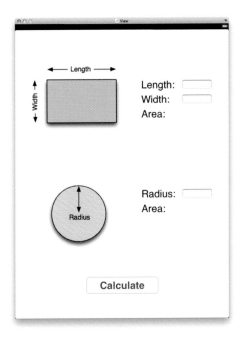

Notice that we've included two images (UIImageView) in sample application view. These serve as cues for users so that they understand what is meant by length, width, radius, and so on. (Hey, you never know!) If you want to add these to your version of the application, drag the CircleArea.png and RectArea.png files to your Xcode Resources folder. You can also add the SphereVolume.png and BoxVolume.png images, which are used in the Volume view.

Now it's your turn to build the view. Open AreaView.xib, and begin by dragging three instances of UITextField to the view. Two should be grouped together for the length and width entry for a rectangle, the third will be for the radius. After you've added the fields to the view, select each and open the Attributes Inspector (Command+1). Set the text field traits so that the keyboard is set to a number pad, as shown in Figure 14.16.

FIGURE 14.16
Because we need only numeric input, set the keyboard to be a number pad.

Drag instances of UILabel to the view and use them to label each of the fields.

The results of the area calculations need to be displayed near the entry fields, so add two additional UILabel instances to the view—one located near the fields for the rectangle, the other near the radius field. Double-click to edit and clear their contents, or set them to zero as the default. Use two more UILabels to create Area labels. Visit all the labels and fields with the Attributes Inspector (Command+1) and set a size that is appropriate for the iPad's screen.

If you'd like to add the images to the view, add two image views from the Library, positioning one beside the rectangle fields, the other beside the radius fields. Open the Attributes Inspector (Command+1) for each image view, and choose the RectArea.png or CircleArea.png images.

To finish the view, we need two buttons. Add the first button to the bottom of the view and title it **Calculate**. The second button will trap background touches and trigger the hideKeyboard method. Add a button that spans the entire background. Use the Layout menu to send it to the back, or drag its icon in the Interface Builder Document window so that it falls at the top of the View hierarchy. Open the Attributes Inspector (Command+1) for the button, and choose Custom for the button type to make the button invisible, as demonstrated in Figure 14.17.

FIGURE 14.17
Set a custom button type for the large background button.

By the Way

For a quick refresher on how we're going about hiding the keyboard, see Hour 7, "Working with Text, Keyboards, and Buttons."

When you have finished with the view layout, you'll have quite a few objects in the hierarchy. If you expand the Document window, it should resemble what we've created in Figure 14.18.

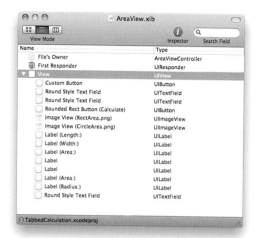

FIGURE 14.18
There are quite a few objects in the view.

Connecting Outlets and Actions

After creating an appropriate user interface for the area view, connect the objects to the instance variables that we defined earlier. Control-drag from the File's Owner icon to each of the three `UITextField` instances. When prompted, create the connection from the field to the correct variable.

Assign `rectResult` and `circleResult` by Control-dragging from the File's Owner icon to the two `UILabels` that will hold the results for the area calculations.

For the two buttons, Control-drag from the button to the File's Owner icon. Set `calculate` as the event for the calculate button, and `hideKeyboard` for the custom background button.

Implementing the Area Calculation Logic

We have our inputs, our outputs, and a trigger for the `calculate` method. Let's tie them together to finish up the area view. Switch back to Xcode and edit the AreaViewController.m file.

Although it isn't quite necessary for a project this size, defining constants for commonly used values can be helpful in creating readable code. With this in mind, define a constant, `Pi`, near the top of the file. We'll use this in the calculation of the circle's area:

```
#define Pi 3.1415926
```

Next, after the @implementation directive, synthesize the getters/setters for all the
properties defined in the header file:

```
@synthesize rectWidth;
@synthesize rectLength;
@synthesize rectResult;
@synthesize circleRadius;
@synthesize circleResult;
```

Now for the real work: implementing the calculate method. Add the method definition shown in Listing 14.6 to the class.

LISTING 14.6

```
 1: -(IBAction)calculate:(id)sender {
 2:     float floatRectResult=[rectWidth.text floatValue]*
 3:            [rectLength.text floatValue];
 4:     float floatCircleResult=[circleRadius.text floatValue]*
 5:            [circleRadius.text floatValue]*Pi;
 6:     NSString *stringRectResult=[[NSString alloc]
 7:                       initWithFormat:@"%1.2f",floatRectResult];
 8:     NSString *stringCircleResult=[[NSString alloc]
 9:                       initWithFormat:@"%1.2f",floatCircleResult];
10:     rectResult.text=stringRectResult;
11:     circleResult.text=stringCircleResult;
12:     [stringRectResult release];
13:     [stringCircleResult release];
14:
15:     [summaryViewController updateTotal];
16: }
```

We're working with the assumption that you're comfortable with the equations for
calculating the area of a rectangle (l*w) and a circle (Pi*r^2), but there are a few
pieces of the code that might be unfamiliar. Lines 2–3 and 4–5 calculate the area for
the rectangle and circle, respectively, and store the results in two new floating point
variables (floatRectResult, floatCircleResult). The calculations take advantage
of the NSString class method floatValue to provide a floating-point number from
the user's input.

By the Way

The floatValue method will return 0.0 if the user types in gibberish. This means
we'll always have a valid calculation to perform, even if the user enters bad information.

Lines 6–7 and 8–9 allocation and initialize two strings to hold the formatted results.
Using initWithFormat: and the format %1.2f to create the strings, we ensure that
there will always be at least one digit before the decimal, and two decimal places in
the result.

Lines 10–13 set the results within the view, then release the temporary strings. The last step, in line 15, uses an instance method of the SummaryViewController, updateTotal, to update the total number of calculations performed. Defining this method will be one of the last things we do this hour.

All in all, the calculation logic isn't difficult to understand. The only pieces missing are the implementation of hideKeyboard and releasing our objects in dealloc. Go ahead and define hideKeyboard as follows:

```
-(IBAction)hideKeyboard:(id)sender {
    [rectWidth resignFirstResponder];
    [rectLength resignFirstResponder];
    [circleRadius resignFirstResponder];
}
```

Wrap up the implementation of the area view controller by editing dealloc to release the objects we used:

```
- (void)dealloc {
    [rectWidth release];
    [rectLength release];
    [circleRadius release];
    [rectResult release];
    [circleResult release];
    [super dealloc];
}
```

AreaViewController and AreaView are complete. Building the volume view and view controller will follow a very similar process, so we'll move quickly through the next section.

Implementing the Volume View

In the volume view, the application will accept input for the dimensions of a box (length, width, height) and a sphere (radius), and calculate the volume of the object based on these values. The interface elements will be largely identical to the area view, but will require an additional field (height) for the box calculation. Begin the implementation by editing the VolumeViewController header.

Adding Outlets and Actions

With the exception of some terminology changes required by our switch from 2D to 3D, the outlets and actions that will be required in the volume view should be very familiar:

boxWidth (UITextField)—Field for entering the width of a box

boxLength (UITextField)—Field for entering the length of a box

boxHeight (UITextField)—Field for entering the height of a box sphereRadius (UITextField)—Field for entering the radius of a sphere

boxResult (UILabel)—The calculated area of the rectangle

sphereResult (UILabel)—The calculated area of the circle

summaryViewController (SummaryViewController)—The instance of the summary view

calculate (method)—Performs the area calculation

hideKeyboard (method)—Hides the onscreen keyboard

Edit the VolumeViewController.h file to include the necessary outlets and actions for the view. When you finish, your code should look like Listing 14.7.

LISTING 14.7

```
 1: #import <UIKit/UIKit.h>
 2: #import "SummaryViewController.h"
 3:
 4: @interface VolumeViewController : UIViewController {
 5:     IBOutlet UITextField *boxWidth;
 6:     IBOutlet UITextField *boxHeight;
 7:     IBOutlet UITextField *boxLength;
 8:     IBOutlet UITextField *sphereRadius;
 9:     IBOutlet UILabel *boxResult;
10:     IBOutlet UILabel *sphereResult;
11:     IBOutlet SummaryViewController *summaryViewController;
12: }
13:
14: @property (retain, nonatomic) UITextField *boxWidth;
15: @property (retain, nonatomic) UITextField *boxHeight;
16: @property (retain, nonatomic) UITextField *boxLength;
17: @property (retain, nonatomic) UITextField *sphereRadius;
18: @property (retain, nonatomic) UILabel *boxResult;
19: @property (retain, nonatomic) UILabel *sphereResult;
20:
21: -(IBAction)calculate:(id)sender;
22: -(IBAction)hideKeyboard:(id)sender;
23:
24: @end
```

Because of the similarity to the area view, we won't go into detail on the individual lines. Let's move on to the VolumeView itself.

Creating the View

Like the layout of the area view, the volume view will collect data, provide the user with a calculate button, and of course, display the results. Figure 14.19 shows our finished version of the view.

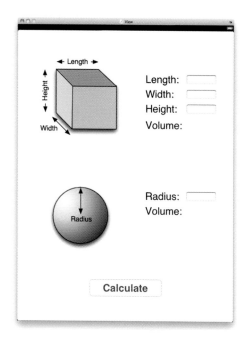

FIGURE 14.19
Once again, collect data, calculate, and provide the results!

> The volume view includes images to help users identify the values that they will need to enter. If you didn't drag the SphereVolume.png and BoxVolume.png images to your Xcode resources when building the area view, this would be a good time to add them!

By the Way

Open VolumeView.xib in Interface Builder and drag four text fields to the view. For the volume calculations, three fields should be grouped for length, width, and height of the box. A single field is all that is required for the sphere. Be sure to set the field attributes so that the keyboard displayed is a number pad. Add labels to the view to identify each of the fields for the user.

Position two additional UILabel instances below the box/sphere input fields—these will be used for the output of the calculations. Be sure to clear the default contents of these labels, or set them to 0. Using the Attributes Inspector (Command+1), size all the labels and fields to a size that is appropriate for the iPad's screen.

To add the images, drag to image views from the Library to the view. Set the contents of the image views by opening the Attributes Inspector (Command+1) for each view and choosing the BoxVolume.png or SphereVolume.png images.

Finish the view by adding two buttons: the Calculate button at the bottom of the view, and the invisible button used to hide the keyboard. Remember to expand the "hide keyboard" button to fill the view, and send it to the back. Open the Attributes Inspector (Command+1) for the button, and choose Custom for the button type to make the button invisible.

Connecting Outlets and Actions

Connect the fields, labels, and buttons in Interface Builder to the appropriate outlets that you created in the VolumeViewController.h file. Control-drag from the File's Owner icon in the Document window to each of the input fields and output labels; choose the appropriate outlet when prompted.

To connect the button controls to the actions, Control-drag from the two UIButton instances to the File's Owner, choosing the fitting calculate and hideKeyboard method when prompted.

Implementing the Volume Calculation Logic

Switch back to Xcode and edit the VolumeViewController.m file. As before, define the Pi constant at the top of the file:

```
#define Pi 3.1415926
```

Next, use the @synthesize directive to create the getters and setters after the @implementation directive:

```
@synthesize boxWidth;
@synthesize boxHeight;
@synthesize boxLength;
@synthesize sphereRadius;
@synthesize boxResult;
@synthesize sphereResult;
```

Create and edit the calculate method to determine the volume of the two shapes. For the box, this is length*width*height, and for the sphere, 4/3*Pi*R^3. Use the results to populate the boxResult and sphereResult labels in the view. Our implementation of this method is provided in Listing 14.8.

LISTING 14.8

```
-(IBAction)calculate:(id)sender {
    float floatBoxResult=[boxWidth.text floatValue]*
                        [boxLength.text floatValue]*[boxHeight.text floatValue];
    float floatSphereResult=(4/3)*Pi*[sphereRadius.text floatValue]*
         [sphereRadius.text floatValue]*[sphereRadius.text floatValue];
    NSString *stringBoxResult=[[NSString alloc]
                        initWithFormat:@"%1.2f",floatBoxResult];
    NSString *stringSphereResult=[[NSString alloc]
                        initWithFormat:@"%1.2f",floatSphereResult];
    boxResult.text=stringBoxResult;
    sphereResult.text=stringSphereResult;
```

```
    [stringBoxResult release];
    [stringSphereResult release];

    [summaryViewController updateTotal];
}
```

Because only the logic for the calculations has changed, you should refer to the area view calculation for detailed description of the methods used here.

By the Way

Add the hideKeyboard method so that the user can dismiss the onscreen keyboard by touching the background of the view:

```
-(IBAction)hideKeyboard:(id)sender {
    [boxWidth resignFirstResponder];
    [boxLength resignFirstResponder];
    [boxHeight resignFirstResponder];
    [sphereRadius resignFirstResponder];
}
```

Lastly, release the objects in the dealloc method:

```
- (void)dealloc {
    [boxWidth release];
    [boxHeight release];
    [boxLength release];
    [sphereRadius release];
    [boxResult release];
    [sphereResult release];
    [super dealloc];
}
```

Implementing the Summary View

Of all the views, the summary view is the easiest to implement. This view will provide a single count of the number of calculations performed, as determined by the number of times the calculate button is pressed. Just a single outlet and a single counter—no problem!

Adding the IBOutlet, Instance Variable, and Method

The SummaryViewController class will need a single outlet, totalCalculations, that will be connected to a UILabel in the summary view and used to display the calculation summary to the user. It will also use a single integer value, calcCount, to internally track the number of calculations performed.

Finally, the class will implement an instance method updateTotal that will update the calcCount value. Edit the SummaryViewController.h file to include these requirements, as demonstrated in Listing 14.9.

LISTING 14.9

```
#import <UIKit/UIKit.h>

@interface SummaryViewController : UIViewController {
    IBOutlet UILabel *totalCalculations;
    int calcCount;
}

@property (retain, nonatomic) UILabel *totalCalculations;

-(void) updateTotal;

@end
```

Creating the View and Connecting the Outlet

To create the summary view, open the SummaryView.xib file in Interface Builder. As promised, this view is extremely easy to set up. Drag a UILabel object to the view. This will serve as the output of the total calculation count, so set the default text of the label to 0.

Finish the view by adding another label with the text **Total Calculations:** positioned above or beside the output label. The result should be similar to the view pictured in Figure 14.20.

FIGURE 14.20
Add one label for the output value and one to serve as a description.

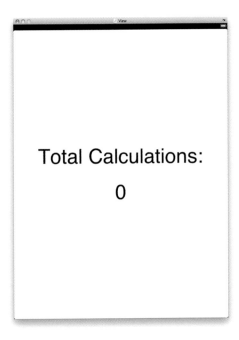

Total Calculations:

0

Connect the output label to the `totalCalculations` outlet by Control-dragging from the File's Owner icon to the `UILabel` instance within the Interface Builder document view.

Connecting the Area, Volume, and Summary Views

If you recall, the previous two views call the `updateTotal` method of the summary view. For these views to have access to the `summaryViewController` instance variable, we must create two additional connections—this time in the MainWindow.xib file.

Open the MainWindow.xib Document window and expand the Tab Bar Controller hierarchy. Control-drag from the area view controller instance to the summary view. Choose the `summaryViewController` outlet, as demonstrated in Figure 14.21.

FIGURE 14.21
Connect the summary view controller to the area and volume view controllers.

Repeat this for the volume view controller. The area and volume view controllers will now be able to successfully call the `updateTotal` method.

Implementing the Volume Calculation Logic

All that remains for the TabbedCalculation project is implementing the logic to track the calculation total and update the summary view. Let's open the SummaryViewController.m file and wrap this up! First use the `@synthesize` directive to create the getter/setter for the `totalCalculations` UILabel:

```
@synthesize totalCalculations;
```

Next, add the `updateTotal` method so that it will increment the `calcCount` variable when invoked:

```
-(void) updateTotal {
    calcCount++;
}
```

Now, the tough part. Notice that we don't display the new total in the `updateTotal` method? The reason for this is that until the view is displayed, there aren't any `UILabel` values to update, so if we try to update before the view is shown, the count will be wrong. Subsequent views *would* work, but initially the displayed result would be incorrect.

So, how do we get around this? The easiest way is to only update the view just before it is displayed onscreen. At that point in time, we have access to all the objects, so everything will be copacetic. Overriding the `viewWillAppear:` method will provide us with the right hook into the display process. Implement the `viewWillAppear:` method as follows:

```
- (void)viewWillAppear:(BOOL)animated {
    NSString *calcResult=[[NSString alloc] initWithFormat:@"%d",calcCount];
    totalCalculations.text=calcResult;
    [calcResult release];
    [super viewWillAppear:animated];
}
```

Nothing here should be a surprise. We format a temporary string using the `calcCount` variable, set the `totalCalcuations` (`UILabel`) "text" property to the string, release the string, and pass the method invocation up the chain.

The code isn't finished until the objects are released, so edit the `dealloc` method to release `totalCalculations`:

```
- (void)dealloc {
    [totalCalculations release];
    [super dealloc];
}
```

Congratulations! You just completed a tab bar-based multiview application with basic inter-view communication. Your experience working with multiple views will open up a whole new range of applications that you can develop.

Further Exploration

By now, you should have a good idea of how to implement multiple views and switch between them either manually or view a tab bar controller. There was quite a bit of information covered in this hour, so I recommend reviewing the topics that we covered and spending some time in the Apple documentation reviewing the classes, the properties, and their methods. Inspecting the UI elements in Interface Builder will give you additional insight into how they can be integrated into your apps.

The toolbar (`UIToolbar`), for example, can be customized with image-based buttons rather than the round rectangles we used in the example. Apple provides a wide range of standard toolbar images/buttons covering everything from audio/video playback controls to a camera button for starting the built-in camera. If you have a set of actions that the user should be able to choose from within a view, implementing these with a toolbar will keep your screen free from clutter, and provide a convenient UI anchor that can be updated from view to view, or used across multiple views (as demonstrated in the first example).

The tab bar controller (`UITabBarController`) also offers additional features beyond what was covered here. If there are too many buttons to be displayed in a single tab bar, for example, the tab bar controller provides its own "more" view in the form of a navigation controller (which you learn about in the next hour). This gives you the ability to expand the user's options beyond the buttons immediately visible onscreen. The `UITabBarControllerDelegate` protocol, which we conformed to, and the `UITabBarDelegate` can even implement optional methods to enable the user to customize the tab bar within the application. You can see this level of functionality within Apple's iPod application.

Another area that you will eventually want to review is the loading of multiple views/view controllers. In these projects, the view controllers were instantiated when the application was loaded. In small apps, this is fine, but in larger projects with more complex views, this can add to the load time and potentially uses memory for views that user may never select. To get around this, we can programmatically instantiate a view controller.

Apple Tutorials

The following Apple Tutorials can help demonstrate the concepts discussed in this hour's lesson. You can access them through the Xcode developer documentation:

MoviePlayer (accessible via the Xcode developer documentation): This example demonstrates a complex multiview interface including a tab bar controller.

AccelerometerGraph (accessible via the Xcode developer documentation): A simple example that uses a toolbar to choose between multiple functions within an application.

Summary

In this hour, you learned how to create applications that extend beyond a single view and view controller. This will ultimately enable you to create more involved and meaningful user experiences. You also made use of the toolbar UI element (UIToolbar) to provide a simple button bar for common user activities within a view.

After creating a multiview application from scratch, we examined how a tab bar controller (UITabBarController) can handle much of the behind-the-scenes work of switching between parallel views automatically. With so much time freed up by the tab bar, we were able to implement a multiview calculator application that included a tab bar with images, multiple independent user interfaces, and inter-view communications.

Q&A

Q. *Why can't a single view (with appropriate hiding and showing of elements) do the same thing as multiple views?*

A. Technically, you could accomplish the same thing within a single view, but the complexity of maintaining your views, even with the drag-and-drop capabilities of Interface Builder will quickly become overwhelming in more advanced applications.

Q. *Can tab bar be used for the same purpose as a toolbar?*

A. No. A tab bar should always be used to switch between similar views. This is its intended purpose within the Apple UI guidelines. A toolbar, however, can serve a more general role and be used to trigger any number of events that are relevant to the current state of the application.

Workshop

Quiz

1. How many methods of the UITabBarControllerDelegate protocol are required to implement to gain the view-switching functionality?

2. What image should you use in a toolbar for a "rewind" control?

3. What is one way that you can implement communications between multiple view controllers?

Answers

1. None! All the `UITabBarControllerDelegate` protocol methods are optional.

2. Apple provides preset buttons for *many* common application activities. Just add a button bar item (`UIButtonBarItem`) and use the Interface Builder Attributes Inspector to set the identifier.

3. View controllers, like any other objects, can communicate if you add the appropriate `IBOutlets` and define the connections in Interface Builder.

Activities

1. Update the TabbedCalculation application so that the area and volume views share user input data. In other words, when a user enters length, width, or radius in the area view, the corresponding fields should be updated in the volume view.

2. Create a new tab bar application using the provided Apple template. As mentioned earlier, this template seems to be at odds with itself in terms of the intended development direction. Even so, you can probably save yourself a few keystrokes if you learn to work around the initial configuration.

HOUR 15

Navigating Information Using Table Views and Split View-Based Applications

What You'll Learn in This Hour:

▶ The types of table views

▶ How to implement a simple table view and controller

▶ Ways of adding more structure and impact to a table with sections and cell images

▶ How to use a Split View-based Application template

So far, our exploration of iPad development has included typical interface elements—fields, buttons, dialog boxes, views, and of course, a variety of output mechanisms. However, what's missing is the ability to present categorized information in a structured manner. Everywhere you look (websites, books, applications on your computer), you see methods for displaying information in an attractive and orderly manner. The iPad has its own conventions for displaying this type of information.

First, the table view. This UI element is essentially a categorized list, like what you see when browsing your iPad contacts. Second, the iPad provides a SplitViewController object that combines tables, popovers, and a detail view into an experience very similar to using Apple's iPad Mail. In this hour, we explore how to implement a table view, and then how to take that knowledge and apply it to a Split View-based Application template.

Understanding Table Views and Split Views

Let's begin by understanding what table views are, how they are used, and how they apply to the split view-based application template. This hour introduces new information while building on the past few hours' lessons.

Tables

Like the other views you've seen in this book, a table view (`UITable`) holds information. A table view's appearance, however, is slightly counterintuitive. Instead of showing up as a true table (like an Excel worksheet), a table view displays a single list of cells onscreen. Each cell can be structured to contain multiple pieces of information, but is still a single unit. In addition, the cells can be broken into sections so that the clusters of information can be communicated visually. You might, for example, list computer models by manufacturers, or models of the Macintosh by year. Table views respond to touch events and enable the user to easily scroll up and down through long lists of information and select individual cells through the help of a table view controller (`UITableViewController`)

Types of Tables

There are two basic styles of table views: plain and grouped, as demonstrated in Figure 14.1 and Figure 14.2, respectively. Plain tables lack the clear visual separation of sections of the grouped tables, but are frequently implemented with a touchable index (like the iPad contact list). Because of this, they are sometimes called indexed tables. This text will continue to refer to them by the names (plain/grouped) designated in Interface Builder. For the most part, the appearance of tables is configured in code, but a table's style can also be set in Interface Builder.

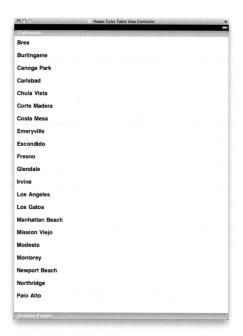

FIGURE 15.1
Plain tables look like simple lists.

FIGURE 15.2
Grouped tables have emphasized sections.

Split View-Based Applications

The second interface element that we'll be working with this hour isn't exactly an "element," per se; it's an entire application interface called the Split View-based Application template. The Split View-based Application template pulls together tables, popovers, and views. It works like this: In landscape mode, a table is displayed on the left, and a detail area on the right. When an element from the table is selected, the detail area shows (guess what) details about the selection. If the iPad is rotated to a portrait mode, the table disappears, and the detail fills the screen. To navigate between different items, the user can touch a toolbar button to display a popover with the table. This approach gives the user the flexibility to easily navigate a large amount of information and focus on a single item, if desired.

The Split View-based Application template is widely used on the iPad in both Apple and third-party applications. Mail, for example, uses a split interface for showing the list of messages and the content of a selected message. Popular file management apps, like Dropbox, show a list of files on the left and the content of the selected file in the detail view, as shown in Figure 15.3.

FIGURE 15.3
The Dropbox file management app.

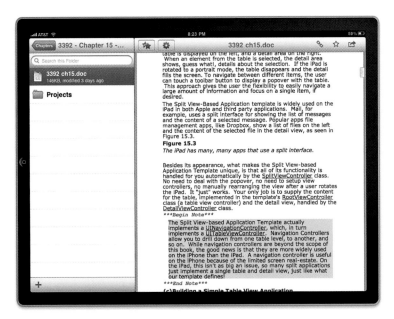

The iPad has many, many apps that use a split interface. Besides its appearance, what makes the Split View-based Application template unique is that all of its functionality is handled for you automatically by the `SplitViewController` class. No need to deal with the popover, no need to set up view controllers, no manually rearranging the view after a user rotates the iPad. It just works. Your only job is to supply the content for the table, implemented in the template's `RootViewController` class (a table view controller) and the detail view, handled by the `DetailViewController` class.

The Split View-based Application template actually implements a `UINavigationController`, which, in turn implements a `UITableViewController`. Navigation controllers allow you to drill down from one table level to another and so on. Although navigation controllers are beyond the scope of this book, the good news is that they are more widely used on the iPhone than the iPad. A navigation controller is useful on the iPhone because of the limited screen real estate. On the iPad, this isn't as big an issue, and therefore many split applications just implement a single table and detail view, just like what our template defines!

By the Way

Building a Simple Table View Application

To begin this hour's tutorials, we'll create a table that lists the names of flowers under a heading that describes their colors. When the user touches an entry in the table, an alert will appear showing chosen flower name and color. The final application will look similar to Figure 15.4.

FIGURE 15.4
In our first application, we'll create a table that can react to a user's interactions.

Implementation Overview

The skills needed to add table views to your projects are very similar to what you learned when working with pickers in Hour 12, "Making Multivalue Choices with Pickers and Action Sheets." A table view is created by an instance of UITableView and classes that implement the UITableViewDataSource and UITableViewDelegate protocols to provide the data that the table will display. Specifically, the data source needs to provide information on the number of sections in the table and the number of rows in each section. The delegate handles creating the cells within the table and reacting to the user's selection.

Unlike the picker, where we implemented the required protocols within a standard UIViewController, we'll be creating an instance of UITableViewController, which conforms to both of the needed protocols. This simplifies our development and keeps things as streamlined as possible. In a large project with complex data needs, you may want to create one or more new classes specifically for handling the data.

Preparing the Project

Begin by creating a new Xcode project named **FlowerColorTable** using the Window-based iPad Application template.

We will need a new subclass of the UITableViewController class to the project to handle interactions with our table view. To add the new class, complete the following steps:

1. Create a new file in Xcode (File, New).

2. Within the New File dialog box, select Cocoa Touch Class, UIViewController subclass, and then check the UITableViewController Subclass and Targeted for iPad check boxes, as shown in Figure 15.5. Note that because we'll be generating the content of table view programmatically, we don't need a separate XIB file.

3. Click Next.

4. Type **FlowerColorTableViewController.m** as the filename, and be sure that Also Create FlowerColorTableViewController.h is selected.

5. Finally, click the Finish button. The new subclass will be added to your project.

FIGURE 15.5
Create the files for implementing a new subclass of UITableView-Controller.

The FlowerColorTableViewController.m will include all the method stubs you need to get your table up and running quickly. In a few minutes, we'll add an instance of this new table view controller subclass to the MainWindow.xib file. This will create an instance of the FlowerColorTableViewController when the application launches.

Adding Outlets

Before we can make our connections in Interface Builder, we need to create an outlet for the application delegate to access the FlowerColorTableViewController that we're adding to the system.

Edit FlowerColorTableAppDelegate.h and add a line that imports the FlowerColorTableViewController interface file. Also, add an outlet for the instance of FlowerViewController that we will be creating; we'll call it **flowerColorTableViewController** for consistency.

Why do we import the FlowerColorTableViewController.h file? If we didn't, Xcode wouldn't "know" what a FlowerColorTableViewController is, and we wouldn't be able to declare an instance of it.

The FlowerColorTableAppDelegate.h code should read as shown in Listing 15.1.

LISTING 15.1

```
 1: #import <UIKit/UIKit.h>
 2: #import "FlowerColorTableViewController.h";
 3:
 4: @interface FlowerColorTableAppDelegate : NSObject <UIApplicationDelegate> {
 5: IBOutlet FlowerColorTableViewController *flowerColorTableViewController;
 6:     UIWindow *window;
 7: }
 8:
 9: @property (nonatomic, retain) IBOutlet UIWindow *window;
10:
11: @end
```

Lines 2 and 5 are the only additions to the app delegate interface file.

Adding the View

Once the view controller has been instantiated, it will need to add its subview to the application window. Make these implementation changes within the `FlowerColorTableAppDelegate` class.

Start by editing `application:didFinishLaunchingWithOptions`, using the `addSubview` method to add the following:

```
- (BOOL)application:(UIApplication *)application
 didFinishLaunchingWithOptions:(NSDictionary *)launchOptions {

    // Override point for customization after application launch
    [window addSubview:flowerColorTableViewController.view];
    [window makeKeyAndVisible];

    return YES;
}
```

Next, release the table view controller (`flowerColorTableViewController`) when the application is finished. Edit the `dealloc` method to read as follows:

```
- (void)dealloc {
    [flowerColorTableViewController release];
    [window release];
    [super dealloc];
}
```

Although we've already added references to a table view controller (`flowerColorTableViewController`) in our code, we haven't created the object yet. It's time to open Interface Builder and add an instance of our class.

Adding a Table View and Table View Controller Instance

Double-click the MainWindow.xib file to open it within Interface Builder. Open the
Library, and drag the Table View Controller icon into the MainWindow.xib file.
Double-click the Table View Controller within the Interface Builder Document win-
dow (Window, Documents) to show what a sample UITable looks like in Interface
Builder. Click and drag on the corners of the table so that it is expanded to fill the
full iPad screen, as shown in Figure 15.6.

FIGURE 15.6
Expand the
table to fill the
iPad's screen.

Okay, so we've added an instance of UITableViewController to the project, but
that's not quite what we need. The FlowerColorTableViewController class is our
subclass of UITableViewController, so that's what we want to instantiate and use
in the application.

The UITableViewController instance that you just added includes an instance
of a table view (UITableView), so this is the only object needed in Interface
Builder.

Select the Table View Controller icon in the XIB file, and open the Identity Inspector
(Command+4). Edit the class identity to read **FlowerColorTableViewController**,
as shown in Figure 15.7.

FIGURE 15.7
Update the class identity to FlowerColor TableView Controller within the Identity Inspector.

The application will now instantiate our table view controller when it launches, but the controller still isn't connected to anything. To connect to the `flowerColorTableViewController` outlet created earlier, Control-drag from Flower Color Table App Delegate to the Flower Color Table View Controller icon. When the Outlets pop-up window appears, choose `flowerColorTableViewController` (see Figure 15.8).

FIGURE 15.8
Connect the application delegate to the `flowerColor-TableView Controller`.

All the connections are in place for the table view controller and a table view. Switch back to Xcode, and click Build and Go to test the application. An empty table will appear. It's empty, but it's a table! Next step? Data!

Providing Data to the Table View

With all the structural work out of the way, the table is ready to display something. As mentioned earlier, implementing the required methods for the `UITableViewDataSource` and `UITableViewDelegate` protocols is very similar to creating a picker. For this example, we're going to create a table that lists flowers divided into sections by color.

Creating Sample Data

To keep things simple, we'll only consider two colors: red and blue. We'll populate two arrays (`redFlowers`, `blueFlowers`) with a few appropriate flower names.

Begin by updating FlowerColorTableViewController.h to include the two `NSMutableArrays` we'll be using:

```
@interface FlowerColorTableViewController : UITableViewController {
    NSMutableArray *redFlowers;
    NSMutableArray *blueFlowers;
}
```

Turning to the implementation in FlowerColorTableViewController.m, find the `viewDidLoad` method and uncomment it. We will implement this method so that we have a convenient place to populate the arrays. Add the code in Listing 15.2 to initialize of the `redFlowers` and `blueFlowers` arrays with several flowers in each.

LISTING 15.2

```
- (void)viewDidLoad {
    [super viewDidLoad];
    redFlowers = [[NSMutableArray alloc]
                initWithObjects:@"Gerbera",@"Peony",@"Rose"
                ,@"Poppy",@"Tulip",@"Anthurium",@"Anemone",nil];
    blueFlowers = [[NSMutableArray alloc]
                initWithObjects:@"Hyacinth",@"Hydrangea"
                ,@"Sea Holly",@"Phlox",@"Iris",@"Bluebell"
                ,@"Cyanus",nil];
}
```

As always, make sure that you release the two arrays when finished. Edit the `dealloc` method to read as follows:

```
- (void)dealloc {
    [redFlowers release];
    [blueFlowers release];
    [super dealloc];
}
```

As a last step, add constants that we can use to refer to our color sections. At the top of FlowerColorTableViewController.m, enter the following constant definitions:

```
#define sectionCount 2
#define redSection 0
#define blueSection 1
```

The first constant, sectionCount, is the number of sections that will be displayed in the table. Because we're implementing red and blue flower lists, this value is 2. The next constant, redSection, denotes that the listing of red flowers in the table will be shown first (section 0), while the third and final constant, blueSection, identifies that the blue section of flowers will appear second (section 1).

Implementing the Table View Controller Data Source Methods

Our application now has the data it needs to create a table, but it doesn't yet "understand" how to get that data into the table view itself. Thankfully, the methods that a table requires to display information are easy to understand, and more important, easy to implement. Because this example includes sections (red and blue), we need to include these three methods in FlowerColorViewController.m as part of the UITableViewDataSource protocol:

> numberofSectionsInTableView:—Returns the number of sections within a given table.

> tableView:tableViewnumberOfRowsInSection:—Returns the number of rows in a section.

> tableView:titleForHeaderInSection:—Returns a string to be used as the title for a given section number.

The number of sections has already been defined in the constant sectionCount, so implementing the first method requires nothing more than returning this constant. Add this code to FlowerColorViewController.m:

```
- (NSInteger)numberOfSectionsInTableView:(UITableView *)tableView
{
    return sectionCount;
}
```

The second method requires us to return the number of rows (cells) that will be displayed in a given section. Because the rows in each section will be filled with the strings in the redFlowers and blueFlowers arrays, we can return the count of elements in each array using the array count method.

Use a switch statement along with the redSection and blueSection constants that were defined earlier to return the appropriate counts for each of the two arrays. The final implementation is shown in Listing 15.3. Be sure to add this to FlowerColorViewController.m.

LISTING 15.3

```
- (NSInteger)tableView:(UITableView *)tableView
            numberOfRowsInSection:(NSInteger)section
{
    switch (section) {
        case redSection:
            return [redFlowers count];
        case blueSection:
            return [blueFlowers count];
        default:
            return 0;
    }
}
```

> Even though it is impossible for our application to reach a section other than red or blue, it is still good practice to provide a default case to the switch statement. This ensures that even if we haven't properly identified all of our potential cases, it will still be caught by the default case.

By the Way

For the third data source method, `tableView:titleForHeaderInSection`, you can turn again to the defined constants and a switch statement to very easily return an appropriate string for a given section number. Implement the method as shown in Listing 15.4.

LISTING 15.4

```
- (NSString *)tableView:(UITableView *)tableView
            titleForHeaderInSection:(NSInteger)section {
    switch (section) {
        case redSection:
            return @"Red";
        case blueSection:
            return @"Blue";
        default:
            return @"Unknown";
    }
}
```

That wraps up what needs to be provided to satisfy the `UITableViewDataSource` protocol. However, as you've seen, these methods don't provide the actual data that will be visible in the table cells.

Populating the Cells

At long last, we've reached the method that actually make our table display something! These `tableView:cellForRowAtIndexPath` will do the "heavy lifting" in the application. This single method, which needs to implemented within your table view controller, returns a cell (`UITableViewCell`) object for a given table section and row.

> The methods required for working with table views frequently use an NSIndexPath object to communicate row and section information. When dealing with an incoming NSIndexPath object in your table methods, you can use the accessors IndexPath.section and IndexPath.row to get to the current section and row.

To implement the tableView:cellForRowAtIndexPath method properly, we must create and return a properly formatted UITableViewCell.

What makes this process interesting is that as cells move on and off the screen, we don't want to keep releasing and reallocating memory. We also don't want to allocate memory for every single cell that the table could display. So, what's the alternative? To reuse cells that are no longer needed to generate the current display. The good news is that Apple has already set up methods and a process for this to occur automatically.

Take a close look at the method stub for tableView:cellForRowIndexPath (specifically, the following snippet):

```
UITableViewCell *cell = (UITableViewCell*)[tableView
                        dequeueReusableCellWithIdentifier:CellIdentifier];
    if(cell == nil)
    {
        cell = [[[UITableViewCell alloc]
                initWithFrame:CGRectZero
                reuseIdentifier:CellIdentifier] autorelease];
    }
```

This code attempts to use the dequeueReusableCellWithIdentifier UITableView method to find a cell that has already been allocated but that is ready to be reused. In the event that an appropriate cell can't be found (such as the first time the table view loads its cells), a new cell is allocated and initialized. You shouldn't have any reason to change this prewritten logic for most table-based applications.

After a cell object has been appropriately allocated, the method must format the cell for the indexPath object provided. In other words, we must make sure that for whatever section is specified in indexPath.section and whatever row is passed in indexPath.row, the cell object is given the necessary label.

To set a cell's label to a given string, first use textLabel to return the UILabel object for the cell, then the setText method to update the label. For example:

```
[[cell textLabel]setText: @"My Cell Label"]
```

Because we don't want to set a static string for the cell labels and our labels are stored in arrays, we need to retrieve the appropriate label string from the array, and then pass it to setText. Remember that the individual cell row that we need to return will be provided by `indexPath.row`, so we can use that to index into our array. To retrieve the current text label for a member of the `redFlowers` array, we can use the following:

```
[redFlowers objectAtIndex:indexPath.row]
```

These two lines can be combined into a single statement that sets the cell label text to the current row of the `redFlowers` array:

```
[[cell textLabel] setText:[redFlowers objectAtIndex:indexPath.row]]
```

This is good, but not quite the solution to all our problems. We need to account for both the `redFlowers` and `blueFlowers` arrays and display each within the appropriate section. Once again, we'll turn to the `switch` statement to make this happen, this time using `indexPath.section` to determine whether the cell should be set to a member of the `redFlowers` array or the `blueFlowers` array.

Your final code, shown in Listing 15.5, should be an addition to the existing `tableView:cellForRowAtIndexPath` method stub.

LISTING 15.5

```
 1: - (UITableViewCell *)tableView:(UITableView *)tableView
 2:          cellForRowAtIndexPath:(NSIndexPath *)indexPath
 3: {
 4:      static NSString *CellIdentifier = @"Cell";
 5:
 6:      UITableViewCell *cell = (UITableViewCell*)[tableView
 7:          dequeueReusableCellWithIdentifier:CellIdentifier];
 8:      if(cell == nil)
 9:      {
10:          cell = [[[UITableViewCell alloc]
11:                  initWithFrame:CGRectZero
12:                  reuseIdentifier:CellIdentifier] autorelease];
13:      }
14:
15:      switch (indexPath.section) {
16:          case redSection:
17:              [[cell textLabel]
18:               setText:[redFlowers objectAtIndex:indexPath.row]];
19:              break;
20:          case blueSection:
21:              [[cell textLabel]
22:               setText:[blueFlowers objectAtIndex:indexPath.row]];
23:              break;
24:          default:
25:              [[cell textLabel]
26:               setText:@"Unknown"];
27:      }
28:      return cell;
29: }
```

The moment you've been waiting for has arrived! You should now be able to launch your application and view the result. Congratulations, you've just implemented a table view from scratch!

Reacting to a Row Touch Event

A table that displays information is all fine and dandy, but it would be nice if the user had a means of interacting with it. Unlike other UI elements where we'd need to define an action and make connections in Interface Builders, we can add some basic interactivity to the FlowerColorTable application by implementing a method from the UITableViewDelegate - tableView:didSelectRowAtIndexPath. This method is called when a table row has been touched by the user. The key to identifying the specific row and section that was selected is indexPath, an instance of NSIndexPath.

How you react to a row selection event is up to you. For the sake of this example, we're going to use UIAlertView to display a message. The implementation, shown in Listing 15.6, should look very familiar by this point. Add this delegate method to the FlowerColorTableViewController.m file.

LISTING 15.6

```
 1: - (void)tableView:(UITableView *)tableView
 2:         didSelectRowAtIndexPath:(NSIndexPath *)indexPath {
 3:     UIAlertView *showSelection;
 4:     NSString    *flowerMessage;
 5:     switch (indexPath.section) {
 6:         case redSection:
 7:             flowerMessage=[[NSString alloc]
 8:                         initWithFormat:
 9:                         @"You chose the red flower - %@",
10:                         [redFlowers objectAtIndex: indexPath.row]];
11:             break;
12:         case blueSection:
13:             flowerMessage=[[NSString alloc]
14:                         initWithFormat:
15:                         @"You chose the blue flower - %@",
16:                         [blueFlowers objectAtIndex: indexPath.row]];
17:             break;
18:         default:
19:             flowerMessage=[[NSString alloc]
20:                         initWithFormat:
21:                         @"I have no idea what you chose!?"];
22:             break;
23:     }
24:
25:     showSelection = [[UIAlertView alloc]
26:                     initWithTitle: @"Flower Selected"
27:                     message:flowerMessage
28:                     delegate: nil
29:                     cancelButtonTitle: @"Ok"
```

```
30:                        otherButtonTitles: nil];
31:     [showSelection show];
32:     [showSelection release];
33:     [flowerMessage release];
34: }
```

Lines 3 and 4 declare `flowerMessage` and `showSelection` variables that will be used for the message string shown to the user and the `UIAlertView` instance that will display the message, respectively.

Lines 5–23 use a `switch` statement with `indexPath.section` to determine which flower array our selection comes from and the `indexPath.row` value to identify the specific element of the array that was chosen. A string (`flowerMessage`) is allocated and formatted to contain the value of the selection.

Lines 25–31 create and display an alert view instance (`showSelection`) containing the message string (`flowerMessage`).

Lines 32–33 release the instance of the alert view and the message string.

After implementing this function, build and test the application again. Touch a row and review the result. The application will now display an alert box with the results of your selection, as shown in Figure 15.9.

FIGURE 15.9
The application now reacts to row selection and identifies the item that was selected.

Fine-Tuning the Table Appearance

Most of the customization of a table's appearance happens through code (we'll be seeing a bit more of this in the next tutorial), but a few tweaks can be made in Interface Builder. If you followed the steps exactly, for example, your table will have a slightly different appearance, with less line spacing and the "plain" table styling.

Changing the Row Size

To update the height of the rows in the table, open the MainWindow.xib file, and then open the Document window. Select the Table View within the Flower Color Table View Controller and open the Attributes Inspector. Press Command+3 to open the Size Inspector window. Update the row height size to at least 75 (pixels), as shown in Figure 15.10. You can also choose to update the header and footer spacing.

FIGURE 15.10
Update the row height to loosen the table spacing.

Setting the Table Style

To switch to a Grouped table appearance, again select the table view, and then open the Attributes Inspector (Command+1). Use the Style drop-down menu to switch between the Plain and Grouped options.

> If you set sizing information for one style of table, then change the style, your previous size selections will be lost.

Creating a Split View-Based Application

With a basic understanding of table controllers under our belt, we can move on to building an application that combines a table view with a popover, a detail view, and dynamic resizing/repurposing of onscreen content. Sound difficult? It's not. Apple's Split View-based Application template takes care of the tough stuff; we just need to provide content.

This tutorial uses what we know about tables to create a list of flowers, by color, including images for each row. It will also enable the user to touch a specific flower and show a detail view. The detail view will load the content of a Wikipedia article for the selected flower. The finished application will resemble Figure 15.11.

FIGURE 15.11
Our split view application will show flowers, including thumbnails, and details on specific flower types.

Implementation Overview

In the preceding example, we created a table view controller and went through all the steps of adding methods to display content. This time, however, the project template will take care of building out nearly all the classes and method stubs for us. We will implement the necessary methods for a UITableViewController object (and associated delegate protocols), and a corresponding detail view that contains a single web view (UIWebView) object.

To manage the data, we'll use a combination of NSMutableDictionaries and NSMutableArrays. In Hour 16, "Reading and Writing Application Data," you'll be learning about persistent data storage, which will simplify the use of data even more in your future projects.

Time to code!

Preparing the Project

Instead of starting with the Window or View-based Application template, start Xcode and create a new project using the Split View-based Application template. Name the project **FlowerInfoViewer**.

The Split View-based template does all the hard work of setting up a detail view and controller (DetailView.xib and `DetailViewController`) and a table view controller (`RootViewController`). This is the "heart and soul" of many applications and gives us a great starting point for adding functionality.

Understanding the `SplitViewController` Hierarchy

After creating the new project, explore the MainWindow.xib file. You'll notice an interesting hierarchy located within the `SplitViewController` object, as shown in Figure 15.12.

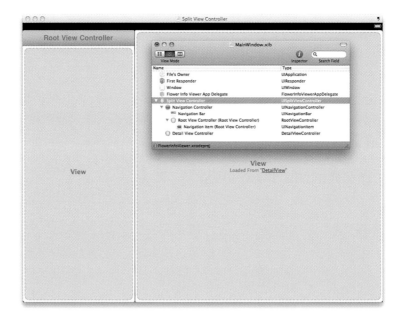

Within the `SplitViewController` is a navigation controller (`UINavigationController`) with navigation bar (`UINavigationBar`). The controller provides the ability to drill down from one table to another, and the `UINavigationBar` instance creates the horizontal bar that can provide UI elements for navigating through multiple tables. As mentioned earlier, this isn't nearly as necessary as it is on the iPhone, so we will only use a single table view controller in the tutorial. Conveniently, the table view controller is already accounted for in the XIB file, too: `RootViewController`. Finally, a `UINavigationItem` object is included in the table view controller. We can use this to set the title that will appear above the section when the application is in landscape mode.

Also inside the `SplitViewController` object is an instance view controller `DetailViewController`. This view controller loads is view from the DetailView.xib file.

As our first act of configuration, double-click the `SplitViewController` object to open its view onscreen, and then rotate it to a landscape orientation. Double-click the text in the `UINavigationBar` that reads "Root View Controller" and change it to read **Flower Types.** You've just edited the `UINavigationItem`'s `Title` attribute and completed the only configuration needed in the MainWindow.xib file!

Feel free to build the app and try it out. Even though we're starting with an empty template, you'll still be able to see the basic functionality provided by the template, as demonstrated in Figure 15.13.

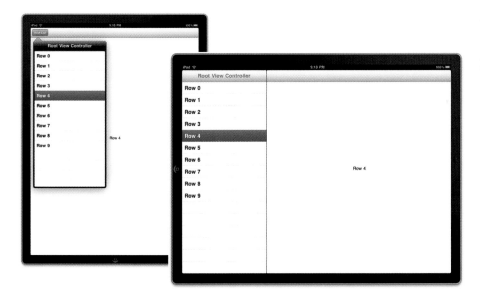

FIGURE 15.13
There's quite a bit of functionality provided within the Split View-based template.

Preparing for the Detail View

Although we don't need to edit anything in MainWindow.xib, we will want to make some changes to the `DetailView` and `DetailViewController` files. Our detail view will contain a `UIWebView` that shows a Wikipedia article about a chosen flower. The default detail view contains `UILabel` called `detailDescriptionLabel` that we don't need.

Edit DetailViewController.h to remove the unnecessary UILabel and add the web view, which we will call detailWebView. Include the appropriate @property directive, as shown in Listing 15.7.

LISTING 15.7

```
#import <UIKit/UIKit.h>

@interface DetailViewController : UIViewController
    <UIPopoverControllerDelegate, UISplitViewControllerDelegate> {

    UIPopoverController *popoverController;
    UINavigationBar *navigationBar;

    id detailItem;

    IBOutlet UIWebView *detailWebView;
}

@property (nonatomic, retain) IBOutlet UINavigationBar *navigationBar;
@property (nonatomic, retain) id detailItem;

@property (nonatomic, retain) UIWebView *detailWebView;


@end
```

Next, add a @synthesize line to DetailViewController.m for the web view:

```
@synthesize detailWebView;
```

Finally, edit the DetailViewController.m dealloc method to release the web view when finished:

```
- (void)dealloc {
    [detailWebView release];
    [popoverController release];
    [navigationBar release];

    [detailItem release];
    [super dealloc];
}
```

Now we'll create the UIWebView and connect it to the outlet, finishing the basics of the detail view.

Creating the Detail View

Open the DetailView.xib file and drag a UIWebView onto the existing view. Size it to fill the view, from top to bottom.

Next, drag a navigation item (UINavigationItem) from the Library into the navigation bar. Double-click the title in the navigation bar at the top of the view and change the text "Title" to read **Flower Details**. This gives us a label in the navigation bar that we can set to the name of the chosen flower. The finished view should resemble Figure 15.14.

FIGURE 15.14
Add a
UIWebView and
UINavigation
Item to the
view.

Finish the view up by connecting the detailWebView outlet to the web view. Just Control-drag from the File's Owner icon to the web view, choosing detailWebView when prompted.

Save your work, and then return to Xcode. All the rest of our work will take place there.

Providing Data to the Application

In the previous table implementation project, we used multiple arrays and switch statements to differentiate between the different sections of flowers. This time around, however, we need to track the flower sections, names, image resources, and the detail URL that will be displayed.

Creating the Application Data Structures

What the application needs to store is quite a bit of data for simple arrays. Instead, we'll make use of an NSMutableArray of NSMutableDictionaries to hold the specific attributes of each flower and a separate array to hold the names of each section. We'll index into each based on the current section/row being displayed, so no more switch statements!

To begin, edit RootViewController.h to read as shown in Listing 15.8.

LISTING 15.8

```
#import <UIKit/UIKit.h>

@class DetailViewController;

@interface RootViewController : UITableViewController {
    DetailViewController *detailViewController;
        NSMutableArray *flowerData;
          NSMutableArray *flowerSections;
}

-(void) createFlowerData;

@property (nonatomic, retain) IBOutlet DetailViewController
*detailViewController;

@end
```

We've added two NSMutableArrays: flowerData and flowerSection. These will hold our flower and section information, respectively. We've also declared a method createFlowerData, which will be used to add the data to the arrays.

Next, open the RootViewController.m implementation file and add the createFlowerData method shown in Listing 15.9.

LISTING 15.9

```
 1: - (void)createFlowerData {
 2:
 3:     NSMutableArray *redFlowers;
 4:     NSMutableArray *blueFlowers;
 5:
 6:     flowerSections=[[NSMutableArray alloc] initWithObjects:
 7:                     @"Red Flowers",@"Blue Flowers",nil];
 8:
 9:     redFlowers=[[NSMutableArray alloc] init];
10:     blueFlowers=[[NSMutableArray alloc] init];
11:
12:     [redFlowers addObject:[[NSMutableDictionary alloc]
13:                     initWithObjectsAndKeys:@"Poppy",@"name",
14:                     @"poppy.png",@"picture",
```

```
15:                        @"http://en.wikipedia.org/wiki/Poppy",@"url", nil]];
16:    [redFlowers addObject:[[NSMutableDictionary alloc]
17:                    initWithObjectsAndKeys:@"Tulip",@"name",
18:                    @"tulip.png",@"picture",
19:               @"http://en.wikipedia.org/wiki/Tulip",@"url",nil]];
20:
21:    [blueFlowers addObject:[[NSMutableDictionary alloc]
22:                    initWithObjectsAndKeys:@"Hyacinth",@"name",
23:                    @"hyacinth.png",@"picture",
24:               @"http://en.wikipedia.org/wiki/Hyacinth_(flower)",
25:                    @"url",nil]];
26:    [blueFlowers addObject:[[NSMutableDictionary alloc]
27:                    initWithObjectsAndKeys:@"Hydrangea",@"name",
28:                    @"hydrangea.png",@"picture",
29:                    @"http://en.wikipedia.org/wiki/Hydrangea",
30:                    @"url",nil]];
31:
32:    flowerData=[[NSMutableArray alloc] initWithObjects:
33:               redFlowers,blueFlowers,nil];
34:
35:    [redFlowers release];
36:    [blueFlowers release];
37: }
```

Don't worry if you don't understand what you're seeing; an explanation is definitely in order! The createFlowerData method creates two arrays: flowerData and flowerSections.

The flowerSections array is allocated and initialized in lines 6 and 7. The section names are added to the array so that their indexes can be referenced by section number. For example, Red Flowers is added first, so it is accessed by index (and section number) 0, Blue Flowers is added second and will be accessed through index 1. When we want to get the label for a section, we'll just reference it as [flowerSections objectAtIndex:section].

The flowerData structure is a bit more complicated. As with the flowerSections array, we want to be able to access information by section. We also want to be able to store multiple flowers per section, and multiple pieces of data per flower. So, how can we get this done?

First, let's concentrate on the individual flower data within each section. Lines 3 and 4 define two NSMutableArrays: redFlowers and blueFlowers. These need to be populated with each flower. Lines 12–30 do just that; the code allocates and initializes an NSMutableDictionary with key/value pairs for the flower's name (name), image file (picture), and Wikipedia reference (url) and inserts it into each of the two arrays.

Wait a second. Doesn't this leave us with two arrays when we wanted to consolidate all the data into one? Yes, but we're not done. Lines 32 and 33 create the final `flowerData` NSMutableArray using the `redFlowers` and `blueFlowers` arrays. What this means for our application is that we can reference the red flower array as `[flowerData objectAtIndex:0]` and `[flowerData objectAtIndex:1]` (corresponding, as we wanted, to the appropriate table sections).

Finally, lines 35 and 36 release the temporary `redFlowers` and `blueFlowers` arrays. The end result will be a structure in memory that resembles Figure 15.4.

FIGURE 15.4
The data structure that will populate our table view

flowerData (NSMutableArray)			
Index	**NSMutableArray**		
0	**Red Flowers**		
	Index	**NSMutableDictionary**	
	0	**Name**	**Picture**	**URL**
		Poppy	poppy.png	http://en.wikipedia.org/wiki/Poppy
	1	**Name**	**Picture**	**URL**
		Tulip	tulip.png	http://en.wikipedia.org/wiki/Tulip
1	**Blue Flowers**		
	Index	**NSMutableDictionary**	
	0	**Name**	**Picture**	**URL**
		Hyacinth	Hyacinth.png	http://en.wikipedia.org/wiki/Hyacinth_(flower)
	1	**Name**	**Picture**	**URL**
		Hydrangea	hydrangea.png	http://en.wikipedia.org/wiki/Hydrangea

---

By the Way

The data that we included in the listing of the `createFlowerData` method is a small subset of what is used in the actual project files. If you would like to use the full dataset in your code, you can copy it from this hour's project files, or add it manually to the method using these values:

Red Flowers

Name	Picture	URL
Gerbera	gerbera.png	http://en.wikipedia.org/wiki/Gerbera
Peony	peony.png	http://en.wikipedia.org/wiki/Peony
Rose	rose.png	http://en.wikipedia.org/wiki/Rose
Hollyhock	hollyhock.png	http://en.wikipedia.org/wiki/Hollyhock
Straw Flower	strawflower.png	http://en.wikipedia.org/wiki/Strawflower

Blue Flowers		
Name	**Picture**	**URL**
Sea Holly	seaholly.png	http://en.wikipedia.org/wiki/Sea_holly
Grape Hyacinth	grapehyacinth.png	http://en.wikipedia.org/wiki/Grape_hyacinth
Phlox	phlox.png	http://en.wikipedia.org/wiki/Phlox
Pin Cushion Flower	pincushionflower.png	http://en.wikipedia.org/wiki/Scabious
Iris	iris.png	http://en.wikipedia.org/wiki/Iris_(plant)

Populating the Data Structures

The createFlowerData method is now ready for use. We can call it from within the RootViewController's viewDidLoad method. Because an instance of the RootViewController class is calling one of its own methods, it is invoked as [self createFlowerData]:

```
- (void)viewDidLoad {
    [self createFlowerData];
    [super viewDidLoad];
}
```

Remember, we need to release the flowerData and flowerSections when we're done with them. Be sure to add the appropriate releases to the dealloc method:

```
- (void)dealloc {
    [flowerData release];
    [flowerSections release];
    [detailViewController release];
    [super dealloc];
}
```

Adding the Image Resources

As you probably noticed when entering the data structures, the application references images that will be placed alongside the flower names in the table. In the project files provided online, find the Flowers folder, select all the images, and drag them into your Xcode resources folder for the project. If you want to use your own graphics, size them at 100x75 pixels, and make sure the names of the images stored with the picture NSMutableDictionary key match what you add to your project.

Implementing the Root View Table Controller

We've now reached the point where we can build out our table view in the `RootViewController`. Very little changes between how we implemented our initial tutorial table view controller and how we will be building this one. Once again, we need to satisfy the appropriate data source and delegate protocols to add an interface and event handling to our data.

The biggest change to the implementation will be how we access our data. Because we've built a somewhat complex structure of arrays of dictionaries, we need to make absolutely sure we're referencing the data that we intend to be.

Creating the Table View Data Source Methods

Instead of completely rehashing the implementation details, let's just review how we can return the needed information to the various methods.

As with the previous example, start by implementing the data source methods within RootViewController.m. Remember, these methods (`numberOfSectionsInTableView`, `tableView:numberOfRowsInSection`, and `tableView:titleforHeaderInSection`) must return the number of sections, the rows within each section, and the titles for the sections, respectively.

To return the number of sections, we just need the count of the elements in the `flowerSections` array:

```
[flowerSections count]
```

Retrieving the number of rows within a given section is only slightly more difficult. Because the `flowerData` array contains an array for each section, we must first access the appropriate array for the section, and then return its count:

```
[[flowerData objectAtIndex:section] count]
```

Finally, to provide the label for a given section via the `tableView:titleforHeaderInSection` method, the application should index into the `flowerSections` array by the section value, and return the string at that location:

```
[flowerSections objectAtIndex:section]
```

Edit the appropriate methods in RootViewController.m so that they return these values.

Populating the Cells with Text and Images

The final mind-bending hurdle that we need to deal with is how to provide actual content to the table cells. As before, this is handled through the `tableView:cellForRowAtIndexPath`, but unlike the previous example, we need to dig down into our data structures to retrieve the correct results.

Recall that we will be setting the cell's label using an approach like this:

```
[[cell textLabel]setText:@"My Cell Label"]
```

In addition to the label, however, we also need to set an image that will be displayed alongside the label in the cell. Doing this is very similar to setting the label:

```
[[cell imageView] setImage:[UIImage imageNamed:@"MyPicture.png"]]
```

To use our own labels and images, however, things get a bit more complicated. Let's quickly review the three-level hierarchy of our `flowerData` structure:

```
flowerData(NSMutableArray)→NSMutableArray→NSMutableDictionary
```

The first level, the top `flowerData` array, corresponds to the sections within the table. The second level, another array contained within the `flowerData` array, corresponds to the rows within the section, and, finally, the `NSMutableDictionary` provides the individual pieces of information about each row. Refer back to Table 15.1 if you're still having trouble picturing how information is organized.

So, how do we get to the individual pieces of data that are three layers deep? By first using the section value to return the right array, and then, from that, using the row value to return the right dictionary, and then finally, using a key to return the correct value from the dictionary.

For example, to get the value that corresponds to the `"name"` key for a given section and row, we can write the following:

```
[[[flowerData objectAtIndex:indexPath.section] objectAtIndex: indexPath.row]
objectForKey:@"name"]
```

Likewise, we can return the image file with this:

```
[[[flowerData objectAtIndex:indexPath.section] objectAtIndex: indexPath.row]
objectForKey:@"picture"]
```

Substituting these values into the statements needed to set the cell label and image, we get the following:

```
[[cell textLabel] setText:[[[flowerData objectAtIndex:indexPath.section]
objectAtIndex: indexPath.row] objectForKey:@"name"]]
```

and

```
[[cell imageView] setImage:[UIImage imageNamed:[[[flowerData
objectAtIndex:indexPath.section] objectAtIndex: indexPath.row]
objectForKey:@"picture"]]]
```

Add these lines to the `tableView:cellForRowAtIndexPath` method, before the statement that returns the cell.

As a final decoration, the cell can display an arrow on the right side to show that it can be touched to drill down to a detail view. This UI element is called a *disclosure indicator* and can be added just by setting the `accessoryType` property for the cell object:

```
cell.accessoryType=UITableViewCellAccessoryDisclosureIndicator
```

Add this line after your code to set the cell text and image. The table display setup is now complete.

> I've intentionally left out the full method implementations in this section because, with the exception of how values are accessed, the code is nearly identical to the previous example. Remember that you can always review the full implementations in the hour's project files.

Unfortunately, if you Build and Run the application, your table is going to look a bit squished. Unlike the previous tutorial where we could adjust the row height in Interface Builder, we have to do this through code. To update the height of the rows in the table to be 75 pixels, add the `tableView:heightForRowAtIndexPath` method. All we need to do is return the number of pixels tall a row should be, as follows:

```
- (CGFloat)tableView:(UITableView *)tableView
  heightForRowAtIndexPath:(NSIndexPath *)indexPath  {
    return 75.0;
}
```

Now the table should look nicely spaced, with plenty of room for finger tapping! Of course, the detail view doesn't yet know how to respond to the selection of a flower in the root table view, but we'll get there shortly.

Handling Navigation Events

In the previous example application, we handled a touch event with the `tableView:didSelectRowAtIndexPath` method and displayed an alert to the user. This time, our implementation will need to tell the `DetailViewController` that it should update and display the contents of the URL in our data structure.

We'll be communicating with the detailViewController through one of its properties (of type id) called detailItem. Since detailItem can point to any object, we'll
set it to the NSDictionary of the chosen flower; this will give us access to the
name,url, and other keys directly within the detail view.

Implement tableView:didSelectRowAtIndexPath like this:

```
- (void)tableView:(UITableView *)aTableView
        didSelectRowAtIndexPath:(NSIndexPath *)indexPath {

detailViewController.detailItem =
        [[flowerData objectAtIndex:indexPath.section]
          objectAtIndex: indexPath.row];

}
```

Now, when a flower is selected, it is passed to the detailViewController's
detailItem property.

Well now, that seems too easy, doesn't it? There's probably lots of work to be done
trapping the event in the detail view controller and updating the view, right? Nope.
To implement the detail view controller, we'll need to update a single method,
configureView.

Implementing the Detail View Controller

We've already created the detail view controller interface, and we know how it
should work. When the user picks one of our flowers, the UIWebView instance
(detailWebView) should be instructed to load the web address stored within the
detailItem property. The method were we can implement this logic is
configureView. It is automatically invoked whenever the detail view should update
itself. Because we have configureView and detailItem already in place, all that
we need is a tiny bit of logic.

Updating the Detail View

Because detailItem is a single NSDictionary for one of our flowers, we'll need to
use the "url" key to access the URL string, and then turn that into a value NSURL.
This is accomplished quite simply:

```
NSURL*detailURL;
detailURL=[[NSURL alloc] initWithString:[detailItem objectForKey:@"url"]];
```

First we declare the NSURL object detailURL, and then allocate and initialize it using
the URL stored in the dictionary.

You might remember from earlier lessons that loading a web page in a web view is
accomplished with the loadRequest method. This method takes an NSURLRequest

object as its input parameter. Because we only have an NSURL (detailURL), we also need to use the NSURLRequest class method requestWithURL to return the appropriate object type. One additional line of code takes care of all of this:

```
[detailWebView loadRequest:[NSURLRequest requestWithURL:detailURL]]
```

Finally, remember that navigation item that we added to the navigation bar in the detail view? We want to access that object and set its title to the name of the flower ([detailItem objectForKey:@"name"]) that we're viewing. Unfortunately, we don't have an outlet for the item, how will we access it?

The navigation bar already has an instance variable itself, navigationBar, built in to the template. Using its property topItem, we can access the navigation item without a separate outlet. With that in mind, the code to set the title in the bar at the top of the detail view becomes the following:

```
navigationBar.topItem.title = [detailItem objectForKey:@"name"];
```

Update the configureView method in DetailViewController.m to read as follows:

```
- (void)configureView {
    // Update the user interface for the detail item.
    NSURL *detailURL;
    detailURL=[[NSURL alloc] initWithString:[detailItem objectForKey:@"url"]];
    [detailWebView loadRequest:[NSURLRequest requestWithURL:detailURL]];
    navigationBar.topItem.title = [detailItem objectForKey:@"name"];
    [detailURL release];
}
```

Setting the Detail View Popover Button

We need to make to one final tweak to the project to get things "just right." The popover that displays when the split view is in portrait mode reads Root List by default. We want to update it to say Flower Types.

Find the method splitViewController:willHideViewController:withBarButtonItem: forPopoverController in the DetailViewController.m file. Specifically, find the one line that reads as follows:

```
barButtonItem.title = @"Root List";
```

Update the line to this:

```
barButtonItem.title = @"Flower Types";
```

Make sure you save all of your files, because you are finished! Build and Run the FlowerInfoViewer application. Try navigating through a few flowers. With a reasonably minor amount of coding, we've created what feels like a very complex iPad application!

Further Exploration

Although the most "dramatic" part of this hour was implementing the `UISplitViewController`, there is a wealth of additional features to be uncovered in the topic of tables. To continue your experience in working with tables, I suggest focusing on a few important enhancements.

The first is expanding what you can do with table cells. Review the property list for `UITableViewCell`. In addition to the `TextLabel` and `ImageView` properties, you can make numerous other customizations—including setting backgrounds, detail labels, and much, much more. In fact, if the default table cell options do not provide everything you need, Interface Builder supports visual customization of table cells by creating a customized instance of `UITableViewCell`.

Once you have a handle on the presentation of the table views, you can increase their functionality by implementing a few additional methods in your table view controller. Read the reference for `UITableViewController`, `UITableViewDataSource`, and `UITableViewDelegate`. You can quickly enable editing functionality for your table by implementing a handful of additional methods. You'll need to spend some time thinking of what editing controls you want to use and what the intended result will be, but the basic functionality of deleting, reordering, and inserting rows (along with the associated graphic controls you're used to seeing in iPad applications) will come along "for free" as you implement the methods.

Apple Tutorials

Customizing table cells and views – TableViewSuite (accessible via the Xcode developer documentation): The TableViewSuite tutorial is an excellent look at how table views can be customized to suit a particular application.

Editing table cells – EditableDetailView (accessible via the Xcode developer documentation): The EditableDetailView tutorial implements row editing, including inserting, reordering, and deleting, within a table view.

Summary

This hour introduced two of the most important iPad interface elements: the table view and the complementary split view controller. Table views enable users to sort through large amounts of information in an orderly manner. We covered how table cells are populated, including text and images, as well as the mechanism by which cell selection occurs.

We also explored the role of the split view controller in managing a table view and detail view and in presenting an intuitive and efficient interface to the user.

Coming away from this hour, you should feel comfortable working with tables in your applications and building basic apps using a split view controller.

Q&A

Q. *What is the most efficient way to provide data to a table?*

A. You've almost certainly come to the conclusion that there has got to be a better way to provide data to complex views rather than manually defining all the data within the application itself. Starting in Hour 16, you'll learn about persistent data and how it can be used within applications. This will become the preferred way of working with large amounts of information as you move forward.

Q. *Can a table row have more than a single cell?*

A. No, but a customized cell can be defined that presents information in a more flexible manner than the default cell. As described in the "Further Exploration" section, custom cells can be defined in Interface Builder through the UITableViewCell class.

Q. *Do split view controllers have to be implemented using the Apple template?*

A. Absolutely not. The template, however, provides all the right methods for many split view applications and is a great starting place for beginners.

Workshop

Quiz

1. When working with the NSIndexPath object in the table view controller methods, which two properties will come in handy?

2. Which two protocols, both conformed to by the UITableViewController class, are required for a table view to be displayed and events to be handled?

3. Where does the title for a navigation bar come from?

Answers

1. The section property will identify the section within the table, while the row property refers to the specific cell inside of that section.

2. A table view requires methods defined within the `UITableViewDataSource` and `UITableViewDelegate` protocols in order to display information.

3. If a view controller contains a navigation item (`UINavigationItem`), the title property of the navigation item will be used. If it doesn't, the view controller's title property will be substituted instead.

Activities

1. Update the first tutorial to display thumbnails of the flowers using the techniques you learned in the split view-based application example.

2. Use Interface Builder to create and customize an instance of the `UITableViewCell` class.

HOUR 16

Reading and Writing Application Data

What You'll Learn in This Hour:

▶ Good design principles for using application preferences
▶ How to store application preferences and read them later
▶ How to expose your application's preferences to the Settings application
▶ How to store data from your applications

Most substantial applications, whether on the computer or the iPad, enable users to customize their operation to their own needs and desires. You have probably cursed an application before, only to later find a setting that removes the unholy annoyance, and you probably have a favorite application that you've customized to your exact needs, so that it fits like a well-worn glove. In eferences>this hour, you learn how your application can use application preferences to enable the user to customize its behavior and how, in general, applications can store data on the iPad.

 By the Way

> *Application preferences* is Apple's chosen term, but you might be more familiar with other terms such as *settings*, *user defaults*, *user preferences*, or *options*. These are all essentially the same concept.

Design Considerations

The dominant design aesthetic of iPad applications is for simple, single-purpose applications that start fast and do one task quickly and efficiently. Being fun, clever, and beautiful is an expected bonus. How do application preferences fit into this design view?

You want to limit the number of application preferences by creating opinionated software. There might be three valid ways to accomplish a task, but your application should have an opinion on the one best way to accomplish it, and then should implement this one approach in such a polished and intuitive fashion that your users instantly agree it's the best way. Leave the other two approaches for someone else's application. It may seem counterintuitive, but there is a much bigger market for opinionated software than for applications that try to please everyone.

This might seem like odd advice to find in a chapter about application preferences, but I'm not suggesting that you avoid preferences altogether. There are some very important roles for application preferences. Use preferences for the choices your users must make, rather than for all the choices they could possibly make. For example, if you are connecting to the application programming interface (API) of a third-party web application on behalf of your user, and the user must provide credentials to access the service, this is something the user must do, not just something users might want to do differently, and so it is a perfect case for storing as an application preference.

Another strong consideration for creating an application preference is when a preference can streamline the use of your application (for example, when users can record their default inputs or interests so that they don't have to make the same selections repeatedly). You want user preferences that reduce the amount of onscreen typing and taps that it takes to achieve the user's goal for using your application.

After you've decided a preference is warranted, you have an additional decision to make. How will you expose the preference to the user? One option is to make the preference implicit based on what the user does while using the application. An example of an implicitly set preference is returning to the last state of the application. For example, suppose a user flips a toggle to see details. When the user next uses the application, the same toggle should be flipped and showing details.

Another option is to expose your application's preference in Apple's Settings application, shown in Figure 16.1. Settings is an application built in to the iPad. It provides a single place to customize the iPad. Everything from the hardware, built-in applications from Apple, and third-party applications can be customized from the Settings application.

A settings bundle lets you declare the user preferences of your application so that the Settings application can provide the user interface for editing those preferences. There is less coding for you to do if you let Settings handle your application's preferences, but less coding is not always the dominant consideration. A preference that is set once and rarely changes, such as the username and password for a web service, is ideal for configuring in Settings. In contrast, an option that the user might change with each use of your application, such as the difficulty level in a game, is not appropriate for Settings.

Users will be annoyed if they have to repeatedly exit your application, launch Settings to change the preference, and then relaunch your application. Decide whether each preference belongs in the Settings application or in your own application, but it's generally not a good idea to put them in both.

Also keep in mind that the user interface that Settings can provide for editing your application preferences is limited. If a preference requires a custom interface component or custom validation code, it can't be set in Settings and it must be set from within your application.

We don't strictly heed every aspect of this design advice because we are creating an application whose main purpose is to teach us about application preferences rather than to be an example of excellent product design.

Reading and Writing User Defaults

Application preferences is Apple's name for the overall preference system by which applications can customize themselves for the user. The application preferences system takes care of the low-level tasks of persisting preferences to the device, keeping each application's preferences separate from other applications' preferences, and backing up application preferences to the computer via iTunes so that users won't lose their preferences in case the device needs to be restored. Your interaction with the application preferences system is through an easy-to-use API that consists mainly of the NSUserDefaults singleton class.

The NSUserDefaults class works similarly to the NSDictionary class. The main differences are that NSUserDefaults is a singleton and is more limited in the types of objects it can store. All the preferences for your application are stored as key/value pairs in the NSUserDefaults singleton.

> A *singleton* is just an instance of the Singleton pattern, and a pattern in programming is just a common way of doing something. The Singleton pattern is fairly common in the iPhone OS SDK, and it is a technique used to ensure that there is only one instance (object) of a particular class. In the iPhone OS SDK, it is most often used to represent a service provided to your program by the hardware or operating system.

Creating Implicit Preferences

In our first example, we will create a (admittedly ridiculous) flashlight application. The application will have an on/off switch and will shine a light from the screen when it is on. A slider will control the brightness level of the light. We will use preferences to return the flashlight to the last state the user left it in.

Setting Up the Project

Create a new view-based iPad application in Xcode and call it **Flashlight**. Click the FlashlightViewController.h file in the Classes group and add outlets for our on/off switch, brightness slider, and light source. Add an action called setLightSourceAlpha that will respond when toggling the switch or sliding the brightness control. The FlashlightViewController.h file should read as shown in Listing 16.1.

LISTING 16.1

```
#import <UIKit/UIKit.h>

@interface FlashlightViewController : UIViewController {

        IBOutlet UIView *lightSource;
        IBOutlet UISwitch *toggleSwitch;
        IBOutlet UISlider *brightnessSlider;

}

@property (nonatomic, retain) UIView *lightSource;
@property (nonatomic, retain) UISwitch *toggleSwitch;
@property (nonatomic, retain) UISlider *brightnessSlider;

-(IBAction) setLightSourceAlphaValue;

@end
```

Next, edit the FlashlightViewController.m implementation file and add corresponding @synthesize directives for each property, following the @implementation line:

```
@synthesize lightSource;
@synthesize toggleSwitch;
@synthesize brightnessSlider;
```

To make sure we don't forget to clean up the retained objects later, edit the dealloc
method to release the lightSource, toggleSwitch, and brightnessSlider objects:

```
- (void)dealloc {
    [lightSource release];
    [toggleSwitch release];
    [brightnessSlider release];
    [super dealloc];
}
```

Now, let's lay out the UI for the flashlight.

Creating the Interface

Open Interface Builder by double-clicking the FlashlightViewController.xib file in the
Resources group.

1. In Interface Builder, click the empty view and open the Attribute Inspector
   (Command+1).

2. Set the background color of the view to black. (We want our flashlight to have
   a black background.)

3. Drag a UISwitch from the Library onto the bottom left of the view.

4. Drag a UISlider to the bottom right of the view. Size the slider to take up all the horizontal space not used by the switch.

5. Finally, add a UIView to the top portion of the view. Size it so that it is full width and takes up all the vertical space above the switch and slider. Your view should now look like Figure 16.2.

Connect the Outlets and Action

The code we will write to operate the flashlight and deal with the application preferences will need access to the switch, slider, and light source. Control-drag from the File's Owner icon and connect the lightSource IBOutlet to the new UIView, the toggleSwitch IBOutlet to the UISwitch, and the brightnessSlider IBOutlet to the UISlider.

In addition to being able to access the three controls, our code needs to respond to changes in the toggle state of the switch and changes in the position of the slider. Select the UISwitch and open the Connections Inspector (Command+2). Connect the UISwitch to the setLightSourceAlphaValue method by dragging from the circle beside the Value Changed event to the File's Owner icon. Choose setLightSourceAlphaValue when prompted to make the connection, as shown in Figure 16.3.

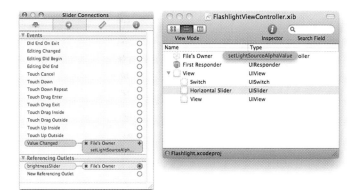

FIGURE 16.3
Connect the
switch and
slider to the set
LightSource
AlphaValue
method.

Repeat this process for the UISlider, having its Value Changed event also call the
setLightSourceAlphaValue method. This ensures immediate feedback when the
user adjusts the slider value.

Save your work, then switch back to Xcode.

Implementing the Application Logic

What can I say? Flashlights don't have much logic!

When the user toggles the flashlight on or off and adjusts the brightness level, the
application will respond by adjusting the alpha property of the lightSource view.
The alpha property of a view controls the transparency of the view, with 0.0 being
completely transparent and 1.0 being completely translucent. The lightSource
view is white, and is on top of the black background. When the lightSource view is
more transparent, more of the black will be showing through and the flashlight will
be darker. When we want to turn the light off, we just set the alpha property to 0.0
so that none of the white background of the lightSource view will be showing.

To make the flashlight work, we can add this method in Listing 16.2 to
FlashlightViewController.m.

LISTING 16.2

```
-(IBAction) setLightSourceAlphaValue {
        if (toggleSwitch.on) {
                lightSource.alpha = brightnessSlider.value;
        } else {
                lightSource.alpha = 0.0;
        }
}
```

This simple method checks the on property of the toggleSwitch object, and if it *is* on, sets the alpha property of the lightSource UIView to the value property of the slider. The slider's value property returns a floating point number between 0 and 100, so this is already enough code to make the flashlight work. You can run the project yourself and see.

Storing the Flashlight Preferences

We don't just want the flashlight to work; we want it to return to its last state when the user uses the flashlight application again later. We'll store the on/off state and the brightness level as implicit preferences. First we need two constants to be the keys for these preferences. Add these constants to the top of the FlashlightViewController.h interface file:

```
#define kOnOffToggle @"onOff"
#define kBrightnessLevel @"brightness"
```

Then we will persist the two values of the keys in the viewWillDisappear event of the FlashlightViewController. We will get the NSUserDefault singleton using the standardUserDefaults method and then use the setBool and setFloat methods. Because NSUserDefaults is a singleton, we are not creating it and are not responsible for managing its memory.

Add the viewWillDisappear method, shown in Listing 16.3 to the FlashLightViewController.m implementation file.

LISTING 16.3

```
-(void) viewWillDisappear:(BOOL)animated {

    NSUserDefaults *userDefaults = [NSUserDefaults standardUserDefaults];
    [userDefaults setBool:toggleSwitch.on forKey:kOnOffToggle];
    [userDefaults setFloat:brightnessSlider.value forKey:kBrightnessLevel];

    [super viewWillDisappear:animated];
}
```

Our code now saves the values for our two keys, but where do they go? The idea here is that *we don't have to know* because we are using the NSUserDefaults API to shield us from this level of detail and to allow Apple to change how defaults are handled in future versions of the iPhone OS.

It can still be useful to know, however, and the answer is that our preferences are stored in a plist file. If you are an experienced Mac user, you may already be familiar with plists, which are used for Mac applications, too. When running on a device, the plist will be local to the device, but when we run our application in the iPhone Simulator, the simulator uses our computer's hard drive for storage, making it easy for us to peek inside the plist.

Run the Flashlight application in the iPhone Simulator, and then use Finder to navigate to /Users/<your username>/Library/Application Support/iPhone Simulator/<Device OS Version>/Applications. The directories in Applications are generated globally unique IDs, but it should be easy to find the directory for Flashlight by looking for the most recently modified data. You'll see Flashlight.app in the most recently modified directory, and you'll see the com.yourcompany.Flashlight.plist inside the ./Library/Preferences subdirectory. This is a regular Mac plist file, and so when you double-click it, it will open with the Property List Editor application and show you the two preferences for Flashlight.

Reading the Flashlight Preferences

Now our application is writing out the state of the two controls anytime our view disappears (for this application, essentially when the application closes). So, to complete the desired behavior, we need to do the opposite and read in and use the preferences for the state of the two controls anytime our flashlight view appears (essentially when the application launches). For this, we will use the viewDidLoad method, which is provided for us by Xcode as a commented-out stub, and the floatForKey and boolForKey methods of NSUserDefaults. Uncomment viewDidLoad and get the NSUserDefaults singleton in the same way as before, but this time we will set the value of the controls from the value returned from the preference rather than the other way around.

In the FlashlightViewController.m file in the Classes group, implement viewDidLoad as shown in Listing 16.4

LISTING 16.4

```
- (void)viewDidLoad {
      NSUserDefaults *userDefaults = [NSUserDefaults standardUserDefaults];
      brightnessSlider.value = [userDefaults floatForKey:kBrightnessLevel];
      toggleSwitch.on = [userDefaults boolForKey:kOnOffToggle];
      if ([userDefaults boolForKey: kOnOffToggle]) {
              lightSource.alpha = [userDefaults floatForKey:kBrightnessLevel];
      } else {
              lightSource.alpha = 0.0;
      }
    [super viewDidLoad];
}
```

That's all there is to it. All we need now is a snazzy application icon and we too can make millions in the App Store with our Flashlight application (see Figure 16.4).

FIGURE 16.4
Flashlight appli-
cation in action.

While we are waiting for the cash to pour in (it may be awhile), let's look at an application where the user takes more direct control of the application's preferences.

Implementing System Settings

One option to consider for providing application preferences is to use the Settings application. You do this by creating and editing a settings bundle for your application in Xcode rather than by writing code and designing a UI, so this is a very fast and easy option.

For our second application of the hour, we'll create ReturnMe, an application that tells someone who finds a lost device how to return it to its owner. The Settings application will be used to edit the contact information of the owner and to select a picture to evoke the finder's sympathy.

Setting Up the Project

As we frequently do, begin by creating a new view-based iPad application in Xcode called **ReturnMe**.

We want to provide the finder of the lost device with a sympathy-invoking picture and the owner's name, email address, and phone number. Each of these items will be configurable as an application preference, so we'll need outlets to set the values of a UIImageView and three UILabels.

Open the ReturnMeViewController.h file in the Classes group and add outlets and properties for each control. The completed ReturnMeViewController.h file should look like Listing 16.5.

LISTING 16.5

```
#import <UIKit/UIKit.h>

@interface ReturnMeViewController : UIViewController {
    IBOutlet UIImageView *picture;
    IBOutlet UILabel *name;
    IBOutlet UILabel *email;
    IBOutlet UILabel *phone;
}

@property (nonatomic, retain) UIImageView *picture;
@property (nonatomic, retain) UILabel *name;
@property (nonatomic, retain) UILabel *email;
@property (nonatomic, retain) UILabel *phone;

@end
```

After updating the interface file, add corresponding @synthesize lines within the ReturnMeViewController.m file for each property:

```
@synthesize picture;
@synthesize name;
@synthesize email;
@synthesize phone;
```

And, of course, release all of these objects in the dealloc method:

```
- (void)dealloc {
    [picture release];
    [name release];
    [email release];
    [phone release];
    [super dealloc];
}
```

We want a few images that will help goad our Good Samaritan into returning the lost device rather than selling it to Gizmodo. Drag the dog1.png, dog2.png, and coral.png files from the project's Images folder into the Resources group. When you drag the images into Xcode, make sure you click the option to copy them into the destination group's folder so that copies of the images will be placed in your Xcode project's directory.

Creating the Interface

Now let's lay out the ReturnMe application's UI. Open Interface Builder by double-clicking the ReturnMeViewController.xib file in the Resources group:

1. First, open the XIB file's view.

2. Drag three `UILabels` onto the view. Click each label and open the Attribute Inspector (Command+1) and set the text to a default value of your choosing for name, email, and phone number.

3. Drag a `UIImageView` to the view. Size the image view to take up the majority of the iPad's display area.

4. With the image view selected, open the Attributes Inspector (Command+1). Set the mode to be Aspect Fill, and pick one of the animal images you added to the Xcode project from the Image drop-down.

5. Add some additional `UILabels` to explain the purpose of the application and labels that explain each preference value (name, email, and phone number).

As long as you have the three labels and the image view in your UI, as shown in Figure 16.5, you can design the rest as you see fit. Have fun with it!

FIGURE 16.5
Create an interface with an image, labels, and anything else you'd like!

When you have finished building the interface, connect the UIImageView and three UILabels to their corresponding outlets: picture, name, email, and phone. There aren't any actions to connect, so just Control-drag from the File's Owner icon to each of these interface items, choosing the appropriate outlet when prompted.

Now that the interface is built, we'll create the Settings Bundle, which will enable us to integrate with the iPad's Settings application.

Creating the Settings Bundle

Create a new settings bundle in Xcode by selecting File, New File from the menu and selecting Settings Bundle from the iPhone OS Resource group in the sidebar, as shown in Figure 16.6.

FIGURE 16.6
Settings bundle in Xcode's New File dialog.

Keep the default name of Settings.bundle when you create it. Drag the newly created settings bundle into the Resources group if it does not get created there.

The file that controls how our ReturnMe application will appear in the Settings application is the Root.plist file in the settings bundle. We can edit this file with the Property List Editor that is built in to Xcode. We will add preference types to it (see Table 16.1) that will be read and interpreted by the Settings application to provide the UI to set our application's preferences.

TABLE 16.1   Preference Types

Type	Key	Description
Text field	PSTextFieldSpecifier	Editable text string
Toggle switch	PSToggleSwitchSpecifier	On/off toggle button
Slider	PSSliderSpecifier	Slider across a range of values
Multivalue	PSMultiValueSpecifier	Drop-down value picker
Title	PSTitleValueSpecifier	Read-only text string
Group	PSGroupSpecifier	Title for a logical group of preferences
Child pane	PSChildPaneSpecifier	Child preferences page

The ReturnMe preferences will be grouped into three groups: Sympathy Image, Contact Information, and About. The Sympathy Image group will contain a multivalue preference to pick one of the images, the Contact Information group will contain three text fields, and the About group will link to a child page with three read-only titles.

Expand the Settings.bundle in Xcode and click the Root.plist file. You'll see a table of three columns: Key, Type, and Value. Expand the PreferencesSpecifiers property in the table and you'll see a series of four dictionary properties. These are provided by Xcode as samples, and each of them will be interpreted by Settings as a preference. You will follow the simple schema in the *Settings Application Schema Reference* in the iPhone OS Reference Library to set all the required properties, and some of the optional properties, of each preference.

Expand the first dictionary property under PreferenceSpecifiers called Item 0, and you'll see that its Type is PSGroupSpecifier. This is the correct Type to define a preference group, but change the Title property's value to **Sympathy Image** by clicking it and typing the new title. Expand the second item (Item 1) and you'll see that its Type is PSTextFieldSpecifier. Our Sympathy Image will be selected as a multivalue, not a text field, so change the Type to PSMultiValueSpecifier. Change the Title to **Image Name**, the Key to **picture**, and the DefaultValue to **Dog**. The remaining four keys under Item 1 apply to text fields only, so delete them by selecting them and pressing the Delete key.

The values for a multivalue picker come from two arrays, an array of item names and an array of item values. In our case, the name and value arrays will be the same, but we still must provide both of them. To add another property under DefaultValue, click the plus sign at the end of the row (see Figure 16.7) to add another property at the same level.

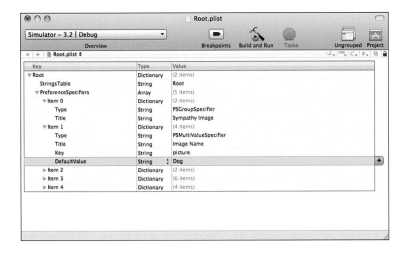

FIGURE 16.7
Add another property in Xcode's Property List Editor.

The new item will have the default name of New Item, so change that to **Values**. The Type column defaults to `String`, so change it to **Array**. Each of the three possible image names needs a property under the Values property. Expand the Values item's disclosure triangle and notice that the plus sign at the end of the row changes to an icon with three lines (see Figure 16.8). This icon adds child properties, rather than properties at the same level. Click the icon three times to add properties that'll be called Item 0, Item 1, and Item 2.

FIGURE 16.8
Add child items in Xcode's Property List Editor.

Change the Value of the three new child properties to **Dog**, **Mean Dog**, and **Coral**. Repeat this step to add a peer of Values called **Titles**. Titles is also an `Array` type and has the same three `String` type children with the same values, as shown in Figure 16.9.

FIGURE 16.9
The completed
image selector
preference in
Xcode's
Property List
Editor.

The third property (Item 2) in our plist `PreferenceSpecifiers` should be a
`PSGroupSpecifier` with a title of **Contact Information**. Change the Type and Title
of Item 2 and remove the extra items.

The fourth property (Item 3) is the name preference. Change the Type to
PSTextFieldSpecifier, the Key to **name**, and the DefaultValue to **Your Name** with a
Type of `String`. Add three more keys to Item 3. These should be `String` types and
are optional parameters that set up the keyboard for text entry. Set the keys to
`KeyboardType`, `AutocapitalizationType`, and `AutocorrectionType`, and the values to **Alphabet**, **Words**, and **No**, respectively.

You can test your settings so far by saving the plist, building and running the
ReadMe application in the iPhone Simulator, exiting the application with the Home
button, and then running the Settings application in the simulator. You should see a
Settings selection for the ReturnMe application and settings for the Sympathy Image
and Name.

Add two more `PSTextFieldSpecifier` preferences to the plist, mirror what you set
up for the Name preference—one for Email and one for Phone Number. Use the keys
of `email` and `phone` and change the KeyboardType to **EmailAddress** and
NumberPad, respectively.

The final preference is About, and it opens a child preference pane; we'll add two
more items to accomplish this. First, add a new item, Item 6, to the plist. Configure
the item as a dictionary, and then add a Type of **PSGroupSpecifier** and a Title of
About ReturnMe.

Next, add Item 7, configured as a dictionary. Expand the new item and set a property with a Type of `PSChildPaneSpecifier`, a Title of **About**, and a `String` property with a Key of **File** and a Value of **About**. The child pane element assumes the value of File exists as another plist in the settings bundle. In our case, this is a file called About.plist.

The easiest way to create this second plist file in the settings bundle is by copying the Root.plist file we already have. Right-click the Root.plist file in Xcode and select the Open with Finder menu option. This opens the plist in the external Property List Editor. Select File, Save As, and change the name to **About.plist** before clicking Save. Xcode won't immediately notice that your settings bundle has a new plist file. Collapse and expand Settings.bundle to refresh the contents.

Edit About.plist to have one group property titled **About ReturnMe** and three `PSTitleSpecifier` properties for **Version**, **Copyright**, and **Website**. `PSTitleSpecifier` properties have four properties: Type, Title, Key, and DefaultValue. If you have any difficulties setting up your plist files, compare your preferences UI to Figure 16.10 and your plists to the plists in the settings bundle in the project's source code to see where you might have made a misstep.

FIGURE 16.10
ReturnMe's settings in the Settings application.

Connecting Preferences to the Application

We have four preferences we want to retrieve from the preferences database: the
selected image and the device owner's name, email, and alternate phone number.
Add a key constant for each of these to the top of the ReturnMeViewController.h file
in Xcode:

```
#define kName @"name"
#define kEmail @"email"
#define kPhone @"phone"
#define kReward @"reward"
#define kPicture @"picture"
```

We have now bundled up our preferences so that they can be set by the Settings
application, but our ReturnMe application also has to be modified to use the preferences. We do this in the ReturnMeViewController.m file's `viewDidLoad` event. Here
we will call a helper method we write called `setValuesFromPreferences`. Our code
to use the preference values with the `NSUserDefaults` API looks no different from
the Flashlight application. It doesn't matter if our application wrote the preference
values or if the Settings application did; we can simply treat `NSUserDefaults` like a
dictionary and ask for objects by their key.

We provided default values in the settings bundle, but it's possible the user just
installed ReturnMe and has not run the Settings application. We should provide the
same default settings programmatically to cover this case, and we can do that by
providing a dictionary of default preference keys and values to the `NSUserDefaults`
`registerDefaults` method. Add the methods in Listing 16.6 to the
ReturnMeViewController.m file.

LISTING 16.6

```
- (NSDictionary *)initialDefaults {
    NSArray *keys = [[[NSArray alloc] initWithObjects:
                      kPicture, kName, kEmail, kPhone, nil] autorelease];
    NSArray *values = [[[NSArray alloc] initWithObjects:
                        @"Dog", @"Your Name", @"you@yours.com",
                        @"(555)555-1212", nil] autorelease];
    return [[[NSDictionary alloc] initWithObjects: values
                        forKeys: keys] autorelease];
}

-(void)setValuesFromPreferences {

    NSUserDefaults *userDefaults = [NSUserDefaults standardUserDefaults];
    [userDefaults registerDefaults: [self initialDefaults]];
    NSString *picturePreference = [userDefaults stringForKey:kPicture];
    if ([picturePreference isEqualToString:@"Dog"]) {
        picture.image = [UIImage imageNamed:@"dog1.png"];
    } else if ([picturePreference isEqualToString:@"Mean Dog"]) {
        picture.image = [UIImage imageNamed:@"dog2.png"];
```

```
    } else {
        picture.image = [UIImage imageNamed:@"coral.png"];
    }

    name.text = [userDefaults stringForKey:kName];
    email.text = [userDefaults stringForKey:kEmail];
    phone.text = [userDefaults stringForKey:kPhone];

}
```

With this supporting code in place, we have the ability to set some default prefer-ences, and load preferences that are configured in the iPad Settings application. That said, we still need to load the preferences when the application starts. Edit ReturnMeViewController.m, implementing the viewDidLoad method to invoke setValuesFromPreferences:

```
- (void)viewDidLoad {
    [self setValuesFromPreferences];
    [super viewDidLoad];
}
```

Build and Run the modified ReturnMe application and switch back and forth between the Settings and ReturnMe applications. You can see that with very little code on our part we were able to provide a sophisticated interface to configure our application. The Settings application's plist schema provides a fairly complete way to describe the preference needs of our application.

Understanding the iPad File System Sandbox

Up to this point, the applications we've built have not allowed the user to create and store a lot of new data. Quite a few types of applications, however, do need to store a substantial amount of new information. Consider some of Apple's applica-tions, such as Notes and Contacts. These are data management applications whose main function is to reliably store and retrieve data for the user. Where does this data go when the application is not running? Just like with a desktop application, iPad applications persist their data to the file system.

In creating the iPhone OS SDK, Apple introduced a wide range of restrictions designed to protect users from malicious applications harming their devices. The restrictions are collectively known as the application sandbox. Any application you create with the SDK exists in a sandbox. There is no opting out of the sandbox and no way to get an exemption from the sandbox's restrictions.

Some of these restrictions affect how application data is stored and what data can be accessed. Each application is given a directory on the device's file system, and applications are restricted to reading and writing files in their own directory. This means a poorly behaved application can, at worst, wipe out its own data, but not the data of any other application.

It also turns out that this restriction is not terribly limiting. The information from Apple's applications, such as contacts, calendars, and the photo and music libraries, is for the most part already exposed through APIs in the iPhone OS SDK. (For more information, see Hour 20, "Working with Rich Media," and Hour 21 "Interacting with Other Applications.")

> With each version of the iPhone OS SDK, Apple has been steadily ramping up what you can't do because of the application sandbox, but parts of the sandbox are still enforced via policy rather than as technical restrictions. Just because you find a location on the file system where it is possible to read or write files outside the application sandbox doesn't mean you should. Violating the application sandbox is one of the surest ways to get your application rejected from the iTunes Store.

Storage Locations for Application Data

Within an application's directory, four locations are provided specifically for storing the application's data: the Library/Preferences, Library/Caches, Documents, and tmp directories.

> When you run an application in the iPhone Simulator, the application's directory exists on your Mac in /Users/<your user>/Library/Applications Support/iPhone Simulator/<Device OS Version>/Applications. There are any number of applications in this directory, each with a directory named after a unique ApplicationID (a series of characters with dashes) that is provided by Xcode. The easiest way to find the directory of the current application you are running in the iPhone Simulator is to look for the most recently modified application directory. Take a few minutes now to look through the directory of a couple applications from previous hours.

You encountered the Library/Preferences directory earlier this hour. It's not typical to read and write to the Preferences directory directly. Instead, you use the NSUserDefaults API. The Library/Caches, Documents, and tmp directories are, however, intended for direct file manipulation. The main difference between them is the intended lifetime of the files in each directory.

The Documents directory is the main location for storing application data. It is backed up to the computer when the device is synced with iTunes, so it is important to store any data users would be upset to lose in the Documents directory.

The Library/Caches directory is used to cache data retrieved from the network or from any computationally expensive calculation. Files in Library/Caches persist between launches of the application, and caching data in the Library/Caches directory can be an important technique used to improve the performance of an application.

Lastly, any data you want to store outside of the device's limited volatile memory, but that you do not need to persist between launches of the application, belongs in the tmp directory. The tmp directory is a more transient version of Library/Caches; think of it as a scratch pad for the application.

> Applications are responsible for cleaning up all the files they write, even those written to Library/Caches or tmp. Applications are sharing the limited file system space (typically 4GB to 32GB) on the device. The space an application's files take up is not available for music, podcasts, photos, and other applications. Be judicious in what you choose to persistently store and be sure to clean up any temporary files created during the lifetime of the application.

Watch Out!

File Paths

Every file in an iPad file system has a path, which is the name of its exact location on the file system. For an application to read or write a file in its sandbox, it needs to specify the full path of the file.

Core Foundation provides a C function called `NSSearchPathForDirectoriesInDomains` that returns the path to the application's Documents or Library/Caches directory. Asking for other directories from this function can return multiple directories, so the result of the function call is an `NSArray` object. When this function is used to get the path to the Documents or Library/Caches directory it returns exactly one `NSString` in the array, and the `NSString` of the path is extracted from the array using `NSArray`'s `objectAtIndex` method with an index of 0.

`NSString` provides a method for joining two path fragments together called `stringByAppendingPathComponent`. By putting the result of a call to `NSSearchPathForDirectoriesInDomains` together with a specific filename, it is possible to get a string that represents a full path to a file in the application's Documents or Library/Caches directory.

Suppose, for example, your next blockbuster iPad application calculates the first 100,000 digits of pi, and you want the application to write the digits out to a cache file so that they won't need to be calculated again. To get the full path to this file's location, you need to first get the path to the Library/Caches directory and then append the specific filename to it:

```
NSString *cacheDir =
    [NSSearchPathForDirectoriesInDomains(NSCachesDirectory,
    NSUserDomainMask, YES) objectAtIndex: 0];
NSString *piFile = [cacheDir stringByAppendingPathComponent:@"American.pi"];
```

To get a path to a file in the Documents directory, use the same approach but with NSDocumentDirectory as the first argument to NSSearchPathForDirectoriesInDomains:

```
NSString *docDir =
        [NSSearchPathForDirectoriesInDomains(NSDocumentDirectory,
        NSUserDomainMask, YES) objectAtIndex: 0];
NSString *scoreFile = [docDir stringByAppendingPathComponent:@"HighScores.txt"];
```

Core Foundation provides another C function called NSTemporaryDirectory that returns the path of the application's tmp directory. As before, this can be used to get a full path to a file:

```
NSString *scratchFile =
        [NSTemporaryDirectory() stringByAppendingPathComponent:@"Scratch.data"];
```

Implementing File System Storage

In our final example for this hour, we'll create a flash card application. The application shows the user one card at a time, initially hiding the answer, and then lets users know whether they got the answer right or not. It keeps track of how many times users answer each card right or wrong, and users can create new flash cards and delete existing flash cards. Initially, we'll put the UI and mechanics of the game together without any data persistence. Each time you run the application, you'll need to create the cards all over again. Then we'll look at how to persist the user-created flash cards between application launches using object archiving.

Setting Up the Project

Create a new view-based iPad application in Xcode and call it **FlashCards**. As you'd suspect with an object-oriented flash card application, the first thing that's needed is a class that represents flash cards. Create a new class by selecting File, New File and then the Objective-C class template (NSObject subclass) from the iPhone OS Cocoa

Touch Class category. Name the new file **FlashCard.m**, and be sure the Also Create FlashCard.h check box is selected.

Creating the FlashCard Class Interface

A flash card object needs to keep track of four distinct pieces of information: the question, the correct answer, how often the user knew the correct answer, and how often the user got it wrong. Create NSString properties for the question and answer, NSUInteger properties for the right and wrong counters, and a custom initializer that accepts the question and answer as arguments (see Listing 16.7).

LISTING 16.7

```
#import <Foundation/Foundation.h>

@interface FlashCard : NSObject {
    NSString *question;
    NSString *answer;
    NSUInteger rightCount;
    NSUInteger wrongCount;
}

@property (nonatomic, retain) NSString *question;
@property (nonatomic, retain) NSString *answer;
@property (nonatomic, assign) NSUInteger rightCount;
@property (nonatomic, assign) NSUInteger wrongCount;

- (id)initWithQuestion:(NSString *)thisQuestion
               answer:(NSString *)thisAnswer;

@end
```

Implementing the FlashCard Class Logic

Our next step is to implement the FlashCard class. To do this, we'll synthesize the four properties and write the initWithQuestion:answer method. The FlashCard.m implementation file is shown in Listing 16.8.

LISTING 16.8

```
#import "FlashCard.h"

@implementation FlashCard

@synthesize question, answer, rightCount, wrongCount;

- (id)initWithQuestion:(NSString *)thisQuestion answer:(NSString *)thisAnswer {

    if (self = [super init]) {
        self.question = thisQuestion;
        self.answer = thisAnswer;
    self.rightCount = 0;
```

```
        self.wrongCount = 0;
    }
    return self;
}

@end
```

Now that the FlashCard class is finished, we'll turn our attention back to our main application.

Preparing the Application Interface

Click the FlashCardsViewController.h file in the Classes group and import the FlashCard class. Add outlets for five different labels: a count of the total cards (cardCount), a count of how many times the current card has been answered rightly (rightCount) and how many times wrongly (wrongCount), and the current question (question) and answer (answer). The view controller also needs outlets for four buttons: delete (deleteButton), mark right (rightButton), mark wrong (wrongButton), and next action (actionButton) buttons. There is also some states of the application to track in the controller. Add an NSMutable array (flashcards) property that will hold all the flash card objects, a counter property (currentCardCounter) that tracks which flash card is currently being displayed, and a read-only property (currentCard) that uses the counter and the array to return the currently displayed flash card object.

We also need to consider the user's actions. Users will add (addCard) and delete (deleteCard) flash cards, press the next action button to expose the flash card's answer or flip to the next card (nextAction), and they will mark whether they knew the correct answer or not (markRight and markWrong). Each of these five actions will be connected to the buttons of our UI.

After you've added the outlets, properties, and actions your FlashCardsViewController.h file should look like Listing 16.9.

LISTING 16.9

```
#import <UIKit/UIKit.h>
#import "FlashCard.h"

@interface FlashCardsViewController : UIViewController {

    IBOutlet UILabel *cardCount;
    IBOutlet UILabel *wrongCount;
    IBOutlet UILabel *rightCount;
    IBOutlet UILabel *question;
    IBOutlet UILabel *answer;
```

```
    IBOutlet UIBarButtonItem *deleteButton;
    IBOutlet UIBarButtonItem *rightButton;
    IBOutlet UIBarButtonItem *wrongButton;
    IBOutlet UIBarButtonItem *actionButton;
    NSMutableArray *flashCards;
    NSUInteger currentCardCounter;
    FlashCard *currentCard;
}

@property (nonatomic, retain) UILabel *cardCount;
@property (nonatomic, retain) UILabel *wrongCount;
@property (nonatomic, retain) UILabel *rightCount;
@property (nonatomic, retain) UILabel *question;
@property (nonatomic, retain) UILabel *answer;
@property (nonatomic, retain) UIBarButtonItem *deleteButton;
@property (nonatomic, retain) UIBarButtonItem *rightButton;
@property (nonatomic, retain) UIBarButtonItem *wrongButton;
@property (nonatomic, retain) UIBarButtonItem *actionButton;
@property (nonatomic, retain) NSMutableArray *flashCards;
@property (nonatomic, assign) NSUInteger currentCardCounter;
@property (nonatomic, readonly) FlashCard *currentCard;

-(IBAction) markWrong:(id)sender;
-(IBAction) markRight:(id)sender;
-(IBAction) nextAction:(id)sender;
-(IBAction) addCard:(id)sender;
-(IBAction) deleteCard:(id)sender;

@end
```

Next, add the @synthesize lines for each property to the
FlashCardsViewController.m implementation file:

```
@synthesize cardCount, wrongCount, rightCount;
@synthesize question, answer;
@synthesize deleteButton, rightButton, wrongButton, actionButton;
@synthesize flashCards;
@synthesize currentCardCounter;
```

Update the dealloc method to release all the retained objects:

```
- (void)dealloc {
    [cardCount release];
    [wrongCount release];
    [rightCount release];
    [question release];
    [answer release];
    [deleteButton release];
    [rightButton release];
    [wrongButton release];
    [actionButton release];
    [flashCards release];
    [super dealloc];
}
```

Creating the Interface

It's time to build the first part of the FlashCards interface. Double-click the FlashCardsViewController.xib file in the Resources group to open Interface Builder. Complete the following steps to lay out the UI and connect the outlets and actions:

1. Click the empty view, open the Attributes Inspector (Command+1), and then click the Background attribute's color picker and change the color to white.

2. Open the Library (Shift+Command+L) and drag a toolbar to the very top of the view and another to the very bottom of the view.

3. Click the Item button until just the button is selected, open the Attributes Inspector (Command+1), and choose Add from the Identifier Properties drop-down list.

4. Click the Item button in the bottom toolbar until just the button is selected, open the Attributes Inspector (Command+1), and change the Title attribute to **Right**.

5. From the Library (Shift+Command+L), drag one bar button item to the top toolbar and two bar button items to the bottom toolbar.

6. Click the new button until just the button is selected, open the Attributes Inspector (Command+1), and choose Trash from the Identifier Properties drop-down list.

7. Click the middle button in the bottom toolbar until it is selected, open the Attributes Inspector (Command+1), and change the Title attribute to **Wrong**.

8. Click the rightmost button in the bottom toolbar three times until just the button is selected, open the Attributes Inspector (Command+1), and choose Action from the Identifier Properties drop-down list. The view should now look like Figure 16.11.

9. Within the Library (Shift+Command+L) and search for "space." Drag a flexible space bar button item from the Library search results to the leftmost position in the top toolbar.

10. Drag a fixed space bar button item to the leftmost position in the bottom toolbar.

11. Drag a flexible space bar button item to the position between the Wrong and Action button in the bottom toolbar.

12. Drag the right handle on the fixed space bar button item on the bottom toolbar to the right until the Right and Wrong buttons are centered horizontally in the toolbar. The view should now look like Figure 16.12.

FIGURE 16.11
Add the toolbars to the UI.

FIGURE 16.12
Lay out the toolbars.

13. Open the Library (Shift+Command+L) and search for "label."

14. Drag a label to the left alignment guide on the top toolbar. Size the label to be as wide as the entire toolbar up to the Add button.

15. Click the new label, open the Attributes Inspector (Command+1), and change the Text attribute to **100 of 200**. This label will tell users which card they are on and how many cards they've created in total.

16. Drag four labels onto the view between the two toolbars.

17. Position one of the labels just under the top toolbar and against the left alignment guide. Size the label wider to about the midpoint of the view. Click the label, open the Attribute Inspector (Command+1), and change the Text attribute to **Right: 0**. Click the Color Attribute's Color Picker and change the text color to green.

18. Position another one of the labels just under the top toolbar and against the right alignment guide. Size the label wider to about the midpoint of the view. Click the label, open the Attributes Inspector (Command+1), change the Layout attribute to Right Alignment, and change the Text attribute to **Wrong: 0**. Click the Color Attribute's Color Picker and change the text color to red.

19. Position the third label just under the right and wrong labels and against the left alignment guide. Size the label wider to reach all the way to the right alignment guide. Size the label taller to reach about the midpoint of the view. Click the label, open the Attributes Inspector (Command+1), and change the Layout attribute to center alignment, and change the Text attribute to **Question?** and set the size to 72.

20. Position the final label just under the question label and against the left alignment guide. Size the label wider to reach all the way to the right alignment guide. Size the label taller to reach the bottom toolbar. Click the label, open the Attributes Inspector (Command+1), and change the Layout attribute to Center Alignment, and change the Text attribute to **Answer** and the size to 72. The view should now look like Figure 16.13.

21. Open Document window. Connect the four button outlets (delete, right, wrong, and action) to the respective buttons in the view. Connect the five actions (`addCard`, `deleteCard`, `markRight`, `markWrong`, and `nextAction`) to the respective buttons in the view.

22. Connect the five label outlets (`question`, `answer`, `cardCount`, `rightCount`, and `wrongCount`) to the respective labels in the view as in Figure 16.14. Save the XIB file, quit Interface Builder, and return to Xcode.

FIGURE 16.13
Lay out the labels.

FIGURE 16.14
Connect the labels.

Adding a Create Card View Controller

We now have the complete view for using the flash cards, but users also need to be able to create new cards. When users press the Add button in the top toolbar, we'll show them another view to capture the question and answer for the new flash card. This new view will have its own controller and NIB.

Select the Classes group and then select File, New File, and then the `UIViewController` subclass template. Make sure the Targeted for iPad and With XIB for User Interface check boxes are selected and click the Next button. Name the controller **CreateCardViewController**, make sure the Also Create CreateCardViewController.h check box is selected, and click the Finish button. Drag the new CreateCardController.xib file from the Classes group to the Resources group to keep the project tidy.

Preparing the Second View Controller

The new view controller needs outlets to access the two text fields that'll be on the view that will contain the question and answer the user typed. It also needs a delegate to call back to the `FlashCardsViewController` object when the user wants to save a new card or just dismiss the view. There will be an action for each of the user's two options: save and cancel.

Click the CreateCardViewController.h file in the Classes group. Add a `CreateCardDelegate` protocol with two methods: `didCancelCardCreation` and `didCreateCardWithQuestion:answer`. Both arguments to the second method are `NSString` objects. Add the `save` and `cancel` actions and add an outlet and property for the question and answer text fields and a property for the `CreateCardDelegate`. After you've added the delegate, outlets, actions, and properties, your CreateCardViewController.h file should look like Listing 16.10.

LISTING 16.10

```
#import <UIKit/UIKit.h>

@protocol CreateCardDelegate <NSObject>

-(void) didCancelCardCreation;
-(void) didCreateCardWithQuestion:(NSString *)question
                           answer:(NSString *)answer;

@end

@interface CreateCardViewController : UIViewController {

    IBOutlet UITextField *question;
    IBOutlet UITextField *answer;
    id cardDelegate;
```

```
}

@property (nonatomic, retain) UITextField *question;
@property (nonatomic, retain) UITextField *answer;
@property (nonatomic, assign) id<CreateCardDelegate> cardDelegate;

-(IBAction) save;
-(IBAction) cancel;

@end
```

Sorry to bug you about this, but you know what to do. Edit the
CreateCardViewController.m file to include the necessary @synthesize lines for the
properties:

```
@synthesize cardDelegate;
@synthesize question;
@synthesize answer;
```

Modify dealloc to include the objects that were retained:

```
- (void)dealloc {
    [question release];
    [answer release];
    [super dealloc];
}
```

Now, the user interface for creating cards.

Creating the User Interface

Open Interface Builder by double-clicking the CreateCardViewController.xib file in
the Resources group. Then complete the following steps to lay out the UI and connect the outlets and actions:

1. Open the Library (Shift+Command+L) and drag a toolbar to the very top of
   the view.

2. Click the Item button until just the button is selected, open the Attribute
   Inspector (Command+1), and choose Save from the Identifier Properties drop-
   down list.

3. From the Library, drag one bar button item to the top toolbar.

4. Click the new button until just the button is selected, open the Attributes
   Inspector (Command+1), and choose Cancel from the Identifier Properties
   drop-down list.

5. Within the Library, search for "space." Drag a flexible space bar button item
   to the leftmost position in the top toolbar.

6. Drag two text fields onto the view below the toolbar.

7. Position one of the text fields under the top toolbar and against the left alignment guide. Size the label wider to the right and left alignment guides and about one third of the view. Click the text field, open the Attributes Inspector (Command+1), and change the Text attribute to **Question?**, change the alignment to centered, change the Border attribute to the leftmost style, and change the Correction Text Input Traits attribute to No. Set the font size to 72pts.

8. Position the second text field under the first and against the left alignment guide. Size the label wider to the left and right alignment guides and about one third of the view. Click the text field, open the Attributes Inspector (Command+1), and change the Text attribute to **Answer.**, change the alignment to centered, change the Border attribute to the leftmost style, and change the Correction Text Input Traits attribute to No. Set the font size to 72pts. Your UI should now look like Figure 16.15.

FIGURE 16.15
The create card UI.

9. Connect the two label outlets, `question` and `answer`, to the respective labels.

10. Connect the two actions, `cancel` and `save`, to the respective buttons in the view. Save the XIB file, quit Interface Builder, and return to Xcode.

Implementing the Application Logic

At this point, we've defined a flash card model and two complete views, one for creating flash cards and one for using them. All that remains to have a basic flash card application is to implement the two controllers.

Show Cards and Capture Results

The class header for the `FlashCardsViewController` provides a roadmap for the implementation. It tells us we have to synthesize 11 properties and implement 5 actions. You may have noticed that we defined 12 properties in the class definition but we only synthesized 11. That's because we need to manually implement the getter for the read-only `currentCard` property. To implement this property and get the current flash card, we use the `currentCardCounter` as the index into the `flashCards` array, checking to be sure the array isn't empty. Add the `currentCard` method, shown in Listing 16.11 to the `FlashCardsViewController.m` file.

LISTING 16.11

```
-(FlashCard *) currentCard {
    if (self.currentCardCounter < 0) {
        return nil;
    }
    FlashCard *flashCard = [self.flashCards
                            objectAtIndex:self.currentCardCounter];
    return flashCard;
}
}
```

We've now created all 12 properties of our view controller, so let's start using them to implement the controller. When the view is first loaded, we won't have any flash cards yet, so we need to make sure the UI behaves properly with no flash cards. Consider for a moment that it's possible to get back to this same state of having no cards when the user deletes the last flash card. So it's best to handle the case of no flash cards in the normal flow of the application. Add a method to view controller called `showNextCard`, and make it able to handle populating the UI in each of the three interesting cases: when there are no flash cards, when there is a next flash card in the array, and when there is not a next flash card in the array and so we need to loop back to the beginning of the array of flash cards. Implement `showNextCard` as shown in Listing 16.12.

LISTING 16.12

```
-(void)showNextCard {

    self.rightButton.enabled = NO;
    self.wrongButton.enabled = NO;

    NSUInteger numberOfCards = [self.flashCards count];

    if (numberOfCards == 0) {
        // UI State for no cards
        self.question.text = @"";
        self.answer.text = @"";
        self.cardCount.text = @"Add a flash card to get started";
        self.wrongCount.text = @"";
        self.rightCount.text = @"";
        self.deleteButton.enabled = NO;
        self.actionButton.enabled = NO;
    } else {
        self.currentCardCounter += 1;
        if (self.currentCardCounter >= numberOfCards) {
            // Loop back to the first card
            self.currentCardCounter = 0;
        }
        self.cardCount.text =
        [NSString stringWithFormat:@"%i of %i",
         (self.currentCardCounter + 1), numberOfCards];
        self.question.text = self.currentCard.question;
        self.answer.hidden = YES;
        self.answer.text = self.currentCard.answer;
        [self updateRightWrongCounters];
        self.deleteButton.enabled = YES;
        self.actionButton.enabled = YES;
    }
}
```

Because the showNextCard method can set up the UI, even when we have no cards,
handling the initial load of the view is straightforward. We just need to create and
initialize the array that will hold the flash cards and then call the showNextCard
method. Uncomment the viewDidLoad method and implement it as shown in
Listing 16.13:

LISTING 16.13

```
- (void)viewDidLoad {
    self.flashCards = [NSKeyedUnarchiver
                       unarchiveObjectWithFile:[self archivePath]];
    self.currentCardCounter = -1;
    if (self.flashCards == nil) {
        self.flashCards = [[NSMutableArray alloc] init];
    }
    [self showNextCard];
    [super viewDidLoad];
}
```

The `showNextCard` method uses outlets to set values on the labels in the UI, and to enable and disable the buttons as appropriate. Careful readers will have noticed that it also called a method we haven't written yet, `updateRightWrongCounters`. This method should provide the right text to the labels based on the counters in the current flash card. Add the method in Listing 16.14, to the view controller.

LISTING 16.14

```
- (void) updateRightWrongCounters {
    self.wrongCount.text =
    [NSString stringWithFormat:@"Wrong: %i",
    self.currentCard.wrongCount];
    self.rightCount.text =
    [NSString stringWithFormat:@"Right: %i",
    self.currentCard.rightCount];
}
```

Update the FlashCardViewsController.h file in the Classes group with the two methods we just defined:

```
-(void)showNextCard;
-(void)updateRightWrongCounters;
```

There are three user actions for progressing through the set of flash cards: `nextAction`, `markWrong`, and `markRight`. `nextAction` first reveals the answer and enables the Right and Wrong buttons, and the second time `nextAction` is used on a card it advances to the next card. Implement `nextAction` as in Listing 16.15.

LISTING 16.15

```
- (IBAction) nextAction {
    if (self.answer.hidden) {
        self.answer.hidden = NO;
        self.rightButton.enabled = YES;
        self.wrongButton.enabled = YES;
    } else {
        [self showNextCard];
    }
}
```

The `markWrong` and `markRight` actions increment the counter for the flash card by one. They also handle disabling the button that was pressed so that the user doesn't increment twice for the same card, and they allow the user to change his mind by decrementing the previously incremented counter. Add the two methods in Listing 16.16 to the FlashCardsViewController.m file:

LISTING 16.16

```
- (IBAction) markWrong {

    // Update the flash card
    self.currentCard.wrongCount += 1;
    if (!self.rightButton.enabled) {
        // They had previously marked the card right
        self.currentCard.rightCount -= 1;
    }
    // Update the UI
    self.wrongButton.enabled = NO;
    self.rightButton.enabled = YES;
    [self updateRightWrongCounters];
}

- (IBAction) markRight {

    // Update the flash card
    self.currentCard.rightCount += 1;
    if (!self.wrongButton.enabled) {
        // They had previously marked the card right
        self.currentCard.wrongCount -= 1;
    }
    // Update the UI
    self.wrongButton.enabled = YES;
    self.rightButton.enabled = NO;
    [self updateRightWrongCounters];
}
```

Creating New Cards

We previously created a separate view and view controller to interact with the user and create a new card. Add a statement to the FlashCardsViewController.h file to import the second view controller:

```
#import "CreateCardViewController.h"
```

The addCard action that is called when the user touches the Add button instantiates an instance of our CreateCardViewController and turns control over to it with UIView's presentModalViewController:animated method. Add the action to the FlashCardsViewController.m file as follows in Listing 16.17.

LISTING 16.17

```
- (IBAction) addCard {
    // Show the create card view
    CreateCardViewController *cardCreator =
        [[CreateCardViewController alloc] init];
        cardCreator.cardDelegate = self;

    [self presentModalViewController:cardCreator animated:YES];
    [cardCreator release];
}
```

The addCard IBAction will now show our second view, but we still need to implement the controller for this view. The class header we created for CreateCardViewController tells us we have to synthesize three properties and implement the two actions. The actions just need to call back to the CardCreateDelegate when the user presses the Save or Cancel buttons. Click the CreateCardViewController.m file in the Classes group and update the file as in Listing 16.18.

LISTING 16.18

```
-(IBAction) save {
    [self.cardDelegate  didCreateCardWithQuestion: question.text
                                    answer: answer.text];
}

-(IBAction) cancel {
    [self.cardDelegate didCancelCardCreation];
}
```

Now we need to implement the card delegate in the FlashCardsViewController. If the callback indicates the user canceled, we need to dismiss only the modal view. When the delegate indicates a new card needs to be saved, we also must create a new FlashCard instance. After we create it, we need to insert the new flash card into the array of cards at the current spot or at the end of the array if we are on the last card. Then we show the next card in the array (which will always be the new card we just added). Click the FlashCardsViewController.m file in the Classes group and add the two methods shown in Listing 16.19 to implement the CreateCardDelegate protocol.

LISTING 16.19

```
-(void) didCancelCardCreation {
    [self dismissModalViewControllerAnimated:YES];
}

-(void) didCreateCardWithQuestion:(NSString *)thisQuestion
                           answer:(NSString *)thisAnswer {

    // Add the new card as the next card
    FlashCard *newCard = [[FlashCard alloc]initWithQuestion: thisQuestion
                                              answer:thisAnswer];
    if (self.currentCardCounter >= [self.flashCards count]) {
        [self.flashCards addObject:newCard];
    } else {
        [self.flashCards insertObject:newCard
                          atIndex:(self.currentCardCounter + 1)];
    }

    // Show the new card
    [self showNextCard];
    [self dismissModalViewControllerAnimated:YES];

}
```

Click the FlashCardsViewController.h file in the Classes group to import the CreateCardViewController interface file and modify the class's `@interface` to indicate that we've implemented the `CreateCardDelegate` protocol:

```
#import <UIKit/UIKit.h>
#import "FlashCard.h"
#import "CreateCardViewController.h"

@interface FlashCardsViewController : UIViewController <CreateCardDelegate> {
```

Delete Cards

Because we wrote our showNextCard method to be flexible, deleting a card is just a matter of deleting the current card from the array and showing the next card with showNextCard. showNextCard can handle any of the circumstances that may result from this, such as there being no cards in the array or needing to loop back to the beginning of the array:

```
- (IBAction) deleteCard {
    [self.flashCards removeObjectAtIndex:currentCardCounter];
    [self showNextCard];
}
```

We've now put together a working flash card application that is not too shabby (see Figure 16.16). At this point, the FlashCards application does have one fatal flaw: When the application terminates, all the flash cards the user painstakingly created are gone! In the next section, we rectify this using object archiving for data persistence.

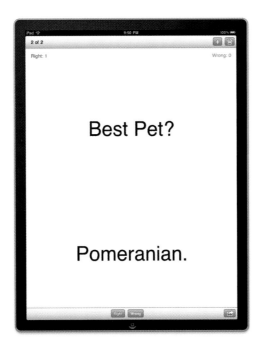

FIGURE 16.16
The FlashCards application in action.

Implementing Object Archiving

A running iPad application has a vast number of objects in memory. These objects are interlinked to one another with references in such a way that if you were to visualize the relationships, they would appear like a tangled spider web. This web of all the objects in an application and all the references between the objects is called an *object graph*.

A running iPad application is not much more than the program itself (which is always the same, at least until the user installs an update) and the unique object graph that is the result of all the activity that has occurred in the running of the application up to that point. One approach to storing an application's data (so that it is available when the application is launched again in the future) is to take the object graph, or a subset of it, and store the object graph on the file system. The next time the program runs, it can read the graph of objects from the file system back into memory and pick up where it left off, executing the same program with the same object graph.

Most object-oriented development environments have a serialization mechanism that is used to stream a graph of objects out of memory and onto a file system and then back into memory again at a later time. Object archiving is the Cocoa version of this process. There are two main parts to object archiving: NSCoder and NSCoding. An NSCoder object can archive (encode and decode) any object that conforms to the NSCoding protocol. Apple supplies NSCoder for most data types, and any custom objects we want to archive implement the NSCoding protocol. We are in luck because the NSCoding protocol consists of just two methods: initWithCoder and encodeWithCoder.

Let's start with encodeWithCoder. The purpose of encodeWithCoder is to encode all the instance variables of an object that should be stored during archival. To implement encodeWithCoder, decide which instance variables will be encoded and which instance variables, if any, will be transient (not encoded). Each instance variable you encode must be a scalar type (a number) or must be an object that implements NSCoding. This means all the instance variables you're likely to have in your custom objects can be encoded because the vast majority of Cocoa Touch and Core Foundation objects implement NSCoding. On the iPad, NSCoder uses keyed encoding, so you provide a key for each instance variable you encode. The encoding for our FlashCard class is shown in Listing 16.20.

LISTING 16.20

```
- (void)encodeWithCoder:(NSCoder *)encoder {

    [encoder encodeObject:self.question forKey:kQuestion];
    [encoder encodeObject:self.answer forKey:kAnswer];
    [encoder encodeInt:self.rightCount forKey:kRightCount];
    [encoder encodeInt:self.wrongCount forKey:kWrongCount];

}
```

Notice that we used the encodeObject:forKey method for NSStrings and you'd use the same for any other objects. For integers, we used encodeInt:forKey. You can check the API reference documentation of NSCoder for the complete list, but a few others you should be familiar with are encodeBool:forKey and encodeDouble:forKey and encodeBytes:forKey. You'll need these for dealing with Booleans, floating-point numbers, and data.

The opposite of encoding is decoding, and for that part of the protocol there is the initWithCoder method. Like encodeWithCoder, initWithCoder is keyed, but rather than providing NSCoder an instance variable for a key, you provide a key and are returned an instance variable. For our FlashCard class, decoding should be implemented as in Listing 16.21.

LISTING 16.21

```
- (id)initWithCoder:(NSCoder *)decoder {

    if (self = [super init]) {
        self.question = [decoder decodeObjectForKey:kQuestion];
        self.answer = [decoder decodeObjectForKey:kAnswer];
        self.rightCount = [decoder decodeIntForKey:kRightCount];
        self.wrongCount = [decoder decodeIntForKey:kWrongCount];
    }
    return self;

}
```

The four keys we used are should be defined as constants in the FlashCard.h header file. Add them now:

```
#define kQuestion @"Question"
#define kAnswer @"Answer"
#define kRightCount @"RightCount"
#define kWrongCount @"WrongCount"
```

The last step is to update the class definition in the FlashCard.h header file to indicate that FlashCard implements the NSCoding protocol:

```
@interface FlashCard : NSObject <NSCoding> {
```

Our FlashCard class is now archivable, and an object graph that includes FlashCard object instances can be persisted to and from the file system using object archiving.

Archiving in the Flash Cards

To fix the fatal flaw in the FlashCards application, we need to store all the flash cards on the file system. Now, because FlashCard implements the NSCoding protocol, each individual flash card is archivable. Remember that object archiving is based on the notion of storing an object graph and we are not looking to store each flash card in an individual file (although we certainly could if we wanted to). We want one object graph with references to all of our flash cards so that we can archive it into a single file.

It turns out that the FlashCards application already has such an object graph in memory in the form of the FlashCardsViewController's NSMuteableArray property called flashCards. The flashCards array has a reference to every flash card the user has defined, and so it forms the root of an object graph that contains all the flash cards. An NSMuteableArray, like all the Cocoa data structures, implements NSCoding, so we have a ready-made solution for archiving an object graph containing all the flash cards.

We need a location for the file that'll store the flash cards. We'd like the flash cards to be safely backed up each time the user syncs her device with iTunes, so we'll put the file in the application's Documents directory. We can call the file anything; object archiving doesn't put any restrictions on the filename or extension. Let's call it **FlashCards.dat**. We'll need the full path to this file both when we store the flash cards to the file system and when we read them from the file system, so let's write a simple helper function that returns the path to the file. Open the FlashCardsViewController.m file in the Classes group and add the method in Listing 16.22.

LISTING 16.22

```
-(NSString *)archivePath {
    NSString *docDir =
        [NSSearchPathForDirectoriesInDomains(NSDocumentDirectory,
        NSUserDomainMask, YES) objectAtIndex: 0];
    return [docDir stringByAppendingPathComponent:@"FlashCards.dat"];
}
```

We need to archive the array of flash cards to the file before the application terminates and then unarchive the array of flash cards from the file when the application starts. To write an archive to a file, use the `archiveRootObject:toFile` method of NSKeyedArchiver. We'll want to do this when the `FlashCardsAppDelegate` receives the applicationWillTerminate event, so define a method in the FlashCardsViewController.m file that `FlashCardsAppDelegate` can call to archive the flash cards:

```
-(void)archiveFlashCards {
    [NSKeyedArchiver archiveRootObject:flashCards toFile:[self archivePath]];
}
```

Add the new method to the FlashCardsViewController.h file:

```
-(void)archiveFlashCards;
```

Open the FlashCardsAppDelegate.m file and add the applicationWillTerminate that will call the archiveFlashCards method of the FlashCardsViewController:

```
- (void)applicationWillTerminate:(UIApplication *)application {
    [viewController archiveFlashCards];
}
```

Each time our application terminates, whatever flash cards are in the array will be written out to the FlashCards.dat file in the Documents directory. On startup, we need to read the archive of the array from the file. To unarchive an object graph, use the unarchiveObjectWithFile method of NSKeyedUnarchiver. It's possible this

is the first time the application has ever been run and there won't yet be a
FlashCards.dat file. In this case, `unarchiveObjectWithFile` returns `nil` and we can
just create a new, empty array like we did before the FlashCards application had
data persistence. Update the `viewDidLoad` method of the
FlashCardsViewController.m file as follows:

```
- (void)viewDidLoad {
    self.flashCards = [NSKeyedUnarchiver
                         unarchiveObjectWithFile:[self archivePath]];
    self.currentCardCounter = -1;
    if (self.flashCards == nil) {
        self.flashCards = [[NSMutableArray alloc] init];
    }
    [self showNextCard];
    [super viewDidLoad];
}
```

That's all there is to it. Once the model objects of an application all implement
`NSCoding`, object archiving is a simple and easy process. With just a few lines of
code, we were able to persist the flash cards to the file system. Run the application
and give it a try!

Further Exploration

There is not much about preferences that you have not been exposed to at this
point. My main advice is to gain some more experience in working with preferences
by going back to previous hours and adding sensible preferences to some of the
example applications you have already worked on. The Application Preferences
system is well documented by Apple, and you should take some time to read
through it.

If you'd like to go further exploring object archiving, your next stop should be
Apple's *Archives and Serializations Programming Guide for Cocoa*, but more complex
data needs, you should begin reviewing the documentation on Core Data.

Core Data is a framework that provides management and persistence for in-memory
application object graphs. Core Data attempts to solve many of the challenges that
face other, simpler forms of object persistence such as object archiving. Some of the
challenging areas Core Data focuses on are multilevel undo management, data
validation, data consistency across independent data assessors, efficient (that is,
indexed) filtering, sorting and searching of object graphs, and persistence to a
variety of data repositories.

Apple Guides

Application Preferences in the iPhone Application Programming is a tutorial-style guide to the various parts of the Application Preference system.

Setting Application Schema References in the iPhone Reference Library is an indispensable guide to the required and optional properties for the preferences in your plist files that will be edited by the Settings application.

Core Data Tutorial for iPhone OS is an Apple tutorial for learning the basics of Core Data. This is a good place to start for an exploration of Core Data.

Summary

In this hour, you've developed three iPad applications, and along the way you learned three different ways of storing the application's data. You captured the user's implicit preferences with the Flashlight application, you allowed the ReturnMe application to be explicitly configured from the Settings application, and stored the FlashCards data through object archiving. You also learned some important design principles that should keep you from getting carried away with too many preferences and should guide you in putting preferences in the right location.

This hour explored a lot of ground, and you have covered the topic of application data storage fairly exhaustively. At this point, you should be ready for most storage needs you encounter while developing your own applications.

Q&A

Q. *What about games? How should game preferences be handled?*

A. Games are about providing the player with an immersive experience. Leaving that experience to go to the Settings application or to interact with a stodgy table view is not going to keep the player immersed. You want users to set up the game to their liking while still remaining in the game's world, with the music and graphical style of the game as part of the customization experience. For games, feel free to use the `NSUserDefaults` API, but provide a custom, in-game experience for the UI.

Q. *I have more complex data requirements. Is there a database I can use?*

A. Although the techniques discussed in this hour's lesson are suitable for most applications, you might want to use Core Data in larger apps. Core Data implements a high-level data model and helps developers manage very complex data requirements.

Workshop

Quiz

1. What is object archiving?

2. What is a plist file?

Answers

1. Object archiving is the ability to save complex objects to files through the process of serialization, and then to read them back into memory at a later time.

2. A plist file is an XML property list file used to store the user's settings for a given application. Plist files can be edited from within Xcode and externally to Xcode with the Property List Editor application.

Activities

1. If you think through the life cycle of the Flashlight application, you may realize there is a circumstance we didn't account for. It's possible that the Flashlight application has never been run before and so has no stored user preferences. To try this scenario, select Reset Content and Settings from the iPhone Simulator menu, and then build and launch the Flashlight application in the simulator. With no prior settings, it defaults to off, with the brightness turned all the way down. This is the exact opposite of what we would like to default to the first time Flashlight is run. Apply the technique we used in the Remember Me application to fix this and default the flashlight's initial state to on and 100% brightness.

2. Return to an earlier application and use implicit preferences to save the state of the program before it exits. When the user relaunches, restore the application to its original state. This is a key part of the user experience on the iPad, and something you should strive for.

HOUR 17

Building Rotatable and Resizable User Interfaces

What You'll Learn in This Hour:

▶ How to make an application "rotation aware"
▶ Ways of laying out an interface to enable automatic rotation
▶ Methods of tweaking interface elements' frames to fine-tune a layout
▶ How to swap views for landscape and portrait viewing

You can use almost every iPad interface widget available, you can create multiple views and view controllers, add sounds and alerts, write files, and even manage application preferences—but until now, your applications suffered from a flaw—if you turn your iPad on its side, the interface can potentially become a jumbled mess! Although Apple's iPad templates enable interface rotation, it's up to you to react and reshape (or replace) the interface depending on the device's orientation. Apple strongly urges developers to create apps that are viewable in all orientations, so this information may be key in getting your application approved for distribution!

This hour's lesson explores three different ways of adding rotatable and resizable interfaces to your apps. You might be surprised to learn that *all* the apps you've built to date can become rotation-aware without a single line of code!

Rotatable and Resizable Interfaces

Years ago, when I bought my ViewSonic Windows Tablet, I was amazed at how difficult it was to switch orientations. Install a device driver, make sure you've booted and logged in, click a little toolbar icon to show a screen menu, choose your orientation, wait... and, eventually, the screen would shift. The iPad features on-the-fly interface rotation that feels natural and doesn't get in the way of what you're trying to do.

As you build your iPad applications, consider how the user will be interfacing with the app. Are there instances when you should force a specific view? Should the interface change when you shift views? The more flexibility you give users to adapt to their own preferred working style, the happier they'll be. Best of all, building rotation-aware apps is a simple process.

Take a few minutes to go back and look at some of the earlier applications we built in nonportrait orientations. Some will probably look just fine, but you'll notice that others, well...don't quite "work" in the different screen orientations, as shown in Figure 17.1.

FIGURE 17.1
Allowing the screen to rotate doesn't mean your application will function perfectly in the new orientation!

Because the iPad screen isn't square, it stands to reason that landscape and portrait views might not match up very well. Everything we've been building has been designed in portrait mode, so how can we create interfaces that look good in portrait or landscape mode? We obviously need to make some tweaks! Let's take a look at what makes rotation possible, then how to control it.

The Key to Interface Rotation

If you start one of the iPad applications you've built and rotate your device, you'll notice that the application's interface rotates (or tries to rotate) to accommodate the change. What makes all this possible is a single method `shouldAutorotateToInterfaceOrientation` that was added automatically to your iPad application's view controller:

```
- (BOOL)shouldAutorotateToInterfaceOrientation:
        (UIInterfaceOrientation)interfaceOrientation {
   return YES;
}
```

When the iPad wants to check to see whether it should rotate your interface, it sends the shouldAutorotateToInterfaceOrientation: message to your view controller, along with a parameter that indicates which orientation it wants to check. By default, the method *always* returns YES, which means that the application should rotate the interface no matter how the user is holding the device.

To limit interface rotation, you can modify shouldAutorotateToInterfaceOrientation: to compare the incoming parameter against the different orientation constants in the iPhone OS, returning TRUE (or YES) if you want to support that orientation.

You'll encounter four basic screen orientation constants:

Orientation	iPad Orientation Constant
Portrait	UIInterfaceOrientationPortrait
Portrait upside-down	UIInterfaceOrientationPortraitUpsideDown
Landscape left	UIInterfaceOrientationLandscapeLeft
Landscape right	UIInterfaceOrientationLandscapeRight

For example, to allow your interface to rotate to either the portrait or landscape left orientations, you would implement shouldAutorotateToInterfaceOrientation: in your view controller like this:

```
- (BOOL)shouldAutorotateToInterfaceOrientation:
        (UIInterfaceOrientation)interfaceOrientation {
   return (interfaceOrientation == UIInterfaceOrientationPortrait ||
           interfaceOrientation == UIInterfaceOrientationLandscapeLeft);
}
```

The return statement handles everything! It returns the result of an expression comparing the incoming orientation parameter, interfaceOrientation, to UIInterfaceOrientationPortrait and UIInterfaceOrientationLandscapeLeft. If either comparison is true, TRUE is returned. If one of the other possible orientations is checked, the expression evaluates to FALSE. In other words, by adding this check to the method, your application will limit rotation to standard portrait or landscape-left modes!

> Remember, you shouldn't artificially limit the allowed orientations of the iPad! If users want to use the application with the device upside-down, they should be able to, unless there is a good reason not to! The examples in this chapter show you what is possible. (They do not imply that supporting one landscape and one portrait mode is appropriate!)

Designing Rotatable and Resizable Interfaces

In the remainder of this hour, we'll be exploring three different techniques for build-ing interfaces that rotate and resize themselves appropriately when the user changes the iPad screen orientation. Before we get started, let's quickly review the different approaches and when you may want to use them.

> ### I Get "Rotatable," but What's with the "Resizable?"
>
> When the iPad rotates, the screen dimensions shift. You still have the same amount of usable space, but it is laid out differently. To make the best use of the available space, you can have your controls (buttons and so on) resize for the new orientation—thus the combination of "rotatable" and "resizable" when discussing screen rotation.

Autorotating and Autoresizing

Interface Builder provides tools for describing how your interface should react when it is rotated. It is possible to define a single view in Interface Builder that positions and sizes itself appropriately when rotated, without writing a single line of code!

This should be the starting point for all interfaces. If you can successfully define por-trait and landscape modes in single view in Interface Builder, your work is done.

Unfortunately, autorotating/autoresizing doesn't work well when there are many irregularly positioned interface elements. A single row of buttons? No problem! Half a dozen fields, switches, and images all mixed together? Probably not going to work.

Reframing

As you've learned, each iPad UI element is defined by a rectangular area on the screen: its `frame` property.

To change the size or location of something in the view, you can redefine the `frame` using the Core Graphics C function `CGRectMake(x,y,width,height)`. `CGRectMake` accepts an x and y coordinate, along with a width and height, and returns a new frame value.

By defining new frames for everything in your view, you have complete control of each object's placement and size. Unfortunately, you need to keep track of the coor-dinate positions for each object. This isn't difficult, per se, but it can be frustrating when you want to shift an object up or down by a few pixels and suddenly find yourself needing to adjust the coordinates of every other object above or below it.

Swapping Views

A more dramatic approach to changing your view to accommodate different screen orientations is to use entirely different views for landscape and portrait layouts! When the user rotates the device, the current view is replaced by another view that is laid out properly for the orientation.

This means that you can define two views in Interface Builder that look exactly the way you want, but it also means that you'll need to keep track of separate IBOutlets for each view! While it is certainly possible for elements in the views to invoke the same IBActions, they cannot share the same outlets, so you'll potentially need to keep track of twice as many UI widgets within a single view controller.

To know *when* to change frames or swap views, you will be implementing the method willRotateToInterfaceOrientation:toInterfaceOrientation:duration in your view controller. This method is called by the iPad when it is about to change orientation.

By the Way

Apple has implemented a screen-locking function on the iPad so that users can set the screen in a particular orientation and rotate the iPad without it changing. (This can be useful for reading while lying on your side.) When the screen lock is enabled, your application will not receive notifications about a change in orientation. In other words, to support the screen lock, you don't need to do a thing!

Did you Know?

Creating Rotatable and Resizable Interfaces with Interface Builder

In the first of our three tutorial projects, we'll look at ways you can use the built-in tools in Interface Builder to control how your views "adapt" to being rotated. For simple views, these features provide everything you need to create orientation-aware apps.

We'll be using a label (UILabel) and a few buttons (UIButton) as our "study subjects" for this tutorial. Feel free to swap them out with other interface elements to see how rotation and resizing is handled across the library.

Setting Up the Project

For this project, we won't even need a project! Open Interface Builder and create a new iPad view by choosing File, New, and then selecting the iPhone OS category and

View template. Be sure to set the product to the iPad,; otherwise, you'll get a tiny iPhone view! Once the template has opened, save it with the name **SimpleSpinView**.

All our work for this example takes place in this file.

Building a Flexible Interface

Creating a rotatable and resizable interface starts out like building any other iPad interface: Just drag and drop!

Open the view you've created, and then populate it with a few items from the Library (Tools, Library). Drag a label (`UILabel`) and four buttons (`UIButton`) to the SimpleSpin view. Center the label at the top of the view, increase the font size to 48, and title it **SimpleSpin**. Name the buttons so you can tell them apart: **Button 1**, **Button 2**, **Button 3**, and **Button 4**. Position them below the label, as shown in Figure 17.2.

FIGURE 17.2
Build your rotatable application interface the same way you would any other interface.

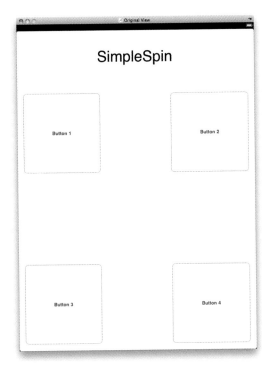

Testing Rotation

You've now built a simple application interface, just as you have in earlier lessons. To get an idea of what the interface looks like when rotated, click the curved arrow in the upper-right corner of the Interface Builder's view window (see Figure 17.3).

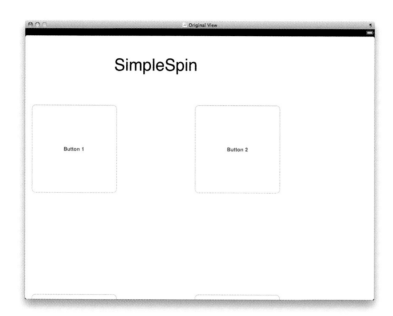

FIGURE 17.3
Use Interface Builder to immediately test the effects of rotating the view.

As you might expect, the reoriented view does not look "quite right." The reason is that objects you add to the view are, by default, "anchored" by their upper-left corner. This means that no matter what the screen orientation is, they'll keep the same distance from the top of the view to their top, and from left of the view to their left side. Objects also, by default, are not allowed to resize within the view. As a result, all elements have the exact same size in portrait or landscape orientations, even if they won't fit in the view.

To fix our problem and create an iPad-worthy interface, we'll need to use the Size Inspector.

Understanding Autosizing in the Size Inspector

As you've grown more experienced building iPad applications, you've gotten accustomed to using the Interface Builder inspectors. The Attributes and Connections Inspectors have been extremely valuable in configuring the appearance and functionality of your application. The Size Inspector (Command+3), on the other hand, has remained largely on the sidelines, occasionally called on to set the coordinates of a control, but never used to enable functionality—until now.

The magic of autorotating and autoresizing views is managed entirely through the Size Inspector's Autosizing settings, shown in Figure 17.4. This deceptively simple "square in a square" interface provides everything you need to tell Interface Builder where to anchor your controls, and in which directions (horizontally or vertically) they can stretch.

FIGURE 17.4
The Autosizing settings control anchor and size properties for any onscreen object.

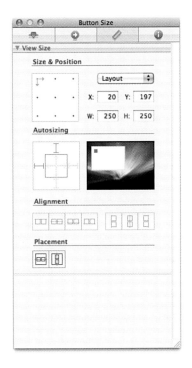

To understand how this works, imagine that the inner square represents one of your interface elements, and the outer square is the view that contains the element. The lines between the inner and outer square are the anchors. When clicked, they toggle between solid and dashed lines. Solid lines are anchors that are set. This means that those distances will be maintained when the interface rotates.

Within the inner square are two double-headed arrows, representing horizontal and vertical resizing. Clicking these arrows toggles between solid and dashed lines. Solid arrows indicate that the item is allowed to resize horizontally, vertically, or both. As mentioned earlier, by default, objects are anchored on their top and left, and are not allowed to resize. This configuration is visible in Figure 17.4.

Did you
Know?

If you need a more "visual" means of understanding the autosizing controls, just look to the right of the two squares. The rectangle to the right shows an animated preview of what will happen to your control (represented as a red rectangle) when the view changes size around it. The easiest way to start understanding the relationship between anchors, resizing, and view size/orientation is to configure the anchors/resize-arrows, and then watch the preview to see the effect.

Applying Autosize Settings to the Interface

To modify our SimpleSpin interface with appropriate autosizing attributes, let's analyze what we want to have happen for each element and translate that into anchors and resizing information.

As we work through the list, select each of the interface elements, and then open the Size Inspector (Commnd+3) and configure their anchors and resizing attributes as described here:

The "SimpleSpin" label: The label should float at the top center of the view. The distance between the top of the view and the label should be maintained. The size of the label should be maintained. (Anchor: Top, Resizing: None).

Button 1: The button should maintain the same distance between its left side and the left side of the view, but it should be allowed to float up and down as needed. It can resize horizontally to better fit a larger horizontal space. (Anchor: Left, Resizing: Horizontal).

Button 2: The button should maintain the same distance between its right side and the right side of the view, but it should be allowed to float up and down as needed. It can resize horizontally to better fit a larger horizontal space. (Anchor: Right, Resizing: Horizontal).

Button 3: The button should maintain the same distance between its left side and the left side of the view, as well as its bottom and the bottom of the view. It can resize horizontally to better fit a larger horizontal space. (Anchor: Left and Bottom, Resizing: Horizontal).

Button 4: The button should maintain the same distance between its right side and the right side of the view, as well as its bottom and the bottom of the view. It can resize horizontally to better fit a larger horizontal space. (Anchor: Right and Bottom, Resizing: Horizontal).

After you've worked through one or two of the UI objects, you'll realize that it took longer to describe what we needed to do, than to do it! Once the anchors and resize settings are in place, the application is ready for rotation! Click the rotate arrow in the Interface Builder's view window and review the result. Your view should now resize and resemble Figure 17.5.

FIGURE 17.5
The finished
view now prop-
erly positions
itself when
rotated into a
landscape orien-
tation.

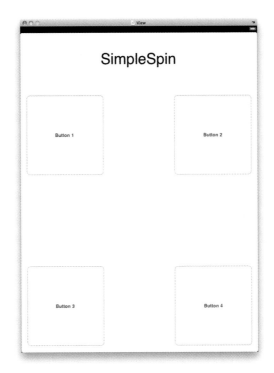

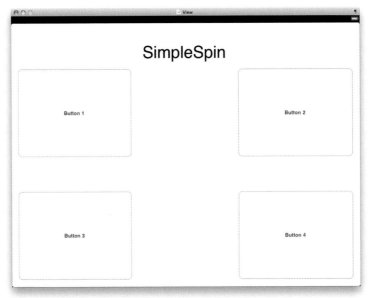

You can, if you choose, save the SimpleSpinView.xib changes, and then choose File, Simulate Interface (Command+R) in Interface Builder. This will run the interface in the iPhone Simulator and give you a better sense of how the interface will look in action on a real device.

Reframing Controls on Rotation

In the previous example, you learned how Interface Builder can help quickly create interface layouts that look as good horizontally as they do vertically. Unfortunately, there are plenty of situations that Interface Builder can't quite accommodate. Irregularly spaced controls and tightly packed layouts will rarely work out the way you expect. You may also find yourself wanting to tweak the interface to look completely different—positioning objects that were at the top of the view down by the bottom, and so on.

In either of these cases, you'll likely want to consider reframing the controls to accommodate a rotated iPad screen. The logic is simple: When the device interface rotates, we'll identify which orientation it will be rotating *to*, and then set new frame properties for everything in the UI that we want to reposition or resize. You'll learn how to do this now.

Setting Up the Project

Unlike the previous example, we can't rely on Interface Builder for everything, so there will be a small amount of code in this tutorial. Create a new iPadView-Based Application project, named **Reframe**.

Adding Outlets and Properties

In this exercise, you'll be manually resizing and repositioning three UI elements: two buttons (UIButton), and one label (UILabel). Because we'll need to access these programmatically, we'll first edit the interface and implementation files to include outlets and properties for each of these objects.

Open the ReframeViewController.h file and edit it to include IBOutlet declarations and @property directives for buttonOne, buttonTwo, and viewLabel, as seen in Listing 17.1.

LISTING 17.1

```
#import <UIKit/UIKit.h>

@interface ReframeViewController : UIViewController {
    IBOutlet UIButton *buttonOne;
    IBOutlet UIButton *buttonTwo;
    IBOutlet UILabel *viewLabel;
}

@property (nonatomic,retain) UIButton *buttonOne;
@property (nonatomic,retain) UIButton *buttonTwo;
@property (nonatomic,retain) UILabel *viewLabel;

@end
```

Save your changes, and then edit `ReframeViewController.m`, adding the appropriate `@synthesize` directives for `buttonOne`, `buttonTwo`, and `viewLabel`, immediately following the `@implementation` line:

```
@synthesize buttonOne;
@synthesize buttonTwo;
@synthesize viewLabel;
```

Releasing the Objects

Edit the `dealloc` method in ReframeViewController.m to release the label and button we've retained:

```
- (void)dealloc {
    [buttonOne release];
    [buttonTwo release];
    [viewLabel release];
    [super dealloc];
}
```

With the exception of the logic to detect and handle the reframing of our interface elements, that finishes the setup of our application. Now, let's create the default view that will be displayed when the application first loads.

Creating the Interface

We've now reached the point in the project where the one big caveat of reframing becomes apparent: keeping track of interface coordinates and sizes. Although we have the opportunity to lay out the interface in Interface Builder, we need to note where all the different elements *are*. Why? Because each time the screen changes rotation, we'll be resetting their position in the view. There is no "return to default positions" method, so even the initial layout we create will have to be coded using x,y coordinates and sizes so that we can call it back up when needed. Let's begin.

Open the ReframeViewController.xib file and its view in Interface Builder.

Disabling Autoresizing

Before doing anything else, click within the view to select it, and then open the Attribute Inspector (Command+1). Within the View settings section, uncheck the Autoresize Subviews check box (see Figure 17.6).

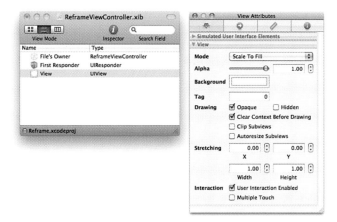

FIGURE 17.6
Disabling autoresizing when manually resizing and positioning controls.

If you forget to disable the autoresize attribute in the view, your application code will manually resize/reposition the UI elements at the same time the iPhone OS tries to do it for you. The result can be a jumbled mess and several minutes of head scratching!

Laying Out the View... Once

Your next step is to lay out the view exactly as you would in any other app. Recall that we added outlets for two buttons and a label; using the Library, click and drag those elements into your view now. Title the label **Reframing** and position it at the top of the view. Set the button titles to **Button 1** and **Button 2**, and place them under the label. Your final layout should resemble Figure 17.7.

FIGURE 17.7
Start by laying
out the view
like a normal
application.

When you have the layout you want, determine what the current frame attributes are for each of your objects. We can get this information from the Size Inspector.

Start by selecting the label and opening the Size Inspector (Command+3). Click the dot in the upper-right corner of the Size & Position settings to set the upper-right corner as the origin point for measuring coordinates. Next, make sure that the drop-down menu is set to Frame, as shown in Figure 17.8.

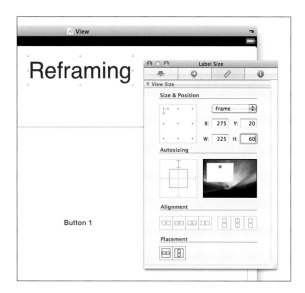

FIGURE 17.8
Configure the
Size & Position
settings to
show the infor-
mation you
need to collect.

Now, write down the X, Y, W (width), and H (height) attributes for the label. This
represents the frame property of the object within your view. Repeat this process for
the two buttons. You should end up with a list of four values for each of your
objects. Our frame values are listed here for comparison:

Label	X: 275.0, Y: 20.0, W: 225.0, H: 60.0
Button 1	X: 20.0, Y: 168.0, W: 728.0, H: 400.0
Button 2	X: 20.0, Y: 584.0, W: 728.0, H: 400.0

Before doing anything else, *save your view*! We'll be making some changes in the
next section that you'll want to undo.

If you want to follow our example *exactly*, feel free to substitute the X, Y, W, and H
values we've provided for the values of your objects in the Size Inspector. Doing
this will resize and reposition your view elements to match ours!

*Did you
Know?*

Laying Out the View... Again

Your next step is to lay out the view exactly as you would in any other app. Wait a
sec... this sounds very familiar. Why do we want to lay out the view again? The
answer is simple. We've collected all the frame properties that we need to configure
the portrait view, but we haven't yet defined where the label and buttons will be in
the *landscape* view. To get this information, we lay the view out again, in landscape
mode, collect all the location and size attributes, and then discard those changes.

The process is identical to what you've already done; the only difference is that you need to click the rotate arrow in Interface Builder to rotate the view. Once you've rotated the view, resize and reposition all the existing elements so that they look the way you want them to appear when in landscape orientation on your iPad. Because we'll be setting the positions and sizes programmatically, the sky is the limit for how you arrange the display. To follow our example, stretch Button 1 across the top of the view and Button 2 across the button. Position the Reframing label in the middle, as shown in Figure 17.9.

FIGURE 17.9
Lay the view out as you want it to appear in landscape mode.

As before, when the view is exactly as you want it to appear, use the Size Inspector (Command+3) to collect the x,y coordinates and height and width of all the UI elements. Our landscape frame values are provided here for comparison:

Label   X: 400.0, Y: 340.0, W: 225.0, H: 60.0

Button 1   X: 20.0, Y: 20.0, W: 983.0, H: 185.0

Button 2   X: 20.0, Y: 543.0, W: 983.0, H: 185.0

When you've collected the landscape frame attributes, undo the changes by using Edit, Undo (Command+Z), or close ReframeViewController.xib (*not* saving the changes).

Connecting the Outlets

Before jumping back into Xcode to finish the implementation, we still need to connect the label and buttons to the outlets (`viewLabel`, `buttonOne`, and `buttonTwo`) that we added at the start of the project. Open ReframeViewController.xib again (if you closed it in the last step), and make sure that the view window and Document window are both visible onscreen.

Next, Control-drag from the File's Owner icon to the label and two buttons, choosing `viewLabel`, `buttonOne`, and `buttonTwo` as appropriate. Figure 17.10 demonstrates the connection from the Reframing label to the `viewLabel` outlet.

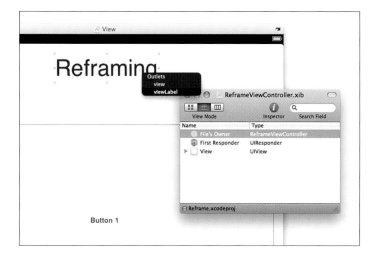

FIGURE 17.10
Finish up the interface by connecting the label and buttons to their corresponding outlets.

Save the XIB file and return to Xcode to finish up the project!

Implementing the Reframing Logic

Now that you've built the view and captured the values for the label and button frames in both portrait and landscape views, the only thing that remains is detecting when the iPad is ready to rotate and reframing appropriately.

The `willRotateToInterfaceOrientation:toInterfaceOrientation:duration:` method is invoked automatically whenever the interface needs to rotate. We'll compare the `toInterfaceOrientation` parameter to the different iPad orientation constants to identify whether we should be using the frames for a landscape or portrait view.

Open the ReframeViewController.m file in Xcode and add the method shown in Listing 17.2:

LISTING 17.2

```
 1: -(void)willRotateToInterfaceOrientation:
 2:        (UIInterfaceOrientation)toInterfaceOrientation
 3:                  duration:(NSTimeInterval)duration {
 4:
 5:        [super willRotateToInterfaceOrientation:toInterfaceOrientation
 6:                                duration:duration];
 7:
 8:        if (toInterfaceOrientation == UIInterfaceOrientationLandscapeRight ||
 9:            toInterfaceOrientation == UIInterfaceOrientationLandscapeLeft) {
10:            viewLabel.frame=CGRectMake(400.0,340.0,225.0,60.0);
11:            buttonOne.frame=CGRectMake(20.0,20.0,983.0,185.0);
12:            buttonTwo.frame=CGRectMake(20.0,543.0,983.0,185.0);
13:        } else {
14:            viewLabel.frame=CGRectMake(275.0,20.0,225.0,60.0);
15:            buttonOne.frame=CGRectMake(20.0,168.0,728.0,400.0);
16:            buttonTwo.frame=CGRectMake(20.0,584.0,728.0,400.0);
17:        }
18: }
```

The logic is straightforward. To start, we need to make sure that any parent objects are notified that the view is about to rotate. So, in lines 5–6, we pass the same `willRotateToInterfaceOrientation:toInterfaceOrientation:duration:` message to the parent object `super`.

In lines 8–12 we compare the incoming parameter `toInterfaceOrientation` to the landscape orientation constants. If either of these match, we reframe the label and buttons to their landscape layouts by assigning the `frame` property to the output of the `CGRectMake()` function. The input to `CGRectMake()` is nothing more than the X,Y,W, and H values we collected earlier in Interface Builder.

Lines 13–16 handle the "other" orientation: portrait orientation. If the iPad isn't rotated into a landscape orientation, the only other possibility is portrait. Again, the frame values that we assign are nothing more than the values identified using the Size Inspector in Interface Builder.

And, with this simple method, the Reframe project is now complete! You now have the capability of creating interfaces that rearrange themselves when users rotate their iPad.

We still have one more approach to cover. In this final project, rather than rearranging a view in the landscape orientation, we'll replace the view altogether!

Swapping Views on Rotation

Some applications display entirely different user interfaces depending on the iPad's orientation. The Mail application, for example, displays a full view of a message in portrait mode, and a split view with a message list *and* the message when held in landscape. You too can create applications that dramatically alter their appearance by simply switching between views when the device is rotated. Our last tutorial this hour will be short, sweet, and give you the flexibility to manage your landscape and portrait views all within the comfort of Interface Builder.

Setting Up the Project

Create a new project named **Swapper** using the iPad View-Based Application template. Although this includes a single view already (which we'll use for the default portrait display), we'll need to supplement it with a second landscape view.

Adding Outlets and Properties

This application won't implement any real user interface elements, but we will need to access two UIView instances programmatically.

Open the SwapperViewController.h file and edit it to include IBOutlet declarations and @property directives for portraitView, and landscapeView. The result should match Listing 17.3.

LISTING 17.3

```
#import <UIKit/UIKit.h>

@interface ReframeViewController : UIViewController {
    IBOutlet UIView *portraitView;
    IBOutlet UIView *landscapeView;
}

@property (nonatomic,retain) UIView *portraitView;
@property (nonatomic,retain) UIView *landscapeView;

@end
```

You know the routine. Save your changes, and then edit the SwapperViewController.m implementation file, adding the appropriate @synthesize directives immediately following the @implementation line:

```
@synthesize portraitView;
@synthesize landscapeView;
```

Releasing the Objects

Edit the `dealloc` method in ReframeViewController.m to release the two views we've retained:

```
- (void)dealloc {
    [landscapeView release];
    [portraitView release];
    [super dealloc];
}
```

Limiting Rotation

To mix things up a bit, let's limit the rotation options available in this last project. This time, we'll allow only rotation between the two landscape modes and upright portrait.

Update `ReframeViewController.m` to include this implementation:

```
- (BOOL)shouldAutorotateToInterfaceOrientation:
            (UIInterfaceOrientation)interfaceOrientation {
    return (interfaceOrientation == UIInterfaceOrientationPortrait ||
            interfaceOrientation == UIInterfaceOrientationLandscapeRight ||
            interfaceOrientation == UIInterfaceOrientationLandscapeLeft);
}
```

The incoming `interfaceOrientation` parameter is compared to the `UIInterfaceOrientationPortrait`, `UIInterfaceOrientationLandscapeRight`, and `UIInterfaceOrientationLandscapeLeft`. If it matches, rotation is allowed. As you might surmise, this covers all the possible orientations except upside-down portrait (`UIInterfaceOrientationPortraitUpsideDown`), which we're disabling this time around.

Adding a Degree to Radians Constant

Later in this exercise, we're going to need to call a special Core Graphics method to define how to rotate views. The method requires a value to be passed in radians rather than degrees. In other words, instead of saying we want to rotate the view 90 degrees, we have to tell it we want to rotate 1.57 radians. To help us handle the conversion, we will define a constant for the conversion factor. Multiplying degrees by the constant gets us the resulting value in radians.

To define the constant, add the following line after the `#import` line in SwapperViewController.m:

```
#define deg2rad (3.1415926/180.0)
```

Creating the Interface

When swapping views, the sky is the limit for the design. You build them exactly as you would in any other application. The only difference is that if you have multiple views handled by a single view controller, you'll need to define outlets that encompass all the interface elements.

In this example, we'll just be demonstrating how to swap views, so our work in Interface Builder will be quite simple.

Creating the Views

Open SwapperViewController.xib and drag a new instance of the UIView object from the Library to the Document window. Don't put the UIView inside of the existing view. It should be added as a new separate view within the XIB file, as seen in Figure 17.11.

FIGURE 17.11
Add a second view to the XIB file.

Now, open each of the views and add a label to tell them apart. We've set the background color of each view to be different as well. You're welcome to add other controls and design the view as you see fit. Figure 17.12 shows our finished landscape and portrait views.

To differentiate between the two views within the Interface Builder document window, you can switch to icon view, and then edit the name of each view just like you would in the Finder!

Did you Know?

FIGURE 17.12
Edit the two
views so that
you can tell
them apart.

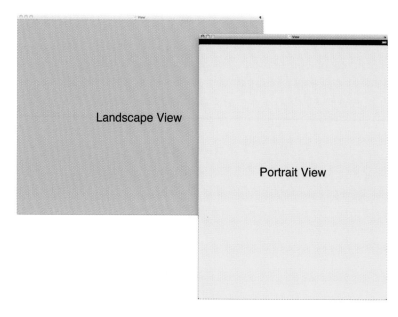

Connecting the Outlets

To finish up in Interface Builder, Control-drag from the File's Owner icon to each of the views. Connect the portrait view to the portraitView outlet, as shown in Figure 17.13, and the landscape view to landscapeView.

FIGURE 17.13
Connect the
views to their
corresponding
outlets.

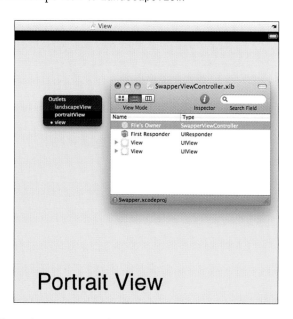

Save the XIB file and return to Xcode to finish up the Swapper implementation.

Implementing the View-Swapping Logic

For the most part, swapping views is actually easier than the reframing logic that we had to implement in the last project—with one small exception. Even though we designed one of the views to be a landscape view, it doesn't "know" that it is supposed to be displayed in a landscape orientation. Before we can display it, we need to rotate it and define how big it is.

Understanding the View-Rotation Logic

Each time we change orientation, we'll go through three steps: swapping the view, rotating the view to the proper orientation through the transform property, and setting the view's origin and size via the bounds property.

For example, assume we're rotating to right landscape orientation:

1. First, we swap out the view by assigning self.view, which contains the current view of the view controller, to the landscapeView instance variable. If we left things at that, the view would properly switch, but it wouldn't be rotated into the landscape orientation. A landscape view displayed in a portrait orientation isn't a pretty thing! For example:

   ```
   self.view=landscapeView;
   ```

2. Next, to deal with the rotation, we define the transform property of the view. This property determines how the view will be altered before it is displayed. To meet our needs, we'll have to rotate the view 90 degrees to the right (for landscape right), –90 degrees to the left (for landscape left), and 0 degrees for portrait. As luck would have it, the Core Graphics C function CGAffineTransformMakeRotation() accepts a rotation value in radians and provides an appropriate structure to the transform property to handle the rotation. For example:

   ```
   self.view.transform=CGAffineTransformMakeRotation(deg2rad*(90));
   ```

> Note that we multiply the rotation in degrees (90, –90, and 0) by the constant deg2rad that we defined earlier so that CGAffineTransformMakeRotation() has the radian value it expects.

3. The final step is to set the bounds property of the view. The bounds define the origin point and size of the view after it undergoes the transformation. A portrait iPad view has an original point of 0,0 and a width and height of 768 and 1004. A landscape view has the same origin point (0,0), but a width of 1024,

and a height of 748. As with the `frame` property, we can set bounds using the results of `CGRectMake()`. For example:

```
self.view.bounds=CGRectMake(0.0,0.0,1024.0,748.0);
```

What Happened to 768x1024 (or 1024x768)? Where Are the Missing 20 Pixels?

The missing 20 pixels are taken up by the iPad status bar. When the device is in portrait mode, the pixels come off of the large (1024) dimension. In landscape orientation, however, the status bar eats up the space on the smaller (768) dimension. Apple strongly recommends against disabling the status bar in iPad applications, so we're simply removing the 20 pixels it occupies from our calculations.

Now that you understand the steps, let's take a look at the actual implementation.

Writing the View-Rotation Logic

As with the Reframing project, all this magic happens within a single method, `willRotateToInterfaceOrientation:toInterfaceOrientation:duration:`.

Open the SwapperViewController.m implementation file and implement the method as shown in Listing 17.4.

LISTING 17.4

```
 1: -(void)willRotateToInterfaceOrientation:
 2:             (UIInterfaceOrientation)toInterfaceOrientation
 3:             duration:(NSTimeInterval)duration {
 4:
 5:     [super willRotateToInterfaceOrientation:toInterfaceOrientation
 6:                               duration:duration];
 7:
 8:     if (toInterfaceOrientation == UIInterfaceOrientationLandscapeRight) {
 9:         self.view=landscapeView;
10:         self.view.transform=CGAffineTransformMakeRotation(deg2rad*(90));
11:         self.view.bounds=CGRectMake(0.0,0.0,1024.0,748.0);
12:     } else if (toInterfaceOrientation ==
➥UIInterfaceOrientationLandscapeLeft) {
13:         self.view=landscapeView;
14:         self.view.transform=CGAffineTransformMakeRotation(deg2rad*(-90));
15:         self.view.bounds=CGRectMake(0.0,0.0,1024.0,748.0);
16:     } else {
17:         self.view=portraitView;
18:         self.view.transform=CGAffineTransformMakeRotation(0);
19:         self.view.bounds=CGRectMake(0.0,0.0,768.0,1004.0);
20:     }
21: }
```

Lines 5–6 pass the interface rotation message up to the parent object so that it can react appropriately.

Lines 8–11 handle rotation to the right (landscape right). Lines 12–15 deal with rotation to the left (landscape left). Finally, lines 16–19 configure the view for the default orientation: portrait.

Save the implementation file, and then choose Build and Run to test the application. As you rotate the device or the iPhone Simulator, your views should be swapped in and out appropriately.

> Although we used an if-then-else statement in this example, you could easily use a `switch` structure instead. The `toInterfaceOrientation` parameter and orientation constants are integer values, which means they can be evaluated directly in a `switch` statement.

Did you Know?

Further Exploration

Although we covered several different ways of working with rotation in the iPad interface, you might want to explore additional features outside of this hour's lesson. Using the Xcode documentation tool, review the `UIView` instance methods. You'll see that there are additional methods that you can implement, such as `willAnimateRotationToInterfaceOrientation:duration:`, which is used to set up a single-step animated rotation sequence. Even more advanced transitions can be accomplished with the `willAnimateFirstHalfOfRotationToInterfaceOrientation:duration:` and `willAnimateSecondHalfOfRotationFromInterfaceOrientation:duration:` methods, which implement a two-stage animated rotation process.

In short, there is more to learn about how to smoothly change from one interface layout to another. This hour gave you the basics to begin implementation, but as your needs grow, additional rotation capabilities in the SDK are just waiting to be tapped.

Summary

The iPad is all about the user experience: a touchable display, intuitive controls, and now, rotatable and resizeable interfaces. Using the techniques described in this hour's lesson, you can adapt to almost any type of rotation scenario. To handle simple interface size changes, for example, you can take advantage of the autosizing attributes in Interface Builder. For more complex changes, however, you might want to redefine the frame properties for your onscreen elements, giving you complete control over their size and placement. Finally, for the ultimate in flexibility, you can create multiple different views and swap them as the device rotates.

By implementing rotation-aware applications, you enable your users to use their iPad in the way that feels most comfortable to them.

Q&A

Q. *Why does Apple want orientation-agnostic applications?*

A. The iPhone has a definite orientation based on its primary purpose of taking and making calls. The iPad, on the other hand, doesn't need to be in a specific orientation to perform its primary function. Users determine what orientation they like, and Apple wants you to respect that!

Q. *I implemented the first exercise, but the buttons overlapped one another. What did I do wrong?*

A. Probably nothing! Make sure that your anchors are set correctly, and then try shifting the buttons up or down a bit in the view. Nothing in Interface Builder prevents elements from overlapping. Chances are, you just need to tweak the positions and try again.

Workshop

Quiz

1. The iPad interface can rotate through three different orientations. True or false?

2. How does an application communicate which rotation orientations it supports?

3. What was the purpose of the deg2rad constant that we defined in the final exercise?

Answers

1. False. There are four primary interface orientations: landscape right, landscape left, portrait, and upside-down portrait.

2. The `shouldAutorotateToInterfaceOrientation:` method in the view controller identifies which of the four orientations it will operate in.

3. We defined the deg2rad constant to give us an easy way to convert degrees to radians for the Core Graphics C function `CGAffineTransformMakeRotation()`.

Activities

1. Edit the Swapper example so that each view presents and processes user input. Keep in mind that because both views are handled by a single view controller you'll need to add all the outlets and actions for both views to the view controller interface and implementation files.

2. Return to an earlier lesson and revise the interface to support multiple different orientations. Use any of the techniques described in this hour's exercises for the implementation.

HOUR 18

Extending the Touch Interface

What You'll Learn in This Hour:

▶ The multitouch gesture recognition architecture
▶ How to detect taps
▶ How to detect swipes
▶ How to detect pinches
▶ How to detect rotations
▶ How to use the built-in shake gesture

A multitouch screen allows applications to use a wide variety of natural finger gestures for operations that would otherwise be hidden behind layers of menus, buttons, and text. From the very first time you use a pinch to zoom in and out on a photo, map, or web page, you realize that's exactly the right interface for zooming. Nothing is more human than manipulating the environment with your fingers.

The iPhone OS provides advanced gesture-recognition capabilities to the iPad platform. This hour shows how you can implement and respond to these gestures within your application.

For most applications in this book, using the iPhone Simulator is perfectly acceptable, but the simulator cannot re-create all the gestures you can create with your fingers. For this hour, be sure to have a physical device that is provisioned for development. To run this hour's applications on your device, follow the steps in Hour 1, "Preparing Your System and iPad for Development."

Multitouch Gesture Recognition

While multitouch has been implemented since day one on the iPhone, a definite limitation applies to what you can do on the small screen: The more you pack onto the display, the harder it is to effectively use it. The iPad liberates developers to design and implement large, highly usable touchable interfaces. Controls can be sized naturally, without worry of a user's fingers missing their targets.

As you've been working through the book's examples, you've gotten used to responding to events, such as `Touch Up Inside`, for onscreen buttons. Gesture recognition is a bit different. Consider a "simple" swipe. The swipe has direction, it has velocity, and it has a certain number of touch points (fingers) that are engaged. It would be unfeasible for Apple to implement events for every combination of these variables, and, at the same time, it would be extremely taxing on the system to just detect a "generic" swipe event and force you, the developer, to check the number of fingers, direction, etc. each time the event was triggered.

To make life simple, Apple has created gesture recognizer classes for almost all the common gestures that you will want to implement in your applications, specifically the following:

> **Tapping (`UITapGestureRecognizer`):** Tapping one or more fingers on the screen
>
> **Pressing (`UIPressGestureRecognizer`):** Pressing one or more fingers to the screen
>
> **Pinching (`UIPinchGestureRecognizer`):** Pinching to close or expand something
>
> **Rotating (`UIRotationGestureRecognizer`):** Sliding two fingers in a circular motion
>
> **Swiping (`UISwipeGestureRecognizer`):** Swiping with one or more fingers in a specific direction
>
> **Panning (`UIPanGestureRecognizer`):** Touching and dragging
>
> **Shaking (`UIEvent`):** Physically shaking the iPad device.

Prior to the iPad's version of iPhone OS, a developer had to read and recognize low-level touch events to determine if, for example, a pinch was happening. For example, are two points represented on the screen? Are they moving toward each other?

On the iPad, you will define what type of recognizer you're looking for, add the recognizer to a view (UIView), and you will automatically receive any multitouch events that are triggered. You'll even receive values like velocity and scale for gestures like "pinch."

Shaking is not a multitouch gesture and will require a slightly different approach than the others. Note that it doesn't have its own recognizer class.

Did you Know?

Using Gesture Recognizers

In this hour's tutorial, you will be implementing five gesture recognizers (tap, swipe, pinch, rotate, and shake), along with feedback. Each gesture will update a text label with information about the gesture that has been detected. Pinch, rotate, and shake will take things a step further by scaling, rotating, or resetting an image view in response to the gestures.

Perhaps the most surprising element of what you're about to do is just how *easy* it is. I know I say that frequently throughout the book, but gesture recognizers are one of those rare features that "just works." Follow along and find out what I mean!

Implementation Overview

This application, which we'll be naming **Gestures**, will display a screen with four embedded views (UIView), each assigned a different gesture recognizer within the viewDidLoad method. When you perform an action within one of the views, it will call a corresponding method in our view controller to update a label with feedback about the gesture, and depending on the gesture type, update an onscreen image view (UIImageView), too

Figure 18.1 shows the final application.

Setting Up the Project

Start Xcode and create a new view-based iPad application called **Gestures**. Next, open up the GesturesViewController.h interface file and add outlets and properties for four UIViews: tapView, swipeView, pinchView, and rotateView. These are the views that we be attaching gesture recognizers to. Add two additional outlets and properties: outputLabel and imageView, of the classes UILabel and UIImageView, respectively. These will be used to provide feedback to the user.

Listing 18.1 shows the finished interface file.

LISTING 18.1

```
#import <UIKit/UIKit.h>

@interface GesturesViewController : UIViewController {
    IBOutlet UIView *tapView;
    IBOutlet UIView *swipeView;
    IBOutlet UIView *pinchView;
    IBOutlet UIView *rotateView;
    IBOutlet UILabel *outputLabel;
    IBOutlet UIImageView *imageView;
}
```

```
@property (nonatomic, retain) UIView *tapView;
@property (nonatomic, retain) UIView *swipeView;
@property (nonatomic, retain) UIView *pinchView;
@property (nonatomic, retain) UIView *rotateView;
@property (nonatomic, retain) UIView *outputLabel;
@property (nonatomic, retain) UIImageView *imageView;

@end
```

To keep things nice and neat, edit the implementation file
(GesturesViewController.m) to include @synthesize directives after the @implemen-
tation line:

```
@synthesize tapView;
@synthesize swipeView;
@synthesize pinchView;
@synthesize rotateView;
@synthesize outputLabel;
@synthesize imageView;
```

Finish off these preliminary steps by releasing each of these objects in the dealloc
method of the view controller:

```
- (void)dealloc {
    [tapView release];
    [swipeView release];
    [pinchView release];
    [rotateView release];
    [outputLabel release];
    [imageView release];
    [super dealloc];
}
```

Adding the Image Resource

Before you can create your application's gesture-aware interface, you must add an
image to the project. We will be using this to provide visual feedback to the user.
Included in the Hour 18 project's Images folder is flower.png. Drag this file onto the
Resources group for your project, choosing to copy it to the project, if needed, as
shown in Figure 18.2.

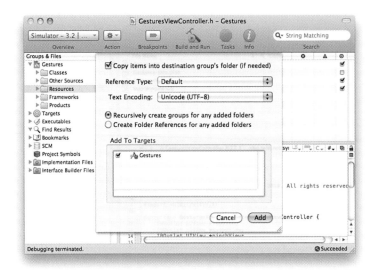

Creating the Interface

Open up the GesturesViewController.xib file in Interface Builder. It's time to create our UI.

As I mentioned when we started, we don't have to concern ourselves with any of the typical actions or events in this project. We'll add some objects and then connect their outlists.

To build the interface, start by dragging four UIView instances to the main view. Size the four views to they are visually square and form a square near the top of the screen. Use the Attributes Inspector (Command+1) to set the background of each view to be something unique.

The views you are adding are convenient objects that we can attach gestures to. In your own applications, you can attach gesture recognizers to your main application view, or the view of any onscreen object.

Next, drag labels into each of the four views. The first label should read Tap Me!, the second, Swipe Me!, Pinch Me! in the third, and Rotate Me! in the last.

Drag a fifth UILabel instance to the main view, and center it at the top of the screen. Use the Attributes Inspector to set it to align center, and increase the font size to 24 pt. This will be the label we use to provide feedback to the user. Change the label's default text to **Do something!**.

Finally, add a UIImageView to the bottom center of the screen. Use the Attributes Inspector (Command+1) and Size Inspector (Command+3) to set the image to flower.png, and the size and location to X: 218, Y:679, W:330, H:310, as shown in Figure 18.3.

FIGURE 18.3
Size and position the UIImageView as shown here.

The finished view should resemble Figure 18.4.

FIGURE 18.4
Your final view
should look like
this.

Connecting the Outlets

To access our gesture views and feedback objects from the main application, we need to connect the outlets defined earlier. Starting with the top-left view, Control-drag from the File's Owner icon to the view. Choose the `tapView` outlet when prompted, as shown in Figure 18.5.

Repeat this process, connecting the top-right view to the `swipeView` outlet, bottom-left view to `pinchView`, and bottom-right view to `rotateView`. Connect the top `UILabel` to `outputLabel` and the bottom `UIImageView` to `imageView`.

We can now close the XIB file and exit Interface Builder. It's time to connect our gesture recognizers.

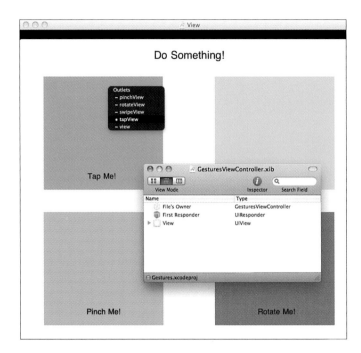

FIGURE 18.5
Connect the
four views,
label, and
image view to
their outlets.

Implementing the Tap Gesture Recognizer

We're going to start implementing the gesture recognizer logic by implementing the "tap" recognizer. What you'll quickly discover is that after you've added one recognizer, the pattern is very, very similar for the others.

Creating the Recognizer

The first thing to consider is this: Where do we want instantiate a gesture recognizer? For this project, it makes sense that the user can start inputting gestures as soon as the application starts and the views are visible, so the `viewDidLoad` method is a good spot. Update the GestureViewController.m file so that the `viewDidLoad` reads as displayed in Listing 18.2.

LISTING 18.2

```
 1:  - (void)viewDidLoad {
 2:      [super viewDidLoad];
 3:
 4:      //Taps
 5:      UITapGestureRecognizer *tapRecognizer;
 6:      tapRecognizer=[[UITapGestureRecognizer alloc]
 7:                          initWithTarget:self
 8:                          action:@selector(foundTap:)];
 9:      tapRecognizer.numberOfTapsRequired=1;
10:      tapRecognizer.numberOfTouchesRequired=1;
11:      [tapView addGestureRecognizer:tapRecognizer];
12:      [tapRecognizer release];
13: }
```

Line 5 kicks things off by declaring an instance of the UITapGestureRecognizer object, tapRecognizer. In line 6, tapRecognizer is allocated and initialized with initWithTarget:action. Working backward, the action is the method that will be called when the tap occurs. Using @selector(foundTap:), we tell the recognizer that we want to use a method called foundTap to handle our taps. The target we specify, self, is the object where foundTap lives. In this case, it will be our view controller (GestureViewController) object, or self.

Lines 9 and 10 set two properties of the tap gesture recognizer:

numberOfTapsRequired — The number of times the object needs to be tapped before the gesture is recognized

numberOfTouchesRequired—The number of fingers that need to be down on the screen before the gesture is recognized

In this example, we're defining a "tap" as one finger tapping the screen once. Feel free to play with these properties as much as you'd like!

In line 11, we use the UIView method addGestureRecognizer to add the tapRecognizer to the tapView. Our view is now tap-aware, and we can release tapRecognizer in line 12.

The next step is to add the code to respond to a tap event.

Amazingly, the iPad supports up to 11 simultaneous touches! Some developers have used this capability to allow applications to be controlled by more than one person at a time.

Responding to the Recognizer

Responding to the tap gesture recognizer is just a matter of implementing the foundTap method. Add this new method to the GestureViewController.m file:

```
- (void)foundTap:(UITapGestureRecognizer *)recognizer {
    outputLabel.text=@"Tapped";
}
```

Ta da! Your first gesture recognizer is done! We'll repeat this process for the other four, and we'll be finished before you know it.

If you'd like to get the coordinate where a tap gesture (or a swipe) takes place you add code like this to gesture handler (replacing <the view> with the name of the recognizer's view):

```
CGPoint location = [recognizer locationInView:<the view>];
```

This will create a simple structure named `location`, with members x and y, accessible as `location.x` and `location.y`.

Did you Know?

Implementing the Swipe Gesture Recognizer

The swipe gesture recognizer will be implemented in almost the same manner as the tap recognizer. Instead of being able to choose the number of taps, however, you can set which direction the swipes can be made in. You can specify a total of four direction constants:

UISwipeGestureRecognizerDirectionLeft—Swipe to the left

UISwipeGestureRecognizerDirectionRight—Swipe to the right

UISwipeGestureRecognizerDirectionUp—Swipe up

UISwipeGestureRecognizerDirectionDown—Swipe down

By using a bitwise OR between the constants (for example, UISwipeGestureRecognizerDirectionLeft | UISwipeGestureRecognizerDirectionRight), you can create a recognizer that detects swipes in multiple directions. Let's do that now.

Add the following code fragment to viewDidLoad method (immediately following the tap gesture recognizer is fine):

```
1:    UISwipeGestureRecognizer *swipeRecognizer;
2:    swipeRecognizer=[[UISwipeGestureRecognizer alloc]
3:                    initWithTarget:self
4:                    action:@selector(foundSwipe:)];
5:    swipeRecognizer.direction=UISwipeGestureRecognizerDirectionLeft |
6:                    UISwipeGestureRecognizerDirectionRight;
```

```
7:    swipeRecognizer.numberOfTouchesRequired=1;
8:    [swipeView addGestureRecognizer:swipeRecognizer];
9:    [swipeRecognizer release];
```

The exact same pattern is followed, this time using the UISwipeGestureRecognizer class. Lines 1 and 2 declare, initialize, and allocate the swipeRecognizer UISwipeGestureRecognizer instance and identify a method foundSwipe to be invoked when the gesture is recognized.

Lines 5 and 6 set the direction property to the allowed swipe directions (either left, or right, in this example).

Line 7 sets the number of finger touches that need to be "seen" for the gesture to be detected.

Lines 8 and 9 add the gesture recognizer to the swipeView object and then release the recognizer.

Responding to the Recognizer

We'll respond to the swipe recognizer in the same way we did with the tap recognizer. Implement the foundSwipe method as follows:

```
- (void)foundSwipe:(UISwipeGestureRecognizer *)recognizer {
    outputLabel.text=@"Swiped";
}
```

If you want to differentiate between different swipe directions, you must implement multiple swipe-gesture recognizers. By adding a recognizer with multiple allowed directions, you're saying that all of the directions are equivalent; they aren't differentiated as separate gestures.

So far, so good! Next up, the pinch gesture. You should really start seeing the pattern now, so we won't spend too much time on the setup.

Implementing the Pinch Gesture Recognizer

Taps and swipes are simple gestures: They either happen or they don't. Pinches and rotations are slightly more complex, returning additional values to give you greater control over the user interface. A pinch, for example, includes a velocity property (how quickly the pinch happened), and scale (a fraction that is proportional to change in distance between your fingers). If you move your fingers 50% closer together, the scale is .5, for example. If you move them twice as far apart, it is 2.

To better show what this means visually, we're going to be scaling imageView
(UIImageView). We'll want to reset this to the original size/location later, so before
we do anything else, add these lines after the #import line in
GesturesViewController:

```
#define originWidth 330.0
#define originHeight 310.0
#define originX 218.0
#define originY 679.0
```

These are the original width, height, and x and y locations of the UIImageView that
was added to the interface in the initial project setup.

Now add the pinch-gesture recognizer code fragment to viewDidLoad method (placing it after the swipe recognizer is fine):

```
UIPinchGestureRecognizer *pinchRecognizer;
    pinchRecognizer=[[UIPinchGestureRecognizer alloc]
                  initWithTarget:self
                  action:@selector(foundPinch:)];
    [pinchView addGestureRecognizer:pinchRecognizer];
    [pinchRecognizer release];
```

As you can see, there's even less going on than with tapping and swiping because
we aren't worried about direction of the number of fingers touching the screen. The
code sets foundPinch as the method that will handle the gesture, then adds the recognizer to pinchView.

Responding to the Recognizer

You've made it to the most complex piece of code in this hour's lesson! The
foundPinch method will accomplish several things. It will reset the UIImageView's
rotation (just in case it gets out of whack when we set up the rotation gesture), create a feedback string with the scale and velocity values returned by the recognizer,
and finally, actually scale the image view so that there is immediate visual feedback
to the user.

Enter the foundPinch method, as shown in Listing 18.3.

LISTING 18.3

```
1: - (void)foundPinch:(UIPinchGestureRecognizer *)recognizer {
2:     NSString *feedback;
3:     double scale;
4:     scale=recognizer.scale;
5:     imageView.transform = CGAffineTransformMakeRotation(0.0);
6:     feedback=[[NSString alloc]
7:                 initWithFormat:@"Pinched, Scale:%1.2f, Velocity:%1.2f",
```

```
 8:                   recognizer.scale,recognizer.velocity];
 9:     outputLabel.text=feedback;
10:     imageView.frame=CGRectMake(originX,
11:                                 originY,
12:                                 originWidth*scale,
13:                                 originHeight*scale);
14:     [feedback release];
15: }
```

Let's walk through this method to make sure we understand what's going on. Lines 2 and 3 declare a string object, feedback, and a floating-point value scale, that will be used to store a feedback string to the user and the scaling value returned by the pinch gesture recognizer.

Line 4 sets scale to the recognizer's scale property.

Line 5 resets the imageView object to a rotation of 0.0 (no rotation at all) by setting its transform property to the transformation returned by the Core Graphics CGAffineTransformMakeRotation function. This function, when passed a value in radians, will return the necessary transformation to rotate a view.

Lines 6–8 allocate and initialize the feedback string to show that a pinch has taken place, and output the values of the recognizer's scale and velocity properties. Line 9 sets the outputLabel in the UI to the feedback string.

For the scaling of the image view itself, lines 10–13 do the work. All that needs to happen is for the imageView object's frame to be redefined to the new size. To do this, we can use CGRectMake to return a new frame rectangle. The top left coordinates (originx, originy) stay the same, but we multiply originWidth and originHeight by the scale factor to increase or decrease the size of the frame according to the user's pinch.

Line 14 cleans up by releasing the feedback string.

Building and running the application will now let you enlarge (even beyond the boundaries of the screen) or shrink the image using the pinch gesture within the pinchView object, as shown in Figure 18.6.

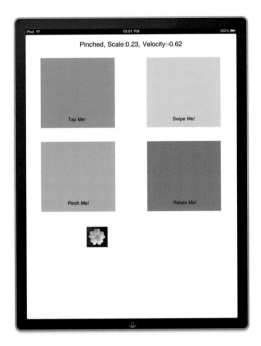

FIGURE 18.6
Enlarge or
shrink the
image in a
pinch (ha ha).

Implementing the Rotation Gesture Recognizer

The last multitouch gesture recognizer that we'll be adding is the rotation gesture
recognizer. Like the pinch gesture, rotation returns some useful information that we
can apply visually to our onscreen objects, notably velocity and rotation. The rotation returned is the number of radians that the user has rotated their fingers, clock-
wise or counterclockwise.

Most of us are comfortable with talking about rotation in "degrees," but the Cocoa
classes usually use radians. Don't worry; it's not a difficult translation to make. If
you'd like, you can calculate degrees from radians using the following formula:

Degrees = Radians * 180/π

There's not really any reason we need to do this in this project, but in your own
applications, you might want to provide a degree reading to your users.

One last time, edit the `viewDidLoad` method and add the following code fragment
for the rotation recognizer:

```
UIRotationGestureRecognizer *rotationRecognizer;
rotationRecognizer=[[UIRotationGestureRecognizer alloc]
                initWithTarget:self
                action:@selector(foundRotation:)];
[rotateView addGestureRecognizer:rotationRecognizer];
[rotationRecognizer release];
```

The rotation gesture recognizer is added to the rotateView and set to trigger foundRotation when a gesture is detected.

Responding to the Recognizer

I'd love to tell you how difficult it is to rotate a view and all the complex math involved, but I kind of gave away the trick to rotation in the foundPinch method earlier. A single line of code will set the UIImageView's transform property to a rotation transformation and visually rotate the view. Of course, we also need to provide a feedback string to the user, but that's not nearly as exciting, is it?

Add the foundRotation method in Listing 18.4 to your GesturesViewController.m file.

LISTING 18.4

```
 1: - (void)foundRotation:(UIRotationGestureRecognizer *)recognizer {
 2:     NSString *feedback;
 3:     double rotation;
 4:     rotation=recognizer.rotation;
 5:     feedback=[[NSString alloc]
 6:             initWithFormat:@"Rotated, Radians:%1.2f, Velocity:%1.2f",
 7:             recognizer.rotation,recognizer.velocity];
 8:     outputLabel.text=feedback;
 9:     imageView.transform = CGAffineTransformMakeRotation(rotation);
10:     [feedback release];
11: }
```

Again, we declare a feedback string and a floating-point value, this time rotation, in lines 2 and 3. Line 4 sets the rotation value to the recognizer's rotation property. This is the rotation in radians detected in the user's gesture.

Line 5 creates the feedback string showing the radians rotated and the velocity of the rotation, while line 8 sets the output label to the string.

Line 9 handles the rotation itself, creating a rotation transformation and applying it to the imageView object's transform property.

Line 10 finishes up by releasing the feedback string.

Try using Build and Run to test your application now. You should be able to freely spin the image view using a rotation gesture in the rotate view, as shown in Figure 18.7.

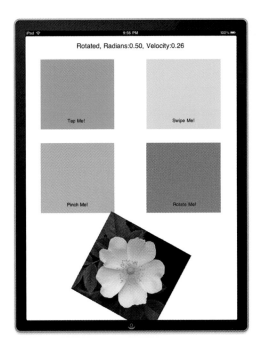

FIGURE 18.7
Spin the image view using the rotation gesture.

Although it might seem like we're done, there's still one gesture we need to cover: a shake.

Implementing the Shake Recognizer

Dealing with a shake is a bit different from the other gestures we've covered this hour. We muse intercept a `UIEvent` of the type `UIEventTypeMotion`. To do this, our view controller or view must be the first responder in the responder chain and must implement one or more of the `motionEnded:withEvent` methods.

Let's tackle these requirements, one at a time.

Becoming First Responder

For our view controller to be a first responder, we have to allow it and then ask for it. Add the following two methods to the GesturesViewController.m file:

```
- (BOOL)canBecomeFirstResponder {
    return YES; // For the shake event
}

- (void)viewDidAppear:(BOOL)animated {
    [self becomeFirstResponder];  // For the shake event
    [super viewDidAppear: animated];
}
```

Our view controller is now prepared to become the first responder and receive the shake event. All that we need to do now is implement `motionEnded:withEvent` to trap and react to the shake itself.

Reacting to a Shake

To react to a shake, implement the `motionEnded:withEvent` method as shown in Listing 18.5.

LISTING 18.5

```
1:  - (void)motionEnded:(UIEventSubtype)motion withEvent:(UIEvent *)event {
2:      if (motion==UIEventSubtypeMotionShake) {
3:          outputLabel.text=@"Shaking things up!";
4:          imageView.transform = CGAffineTransformMakeRotation(0.0);
5:      imageView.frame=CGRectMake(originX,originY,originWidth,originHeight);
6:      }
7:  }
```

First things first: In line 2, we check to make sure that the `motion` value we received (a variable of type `UIEventSubtype`) is, indeed, a motion event. To do this, we just compare it to the constant `UIEventSubtypeMotionShake`. If they match, the user just finished shaking the device!

Lines 3 and 4 react to the shake by setting the output label, rotating the image view back to its default orientation, and setting the image view's frame back to the original size. In other words, shaking the iPad will reset the image to its default state. Pretty nifty, huh?

You can now run the application and use all the gestures that we implemented this hour. Although not a useful app in and of itself, it does illustrate many techniques that you can use in your own applications.

Further Exploration

In addition to the four gestures discussed this hour, there are two other recognizers that you should be able to immediately add to your apps: `UIPressGestureRecognizer` and `UIPanGestureRecognizer`. The `UIGestureRecognizer` class is the parent to all the gesture recognizers that you've learned about in the lesson and offers additional base functionality for customizing gesture recognition. For more information on trapping custom gestures, review the "Creating Custom Gesture Recognizers" section in the *iPad Programming Guide* (found in the Xcode developer documentation.)

You might also want to learn more about the lower-level handling of touches on the iPhone OS platform. See the "Event Handling" section of the *iPhone Application Programming Guide* for more information.

We humans do a lot with our fingers, such as draw, write, play music, and more. Each of these possible gestures has been exploited to great effect in third-party applications. Explore the App Store to get a sense for what's been done with the iPad's multitouch screen.

Finally, for another set of gesture examples, be sure to look at the SimpleGestureRecognizers tutorial project, found within the Xcode documentation. This project will provide many additional examples of implementing gestures on the iPad.

Summary

In this hour, we've given the gesture recognizer architecture a good workout. Using the gesture recognizers provided to the iPad through the iPhone OS, we can easily recognize and respond to taps, swipes, pinches, rotations, and more (without any complex math or programming logic).

You also learned how to make your applications respond to shaking by becoming a first responder and implementing the `motionEnded:withEvent` method. Your ability to present your users with interactive interfaces just increased dramatically!

Q&A

Q. *Why don't the rotation/pinch gestures include configuration options for the number of touches?*

A. The gesture recognizers are meant to recognize common gestures. While it is possible that you could manually implement a rotation or pinch gesture with multiple fingers, it wouldn't be consistent with how users expect their applications to work, and isn't included as an option with these recognizers.

Workshop

Quiz

1. What gesture recognizer detects the user briefly touching the screen?

2. How can you respond to multiple swipe directions in a single gesture recognizer?

3. The rotation recognizer returns a rotation in degrees. True or false?

4. Add shake sensing to your application is as simple as adding another gesture recognizer. True or false?

Answers

1. The `UITapGestureRecognizer` is used to trap and react to one or more fingers tapping the screen.

2. You can't. You can trap multiple swipe directions in a single recognizer, but you should consider those directions to be a single gesture. To react differently to different swipes, they should be implemented as different recognizers.

3. False. Most Cocoa classes dealing with rotation (including the rotation gesture recognizer) work with radians.

4. False. The shake gesture requires that your view or view controller become the first responder and trap motion `UIEvents`.

Activities

1. Expand the Gestures application to include panning and pressing gestures. These are configured nearly identically to the gestures you used in this hour's tutorial.

2. Improve on the user experience by adding the pinch- and rotation gesture recognizers to the `UIImageView` object itself, giving users the ability to interact directly with the image, rather than another view.

HOUR 19

Sensing Movement with Accelerometer Input

What You'll Learn in This Hour

▶ How to determine the iPad's orientation
▶ How to measure tilt
▶ How to measure movement

The Nintendo Wii introduced motion sensing as an effective input technique for mainstream consumer electronics. Apple applied this technology to great success with the iPhone and iPod Touch—and how now brought the technology to the iPad. Apple's devices are equipped with an accelerometer that can be used to determine the orientation, movement, and tilt of the device. With the iPad's accelerometer, a user can control applications by simply adjusting the physical orientation of the device and moving it in space.

This innovative and natural input mechanism is exposed to third-party applications in the iPhone OS SDK. In Hour 18, "Using Advanced Touches and Gestures," you've already seen how the accelerometer provides the shake gesture. Now you will learn how to take direct readings from the accelerometer. For all the magic an accelerometer-aware application appears to exhibit, you will see that using the accelerometer is surprisingly simple.

By the Way

An accelerometer measures acceleration relative to a free fall. Meaning that if you dropped your iPad into a sustained free fall, say off the Empire State Building, its accelerometer would measure 0g on the way down. (Just trust us, don't try this out.) The accelerometer of an iPad sitting in your lap, on the other hand, measures 1g along the axis it is resting on.

Did you Know?

For most applications in this book, using the iPhone Simulator is perfectly acceptable, but the simulator does not simulate the accelerometer hardware. So for this chapter, you'll want to be sure to have a physical device provisioned for development. To run this hour's applications on your device, follow the steps in Hour 1, "Preparing Your System and iPad for Development."

Accelerometer Background

An accelerometer uses a unit of measure called a g, which is short for gravity. 1g is the force pulling down on something resting at sea level on Earth (9.8 meters/second^2). You don't normally notice the feeling of 1g (that is until you trip and fall, and then 1g hurts pretty bad). You are familiar with g-forces higher and lower than 1g if you've ever ridden on a roller coaster. The pull that pins you to your seat at the bottom of the roller coaster hill is a g-force greater than 1, and the feeling of floating up out of your seat at the top of a hill is negative g-force at work.

The measurement of the 1g pull of Earth's gravity on the device while it's at rest is how the iPad's accelerometer can be used to measure the orientation of the phone. The accelerometer provides a measurement along three axes, called x, y, and z (see Figure 19.1).

FIGURE 19.1
The three measurable axes.

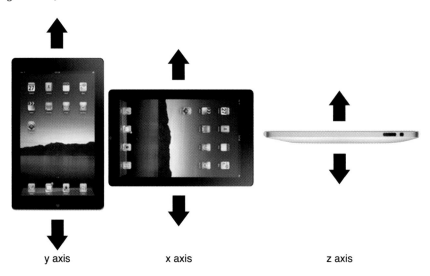

y axis   x axis   z axis

Depending on how your iPad is resting, the 1g of gravity will be pulling differently on the three possible axes. If your device is standing straight up on one of its edges or is flat on its back or on its screen, the entire 1g will be measured on one axis. If the device is tilted at an angle, the 1g will be spread across multiple axes (see Figure 19.2).

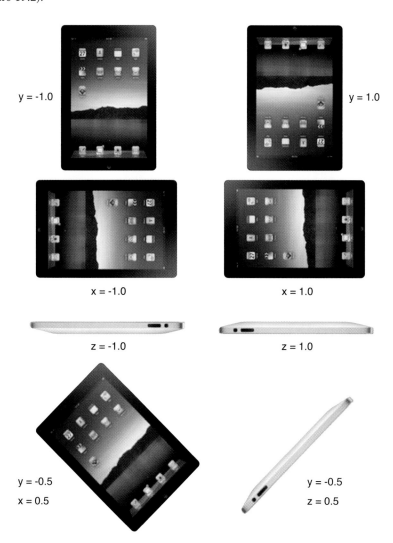

FIGURE 19.2
The 1g of force on an iPad at rest.

y = -1.0

y = 1.0

x = -1.0

x = 1.0

z = -1.0

z = 1.0

y = -0.5
x = 0.5

y = -0.5
z = 0.5

Accelerometer API

You work with the accelerometer through the UIAccelerometer singleton. The UIAccelerometer defines a protocol, the UIAccelerometerDelegateProtocol, which you implement to receive measurements from the accelerometer.

By the Way

> Recall that a singleton is a class that is instantiated once in the lifetime of your application. The services of the iPad's hardware are provided to your application are often provided as singletons. Because there is only one accelerometer in the device, it makes sense that it is accessed as a singleton. Multiple instances of accelerometer objects existing in your application wouldn't add any extra value and would have the added complexity of managing their memory and lifetime, both of which are avoided with a singleton.

Your delegate receives updates as frequently as you request to receive them (up to the limit of 100 updates per second).

Did you Know?

> You need to decide how often your application can benefit from receiving accelerometer updates. You should decide this by experimenting with different update values until you come up with an optimal frequency. Receiving more updates than your application can benefit from can have some negative consequences. Your application will use more system resources processing all the unneeded accelerometer updates, which might negatively impact the performance of the other parts of your application and can certainly affect the battery life of the device. Because you'll probably want fairly frequent updates so that your application responds smoothly, you should take some time to optimize the performance of your UIAccelerometer delegate's code and to make sure it does not allocate and free a lot of memory.

Setting up your application to use the accelerometer is a simple three-step process of retrieving the singleton, registering your delegate, and requesting updates at a specific interval:

```
UIAccelerometer *accelerometer = [UIAccelerometer sharedAccelerometer];
accelerometer.delegate = self;
accelerometer.updateInterval = 0.1; // 10 times per second
```

The UIAccelerometerDelegateProtocol has just one method, accelerometer:didAccelerate. accelerometer:didAccelerate provides the UIAccelerometer singleton and a UIAcceleration object as arguments. The UIAcceleration object has properties for the current reading on each of the three axes and provides a timestamp with the time the reading was taken. This interface to the accelerometer readings is very simple, so the only tricky part in implementing this delegate is making your application respond appropriately to the accelerometer readings. This often involves aggregating numerous separate readings into a single application response. For getting your application to respond naturally, there is no substitute for extensive experimentation.

You may have wondered why a timestamp is included in the UIAcceleration object. The answer is that accelerometer readings aren't timed precisely. The frequency interval is a maximum frequency. Your delegate won't get called more often than the interval that you request, but it's not the case that it will be called exactly as many times as you request, or that each call will be equally spaced out in time. Depending on what you are trying to accomplish with reading the accelerometer, the timestamp may come in very handy because you may need to determine how long it's been since you received the prior reading.

Sensing Orientation

As our first introduction to using the accelerometer, we'll create the Orientation application. Orientation won't be wowing users, it's simply going to say which of six possible orientations the iPad is currently in. The Orientation application will detect standing-up, upside-down, left-side, right-side, face-down, and face-up orientations.

Setting Up the Project

Create a new iPad View-Based Application in Xcode and call it **Orientation**. Click the OrientationViewController.h file in the Classes group and add an outlet property for an orientation label. Also indicate that this controller will be implementing the UIAccelerometerDelegate protocol. The OrientationViewController.h file should read as shown in Listing 19.1.

LISTING 19.1

```
#import <UIKit/UIKit.h>

@interface OrientationViewController : UIViewController
    <UIAccelerometerDelegate> {
    IBOutlet UILabel *orientation;
}

@property (nonatomic, retain) UILabel *orientation;

@end
```

Preparing the Interface

Orientation's UI is simple (and very stylish), just a yellow text label in a field of black, which we construct as follows:

1. Open Interface Builder by double-clicking the OrientationViewController.xib file in the Resources group.

2. Click the empty view and open the Attributes Inspector (Command+1).

3. Click the Background attribute and change the view's background to black using the color picker.

4. Open the Library (Shift+Command+L).

5. Drag a label (UILabel) to the center of the view; expand the size the label to the edge sizing guidelines on each side of the view.

6. Select the label and open the Attributes Inspector (Command+1).

7. Click the Color attribute and change the label's text color to yellow.

8. Click the center button of the Alignment attribute to center the label's text.

9. Click the Font attribute and change the font size to 72 points.

10. Finally, change the label's text to **Face Up**.

Did you Know?

> Now would be good time to put into practice the techniques you learned in Hour 17, "Building Rotatable and Resizable User Interfaces," to keep the text centered on screen while the iPad rotates. It isn't necessary for the completion of the project, but it *is* good practice!

Our UIAccelerometer delegate will need to be able to change the text of the label when the accelerometer indicates that the orientation of the device has changed. To do this, we'll need to connect the outlet we created earlier to the label.

Control-drag from the File's Owner icon in the document window to the label in the view. Choose the orientation outlet when prompted. The view should look like Figure 19.3. Save the XIB file and return to Xcode.

FIGURE 19.3
The Orientation application's UI in Interface Builder.

Implementing the UIAccelerometerDelegate

When our custom view is shown, we need to register our view controller as a UIAccelerometerDelegate. For this application, we don't need very many updates per second from the accelerometer. Two updates a second is frequent enough. We can set up the delegate and the interval in our controller's viewDidLoad method.

The only other thing needed to finish the Orientation application is to implement accelerometer:didAccelerate, which is the only method needed to fulfill the controller's responsibility as a UIAccelerometerDelegate. We use the x, y, and z properties of the UIAcceleration object to determine which axis has the most gravity pulling on it. Because we are trying to measure the device's orientation at rest, we can keep our delegate implementation simple by interpreting any reading of greater than 0.5 or less than –0.5 as meaning that axis has the most gravity. We can ignore the fact that if the phone were moving fast, more than one axis could have a high reading. Modify the OrientationViewController.m file in the Classes group to include the a reference to orientation label, the accelerometer:didAccelerate method, and the changes to viewDidLoad.

Begin by adding the appropriate @synthesize directive following the @implementa-tion line:

```
@synthesize orientation;
```

Next, implement the accelerometer:didAccelerate method and changes to viewDidLoad, as shown in Listing 19.2.

LISTING 19.2

```
- (void)accelerometer:(UIAccelerometer *)accelerometer
        didAccelerate:(UIAcceleration *)acceleration {

    if (acceleration.x > 0.5) {
        orientation.text = @"Right Side";
    } else if (acceleration.x < -0.5) {
        orientation.text = @"Left Side";
    } else if (acceleration.y > 0.5) {
        orientation.text = @"Upside Down";
    } else if (acceleration.y < -0.5) {
        orientation.text = @"Standing Up";
    } else if (acceleration.z > 0.5) {
        orientation.text = @"Face Down";
    } else if (acceleration.z < -0.5) {
        orientation.text = @"Face Up";
    }

}

- (void)viewDidLoad {
    UIAccelerometer *accelerometer = [UIAccelerometer sharedAccelerometer];
    accelerometer.delegate = self;
    accelerometer.updateInterval = 0.5; // twice per second
    [super viewDidLoad];
}
```

Finally, release the label in the implementation file's dealloc method:

```
- (void)dealloc {
    [orientation release];
    [super dealloc];
}
```

Run the application when complete. Your results should resemble Figure 19.4.

FIGURE 19.4
Orientation in
action.

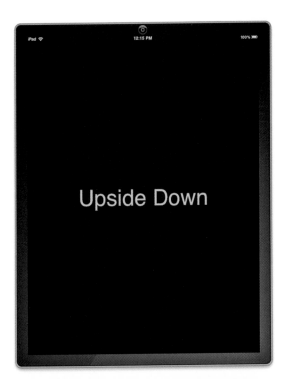

Detecting Tilt

In the Orientation application, we ignored the precise values coming from the accelerometer and instead just looked for the axis getting the dominant amount of gravity to make an all-or-nothing orientation decision. The gradations between these orientations, such as the device being somewhere between its left side and straight up and down, are often interesting to an application.

Imagine you are going to create a car racing game where the device acts as the steering wheel when tilted left and right and the gas and brake pedals when tilted forward and back. It is very helpful to know how far the player has turned the wheel and how hard the user is pushing the pedals to know how to make the game respond.

In this next example application, ColorTilt, we take a solid color and make it progressively more transparent as the user tilts the device left or right. It's not as exciting as a car racing game, but it is something we can accomplish in an hour, and everything learned here will apply when you get down to writing a great iPad application.

Setting Up the Project

Create a new iPad View-Based Application in Xcode and call it **ColorTilt**. Click the ColorViewController.h file in the Classes group and add an outlet property for the view; call it **colorView**. Indicate that this controller will be implementing the UIAccelerometerDelegate protocol. The ColorViewController.h file should read as shown in Listing 19.3.

LISTING 19.3

```
#import <UIKit/UIKit.h>

@interface ColorTiltViewController : UIViewController
    <UIAccelerometerDelegate> {
    IBOutlet UIView *colorView;
    }

@property (nonatomic, retain) UIView *colorView;

@end
```

Preparing the Interface

Now we'll lay out the UI and connect the outlet for the ColorTilt application, as follows:

1. Open Interface Builder by double-clicking the ColorTiltViewController.xib file in the Resources group.

2. Click the empty view and open the Attributes Inspector (Command+1).

3. Click the Background attribute and change the view's background to green using the color picker.

4. Control-drag from the File's Owner icon to the view, as shown in Figure 19.5. Choose colorView when prompted.

5. Save the XIB file and return to Xcode.

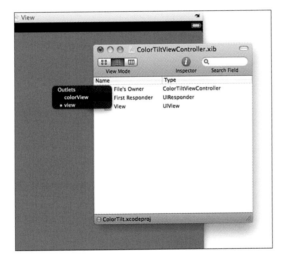

FIGURE 19.5
Connecting the colorView IBOutlet.

Implementing the UIAccelerometerDelegate

Reading the exact tilt of the device results in an even simpler UIAccelerometerDelegate than for the Orientation example because in this case we are only going to pay attention to the x-axis. The closer the x-axis is to being on edge (a reading of 1.0 or –1.0), the more solid (1.0 alpha) we'll make the color. The closer the x-axis reading is to 0, the more transparent (0.0 alpha) the color.

We can use the accelerometer value directly as the alpha with just two bits of data cleansing. We check to make sure a bump or jerk on the device hasn't resulted in an x-axis reading greater than 1.0, and we use the C function `fabs()` to get the absolute value of the reading, because for this example we don't care whether the device is tilting left edge or right.

We'll set up the `UIAccelerometerDelegate` in the same manner as before, but this time ask for an accelerometer reading 10 times a second. Begin by adding the `@syn-thesize` directive following the `@implementation` line in ColorTiltViewController.m:

```
@synthesize colorView;
```

Implement the `accelerometer:didAccelerate` and `viewDidLoad` methods, as shown in Listing 19.4.

LISTING 19.4

```
- (void)accelerometer:(UIAccelerometer *)accelerometer
        didAccelerate:(UIAcceleration *)acceleration {

    UIAccelerationValue value = fabs(acceleration.x);
    if (value > 1.0) { value = 1.0;}
    colorView.alpha = value;

}
- (void)viewDidLoad {

    UIAccelerometer *accelerometer = [UIAccelerometer sharedAccelerometer];
    accelerometer.delegate = self;
    accelerometer.updateInterval = 0.1; // 10 times per second

    [super viewDidLoad];
}
```

Finally, release the colorView in the `dealloc` method:

```
- (void)dealloc {
    [colorView release];
    [super dealloc];
}
```

Build and Run your new application. Figure 19.6 shows the results.

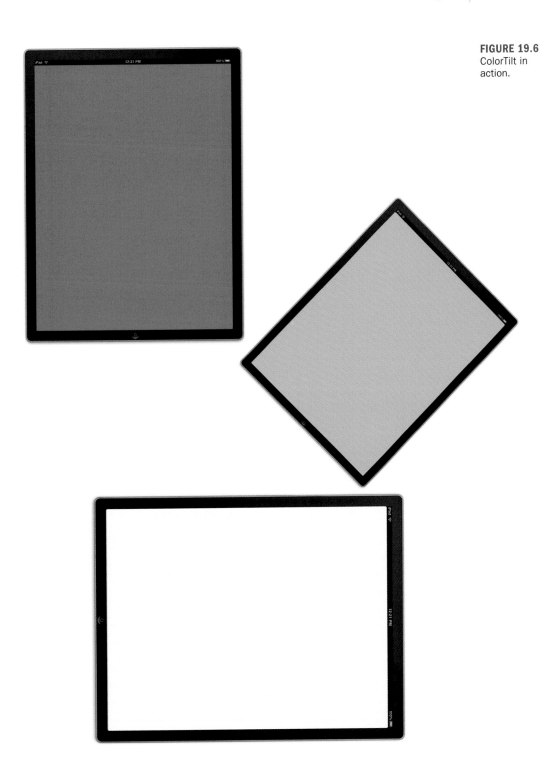

FIGURE 19.6
ColorTilt in
action.

Detecting Movement

So far, we have used the accelerometer to detect the orientation and tilt of the device. In both cases, we relied on gravity acting differently on the three axes.

The accelerometer can also be used to sense movement. One way to do this is to look for g-forces greater than 1g. This is good for detecting quick, strong movements. A more subtle approach is to implement a filter to calculate the difference between gravity and the force the accelerometer is measuring. The measured difference is the subtle movements of the device through space.

Let's expand on the ColorTilt example application by allowing the user to change the color with a sudden movement in any one of six directions. Before setting the alpha of the color based on the tilt, we'll check for a large acceleration along one of the axes. If we detect one, we'll change the view's background color. Modify the ColorTiltViewController.m file to include the method setBaseColor and the changes to accelerometer:didAccelerate, as shown in Listing 19.5.

LISTING 19.5

```
- (void)setBaseColor:(UIAcceleration *)acceleration {

    if (acceleration.x > 1.3) {
        colorView.backgroundColor = [UIColor greenColor];
    } else if (acceleration.x < -1.3) {
        colorView.backgroundColor = [UIColor orangeColor];
    } else if (acceleration.y > 1.3) {
        colorView.backgroundColor = [UIColor redColor];
    } else if (acceleration.y < -1.3) {
        colorView.backgroundColor = [UIColor blueColor];
    } else if (acceleration.z > 1.3) {
        colorView.backgroundColor = [UIColor yellowColor];
    } else if (acceleration.z < -1.3) {
        colorView.backgroundColor = [UIColor purpleColor];
    }
}

- (void)accelerometer:(UIAccelerometer *)accelerometer
        didAccelerate:(UIAcceleration *)acceleration {

    [self setBaseColor:acceleration];

    UIAccelerationValue value = fabs(acceleration.x);
    if (value > 1.0) { value = 1.0;}
    colorView.alpha = value;

}
```

A little experimentation shows that +/–1.3g is a good measure of an abrupt movement. Try it out yourself with a few different values and you may decide another value is better.

Further Exploration

Your challenge now is to use accelerometer readings to implement subtler and more natural interfaces than those in the two applications we created in this hour.

The next step to building effective accelerometer interfaces for your applications is to dust off your old math, physics, and electronics texts and take a quick refresher course.

The simplest and most basic equations from electronics and Newtonian physics are all that is needed to create compelling interfaces. In electronics, a low-pass filter removes abrupt signals over a cutoff value, providing smooth changes in the baseline signal. This is good for detecting smooth movements and tilts of the device and ignoring bumps and the occasional odd, spiked reading from the accelerometer. A high-pass filter does the opposite and detects only abrupt changes; this is good for removing the effect of gravity and detecting only purposeful movements, even when they occur along the axes that gravity is acting upon.

When you have the right signal interpretation in place, there is one more requirement for your interface to feel natural to your users: It must react like the physical and analog world of mass, force, and momentum, and not like the digital and binary world of 1s and 0s. The key to simulating the physical world in the digital is just some basic seventeenth-century physics.

Wikipedia Entries

Low-pass filter: http://en.wikipedia.org/wiki/Low-pass_filter

High-pass filter: http://en.wikipedia.org/wiki/High-pass_filter

Momentum: http://en.wikipedia.org/wiki/Momentum

Newton's laws of motion:
http://en.wikipedia.org/wiki/Newton's_laws_of_motion

Summary

At this point, you know all the mechanics of working with the accelerometer. You used the shake gesture in Hour 18, and in this hour you took direct readings to interpret the orientation, tilt, and movement of the device. You understand how to access the UIAccelerometer singleton, how to write a UIAccelerometerDelegate, and how to interpret the measurements from the UIAcceleration object.

Workshop

Quiz

1. Why is a timestamp provided to your delegate with the accelerometer reading? What might you use this timestamp for?

2. Should you drop your iPad off the Empire State Building to test the accelerometer?

Answers

1. Accelerometer readings don't come at precisely regular intervals. The timestamp can be used to determine how long it's been since the last reading so that the application can take the appropriate amount of action that takes into account the interval of time that has elapsed.

2. We don't recommend it.

Activities

1. When the Orientation application is in use, the label stays put and the text changes. This means that for three of the six orientations (upside down, left side, and right side) the text itself is also upside down or on its side. Fix this by changing not just the label text but also the orientation of the label so that the text always reads normally for the user looking at the screen. Be sure to adjust the label back to its original orientation when the orientation is standing up, face down, or face up.

2. In the final version of the ColorTilt application, sudden movement is used to change the view's color. You may have noticed that it can sometimes be difficult to get the desired color. This is because the accelerometer provides a reading for the deceleration of the device after your sudden movement. So what often happens is that ColorTilt switches the color from the force of the deceleration immediately after switching it to the desired color from the force of the acceleration. Add a delay to the ColorTilt application so that the color can be switched at most once every second. This will make switching to the desired color easier because the acceleration will change the color but the deceleration will be ignored.

3. A high-pass filter that cancels out the effect of gravity is often used to process accelerometer readings to detect slower and subtler movements in space. Modify the ColorTilt application to keep an average reading of gravity over time and to change colors on subtle movements beyond the gravitational average rather than on abrupt jerks. Does this result in a better user experience for ColorTilt? Think about when you would want to use each approach.

HOUR 20

Working with Rich Media

What You'll Learn in This Hour:

- ▶ How to play full-motion video from local or remote (streaming) files
- ▶ Ways of recording and playing back audio files on your iPad
- ▶ How to access the built-in iPod Library from within your applications
- ▶ How to display and access images from the built-in Photo Library
- ▶ Methods of retrieving and displaying information about currently playing media items

There's no denying that the iPad is a compelling platform for rich media playback. To make things even better, Apple provides a dizzying array of Cocoa classes that will help you add media to your own applications—everything from video, to photos, and audio recording. This hour's lesson walks you through a few different features that you may want to consider including in your development efforts.

Exploring Rich Media

Hour 10, "Getting the User's Attention," introduced you to System Sound Services for playing back short (30-second) sound files. This is great for alert sounds and similar applications, but hardly taps the potential of the iPad. This hour takes things a bit further, giving you full playback capabilities, and even audio recording within your own applications.

In this hour, we use two new frameworks: Media Player and AV Foundation. These two frameworks encompass more than a dozen new classes. Although we won't be able to cover everything in this hour, you'll get you a good idea of what's possible and how to get started.

In addition to these frameworks, the UIImagePickerController class is introduced. You can add this simple object to a popover to allow instant access to the iPad's Photo Library from within your application.

Media Player Framework

The Media Player framework is used for playing back video and audio from either local or remote resources. It can be used to call up the iPod interface from your application (presented within a popover), select audio, and manage playback. This is the framework that provides integration with all the built-in media features that your iPad has to offer. We'll be making use of five different classes in our sample code:

> `MPMoviePlayerController` — Allows playback of a piece of media, either located on the iPad file system or through a remote URL. The player controller can provide a GUI for scrubbing through video, pausing, fast forwarding, or rewinding.
>
> `MPMediaPickerController` — Presents the user with an interface for choosing media to play. You can filter the files displayed by the Media Picker or allow selection of any file from the Media Library.
>
> `MPMediaItem` — A single piece of media, such as a song.
>
> `MPMediaItemCollection` — Represents a collection of media items that will be used for playback. An instance of `MPMediaPickerController` returns an instance of `MPMediaItemCollection` that can be used directly with the next class—the music player controller.
>
> `MPMusicPlayerController` — Handles the playback of media items and media item collections. Unlike the movie player controller, the music player works "behind the scenes"—allowing playback from anywhere in your application, regardless of what is displayed on the screen.

Of course, many dozens of methods are available in each of these classes. We'll be using a few simple features for starting and stopping playback, but there is an amazing amount of additional functionality that can be added to your applications with only a limited amount of coding involved.

AV Foundation Framework

Although the Media Player framework is great for all your general media playback needs, Apple recommends the AV Foundation framework for most audio playback functions that exceed the 30 seconds allowed by System Sound Services. In addition, the AV Foundation framework offers audio recording features, making it possible to record new sound files directly in your application. This might sound like a complex programming task, but we'll do exactly that in our sample application.

You need just two new classes to add audio playback and recording to your apps:

> `AVAudioRecorder` — Records audio (in a variety of different formats) to memory or a local file on the iPad. The recording process can even continue while other functions are running in your application.

> `AVAudioPlayer` — Plays back audio files of any length. Using this class, you can implement game soundtracks or other complex audio applications. You have complete control over the playback, including the ability to layer multiple sounds on top of one another.

The Image Picker

The Image Picker (`UIImagePickerController`) works similarly to the `MPMediaPickerController`, but instead of presenting a view where songs can be selected, the user's Photo Library is displayed instead. When the user chooses a photo, the Image Picker will hand us a `UIImage` object based on the user's selection.

Like the `MPMediaPickerController`, an Image Picker must be presented within a popover. The good news is that both of these objects implement their own view and view controller, so we need to do very little work to generate the popover.

As you can see, there's quite a few things to cover, so let's get started using these features in a real iPad application.

Preparing the Media Playground Application

This hour's exercise is less about creating a real-world application and more about building a sandbox for testing out the rich media classes. The finished application will show embedded or fullscreen video, record and play audio, browse and display images from the Photo library, and browse and select music for playback.

Implementation Overview

Because there is *so* much going on in this application, we'll take a similar approach to what we did in Hour 10, "Getting the User's Attention." We'll start by creating an application skeleton with outlets and actions, and then fill them in to implement the features we've been discussing.

There will be four main components to the application. First, a video player that plays an MPEG-4 video file when a button is pressed; fullscreen presentation will be controlled by a toggle switch. Second, we'll create an audio recorder with playback

features. Third, we'll add a button that shows the iPad Photo Library and a
UIImageView that displays the chosen photo. Finally, we'll enable the user to choose
songs from the iPad's iPod Library and start or pause playback. The title of the currently playing song will also be displayed onscreen in a UILabel.

Setting Up the Project Files

Begin by creating a new View-based iPad Application project in Xcode. Name the
new project **MediaPlayground**.

Within Xcode, open the MediaPlaygroundViewController.h file and update the file
to contain the #import directives, outlets, actions, and properties shown in Listing
20.1.

LISTING 20.1

```
#import <UIKit/UIKit.h>
#import <MediaPlayer/MediaPlayer.h>
#import <AVFoundation/AVFoundation.h>
#import <CoreAudio/CoreAudioTypes.h>

@interface MediaPlaygroundViewController : UIViewController
<MPMediaPickerControllerDelegate,AVAudioPlayerDelegate,
UIPopoverControllerDelegate,UIImagePickerControllerDelegate,
UINavigationControllerDelegate> {
    IBOutlet UISwitch *toggleFullscreen;
    IBOutlet UIButton *recordButton;
    IBOutlet UIButton *ipodPlayButton;
    IBOutlet UILabel *nowPlaying;
    IBOutlet UIImageView *chosenImage;

    AVAudioRecorder *soundRecorder;
    MPMusicPlayerController *musicPlayer;

    UIPopoverController *musicPickerPopoverController;
    UIPopoverController *imagePickerPopoverController;
}

-(IBAction)playMedia:(id)sender;
-(IBAction)recordAudio:(id)sender;
-(IBAction)playAudio:(id)sender;
-(IBAction)chooseiPod:(id)sender;
-(IBAction)chooseImage:(id)sender;
-(IBAction)playiPod:(id)sender;

@property (nonatomic,retain) UISwitch *toggleFullscreen;
@property (nonatomic,retain) UIButton *recordButton;
@property (nonatomic, retain) UIButton *ipodPlayButton;
@property (nonatomic, retain) UILabel *nowPlaying;
@property (nonatomic, retain) UIImageView *chosenImage;
@property (nonatomic, retain) AVAudioRecorder *soundRecorder;
@property (nonatomic, retain) MPMusicPlayerController *musicPlayer;

@end
```

Most of this code should look familiar to you. We're defining several outlets, actions, and properties for interface elements, as well as declaring the instance variables soundRecorder and musicPlayer that will hold our audio recorder and iPod music player, respectively. We also need two popover controllers (UIPopoverController) that will be used to display the iPod and Photo interfaces.

> If you've worked through the other hours that cover popovers, you may remember that you don't always need to keep track of the popover controller object. In this example, we have defined two instance variables for the controllers because we will need to dismiss them manually.

By the Way

You might not recognize a few additions. First, we need to import three new interface files so that we can access the classes and methods in the Media Player and AV Foundation frameworks. The CoreAudioTypes.h file is required so that we can specify a file format for recording audio.

Next, you'll notice that we've declared that the MediaPlaygroundViewController class must conform to the MPMediaPickerControllerDelegate, AVAudioPlayerDelegate, UIImagePickerControllerDelegate, UINavigationControllerDelegate, and UIPopoverControllerDelegate protocols. The MPMediaPickerControllerDelegate, UIImagePickerControllerDelegate, and AVAudioPlayerDelegate protocols will help us detect when the user has finished choosing music and photos, and when an audio file has finished playing. The UIPopoverControllerDelegate will be used to properly release the popovers when they're finished being displayed. That leaves UINavigationControllerDelegate; what do we need this for? The navigation controller delegate is required whenever you use an Image Picker. The good news is that you won't need to implement any additional methods for it!

After you've finished the interface file, save your changes and open the view controller implementation file, MediaPlaygroundViewController.m. Edit the file to include the following @synthesize directives and method stubs after the @implementation line:

```
@synthesize toggleFullscreen;
@synthesize soundRecorder;
@synthesize recordButton;
@synthesize musicPlayer;
@synthesize ipodPlayButton;
@synthesize nowPlaying;
@synthesize chosenImage;
```

Finally, for everything that we've retained, be sure to add an appropriate release line within the view controller's dealloc method:

```
- (void)dealloc {
    [toggleScaling release];
    [soundRecorder release];
    [recordButton release];
    [musicPlayer release];
    [ipodPlayButton release];
    [nowPlaying release];
    [chosenImage release];
    [super dealloc];
}
```

Now, we'll take a few minutes to configure the interface XIB file, and then explore the classes and methods that can (literally) make our apps sing.

Creating the Media Playground Interface

Open the MediaPlaygroundViewController.xib file in Interface Builder and begin laying out the view. This application will have a total of six buttons (UIButton), one switch (UISwitch), two labels (UILabel), and a UIImageView. In addition, we need to leave room for an embedded video player that will be added programmatically.

Figure 20.1 represents a potential design for the application. Feel free to use this approach with your layout, or modify it to suit your fancy.

FIGURE 20.1
Create an interface for the different functions we'll be implementing.

> You might want to consider using the Attributes Inspector to set the UIImageView mode to Aspect Fill or Aspect Scale to make sure your photos look right within the view.

Connecting the Outlets and Actions

Finish up the interface work by connecting the buttons and label to the corresponding outlets and actions that were defined earlier.

For reference, the connections that you will be creating are listed in Table 20.1. Be aware that some UI elements need to connect to both an action *and* an outlet so that we can easily modify their properties in the application.

TABLE 20.1   Interface Elements and Actions

Element Name (Type)	Outlet/Action	Purpose
Play Movie (UIButton)	Action: playMedia:	Initiates playback in an embedded movie player, displaying a video file
On/Off Switch (UISwitch)	Outlet: toggleFullscreen	Toggles a property of the movie player, embedding it or presenting the video fullscreen
Record Audio (UIButton)	Action: recordAudio: Outlet: recordButton	Starts and stops audio recording
Play Audio (UIButton)	Action: playAudio:	Plays the currently recorded audio sample
Choose Image	Action: chooseImage:	Opens a popover displaying the user's Photo Library
UIImageView	Outlet: chosenImage	The image view that will be used for displaying a photo from the user's Photo Library
Choose iPod Music	Action: chooseiPod:	Opens a popover displaying the (UIButton) user's Music Library for creating a playlist

TABLE 20.1   continued

Element Name (Type)	Outlet/Action	Purpose
Play iPod Music (UIButton)	Action: playiPod: Outlet: ipodPlayButton	Plays or pauses the current playlist
No Song Playing (UILabel)	Outlet: nowPlaying	Displays the title of the currently playing song (if any)

After creating all the connections to and from the File Owner's icon, save and close the XIB file. We've now created the basic skeleton for all the media capabilities we'll be adding in the rest of the exercise.

Using the Movie Player

The Media Player framework provides access to the built-in media playback capabilities of the iPad. Everything you typically see when playing video or audio—the scrubber control, fast forward/rewind, play, pause—all of these features come "for free" within the classes provided by the Media Player.

In this exercise, we make use of the MPMoviePlayerController class. There are only three methods between us and movie playback bliss:

initWithContentURL: — Provided with an NSURL object, this method initializes the movie player and prepares it for playback.

play — Begins playing the selected movie file.

setFullscreen:animated — Sets the movie playback to fullscreen.

Because the movie controller itself implements controls for controlling playback, we don't need to implement additional features ourselves. If we want to, however, there are many other methods, including stop, that we can call on to control playback.

> These are only a few of the dozens of methods and properties available for the movie player. You can get pointers to additional resources in the "Further Exploration" section at the end of this hour.

Adding the Media Player Framework

To use the MPMoviePlayerController class (and the MPMusicPlayerController we'll be implementing a bit later), we must first add the Media Player framework to the project. To do this, right-click the Frameworks folder icon in Xcode, and choose

Add, Existing Frameworks. Select MediaPlayer.framework in the list that appears, and then click Add.

> Typically, you also need to add a corresponding import line in your header file (#import <MediaPlayer/MediaPlayer.h>), but because we already added this during the application setup, you should be good to go!

Adding Media Files

As you might have noticed earlier when we listed the methods we would be using, initializing an instance of MPMoviePlayerController is performed by passing in an NSURL object. This means that if you pass in a URL for a media file hosted on a web server, as long as it is a supported format, it will work!

Which Formats Are Supported?

Officially, Apple supports the following codecs: H.264 Baseline Profile 3, MPEG-4 Part 2 video in .mov, .m4v, .mpv, or .mp4 containers. On the audio side, AAC-LC, and MP3 formats are supported.

Here is the complete list of audio formats supported by the iPad:

    AAC (16Kbps to 320Kbps)

    AIFF

    AAC Protected (MP4 from iTunes Store)

    MP3 (16Kbps to 320Kbps)

    MP3 VBR

    Audible (formats 2–4)

    Apple Lossless

    WAV

For this example, however, we've chosen to include a local media file so that we can easily test the functionality. Locate the movie.m4v file included in the MediaPlayground project folder and drag it into your Xcode Resources group so that we can access it directly in the application. Be sure to choose to copy the file to the project, when prompted.

Implementing Movie Playback

For movie playback in the MediaPlayground application to work, we need to implement the playMedia: method. This is invoked by the Play Movie button we built in to the interface earlier. Let's add the method, and then walk through how it works.

Add the code from Listing 20.2 to the MediaPlaygroundViewController.m file.

LISTING 20.2

```
 1: -(IBAction)playMedia:(id)sender {
 2:     NSString *movieFile;
 3:     MPMoviePlayerController *moviePlayer;
 4:
 5:     movieFile = [[NSBundle mainBundle]
 6:                     pathForResource:@"movie" ofType:@"m4v"];
 7:     moviePlayer = [[MPMoviePlayerController alloc]
 8:                     initWithContentURL: [NSURL fileURLWithPath: movieFile]];
 9:
10:     [moviePlayer.view setFrame:CGRectMake(100, 150, 568 , 300)];
11:     [self.view addSubview:moviePlayer.view ];
12:
13:
14:     [[NSNotificationCenter defaultCenter] addObserver:self
15:                     selector:@selector(playMediaFinished:)
16:                     name:MPMoviePlayerPlaybackDidFinishNotification
17:                     object:moviePlayer];
18:
19:     [moviePlayer play];
20:
21:     if ([toggleFullscreen isOn]) {
22:         [moviePlayer setFullscreen:YES animated:YES];
23:     }
24:
25: }
```

Things start off simple enough. Line 2 declares a string `movieFile` that will hold the path to the movie file we added in the previous step. Next, we declare the `moviePlayer`, a reference to an instance of `MPMoviePlayerController`.

Next, lines 5–6 grab and store the path of the movie.m4v file in the `movieFile` variable.

Lines 7–8 allocate and initialize the `moviePlayer` itself using an `NSURL` instance that contains the path from `movieFile`. Believe it or not, this is most of the "heavy lifting" of the movie playback method! After we've completed this line, we can (if we want) immediately call the `play` method on the `moviePlayer` object and see the movie play! We've chosen to add an additional feature instead.

Lines 10–11 set the frame dimensions of the movie player that we want to embed in the view, then adds the `moviePlayer` view to the main application view. If this seems familiar, it's because it's the same technique we used to add a field to an alert in Hour 10.

Playback is started using the `play` method in line 19.

Finally, lines 21–23 check to see whether the toggle switch (toggleFullscreen) is turned "on" using the UISwitch instance method isOn. If the switch *is* on, we use the method setFullscreen:animated to expand the movie to fill the iPad's screen. If the switch is off, we do nothing, and the movie plays back within the confines of the frame we defined.

Notice anything missing? We've conveniently skipped over lines 14–17. These lines add a notification for the movie player that will help us identify when the movie has stopped playing. Because this is the first time you've worked with a notification, we'll address it separately.

Receiving a Notification

There is a teensy-weensy problem with implementing the MPMoviePlayerController as we've done here. If we attempt to release the movie player after the play line, the application will crash. If we attempt to autorelease the player, the same thing happens! So, how in the world can we get rid of the player?

The key is that we need to wait until the movie is no longer playing. To do that, we use the NSNotificationCenter class to register an "observer" that will watch for a specific notification message from the mediaPlayer object, and then call a method of our choosing when it receives the notification.

The MPMoviePlayerController sends the MPMoviePlayerPlaybackDidFinishNotification when it has finished playing a piece of media. In lines 16–19, we register that notification for our mediaPlayer object and ask the notification center to invoke the playMediaFinished: method when it receives the notification. Put simply, when the movie player is finished playing the movie (or the user stops playback), the playMediaFinished: method is called.

Implementing the playMediaFinished: method allows us to clean up once we're done with the movie player!

Handling Cleanup

To clean up after the movie playback has finished, we need to release the mediaPlayer object. Add the playMediaFinished: method to the MPMoviePlayerController.m file, as shown in Listing 20.3.

LISTING 20.3

```
 1: -(void)playMediaFinished:(NSNotification*)theNotification
 2: {
 3:     MPMoviePlayerController *moviePlayer=[theNotification object];
 4:
 5:     [[NSNotificationCenter defaultCenter] removeObserver:self
 6:                          name:MPMoviePlayerPlaybackDidFinishNotification
 7:                          object:moviePlayer];
 8:
 9:     [moviePlayer.view removeFromSuperview];
10:     [moviePlayer release];
11: }
```

Three things need to happen in this method. First, in line 3, we assign the local moviePlayer variable to the object that is passed in from the notification. This is the same object that we were using when we initiated the play method in playMedia; it just arrived in this method by way of a notification, so we need to call the object method on the notification to access it again.

In lines 5–7, we tell the notification center that it can stop looking for the MPMoviePlayerPlaybackDidFinishNotification notification. Because we're going to be releasing the movie player object, there's no point in keeping it around.

Line 9 removes the embedded movie player view from the main application view.

Finally, in line 9, we can release the movie player!

Movie playback is now available in the application, as demonstrated in Figure 20.2. Choose Build and Run in Xcode, press the Play Movie button, and sit back and enjoy the show!

FIGURE 20.2
The application
will now play the
video file when
Play Movie is
touched.

Creating and Playing Audio Recordings

In the second part of the tutorial, we'll be adding audio recording and playback to the application. Unlike the movie player, we'll be using classes within the AV Foundation framework to implement these features. As you'll learn, there's very little coding that needs to be done to make this work!

For the recorder, we'll use the AVAudioRecorder class and these methods:

> initWithURL:settings:error:—Provided with an NSURL instance pointing to a local file, and NSDictionary containing a few settings, this method returns an instance of a recorder, ready to use.
>
> record—Begins recording.
>
> stop—Ends the recording session.

Not coincidentally, the playback feature, an instance of AVAudioPlayer, uses some very similar methods:

> initWithContentsOfURL:error:—Creates an audio player object that can be used to play back the contents of the file pointed to by an NSURL object.
>
> play—Plays back the audio.

When you were entering the contents of the MediaPlayground.h file a bit earlier, you may have noticed that we slipped in a protocol: AVAudioPlayerDelegate. By conforming to this protocol, we can implement the method audioPlayerDidFinishPlaying:successfully:, which will automatically be invoked when our audio player finishes playing back the recording. No notifications needed this time around!

Adding the AV Foundation Framework

To use the AVAudioPlayer and AVAudioRecorder classes, we must add the AV Foundation framework to the project. Right-click the Frameworks folder icon in Xcode, and choose Add, Existing Frameworks. Select the AVFoundation.framework, and then click Add.

> Remember, the framework also requires a corresponding import line in your header file (#import <AVFoundation/AVFoundation.h>) to access the classes and methods. We added this earlier when setting up the project.

Implementing Audio Recording

To add audio recording, we need to create the `recordAudio:` method, but before we do, let's think through this a bit. What happens when we initiate a recording? In this application, recording will continue until we press the button again.

To implement this functionality, the "recorder" object itself must persist between calls to the `recordAudio:` method. We'll make sure this happens by using the `soundRecorder` instance variable in the `MediaPlaygroundViewController` class (declared in the project setup) to hold the `AVAudioRecorder` object. By setting the object up in the `viewDidLoad` method, it will be available anywhere and anytime we need it. Edit `MediaPlaygroundViewController.m` and add the code in Listing 20.4 to `viewDidLoad`.

LISTING 20.4

```
 1: - (void)viewDidLoad {
 2:     NSString *tempDir;
 3:     NSURL *soundFile;
 4:     NSDictionary *soundSetting;
 5:
 6:     tempDir=NSTemporaryDirectory();
 7:     soundFile=[NSURL fileURLWithPath:
 8:             [tempDir stringByAppendingString:@"sound.caf"]];
 9:
10:     soundSetting = [NSDictionary dictionaryWithObjectsAndKeys:
11:         [NSNumber numberWithFloat: 44100.0],AVSampleRateKey,
12:         [NSNumber numberWithInt: kAudioFormatMPEG4AAC],AVFormatIDKey,
13:         [NSNumber numberWithInt: 2],AVNumberOfChannelsKey,
14:         [NSNumber numberWithInt:
➥AVAudioQualityHigh],AVEncoderAudioQualityKey,
15:         nil];
16:
17:     soundRecorder = [[AVAudioRecorder alloc] initWithURL: soundFile
18:                                              settings: soundSetting
19:                                                 error: nil];
20:
21:     [super viewDidLoad];
22: }
```

Beginning with the basics, lines 2–3 declare a string, `tempDir`, that will hold the iPad temporary directory (which we'll need to store a sound recording), a URL, `soundFile`, which will point to the sound file itself, and `soundSetting`, a dictionary that will hold several settings needed to tell the recorder how it should be recording.

In line 6, we use `NSTemporaryDirectory()` to grab and store the temporary directory path where your application can store its sound find.

Lines 7 and 8 concatenate `"sound.caf"` onto the end of the temporary directory. This string is then used to initialize a new instance of `NSURL`, which is stored in the `soundFile` variable.

Lines 10–15 create an `NSDictionary` object that contains keys and values for configuring the format of the sound being recorded. Unless you're familiar with audio recording, many of these might be pretty foreign sounding. Here's the 30-second summary:

> `AVSampleRateKey` — The number of audio samples the recorder will take per second.
>
> `AVFormatIDKey` — The recording format for the audio.
>
> `AVNumberofChannelsKey` — The number of audio channels in the recording. Stereo audio, for example, has two channels.
>
> `AVEncoderAudioQualityKey` — A quality setting for the encoder.

> To learn more about the different settings, what they mean, and what the possible options are, read the AVAudioRecorder Class Reference (scroll to the "Constants" section) in the Xcode developer documentation utility.

> The audio format specified in the settings is defined in the CoreAudioTypes.h file. Because the settings reference an audio type by name, you must import this file: `#import <CoreAudio/CoreAudioTypes.h>`.
>
> Again, this was completed in the initial project setup, so no need to make any changes now.

In lines 17–19, the audio recorder, `soundRecorder`, is initialized with the `soundFile` URL and the settings stored in the `soundSettings` dictionary. We pass `nil` to the error parameter because we don't (for this example) care whether an error occurs. If we were to experience an error, it would be returned in a value passed to this parameter.

Controlling Recording

With the `soundRecorder` allocated and initialized, all that we need to do is implement `recordAudio:` so that the `record` and `stop` methods are invoked as needed. To make things interesting, we'll have the `recordButton` change its title between Record Audio and Stop Recording when pressed.

Add the following code in Listing 20.5 to `MediaPlaygroundViewController.m`.

LISTING 20.5

```
-(IBAction)recordAudio:(id)sender {
    if ([recordButton.titleLabel.text isEqualToString:@"Record Audio"]) {
        [soundRecorder record];
        [recordButton setTitle:@"Stop Recording"
                    forState:UIControlStateNormal];
    } else {
        [soundRecorder stop];
        [recordButton setTitle:@"Record Audio"
                    forState:UIControlStateNormal];
    }
}
```

The method first checks the title of the recordButton variable. If it is set to Record Audio, the method uses [soundRecorder record] to start recording, and then sets the recordButton title to Stop Recording. If the title *doesn't* read Record Audio, then we're already in the process of making a recording. In this case, we use [soundRecorder stop] to end the recording and set the button title back to Record Audio.

That's it for recording! Let's implement playback so that we can actually *hear* what we've recorded!

Controlling Audio Playback

To play back the audio that we recorded, we'll create an instance of the AVAudioPlayer class, point it at the sound file we created with the recorder, and then call the play method. We'll also add the method audioPlayerDidFinishPlaying:successfully: defined by the AVAudioPlayerDelegate protocol so that we've got a convenient place to release the audio player object.

Start by adding the playAudio: method, in Listing 20.6, to MediaPlaygroundViewController.m.

LISTING 20.6

```
 1: -(IBAction)playAudio:(id)sender {
 2:     NSURL *soundFile;
 3:     NSString *tempDir;
 4:     AVAudioPlayer *audioPlayer;
 5:
 6:     tempDir=NSTemporaryDirectory();
 7:     soundFile=[NSURL fileURLWithPath:
 8:             [tempDir stringByAppendingString:@"sound.caf"]];
 9:
10:     audioPlayer = [[AVAudioPlayer alloc]
```

```
11:                     initWithContentsOfURL:soundFile error:nil];
12:
13:     [audioPlayer setDelegate:self];
14:     [audioPlayer play];
15: }
```

In lines 2–3, we define variables for holding the iPad application's temporary directory and a URL for the sound file—exactly the same as the record.

Line 4 declares the audioPlayer instance of AVAudioPlayer.

Lines 6–8 should look very familiar, as, once again, they grab and store the temporary directory, and then use it to initialize an NSURL object, soundFile, that points to the sound.caf file we've recorded.

In lines 10 and 11, the audio player, audioPlayer is allocated and initialized with the contents of soundFile.

Line 13 is a bit out of the ordinary, but nothing too strange. The setDelegate method is called with the parameter of self. This tells the audioPlayer instance that it can look in the view controller object (MediaPlaygroundViewController) for its AVAudioPlayerDelegate protocol methods.

Line 14 initiates playback using the play method.

Handling Cleanup

To handle releasing the AVAudioPlayer instance after it has finished playing, we need to implement the protocol method audioPlayerDidFinishPlaying:successfully:. Add the following method code to the view controller implementation file:

```
(void)audioPlayerDidFinishPlaying:
        (AVAudioPlayer *)player successfully:(BOOL)flag {
    [player release];
}
```

We get a reference to the player we allocated via the incoming player parameter, so we just send it the release message and we're done!

Choose Build and Run in Xcode to test recording and playback. Press Record Audio to begin recording. Talk, sing, or yell at your iPad. Touch Stop Recording, as shown in Figure 20.3, to end the recording. Finally, press the Play Audio button to initiate playback.

FIGURE 20.3
Record and play
back audio!

It's time to move on to the next part of this hour's exercise: accessing and displaying photos from the Photo Library.

Using the iPad Photo Library

The iPad is great for storing content, and, with the right apps, great for editing that content. By integrating the iPad Photo Library with your apps, you can directly access any image stored on the device and use it within your application. In this hour's tutorial, we're going to display the library, allow the user to pick a photo, and then display it within a `UIImageView` in the application interface.

The magic that makes this possible is the `UIImagePickerController` class. This class will give us a view controller that we can display via popover, and a corresponding view where the user can navigate their photos and videos.

We will need to implement the `UIImagePickerControllerDelegate` protocol's `imagePickerController:didFinishPickingMediaWithInfo` to detect when an image has been chosen and to properly dismiss the Image Picker and popover.

Implementing the Image Picker

When a user touches the Choose Image button, our application triggers the method `chooseImage`. Within this method, we will allocate the `UIImagePickerController`, configure the type of media that it will be browsing, set its delegate, and then display it within a popover. Because the `UIImagePickerController` is a self-contained view controller and view, using the popover requires very little of the setup that we had to complete in earlier hour's lessons.

Enter the `chooseImage` method shown in Listing 20.7.

LISTING 20.7

```
 1: -(IBAction)chooseImage:(id)sender {
 2:     UIImagePickerController *imagePicker;
 3:     imagePicker = [[UIImagePickerController alloc] init];
 4:     imagePicker.sourceType=UIImagePickerControllerSourceTypePhotoLibrary;
 5:     imagePicker.delegate=self;
 6:     imagePickerPopoverController=[[UIPopoverController alloc]
 7:                             initWithContentViewController :imagePicker];
 8:     [imagePickerPopoverController presentPopoverFromRect:[sender frame]
 9:             inView:self.view
10:             permittedArrowDirections:UIPopoverArrowDirectionAny
                animated:YES];
11:
12:     [imagePicker release];
13: }
```

In lines 2 and 3, `imagePicker` is allocated and initialized as an instance of `UIImagePickerController`.

Line 4 sets the `sourceType` property of the Image Picker to `UIImagePickerControllerSourceTypePhotoLibrary`. This ensures that the picker will show the typical Photo Library view.

There are two other possible sources: `UIImagePickerControllerSourceTypeCamera` and `UIImagePickerControllerSourceTypeSavedPhotosAlbum`. The first provides direct access to built-in cameras on iPhone OS devices, and the second is used to view the camera photo roll. For the iPad, these are currently not as useful as on an iPhone.

Line 5 sets the Image Picker delegate to be the `MediaPlayerViewController` class. This means we will need to implement some supporting methods to handle when the user is finished choosing a photo.

Lines 6–10 allocate and initialize the `imagePickerPopoverController`, adding the `imagePicker` view controller as the content provider and using the rectangle defined by the Choose Image button as the place the popover will "pop" from.

In Line 12, the `imagePicker` is released. The object, however, will not be released from memory until the popover that contains it is released.

Displaying the Chosen Image

With what we've written so far, the user can now touch the Choose Image button, but not much is going to happen once the user navigates to an image. To react to a selection within the Photo Library, we will implement the delegate method `imagePickerController: didFinishPickingMediaWithInfo`.

This method will automatically be called when the user touches a piece of media within the Image Picker. The method is passed an NSDictionary object that can contain several thing: the image itself, an edited version of the image (if cropping/scaling is allowed), or information about the image. We must provide the key value to retrieve the value we want. For this application, we will be accessing the object returned by the UIImagePickerControllerOriginalImage key, a UIImage. This UIImage will then be displayed within the chosenImage UIImageView in our interface.

Did you Know?

To learn more about the data that can be returned by the Image Picker, read the UIImagePickerControllerDelegate Protocol reference within the Apple developer documentation.

Add the imagePickerController:didFinishPickingMediaWithInfo delegate method shown in Listing 20.8 to the MediaPlaygroundViewController.m file.

LISTING 20.8

```
1: - (void)imagePickerController:(UIImagePickerController *)picker
2:        didFinishPickingMediaWithInfo:(NSDictionary *)info {
3:    chosenImage.image=[info objectForKey:
4:                       UIImagePickerControllerOriginalImage];
5:    [imagePickerPopoverController dismissPopoverAnimated:YES];
6:    [imagePickerPopoverController release];
7: }
```

Line 3 does almost all the work! We access the UIImage that the user has chosen by grabbing the object in the info dictionary that is referenced by the UIImagePickerControllerOriginalImage key. This is assigned to the image property of chosenImage, displaying the image, in all its glory, in the application's view.

If we leave the method with just line 3, as soon as the user picks an image, it will display, but the popover will remain. To manually dismiss the popover, we use the dismissPopoverAnimated method in line 5. Line 6 finishes up by dismissing the popover controller.

Cleaning Up After the Image Picker and Popover

Before we can call the image-picking portion of our MediaPlayground application complete, we must account for two more scenarios. First, a user can click a "cancel" button within the Image Picker; this is handled by the imagePickerControllerDidCancel delegate method. If this happens, just dismiss the popover. Nothing else is required. Implement this method as follows:

```
- (void)imagePickerControllerDidCancel:(UIImagePickerController *)picker {
    [imagePickerPopoverController dismissPopoverAnimated:YES];
    [imagePickerPopoverController release];
}
```

Next, the user might dismiss the Image Picker by touching outside of the popover. If that happens, the popover will automatically be dismissed, but still needs to be released. Handle this scenario in the popoverControllerDidCancel method:

```
- (void)popoverControllerDidDismissPopover:
    (UIPopoverController *)popoverController {
    [popoverController release];
}
```

You should now be able to use the Choose Image button and display photos from the iPad Library, as shown in Figure 20.4.

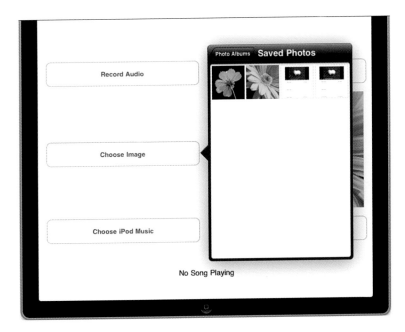

FIGURE 20.4
Choose and display photos in the your application!

Our final step in this hour's lesson is accessing the iPod Library and playing content. You'll notice quite a few similarities to using the Photo Library in this implementation.

Accessing and Playing the iPod Library

When Apple opened the iPhone OS SDK for development, they didn't initially provide a method for accessing the iPod Library. This led to applications implementing their own libraries for background music, and a less-than-ideal experience for the end user.

Thankfully, developers can now directly access the iPod Library and play any of the available music files. Best of all, this is amazingly simple to implement!

First, you'll be using the `MPMediaPickerController` class to choose the music to play. There's only a single method we'll be calling from this class:

> `initWithMediaTypes:` — Initializes the Media Picker and filters the files that are available in the picker.

We'll configure its behavior with a handful of properties that can be set on the object:

> `prompt` — A string that is displayed to the user when choosing songs
>
> `allowsPickingMultipleItems` — Configures whether the user can choose one or more sound files

Like the `AVAudioPlayer`, we're going to conform to the `MPMediaPickerControllerDelegate` protocol so that we can react when the user chooses a playlist. The method that we'll be adding as part of the protocol is `mediaPicker:didPickMediaItems:`.

To play back the audio, we'll take advantage of the `MPMusicPlayerController` class, which can use the playlist returned by the Media Picker. To control starting and pausing the playback, we'll use four methods:

> `iPodMusicPlayer` — This class method initializes the music player as an "iPod" music player, capable of accessing the iPod Music Library.
>
> `setQueueWithItemCollection` — Sets the playback queue using a playlist (`MPMediaItemCollection`) object returned by the Media Picker.
>
> `play` — Starts playing music.
>
> `pause` — Pauses the music playback.

As you can see, once you get the hang of one of the media classes, the others start to seem very "familiar," using similar initialization and playback control methods.

> The iPod music playback features require the same Media Player framework we added previously for the MPMoviePlayerController class. If you skipped that section, return to the "Adding the Media Player Framework" section, earlier in this hour.

Implementing the Media Picker

To use a Media Picker, we'll follow steps very similar to the Image Picker: We'll initialize and configure the behavior of the picker, and then add the picker to a popover. When the user is done with the picker, we'll add the playlist it returns to the music player, and dismiss the popover. If users decide they don't want to pick anything, we simply dismiss the popover and move on.

For all these steps to fall into place, we must already have an instance of the music player so that we can hand off the playlist. Recall that we declared an instance variable musicPlayer for the MediaPlaygroundViewController class. We'll go ahead and initialize this variable in the MediaPlaygroundViewController.m viewDidLoad method. Add the following line to the method now (the location isn't important):

```
musicPlayer=[MPMusicPlayerController iPodMusicPlayer];
```

With that small addition, our instance of the music player is ready, so we can proceed with coding the chooseiPod: method to display the Media Picker.

Update the MediaPlaygroundViewController implementation file with the new method in Listing 20.9.

LISTING 20.9

```
 1: -(IBAction)chooseiPod:(id)sender {
 2:     MPMediaPickerController *musicPicker;
 3:     [musicPlayer stop];
 4:     nowPlaying.text=@"No Song Playing";
 5:     [ipodPlayButton setTitle:@"Play iPod Music"
 6:                     forState:UIControlStateNormal];
 7:
 8:     musicPicker = [[MPMediaPickerController alloc]
 9:                     initWithMediaTypes: MPMediaTypeMusic];
10:
11:     musicPicker.allowsPickingMultipleItems = YES;
12:     musicPicker.delegate = self;
13:
14:     musicPickerPopoverController=[[UIPopoverController alloc]
15:                         initWithContentViewController:musicPicker];
16:     [musicPickerPopoverController
17:         presentPopoverFromRect:[sender frame]
18:         inView:self.view
19:         permittedArrowDirections:UIPopoverArrowDirectionAny animated:YES];
20:
21:     [musicPicker release];
22: }
```

First, line 2 declares the instance of MPMediaPickerController, musicPicker.

Next, lines 3–6 make sure that when the picker is called, the music player will stop playing its current song, the nowPlaying label in the interface is set to the default string "No Song Playing", and the playback button is set to read Play iPod Music. These lines aren't necessary, but they keep our interface from being out of sync with what is really going on in the application.

Lines 8 and 9 allocate and initialize the Media Picker controller instance. It is initialized with a constant, MPMediaTypeMusic, that defines the type of files the user will be allowed to choose with the picker. You can provide any of five values listed here:

> MPMediaTypeMusic — Music files
>
> MPMediaTypePodcast — Podcasts
>
> MPMediaTypeAudioBook — Audio books
>
> MPMediaTypeAnyAudio — Any audio type
>
> MPMediaTypeAny — Any media type

In line 11, we set the allowsPickingMultipleItems property to a Boolean value (YES or NO) to configure whether the user can select one or more media files.

Line 12 sets the delegate music picker's delegate. In other words, it tells the musicPicker object to look in the MediaPlaygroundViewController for the MPMediaPickerControllerDelegate protocol methods.

Lines 14–19, as with the Image Library Picker earlier, initializes and allocates a musicPickerPopoverController object. The popover controller is set to use the musicPicker view controller for its content, and will appear from the rectangle that defines the Choose iPod button.

Finally, line 21 releases the musicPicker.

> If you find it confusing that you release the musicPicker in this method, I don't blame you. Once the music picker is added to the popover, its retain count is incremented, so releasing it essentially means that we aren't responsible for it anymore. When the popover is released later, the music picker will be autoreleased.
>
> What's frustrating is that while this *init, alloc, release* pattern works well *here*, you may find yourself thinking that some other object can be managed similarly, and end up releasing when you shouldn't. Only a thorough read of the corresponding Apple documentation will tell you with certainty how something will behave.

Getting the Playlist

To get the playlist that is returned by Media Picker (an object called MPMediaItemCollection) and clean up after ourselves, we'll add the mediaPicker:didPickMediaItems: protocol method from Listing 20.10 to our growing implementation.

LISTING 20.10

```
1: - (void)mediaPicker: (MPMediaPickerController *)mediaPicker
2:    didPickMediaItems:(MPMediaItemCollection *)mediaItemCollection {
3:       [musicPlayer setQueueWithItemCollection: mediaItemCollection];
4:       [musicPickerPopoverController dismissPopoverAnimated:YES];
5:       [musicPickerPopoverController release];
6: }
```

When the user is finished picking songs in the Media Picker, this method is called and passed the chosen items in a MPMediaItemCollection object, mediaItemCollection. The music player instance, musicPlayer, is subsequently configured with the playlist via the setQueueWithItemCollection: method.

To clean things up, the dismissPopoverAnimated is called to dismiss the musicPickerPopoverController popover, and then the popover controller is released.

Cleaning Up After the Image Picker and Popover

We've got one more situation to account for before we can wrap up the Media Picker: the possibility of a user exiting the Media Picker without choosing anything (touching Done without picking any tracks). To cover this event, we'll add the delegate protocol method mediaPickerDidCancel. As with the Image Picker, we just need to dismiss and release the popover. Add this method to the MediaPlaygroundViewController.m file:

```
- (void)mediaPickerDidCancel:(MPMediaPickerController *)mediaPicker {
    [musicPickerPopoverController dismissPopoverAnimated:YES];
    [musicPickerPopoverController release];
}
```

Now, what about the case of a user touching outside of the popover to dismiss the Media Picker? No problem, we've already got that covered! Our popover delegate protocol method popoverControllerDidDismissPopover handles that just fine for both the Image Picker *and* the Media Picker.

Congratulations! You're almost done! The Media Picker feature is now implemented, so our only remaining task is to add the music player and make sure the corresponding song titles are displayed.

Implementing the Music Player

Because the `musicPlayer` object was created in the `viewDidLoad` method of the view controller (see the start of "Implementing the Media Picker"), and the music player's playlist was set in `mediaPicker:didPickMediaItems:`, the only real work that the `playiPod:` method must handle is starting and pausing playback.

To spice things up a bit, we'll try to be a bit clever—toggling the `ipodPlayButton` title between Play iPod Music (the default) and Pause iPod Music as needed. As a final touch, we'll access a property of `musicPlayer` `MPMusicPlayerController` object called `nowPlayingItem`. This property is an object of type `MPMediaItem`, which contains a string property called `MPMediaItemPropertyTitle` set to the name of the currently playing media file, if available.

To grab the title from `musicPlayer.nowPlayingItem`, we'll use a `MPMediaItem` instance method `valueForProperty:`.

For example: `[musicPlayer.nowPlayingItem valueForProperty: MPMediaItemPropertyTitle]`

If you attempt to use `musicPlayer.nowPlayingItem.MPMediaItemPropertyTitle`, it will fail. You must use the `valueForProperty:` method to retrieve the title or other `MPMediaItem` properties.

Putting this all together, we get the implementation of `playiPod` in Listing 20.11.

LISTING 20.11

```
 1: -(IBAction)playiPod:(id)sender {
 2:     if ([ipodPlayButton.titleLabel.text isEqualToString:@"Play iPod Music"])
{
 3:         [musicPlayer play];
 4:         [ipodPlayButton setTitle:@"Pause iPod Music"
 5:                         forState:UIControlStateNormal];
 6:         nowPlaying.text=[musicPlayer.nowPlayingItem
 7:                         valueForProperty:MPMediaItemPropertyTitle];
 8:     } else {
 9:         [musicPlayer pause];
10:         [ipodPlayButton setTitle:@"Play iPod Music"
11:                         forState:UIControlStateNormal];
12:         nowPlaying.text=@"No Song Playing";
13:     }
14: }
```

Line 2 checks to see whether the `ipodPlayButton` title is set to Play iPod Music. If it is, line 3 starts playback, lines 4 and 5 reset the button to read Pause iPod Music, and lines 6 and 7 set the `nowPlaying` label to the title of the current audio track.

If the ipodPlayButton title is *not* Play iPod Music (line 8), the music is paused, the button title is reset to Play iPod Music, and the onscreen label is changed to display No Song Playing.

After completing the method implementation, save the MediaPlaygroundViewController.m file and choose Build and Run to test the application. Pressing the Choose iPod Music button will open a Media Picker, as shown in Figure 20.5.

FIGURE 20.5
The Media Picker enables browsing the iPad's iPod Music Library.

After you've created a playlist, press the Done button in the Media Picker, and then touch Play iPod Music to begin playing the sounds you've chosen. The title of the current song is displayed at the bottom of the interface.

There was quite a bit covered in this hour's lesson, but consider the capabilities you've uncovered. Your projects can now tie into the same media capabilities that Apple uses in their own iPad apps—delivering rich multimedia to your users with a relatively minimal amount of coding.

Further Exploration

We touched on only a few of the configuration options available for the `MPMoviePlayerController`, `MPMusicPlayerController`, `AVAudioPlayer`, `UIImagePickerController`, and `MPMediaPickerController` classes—but far more customization is possible if you dig through the documentation.

The `MPMoviePlayerController` class, for example, offers the `movieControlMode` property for configuring the onscreen controls for when the movie is playing. You can also programmatically "scrub" through the movie, by setting the playback starting point with the `initialPlaybackTime` property. As mentioned (but not demonstrated) in this lesson, this class can even play back a media file hosted on a remote URL—including streaming media.

Custom settings on `AVAudioPlayer` can help you create background sounds and music with properties such as `numberOfLoops` to set looping of the audio playback and `volume` for controlling volume dynamically. You can even enable and control advanced audio metering, monitoring the audio power in decibels for a given sound channel.

On the image side of things, the `UIImagePickerController` includes properties such as `allowsEditing` to enable the user to trim video clips or scale and crop images directly within the Image Picker. If you intend to write iPhone apps (or apps for a future iPad), you'll want to check out the ability of this class to take pictures and record video.

For those interested in going a step further, you may also want to review the documents "OpenGL ES Programming Guide for iPhone," "Introduction to Core Animation Programming Guide," and "Core Audio Overview." These Apple tutorials will introduce you to the 3D, animation, and advanced audio capabilities available in the iPhone OS.

As always, the Apple Xcode documentation utility provides an excellent place for exploring classes and finding associated sample code.

Apple Tutorials

Getting Started with Audio & Video (accessible through the Xcode documentation): This introduction to the iPad A/V capabilities will help you understand what classes to use for what purposes. It also links to a variety of sample applications demonstrating the media features.

AddMusic (accessible through the Xcode documentation): Demonstrates the use of the `MPMediaPickerController` and the `MPMediaPickerControllerDelegate` protocol as well as playback via the `MPMusicPlayerController` class.

MoviePlayer (accessible through the Xcode documentation): Explores the full range of features in the `MPMoviePlayerController` class, including custom overlaps, control customization, and loading movies over a network URL.

Summary

It's hard to believe, but in the span of an hour, you've learned about eight new media classes, three protocols, and a handful of class methods and properties. These will provide much of the functionality you need to create applications that handle rich media. The AV Foundation framework gives us a simple method for recording and playing back high-quality audio streams. The Media Player framework, on the other hand, handles streaming audio and video and can even tap into the existing resources stored in the iPod Library on the iPad. Finally, the easy-to-use `UIImagePickerController` class gives us surprisingly straightforward access to visual media on the device.

Because there are many more methods available in the Media Player framework, I recommend spending additional time reviewing the Xcode documentation if you are at all interested in building multimedia iPad applications.

Q&A

Q. *How do I make the decision between using* `MPMusicPlayerController` *versus* `AVAudioPlayer` *for sound playback in my applications?*

A. Use the `AVAudioPlayer` for audio that you include in your application bundle. Use the `MPMusicPlayerController` for playing files from the iPod Library. Although the `MPMusicPlayerController` can play back local files, its primary purpose is integrating with the existing iPod media.

Q. *I implemented the Image Picker and Media Picker as fullscreen modal views on the iPhone, and they appear to work fine on the iPad, what gives?*

A. Although you can treat the Image Picker and Media Picker objects the same way on the iPad as on the iPhone, Apple requires that you present these views through a popover, rather than fullscreen. If you happen to try using the pickers as modal views, you'll even notice that they look almost entirely different from the views displayed in the popovers.

Workshop

Quiz

1. What class can be used to implement a high-quality audio recorder?

2. What property and associated class represent the current piece of media being played by an instance of MPMusicPlayerController?

3. What do we take advantage of to determine whether a MPMoviePlayerController object has finished playing a file?

Answers

1. The AVAudioRecorder class enables developers to quickly and easily add audio recording capabilities to their applications.

2. The nowPlaying property of the MPMusicPlayerController is an instance of the MPMediaItem class. This class contains a number of read-only properties, including title, artist, and even album artwork.

3. To determine when a movie has finished playback, the MPMoviePlayerPlaybackDidFinishNotification notification can be registered and a custom method called. We use this approach to release the media player object cleanly in our example code.

Activities

1. Return to an earlier application, adding an instance of AVAudioPlayer that plays a looping background soundtrack. You'll need to use the same classes and methods described in this hour's lesson, as well as the numberOfLoops property.

2. Implement image editing with the UIImagePickerController object. To do this, you'll need to set the allowsImageEditing property and use the UIImagePickerControllerEditedImage key to access the edited image when it is returned by the UIImagePickerControllerDelegate protocol.

Interacting with Other Applications

In previous hours, you learned how your applications can interact with various parts of the iPad hardware and software. In the preceding hour, for example, you accessed the iPod Music Library. In Hour 19, "Sensing Movement with Accelerometer Input," you used the iPad's accelerometer. It is typical of a full-featured application to leverage these unique capabilities of the iPad hardware and software that Apple has made accessible through the iPhone OS SDK. Beyond what you have learned already, the iPad applications you develop can take advantage of some additional built-in capabilities.

Extending Application Integration

In the previous hours, you've learned how to display photos that are stored on your iPad and add web views (essentially mini Safari windows) to your apps. In this hour, you'll take your apps to the next level of integration, by adding access to the iPad's address book, email, and mapping capabilities.

Address Book

The address book is a shared database of contact information that is available to any iPhone application. Having a common, shared set of contact information provides a better experience for the user than if every application manages its own separate list of contacts. With the shared address book, there is no need to add contacts multiple times for different applications, and updating a contact in one application makes the update available instantly in all the other applications.

The iPhone SDK provides comprehensive access to the address book database through two frameworks: the Address Book and the Address Book UI frameworks. With the Address Book framework, your application can access the address book and retrieve and update contact data and create new contacts. The Address Book framework is an older framework based on Core Foundation, which means the APIs and data structures of the Address Book framework are C rather than Objective-C. Don't let this scare you. As you'll see, the Address Book framework is still clean, simple, and easy to use, despite its C roots.

The Address Book UI framework is a newer set of user interfaces that wrap around the Address Book framework and provide a standard way for users to work with their contacts, as shown in Figure 21.1. You can use the Address Book UI framework's interfaces to allow users to browse, search, and select contacts from the address book, display and edit a selected contact's information, and create new contacts. As with the iPod and Photo controls in the previous hour, the address book will be displayed in a popover.

FIGURE 21.1
Access address book details from any application.

Email

In the previous hour, you learned how to show a modal view supplied by the iPhone SDK to allow a user to use Apple's Image Picker interfaces to select a photo for your application. Showing a system-supplied modal view controller is a common pattern in the iPhone SDK, and the same approach is used in the Message UI framework to provide an interface for sending email.

Again, the iPhone SDK provides the UI for your application and interacts with the user to send the email, as shown in Figure 21.2. Your application provides the initial values for the email and then acts as a delegate while temporarily stepping out of the way and letting the user interact with the system-supplied interface for sending email. This is the same interface users use in the Mail application to send email, and so it will be familiar to them.

FIGURE 21.2
Present an email composition view to your users.

Similar to how the previous hour's app did not include any of the details of working with the iPad's database of photos, you do not need to include any of the details about the email service your user is using and how to interact with it to send an email. The iPhone OS SDK takes care of the details of sending email at the expense of some lower-level control of the process. The trade-off makes it very easy to send email from your application.

By the Way

Location and Mapping

Core Location is a framework in the SDK that provides the location of the device. Depending on the version of iPad, any of three technologies can be used: GPS, cellular, or WiFi. GPS is the most accurate of these technologies, and will be used first by Core Location if GPS hardware is present. If the device does not have GPS hardware, or if obtaining the current location with GPS fails, Core Location falls back to cellular and then to WiFi.

Location services, while useful, are even better when combined with a map. The obvious next step after learning the location of the device is to show a map of the immediate area, and to point out locations on the map that are relevant to the application. This is where Core Location's new companion framework, Map Kit, comes in. Map Kit enables you to embed a map into a view and provides all the map tiles (images) needed to display the map. It handles the scrolling, zooming, and loading of new map tiles as they are needed. Applications can use Map Kit to annotate locations on the map. Map Kit can also do reverse geocoding, which means getting place information (country, state, city, address) from coordinates.

> Map Kit map tiles come from the Google Maps/Google Earth API. Even though you aren't making calls to this API directly, Map Kit is making those calls on your behalf, so use of the map data from Map Kit binds you and your application to the Google Maps/Google Earth API terms of service.

You can start using Map Kit with no code at all, just by adding the Map Kit framework to your project and an `MKMapView` instance to one of your views in Interface Builder. Once a map view is added, four attributes can be set within Interface Builder to further customize the view (see Figure 21.3). You can select between map, satellite, and hybrid modes; you can determine whether the map should use Core Location to center on the user's location; and you can control if the user should be allowed to interact with the map through swipes and pinches for scrolling and zooming.

FIGURE 21.3
A map view in Interface Builder's Attribute Inspector.

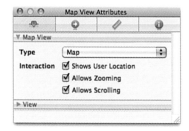

Using Address Book, Email, and Maps... Oh My!

In this hour's example, we will allow users to pick a contact as their best friend from their address book. After they have picked their best friend, we will retrieve information from the address book about their friend and display it nicely on the screen—including their name, photo, and email address. We will also give the user the ability to show their friend's home city in an interactive map, and send them an email—all within a single app screen.

Implementation Overview

This project covers quite a bit of area, but you don't have to enter an extensive amount of code. We'll start by creating the interface, and then add address book, map, and, finally, email features. Each of these will require frameworks to be added, and modifications to the #import lines in our view controller's interface file. In other words, if something doesn't seem to be working, make sure you didn't skip any steps on adding the frameworks!

Setting Up the Project

Start Xcode and create a new View-based iPad application called **BestFriend**, then open the BestFriendViewController.h interface file and add two outlets for UILabels named name and email, an outlet for a UIImageView named photo, and a final outlet for a MKMapView object named map. Because the address book UI will be displayed in a popover, we also need a popoverController instance variable, which we'll call peoplePickerPopoverController.

The application will also implement two actions: newBFF, which will be called to enable the user to choose a new friend from the address book; and sendEmail to send an email to your buddy.

Add these to your interface file, including the appropriate @property directives for each of the outlet variables. Your interface file should now resemble Listing 21.1.

LISTING 21.1

```
#import <UIKit/UIKit.h>

@interface BestFriendViewController : UIViewController {
    IBOutlet UILabel *name;
    IBOutlet UILabel *email;
    IBOutlet UIImageView *photo;
    IBOutlet MKMapView *map;
    UIPopoverController *peoplePickerPopoverController;
}
```

```
@property (nonatomic, retain) UILabel *name;
@property (nonatomic, retain) UILabel *email;
@property (nonatomic, retain) UIImageView *photo;
@property (nonatomic, retain) MKMapView *map;

- (IBAction)newBFF:(id)sender;
- (IBAction)sendEmail:(id)sender;

@end
```

Next, add the corresponding @synthesize lines to the BestFriendViewController.m
file following the @implementation line:

```
@synthesize name;
@synthesize photo;
@synthesize email;
@synthesize map;
```

Next, let's open the BestFriendViewController.xib interface file and build the application UI.

Creating the Application's UI

With all the appropriate outlets and actions in place, we can quickly build the
application's user interface. Instead of trying to describe where everything goes, take
a look at Figure 21.4 to see our approach.

FIGURE 21.4
Create the
application
interface to
resemble this,
or use your own
design!

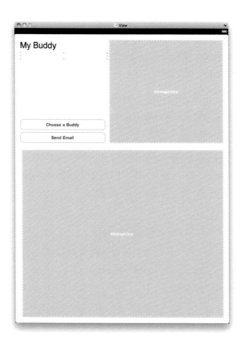

Follow these steps to build the application's UI:

1. Add two labels (`UILabel`) one (larger) for your friend's name, the other for their email address. In my UI, I've chosen to clear the contents of the email label.

2. Add a `UIImageView` that will hold your buddy's photograph from the Address Book. Use the Attributes Inspector to change the image scaling to Aspect Fill or Aspect Fit.

3. Add two buttons (`UIButton`)—one to choose a buddy, and another to email your buddy.

4. Finally, drag a new instance of `MKMapView` into the interface. This is the map view that will ultimately display your location and the city your buddy is in.

Configuring the Map View

After adding the map view, select it and open the Attributes Inspector. Use the Type drop-down menu to pick which type of map to display (satellite, hybrid, and so on), and then activate all the interaction options. This will make the map show the user's current location and enable the user to pan and zoom within the map view (just like in the map application!).

Connecting the Outlets and Actions

You've done this a thousand times (okay, maybe a few dozen), so this should be pretty familiar. Within Interface Builder, Control-drag from the File's Owner icon to the labels, image view, and map view choosing `name`, `email`, `photo`, and `map` as necessary.

Next, use the Connection Inspector for the two buttons to connect the Touch Up Inside events to the `newBFF` and `sendEmail` actions.

With those connections, you're done with the interface! Even though we'll need a popover and will be presenting an email and address book interface—these elements are going to be generated entirely in code.

Accessing the Address Book

There are two parts to accessing the address book: displaying a view that allows the user to choose a contact (an instance of the class `ABPeoplePickerNavigationController`) and reading the data that corresponds to that contact. Two steps... two frameworks that we need to add. Let's do that now.

Adding the Address Book Frameworks and Delegate

Right-click the Frameworks group in your BestFriend project and choose Add, Existing Frameworks from the contextual menu. When prompted, find and add the AddressBook.framework and AddressBookUI.framework (as shown in Figure 21.5).

If the frameworks don't show up in the Frameworks group, drag them there to keep things tidy.

FIGURE 21.5
Add the Address Book and Address Book UI frameworks to your project.

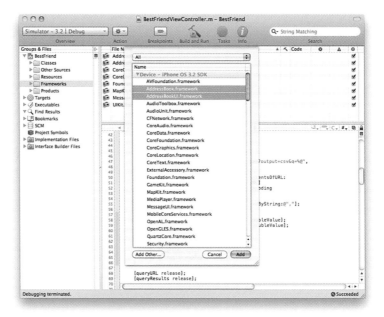

We will also need to import the headers for the Address Book and Address Book UI frameworks and indicate that we implement the `ABPeoplePickerNavigationControllerDelegate` protocol, because our `BestFriendViewController` will be the delegate for our Address Book People Picker, and this protocol is required of its delegate.

Modify the BestFriendViewController.h file, adding these lines to after the existing `#import` line:

```
#import <AddressBook/AddressBook.h>
#import <AddressBookUI/AddressBookUI.h>
```

Next, update the @interface line, adding
<ABPeoplePickerNavigationControllerDelegate> to show that we are conform-
ing to the ABPeoplePickerNavigationControllerDelegate protocol:

```
@interface BestFriendViewController : UIViewController
        <ABPeoplePickerNavigationControllerDelegate> {
```

Choosing a Contact

When the user presses the button to choose a buddy, we want to show the Address
Book Person Picker modal view controller, which will provide the user with the
familiar interface from the Contacts application.

Add the IBAction method shown in Listing 21.2 to the Best_FriendViewController.m
file:

LISTING 21.2

```
 1: - (IBAction)newBFF:(id)sender {
 2:     ABPeoplePickerNavigationController *picker;
 3:
 4:     picker=[[ABPeoplePickerNavigationController alloc] init];
 5:     picker.peoplePickerDelegate = self;
 6:
 7:     peoplePickerPopoverController=[[UIPopoverController alloc]
 8:                             initWithContentViewController:picker];
 9:
10: peoplePickerPopoverController.popoverContentSize= CGSizeMake(320.0,480.0);
11:
12:     [peoplePickerPopoverController presentPopoverFromRect:[sender frame]
13:                     inView:self.view
14:                     permittedArrowDirections:UIPopoverArrowDirectionAny
15:                     animated:YES];
16:
17:     [picker release];
18: }
```

In line 2, we declare picker as an instance of
ABPeoplePickerNavigationController—a GUI object that displays the system's
address book. Lines 4 and 5 allocate the object, and set its delegate to our
BestFriendViewController (self).

Lines 7–15 declare a popover controller (peoplePickerPopoverController) that
will display the contents of the picker object, sets a size for the popover (320 pixels
wide by 480 pixels tall), and, finally, displays the popover from the same Choose a
Buddy button that the user touched.

After the popover is displayed, the picker object can be released in line 17.

Handling Other Address Book Interactions

For the BestFriend application, we need to know only the friend the user has selected; we don't want the user to go on and select or edit the contact's properties. So, we will need to implement the delegate method
`peoplePickerNavigationContoller:peoplePicker:shouldContinueAfterSelect ingPerson` to return NO when it is called—this will be our "workhorse" method. We also need our delegate methods to dismiss the person picker popover to return control of the UI back to our `BestFriendViewController`.

Add the two `ABPersonPickerViewControllerDelegate` protocol methods in Listing 21.3 to the Best_FriendViewController.m file. We need to include these to handle the conditions of the user cancelling without picking someone
(`peoplePickerNavigationControllerDidCancel`), and the user drilling down further than a "person" to a specific attribute
(`peoplePickerNavigationController:shouldContinueAfterSelectingPerson:p roperty:identifier`). Because we're going to capture the user's selection before he or she even *can* drill down, the second method can just return NO—it's never going to get called anyway.

LISTING 21.3

```
// Called after the user has pressed cancel
// The delegate is responsible for dismissing the peoplePicker
- (void)peoplePickerNavigationControllerDidCancel:
        (ABPeoplePickerNavigationController *)peoplePicker {
    [peoplePickerPopoverController dismissPopoverAnimated:YES];
    [peoplePickerPopoverController release];
    [self dismissModalViewControllerAnimated:YES];
}

// Called after a value has been selected by the user.
// Return YES if you want default action to be performed.
// Return NO to do nothing (the delegate is responsible for dismissing the
➥peoplePicker).
- (BOOL)peoplePickerNavigationController:
        (ABPeoplePickerNavigationController *)peoplePicker
        shouldContinueAfterSelectingPerson:(ABRecordRef)person
                        property:(ABPropertyID)property
                        identifier:(ABMultiValueIdentifier)identifier {
    //We won't get to this delegate method
    return NO;
}
```

Choosing, Accessing, and Displaying Contact Information

If the user doesn't cancel the selection, the
`peoplePickerNavigationContoller:peoplePicker:shouldContinueAfterSelect ingPerson:` delegate method will be called, and with it we are passed the selected

person as an ABRecordRef. An ABRecordRef is part of the Address Book framework that we imported earlier.

We can use the C functions of the Address Book framework to read the data about this person from the address book. For this example, we read four things: the person's first name, picture, email address, and ZIP code. We will check whether the person record has a picture before attempting to read it.

Notice that we don't access the person's attributes as the native Cocoa objects you might expect (namely, NSString and UIImage, respectively). Instead, the name string and the photo are returned as Core Foundation C data, and we convert it using the handy ABRecordCopyValue function from the Address Book framework and the imageWithData method of UIImage.

For the email address and ZIP code, we must deal with the possibility of multiple values being returned. For these pieces of data, we'll again use ABRecordCopyValue to grab a reference to the set of data, and the functions ABMultiValueGetCount to make sure that we actually have an email address or ZIP code stored with the contact, and ABMultiValueCopyValueAtIndex to copy the first value that we find.

Sounds complicated? It's not the prettiest code, but it's not difficult to understand.

Add the final delegate method
peoplePickerNavigationController:shouldContinueAfterSelectingPerson to
the BestFriendViewController.m file, as shown in Listing 21.4.

LISTING 21.4

```
 1: - (BOOL)peoplePickerNavigationController:
 2:        (ABPeoplePickerNavigationController *)peoplePicker
 3:        shouldContinueAfterSelectingPerson:(ABRecordRef)person {
 4:
 5:      // Declare variables for temporarily handling the string data
 6:      NSString *friendName;
 7:      NSString *friendEmail;
 8:      NSString *friendZip;
 9:
10:      friendName=(NSString *)
11:                 ABRecordCopyValue(person, kABPersonFirstNameProperty);
12:      name.text = friendName;
13:      [friendName release];
14:
15:
16:      ABMultiValueRef friendAddressSet;
17:      NSDictionary *friendFirstAddress;
18:      friendAddressSet = ABRecordCopyValue(person, kABPersonAddressProperty);
19:
20:      if (ABMultiValueGetCount(friendAddressSet)>0) {
21:          friendFirstAddress = (NSDictionary *)
22:                     ABMultiValueCopyValueAtIndex(friendAddressSet,0);
23:          friendZip = [friendFirstAddress objectForKey:@"ZIP"];
```

```
24:             [friendFirstAddress release];
25:         }
26:
27:       ABMultiValueRef friendEmailAddresses;
28:  friendEmailAddresses = ABRecordCopyValue(person, kABPersonEmailProperty);
29:
30:       if (ABMultiValueGetCount(friendEmailAddresses)>0) {
31:           friendEmail=(NSString *)
32:                        ABMultiValueCopyValueAtIndex(friendEmailAddresses, 0);
33:           email.text = friendEmail;
34:           [friendEmail release];
35:       }
36:
37:       if (ABPersonHasImageData(person)) {
38:           photo.image = [UIImage imageWithData:
39:                          (NSData *)ABPersonCopyImageData(person)];
40:       }
41:
42:       [peoplePickerPopoverController dismissPopoverAnimated:YES];
43:       [peoplePickerPopoverController release];
44:       return NO;
45: }
```

Let's walk through the logic we've implemented here. First, note that when the method is called, it is passed a person variable of the type ABRecordRef—this is a reference to the person who was chosen and will be used throughout the method.

Lines 6–8 declare variables that we'll be using to temporarily store the name, email, and ZIP code strings that we retrieve from the address book.

Lines 10 and 11 use the ABRecordCopyVal method to copy the kABPersonFirstNameProperty property, as a string, to the friendName variable. Lines 12 and 13 set the name UILabel to this string, and then friendName is released.

Accessing an address is a bit more complicated. We must first get the set of addresses (each a dictionary) stored for the person, access the first address, then access a specific field within that set. Within address book, anything with multiple values is represented by a variable of type ABMultiValueRef. We declare a variable, friendAddressSet, of this type in line 16. This will reference *all* addresses of the person. Next, in line 17, we declare an NSDictionary called friendFirstAddress. We will store the first address from the friendAddressSet in this dictionary, where we can easily access its different fields (such as city, state, ZIP, and so on). In line 18, we populate friendAddressSet by again using the ABRecordCopyVal function on the kABPersonAddressProperty of person.

Lines 20–25 execute only if ABMultiValueGetCount returns a copy of greater than zero on the friendAddressSet. If it *is* zero, there are no addresses associated with the person, and we should move on. If there *are* addresses, we store the first address in `friendFirstAddress` by copying it from the `friendAddressSet` using the `ABMultiValueCopyValueAtIndex` method in lines 21 and 22. The index we use with this function is 0—which is the first address in the set. The second address would be 1, third 2, and so on.

Line 23 uses the `NSDictionary` method `objectForKey` to grab the ZIP code string. The key for the ZIP code is simply the string `"ZIP"`. Review the address book documentation to find all the possible keys you may want to access. Finally, line 24 releases the `friendFirstAddress` dictionary.

> In case you're wondering, the code here is not yet complete! We don't actually *do* anything with the ZIP code just yet. This ties into the map function we use later, so, for now, we just get the value and ignore it.

Watch Out!

This entire process is implemented again in lines 27–35 to grab the `person`'s first email address. The only difference is that rather than email addresses being a set of dictionaries, they're simple a set of strings. This means that once we verify that there are email addresses stored for the contact (line 30), we can just copy the first one in the set and use it immediately as a string (lines 31 and 32). Line 33 sets the `email` `UILabel` to the user's email address.

After all of that, you must be thinking to yourself, "Ugh, it's got to be a pain to deal with a person's photo." Wrong! That's actually the easy part! Using the `ABPersonHasImageData` function in line 37, we verify that `person` has an image stored. If he or she does, we copy it out of the address book using `ABPersonCopyImageData`, and use that data along with the `UIImage` method `imageWithData` to return an image object and set the `photo` image within the interface. All of this occurs in lines 38 and 39.

As a final step, the popover is dismissed and released in lines 42 and 43.

Whew! A few new functions were introduced here, but once you get the pattern down, moving data out of the address book becomes almost simple.

So, what about that ZIP code? What are we going to do with it? Let's find out now, by implementing our interactive map!

Using a Map Object

Earlier in the hour, you added a `MKMapView` to your user interface and configured it to show the current location of the device. If you attempted to Build and Run the app, however, you'll have noticed that it fails immediately. The reason for this is that as soon as you add the map view, you need to add a framework to support it. For our example application, we also need to add two frameworks to the project: Core Location, which deals with locations; and Map Kit, which displays the embedded Google Map.

Adding the Location and Map Frameworks

In the Xcode project window, right-click the Frameworks group and choose Add, Existing Frameworks from the menu. In the scrolling list that appears, choose the MapKit.framework and CoreLocation.framework items, and then click Add.

Drag the frameworks into the Frameworks group if they don't appear there automatically.

Next, edit the BestFriendViewController.h interface file so that we have access to the classes and methods in these frameworks. Add these lines after the existing #import lines:

```
#import <CoreLocation/CoreLocation.h>
#import <MapKit/MapKit.h>
```

We can now display the MKMapView, work with locations, and programmatically control the map.

Controlling the Map Display

Because we already get the display of the map and the user's current location for "free" with the MKMapView, the only thing we really need to do in this application is take the user's ZIP code, determine a latitude and longitude for it, and then center and zoom the map on that location.

Unfortunately, Core Location does not provide the ability to turn an address into a set of coordinates, but Google offers a service that does. By requesting the URL http://maps.google.com/maps/geo?output=csv&q=<address> we get back a comma-separated list where the third and fourth values are latitude and longitude, respectively. The address that we send to Google is very flexible—it can be city, state, ZIP, street—whatever information we provide, Google will try to translate it to coordinates. In the case of a ZIP code, it gives us the center of the ZIP code's region on the map—exactly what we want.

Once we have the location, we'll need to use center and zoom the map. We do this by defining a map "region", then using the setRegion:animated method. A region is a simple structure (not an object) called a MKCoordinateRegion. It has members called center, which is another structure called a CLLocationCoordinate2D (containing latitude and longitude); and span, which denotes how many degrees to the east, west, north, and south of the center are displayed. A degree of latitude is 69 miles. A degree of longitude, at the equator, is 69 miles. By choosing small values for the span within the region (like 0.2), we narrow our display down to a few miles around the center point. For example, if we wanted to define a region centered at 40.0 degrees latitude and 40.0 degrees longitude with a span of 0.2 degrees in each direction, we could write the following:

```
MKCoordinateRegion mapRegion;
mapRegion.center.latitude=40.0;
mapRegion.center.longitude=40.0;
mapRegion.span.latitudeDelta=0.2;
mapRegion.span.longitudeDelta=0.2;
```

To center and zoom in on this region in a map object called map, we'd use the following:

```
[map setRegion:mapRegion animated:YES];
```

To keep things nice and neat in our application, we're going to implement all of this functionality in a nice new method called centerMap. centerMap will take a single string (a ZIP code) as input, retrieve the latitude and longitude from Google, and then adjust our map object to display it.

Enter the new centerMap method shown in Listing 21.5 within the BestFriendViewController implementation file.

LISTING 21.5

```
 1: - (void)centerMap:(NSString*)zipCode {
 2:      NSString *queryURL;
 3:      NSString *queryResults;
 4:      NSArray *queryData;
 5:      double latitude;
 6:      double longitude;
 7:      MKCoordinateRegion mapRegion;
 8:
 9:      queryURL = [[NSString alloc]
10:              initWithFormat:
11:              @"http://maps.google.com/maps/geo?output=csv&q=%@",
12:              zipCode];
13:
14:      queryResults = [[NSString alloc] initWithContentsOfURL:
15:              [NSURL URLWithString:queryURL]
16:                  encoding: NSUTF8StringEncoding
17:                  error: nil];
18:      // Autoreleased
19:      queryData = [queryResults componentsSeparatedByString:@","];
20:
21:      if([queryData count]==4) {
22:          latitude=[[queryData objectAtIndex:2] doubleValue];
23:          longitude=[[queryData objectAtIndex:3] doubleValue];
24:          //    CLLocationCoordinate2D;
```

```
25:            mapRegion.center.latitude=latitude;
26:            mapRegion.center.longitude=longitude;
27:            mapRegion.span.latitudeDelta=0.2;
28:            mapRegion.span.longitudeDelta=0.2;
29:            [map setRegion:mapRegion animated:YES];
30:      }
31:
32:      [queryURL release];
33:      [queryResults release];
34:
35: }
```

Let's explore how this works. We kick things off in lines 2–7 by declaring several variables we'll be needing. queryURL, queryResults, and queryData will hold the Google URL we need to request, the raw results of the request, and the parsed data, respectively. The latitude and longitude variables are double-precision floating-point numbers that will be used to store the coordinate information gleaned from queryData. The last variable, mapRegion, will be the properly formatted region that the map should display.

Lines 9–12 allocate and initialize queryURL with the Google URL, substituting in the zipCode string that was passed to the method. Lines 14–17 use the NSString method initWithContentsOfURL:encoding:error to create a new string that contains the data located at the location defined in queryURL. We also make use of the NSURL method URLWithString: to turn the queryURL string into a proper URL object. Any errors are disregarded.

> The initWithContentsOfURL:encoding:error method expects an encoding type. The encoding is the manner in which the string passed to the remote server is formatted. For almost all web services, you'll want to use NSUTF8StringEncoding.

Line 19 uses the NSString method componentsSeparatedByString, which takes a string, a delimiter character, and returns an NSArray that breaks apart the string based on the delimiter. Google is going to hand back data that looks like this: *<number>,<number>,<latitude>,<longitude>*. By invoking this method on the data using a comma delimiter (,), we get an array, queryData, where the third element contains the latitude, and the fourth, the longitude.

Line 21 does a *very* basic sanity check on the information we receive. If there are exactly four pieces of information found, we can assume the results are valid, and lines 22–29 are executed.

Lines 22 and 23 retrieve the strings at indices 2 and 3 of the `queryData` array and convert them to double-precision floating-point values, storing them in the `latitude` and `longitude` variables.

> Remember, an array's index starts at 0. We use an index of 2 to access the *third* piece of data in the array, and an index of 3 to access the *fourth*.

Finally, lines 25–29 define the region of the map to display and then uses `setRegion:animated` to redraw the map accordingly.

Congratulations! Your code now has the smarts needed to locate a ZIP code on the map and zoom in! The last piece of magic we need to finish the mapping is to hook it into the address book selection so that the map is centered when a user picks a contact with an address.

Edit the `peoplePickerNavigationController:shouldContinueAfterSelectingPerson` method, adding the following line

```
[self centerMap:friendZip];
```

immediately following this line:

```
friendZip = [friendFirstAddress objectForKey:@"ZIP"];
```

Our application is nearing completion. All that remains is adding the ability to send email to our chosen buddy. Let the implementation begin!

Using the Message UI

In our example of using the Message UI framework, we will allow users to email a buddy by pressing the Send Mail button. We will populate the To field of the email with the address that we located in the address book. The user can then use the interface provided by the `MFMailComposeViewController` to edit the email and send it. As with the other features discussed this hour, we need to add the Message UI framework before a message will work.

We will also need to conform to the `MFMailComposeViewControllerDelegate`, which includes a method `mailComposeController:didFinishWithResult` that is called after the user is finished sending a message.

Adding the Message UI Framework

Again, in the Xcode project window, right-click the Frameworks group and choose Add, Existing Frameworks from the menu. In the scrolling list, choose MessageUI.framework, and then click Add.

Open the BestFriendViewController.h interface file and add one more #import statement for <MessageUI/MessageUI.h>. Add MFMailComposeViewControllerDelegate to the list of protocols that we're conforming to.

The final version of the interface is displayed in Listing 21.6.

LISTING 21.6

```
#import <UIKit/UIKit.h>
#import <AddressBook/AddressBook.h>
#import <AddressBookUI/AddressBookUI.h>
#import <MessageUI/MessageUI.h>
#import <CoreLocation/CoreLocation.h>
#import <MapKit/MapKit.h>

@interface BestFriendViewController : UIViewController
<ABPeoplePickerNavigationControllerDelegate,MFMailComposeViewControllerDelegate>
{
    IBOutlet UILabel *name;
    IBOutlet UILabel *email;
    IBOutlet UIImageView *photo;
    IBOutlet MKMapView *map;
    UIPopoverController *peoplePickerPopoverController;
}

@property (nonatomic, retain) UILabel *name;
@property (nonatomic, retain) UILabel *email;
@property (nonatomic, retain) UIImageView *photo;
@property (nonatomic, retain) MKMapView *map;

- (IBAction)newBFF:(id)sender;
- (IBAction)sendEmail:(id)sender;

@end
```

Displaying the Message Composer

To compose a message, we'll need to allocate an initialize an instance of MFMailComposeViewController. This modal view is then added to our view with presentModalViewController:animated. To set the To recipients, we'll use the appropriately named MFMailComposeViewController method setToRecipients. One item of interest is that the method expects an array, so we'll need to take the email address for our buddy and create an array with a single element in it so that we can use the method.

Speaking of the email address, where we will access it? Simple! Earlier we set the email UILabel to the address, so we'll just use email.text to get the address of our buddy.

Create the sendEmail method using Listing 21.7 as your guide.

LISTING 21.7

```
 1: - (IBAction)sendEmail:(id)sender {
 2:     MFMailComposeViewController *mailComposer;
 3:     NSArray *emailAddresses;
 4:     emailAddresses=[[NSArray alloc]initWithObjects: email.text,nil];
 5:
 6:     mailComposer=[[MFMailComposeViewController alloc] init];
 7:     mailComposer.mailComposeDelegate=self;
 8:     [mailComposer setToRecipients:emailAddresses];
 9:     [self presentModalViewController:mailComposer animated:YES];
10:
11:     [emailAddresses release];
12:     [mailComposer release];
13: }
```

Unlike some of the other methods we've written this hour, there are few surprises here. Line 2 declares mailComposer as an instance of MFMailComposeViewController—the object that displays and handles message composition. Lines 3 and 4 define an array, emailAddresses, that contains a single element grabbed from the email UILabel.

Lines 6–8 allocate and initialize the MFMailComposeViewController object, setting its delegate to self (BestFriendViewController), and the recipient list to the emailAddresses array. Line 9 presents the message composition window onscreen.

Finally, lines 11 and 12 release the array of email addresses and the mailComposer MFMailComposeViewController object.

Handling Message Completion

When a user is finished composing/sending a message, the modal composition window should be dismissed and the MFMailComposeViewController object released. To do this, we need to implement the mailComposeController:didFinishWithResult method defined in the MFMailComposeViewControllerDelegate protocol.

Add this final method to the BestFriendViewController.m file:

```
- (void)mailComposeController:(MFMailComposeViewController*)controller
        didFinishWithResult:(MFMailComposeResult)result
                    error:(NSError*)error {
    [self dismissModalViewControllerAnimated:YES];
}
```

All that is needed is the single line to dismiss the modal view, and with that, we're done!

Use Build and Run to test the application. Select a contact and watch as the map finds their home location and zooms in. Then use the Email button to compose and send an email (see Figure 21.6).

FIGURE 21.6
Mapping, email, and address book integration—all in one app.

This project, as shown in Figure 21.6, combines mapping, email, and address book features in a single, integrated application. You should now have some ideas about what is possible when you integrate iPad features into your software.

Further Exploration

You've now learned most of what there is to know about picking images and sending email, but we haven't even scratched the surface of the Address Book and Address Book UI frameworks. In fact, the Address Book UI framework contains three additional modal view controllers. You can use the lower-level Address Book framework to create new contacts, set properties, and edit and delete contacts. Anything the Contacts application can do, you can do with the Address Book framework. For more detailed information about the use of these APIs, refer to the excellent guide from Apple iPhone OS Dev Center called the *Address Book Programming Guide for iPhone OS*.

In addition, review the Apple guides for Core Location and Map Kit. Using these complementary tools, you can create annotations, each with its own view, or use simple pushpin views to represent locations. On the 3G iPad, these features can be employed in full-featured GPS applications, giving your users pinpoint accuracy on a large touchable map.

Summary

In this hour, you learned how to allow the user to interact with contacts from the address book, how to send email messages, and how to interact with the Map Kit and Core Location frameworks. Altough there are some challenges to working with address book data (older C functions, for example), after you've established the patterns to follow, it becomes much easier. The same goes for the Map Kit and Core Location features. The more you experiment with the coordinates and mapping functions, the more intuitive it will be to integrate them into your own applications. As for email, there's not much to say—it's easy to implement *anywhere*!

Q&A

Q. *Can I use the* `MKMapView` *when my iPad is offline?*

A. No, the map view requires an Internet connection to fetch its data.

Q. *Is there a way to differentiate between address (mailing or email) types in the address book data?*

A. Yes. Although we did not use these features in our code, you can identify specific types (home, work, and so on) of addresses when reading address book data. Refer to the address book programming guide for a full description of working with address book data.

Workshop

Quiz

1. Map Kit implements discrete zoom levels for MKMapViews that you display. True or false?

2. You can avoid the older Address Book framework and use the new Address Book UI framework instead. True or false?

Answers

1. False. Map Kit requires you to define regions within your map that consist of a center point and a span. The scale of the map display is determined by the size of the span.

2. False. Although the Address Book UI framework provides user interfaces that save you a lot of time and provide familiarity to your users, you must still work with C functions and data structures from the Address Book framework when using the interfaces in your application.

Activities

1. Apply what you learned in Hour 16, "Reading and Writing Application Data," and make the BestFriend application persist the name and photo of the selected friend so that the user doesn't need to repeat the selection each time the application is run.

2. Enhance the BestFriend application to pinpoint your friend's address rather than just a ZIP code. Explore the annotation features of Map Kit to add a pushpin directly on your friend's home location.

HOUR 22

Building Universal Applications

What You'll Learn in This Hour:

- ▶ What makes a universal application "universal"
- ▶ How to use the universal application template
- ▶ Ways of designing universal applications
- ▶ How to detect the device an application is running on
- ▶ Tools for migrating to a universal architecture

Unless you've been ignoring Apple's devices up until the iPad, you've probably heard of the iPhone and the iPod Touch. Both of these platforms use Cocoa Touch as their development language, and as luck would have it, they share nearly all the same classes and methods as the iPad.

In this hour's lesson, you'll be learning how to create an application that runs on both the iPad and the iPhone—termed a *universal* application by Apple. You'll also learn, first hand, some of the problems that come with supporting an application that works on both platforms, and some tips for overcoming them. You're an iPad developer now, but there's no reason why you can't be an iPad *and* iPhone developer!

Universal Application Development

Congratulations are in order! You've reached the point in the book where you should have a good handle on iPad development, so we'll spend the next three hours looking at ways that you can optimize and expand the reach of your projects, as well as ultimately deploy them to the app store. This hour focuses on developing "universal" applications.

A universal application is one that contains the necessary resources to run on the iPad and the iPhone. The iPad already supports running iPhone applications directly, but let's be frank, they don't look all that great when expanded to fullscreen. To build a truly unique iPad experience, you'll likely need different XIB files, images, and maybe even completely different classes. Your code may even need to make decisions on-the-fly about the type of device it is running on.

If this is starting to sound like a bit of a pain, that's because it can be! The iPhone and iPad are not the same device. Users expect a different experience from each of them, so, although an app may have the same functionality, it will likely need to look and work differently depending on where it is running. Depending on how you approach a universal application design, you might end up with duplicate classes, methods, resources, and so on that you will need to support for each device. The good news is that, from your user's perspective, they get a single application that they can run on either their iPhone, iPad, or both; and you get to reach a much larger audience than targeting the iPad alone.

By the Way

> Keep in mind that not all capabilities (such as cameras and GPS) are shared across your development platforms (iPhone/iPad/iPod Touch). Be sure that you plan your universal apps appropriately!

Not all developers have decided that a universal application is the best approach for their projects. Many have created separate HD or XL versions of their apps that are sold at a slightly higher price than the iPhone version. If your application is going to be substantially different on the two platforms, this might be the route you want to take, too. Even if it is, you can consolidate development into a single project that builds two different executables, called *targets*. Later in the hour, we look at the tool available in Xcode that can set this up for you.

By the Way

> There isn't a "right" or "wrong" when deciding how to deal a project that spans the iPad and iPhone devices. As a developer, you will need to evaluate what makes the most sense for your code, your marketing plans, and your users.

If you know upfront that you want to create an application that works on any device, you'll likely begin development with the Universal Window-based Application template.

Understanding the Universal Window Application Template

To aid you in creating a universal application, Apple has included a very helpful template. When creating a new project in Xcode, you can choose the iPhone OS Window-based Application template, and set the Product drop-down to Universal, as shown in Figure 22.1.

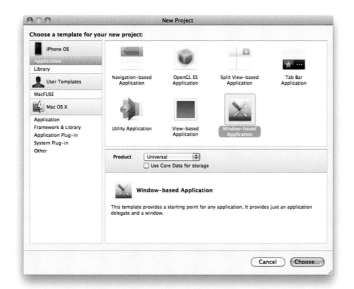

FIGURE 22.1
Begin your universal applications with the universal template.

The universal template is just like a typical window-based application, but with a key difference. Rather than a single Classes group, there are iPad and iPhone groups. Each group contains a separate app delegate and separate MainWindow.xib files, named MainWindow_Pad.xib and MainWindow_Phone.xib, demonstrated in Figure 22.2. As the names suggest, the files with the suffix *Pad* are used when the application executes on the iPad, and *Phone* when it is running on the iPhone.

FIGURE 22.2
A universal
application
includes distinct
project files for
the iPad and
iPhone plat-
forms.

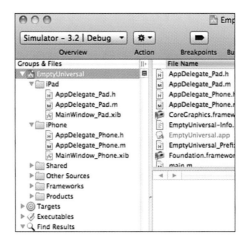

Universal Plist Changes

A universal project's plist file is also slightly different, showing the same differentia-
tion between platforms. This, in fact, is where the actual "magic" takes place. The
keys: `Main nib file base name` and `Main nib file base name (iPad)` are
defined, along with values that point to the previously mentioned platform-specific
XIB files. When the application is launched, the XIB files referenced in the plist are
opened, and every object in them is instantiated. The rest of the application branches out from these important starting points, a fact we put to the test shortly.

Icon Files

One interesting note is that the current universal application template does not provide for multiple application icons. iPhone application icons are 57x57 pixels,
whereas iPad icons are 72x72. To update the template to support the different icons,
you must add a new key to the plist, `CFBundleIconFiles`, of the type `Array`, as
shown in Figure 22.3.

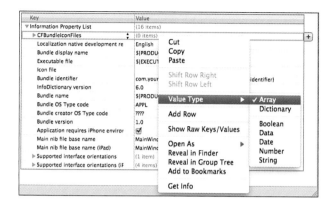

FIGURE 22.3
Add a
CFBundleIcon
Files key, of
type Array, to
reference two
distinct icons
files.

Within the CFBundleIconFiles array, add two strings, each set to the name of an icon file resource that you've added to your project; you don't even need to say which is which. Because the icons are different dimensions, the devices themselves can identify the correct icon and display it to the user.

Launch Images

Another key, or rather, set of keys, that you may want to use with your application is Launch image and Launch image (iPad). Recall that the launch image is the picture that is displayed as an application loads on your device. Because the iPhone and iPad have different screen sizes, it makes sense that there would be multiple types of launch images. Use the Launch image key to set an image for the iPhone, and the Launch image (iPad) variation to configure an image for the iPad.

Beyond those minor tweaks, the universal application template is very much "ready" to go. We could, at this point, just say "use it," but this chapter wouldn't be very useful if we did. Let's go ahead and take the Universal Window-based Application template to a place where it becomes useful. We'll build out an application that launches and displays different views and executes a simple line of code on both the iPad and iPhone platforms.

Creating a Universal Application (Take 1)

We're going to go through the process of building two universal applications. Either approach is valid, but the first application will help demonstrate some of the inefficiencies that you should try to avoid when coding a single app for two platforms.

Both examples have the same purpose: to launch, instantiate a view controller, load a device specific view, and then display a string that identifies the type of device the code is running on. It's not the most exciting thing we've done in the book, but it should give you the background you need to build your apps for all of Apples "i" devices. Figure 22.4 demonstrates the outcome we hope to achieve.

FIGURE 22.4
We will create
an application
that runs and
displays infor-
mation on iPad
and iPhone
devices.

FIGURE 22.4 We will create an application that runs and displays information on iPad and iPhone devices.

Preparing the Project

Begin by creating a new window-based application with a Product setting of Universal. Name the application **Universal**, in case there's any question of what we're trying to do. As we discussed, this template provides us with some MainWindow_<platform>.xib files and an application delegate class, but there really isn't any "meat" to the template. We're used to building things out using view controllers, so adding view controllers for the iPad and iPhone seems like a good first step.

Adding Device-Specific View Controllers and Views

We'll start by adding an iPad-specific view controller. Choose File, New File from the Xcode menu. When prompted, choose the Cocoa Touch Class category and the UIViewController subclass. Be sure that the Targeted for iPad and With XIB for User Interface check boxes are selected. Name the new class **iPadViewController**, and be sure that an interface (.h) file is created, too. After the files are added to your project, drag them into the iPad group within the Groups and Files list.

Now we need to repeat the process for the iPhone. Again, Choose File, New File from the Xcode menu and follow the same steps. This time, however, *do not* check the Targeted For iPad check box (leave the XIB check box checked), and name the class **iPhoneViewController**. Drag the resulting files into the iPhone group.

Adding the View Controllers to the Application Delegates

Our universal application now has view controllers for both our platforms, but they aren't connected to anything. To be useful, we need to instantiate them, and add their views to our windows within AppDelegate_Pad and AppDelegate_Phone.

Concentrating again on the iPad version of the files, open the AppDelegate_Pad.h file and add an outlet named padViewController for an instance of our iPadViewController class. Because we're referencing a new class, we also need to import the iPadViewController.h interface file. Lastly, be sure to add a @property declaration for the view controller. The final AppDelegate_Pad.h file is shown in Listing 22.1.

LISTING 22.1

```
#import <UIKit/UIKit.h>
#import "iPadViewController.h"

@interface AppDelegate_Pad : NSObject <UIApplicationDelegate> {
    UIWindow *window;
    IBOutlet iPadViewController *padViewController;
}

@property (nonatomic, retain) IBOutlet UIWindow *window;
@property (nonatomic, retain) iPadViewController *padViewController;

@end
```

Within the AppDelegate_Pad.h file, add a corresponding @synthesize line after the @implementation line:

```
@synthesize padViewController;
```

Then, as we've done so many times in the past, release the padViewController within the AppDelegate_Pad.m's dealloc method:

```
- (void)dealloc {
    [padViewController release];
    [window release];
    [super dealloc];
}
```

The last change that we need to make to the iPad application delegate is to add the padViewController's view property to the application's window when the app is

launched. Find the `application:didFinishLaunchingWithOptions` method in
AppDelegate_Pad.m and use the window's `addSubview` method to add
`padViewController.view` to the window. The finished method should look like this:

```
- (BOOL)application:(UIApplication *)application
didFinishLaunchingWithOptions:(NSDictionary *)launchOptions {
    // Override point for customization after application launch
    [window addSubview:padViewController.view];
    [window makeKeyAndVisible];
    return YES;
}
```

The application delegate is now configured with the outlets it needs to reference an
instance of the `iPadViewController` class (although we still haven't instantiated it)
and to add the instance's view to the iPad window.

Okay, take a deep breath, now repeat the exact same process for the
AppDelegate_Phone files, but referencing the `iPhoneViewController` class and
naming its instance, `phoneViewController`.

> Are you sure you updated the application delegate for the iPhone? It's easy to
> skim over those last two sentences, thinking its time to move on; but it's not! We
> have two view controllers and two views to deal with in this application. The cod-
> ing is identical in each, so it isn't repeated in the text. But if you accidentally miss
> the code for one device or the other, your application will either be broken or not
> truly be universal.

Once both application delegates are prepared, our next step is to instantiate the
view controllers by adding them to the MainWindow_Pad.xib and
MainWindow_Phone.xib files.

Instantiating the View Controllers

To instantiate the view controllers and connect them to our instances
`padViewController` and `phoneViewController`, we'll use Interface Builder. Double-
click the MainWindow_Pad.xib file to open it. Using the Library (Tools, Library),
drag an instance of `UIViewController` from the Library into the XIB file's
Document window.

Next, select the instance of the `UIViewController` and open the Identity Inspector
(Command+4). Use the drop-down menu to set the class identity for the controller to
`iPadViewController`, as shown in Figure 22.5.

FIGURE 22.5
Set the
`UIViewControl`
`ler` object to
the specific
device-targeted
view controller
class.

Switch to the Attributes Inspector (Command+1) and be sure that the NIB file attribute is set to use `iPadViewController.xib` for its view contents.

Finally, connect the view controller instance to the `padViewController` outlet added earlier. Control-drag from the `AppDelegate_Pad` object to the view controller instance, choosing `padViewController` when prompted. This is demonstrated in Figure 22.6.

FIGURE 22.6
Connect the
view controller
instance to
the `padView`
`Controller`
outlet.

Save the XIB file. You've just finished the setup of the view controller for the iPad. Guess what? The process needs to be repeated for the MainWindow_Phone.xib file. Follow the same steps, but using the `iPhoneViewController` class and connecting the `AppDelegate_Phone` to the `phoneViewController` outlet.

Hold up! I just want to make sure that you did indeed repeat the instructions for the iPhone side of the application. If you skipped over the last paragraph, bad things could happen.

At this point in time, you should have a working universal application that instantiates two separate view controllers and loads two different views, depending on what device it is running on. This, however, isn't readily apparent because the views don't actually *do* anything. We'll finish this project up by editing the iPhoneViewController and iPadViewController to add a teensy bit of functionality to the app.

Detecting and Displaying the Active Device

Our goal for our application is to get and display the name of the device that it is running on. To do this, we'll use a UIDevice class method currentDevice to get an object that refers to the active device, then model to return an NSString that describes the device (such as "iPhone," "iPad Simulator," and so on). The code fragment to return this string is just this:

```
[[UIDevice currentDevice] model]
```

To get this displayed in our views, we'll first concentrate on the iPad. Open the iPadViewController.h file and add a UILabel reference called deviceType, along with the @property declaration, as shown in Listing 22.2.

LISTING 22.2

```
#import <UIKit/UIKit.h>


@interface iPadViewController : UIViewController {
    IBOutlet UILabel *deviceType;
}

@property (nonatomic,retain) UILabel *deviceType;

@end
```

Open the iPadViewController.m implementation file and add a corresponding @syn-thesize directive after the @implementation line:

```
@synthesize deviceType;
```

Keep things clean by releasing deviceType in the dealloc method:

```
- (void)dealloc {
    [deviceType release];
    [super dealloc];
}
```

While we're at it, we might as well add the code to set the deviceType label when the view is loaded. Uncomment the viewDidLoad method and implement it like this:

```
- (void)viewDidLoad {
    deviceType.text=[[UIDevice currentDevice] model];
    [super viewDidLoad];
}
```

The last step is to open the iPadViewController.xib file itself and design the view. In mine, I've added a big label that reads I'm an iPad App!, and then a Device label beneath it, as shown in Figure 22.7.

FIGURE 22.7
Build the view to look however you want; just make sure there's a label (Device here) to connect back to the deviceType outlet.

I'm an iPad App!
Device

Once your design is done, Control-drag from the File's Owner icon to the label you want to use to display the device type. Choose deviceType from the pop-up window when prompted. You can now save and close the iPadViewController.xib file. The iPad view/view controller is complete.

You know what I'm going to say next. You're not done. You need to repeat all of these steps for the iPhoneViewController class, too. Add the deviceType outlet, implement the viewDidLoad method, design the view, connect the outlet... whew... and after you've made it through all of that, *then* you're done.

Watch
Out!

Just checking in to make sure you're still awake! The steps outlined in the text cover the iPad view controller and view. Make sure you also complete the `iPhoneViewController` implementation!

At this point, you can choose Build and Run and finally see the results on the iPhone or iPad. So what have you learned? Hopefully, that universal applications are not necessarily easy to maintain and that if you structure the application so that no classes are shared, you'll end up repeating yourself *a lot*.

Our next example shows a variation of this project. It will do the exact same thing, but instead of using two different view controllers, we use *one* that can load two different views. It isn't perfect, but sharing code between the platforms is a good habit to get into.

Did you
Know?

To target a specific platform in the simulator, the easiest way is to choose your OS version and device from the Overview menu. You might choose "iPad Simulator 3.2" to build and test in the iPad version of the iPhone simulator or "iPhone Simulator 4.0" to test on a simulated iPhone running version 4.0 of the OS.

Creating a Universal Application (Take 2)

Our second pass at building a universal application will really work very similarly to what we just built, but with one distinct difference. Instead of creating `iPhoneViewController` and `iPadViewController` classes, we'll create a view controller class called `GenericViewController` that loads one of two views: an iPad view when instantiated by the iPad application delegate, and an iPhone view when instantiated by the iPhone delegate.

Preparing the Project

Start the second tutorial the same way as the first: Create a new window-based application with a Product setting of Universal. Name the new application **UniversalToo**. Next, we need to create the generic view controller class that will work with both the iPad *and* iPhone views.

Adding a Generic View Controllers and Device-Specific Views

Choose File, New File from the Xcode menu. When prompted, choose the Cocoa Touch Class category and the `UIViewController` subclass. Uncheck *all* the check boxes. (This is a first!) Name the new class **GenericViewController**, and be sure that an interface (.h) file is created, too. After the files are added to your project, drag them into the Shared group within the Groups and Files list.

Next, we need to create the XIB files that will contain the interfaces for the iPad and iPhone. Choose File, New File from the Xcode menu. Select the User Interface category, and then pick the View XIB icon. Set the product to iPad and click Next. Name the new XIB file iPadView.xib. Drag the file into the iPad group after it is created.

Repeat this step, creating a View XIB file targeted to the iPhone. Name the second view **iPhoneView.xib**. Drag it to the iPhone group so that things stay organized.

We now have a single view controller class and two views. Let's see how they get connected to the app.

Adding the View Controller to the Application Delegates

Unlike the previous tutorial, we have only a single view controller to deal with. That said, there is still a bit of duplicate setup work that we need to complete, starting with adding the view controller to both of the application delegates.

Open the AppDelegate_Pad.h file, add an outlet named `viewController` for an instance of `GenericViewController` class, import the GenericViewController.h interface file, and add a `@property` declaration for the view controller. Listing 22.3 shows a completed AppDelegate_Pad.h file.

LISTING 22.3

```
#import <UIKit/UIKit.h>
#import "GenericViewController.h"

@interface AppDelegate_Pad : NSObject <UIApplicationDelegate> {
    IBOutlet GenericViewController *viewController;
    UIWindow *window;
}

@property (nonatomic, retain) IBOutlet UIWindow *window;
@property (nonatomic, retain) IBOutlet GenericViewController *viewController;

@end
```

Within the AppDelegate_Pad.h file, add a corresponding @synthesize line after the @implementation line:

```
@synthesize viewController;
```

Next, `release` the `padViewController` within the AppDelegate_Pad.m's `dealloc` method:

```
- (void)dealloc {
    [viewController release];
    [window release];
    [super dealloc];
}
```

As in the previous tutorial, the last step is to add the view controller's view to the window. Find the `application:didFinishLaunchingWithOptions` method in AppDelegate_Pad.m and use the window's `addSubview` method to add `viewController.view` to the window. The finished method should look like this:

```
- (BOOL)application:(UIApplication *)application
didFinishLaunchingWithOptions:(NSDictionary *)launchOptions {
    // Override point for customization after application launch
    [window addSubview:viewController.view];
    [window makeKeyAndVisible];
    return YES;
}
```

Repeat the process for the `AppDelegate_Phone` class. Unlike last time, however, the view controller class is *not* unique for the iPhone. The code you add to the application delegate will be absolutely identical to what was built for `AppDelegate_Pad`.

> This is one of those rinse-and-repeat moments. Make sure that you've finished building out both `AppDelegate_Phone` and `AppDelegate_Pad` before continuing.

The next step is to instantiate the view controllers by adding it to the MainWindow_Pad.xib and MainWindow_Phone.xib files.

Instantiating the View Controllers

Double-click the MainWindow_Pad.xib file to open it. Using the Library (Tools, Library), drag an instance of `UIViewController` from the Library into the XIB file's Document window.

Select the instance of the `UIViewController` and open the Identity Inspector (Command+4). Use the drop-down menu to set the class identity for the controller to `GenericViewController`, as shown in Figure 22.8.

FIGURE 22.8
Set the `UIView`
`Controller`
object to the
`GenericView-`
`Controller`
class.

Next, use the Attributes Inspector (Command+1) to set the NIB file attribute to
iPadView.xib.

Finish up by connecting the view controller instance to the `viewController` outlet
added earlier. Control-drag from the `AppDelegate_Pad` object to the view controller
instance, choosing `viewController` when prompted, as shown in Figure 22.9.

FIGURE 22.9
Connect the
view controller
instance to the
`viewController`
outlet.

Save the XIB file. Open the MainWindow_Phone.xib file and repeat the setup of the
`GenericViewController` instance and the connection to the `viewController` output. The only change is that you should select the iPhoneView.xib for the interface
NIB file, rather than iPadView.xib.

Watch Out!

Be sure that you've completed setup of the MainWindow xib files for both the iPad and iPhone before continuing; otherwise, only one platform will work.

Setting Up the XIB files

By creating the XIB files without a corresponding view controller, we lose a little bit of configuration that normally we get for free. Specifically, the File's Owner is not set to the appropriate class, nor is the view itself connected to the File's Owner.

Let's rectify this oversight.

Open the iPadView.xib file. Select the File's Owner icon in the Document window, and then open the Identity Inspector (Command+4). Set the class to `GenericViewController`, as shown in Figure 22.10.

FIGURE 22.10
Each XIB must be modified to set the File's Owner to the correct class.

Now, Control-drag from the File's Owner icon to the View icon. Select the `view` outlet, as shown in Figure 22.11.

FIGURE 22.11
Connect the
view to the `view`
outlet.

Configure the iPhoneView.xib file in the same manner. Because we're only dealing with one class, the steps are literally identical.

> Before continuing, be sure that you've configured both the iPhoneView.xib and iPadView.xib files as described.

The application skeleton is now complete. To finish the functionality, we need to implement the logic in `GenericViewController`, including defining the `deviceType` outlet and connect to the outlet from the iPadView.xib and iPhoneView.xib views.

Implementing the Generic View Controller

Open the GenericViewController.h file and add a `UILabel` reference called `deviceType`, along with the `@property` declaration, as shown in Listing 22.4.

LISTING 22.4

```
#import <UIKit/UIKit.h>

@interface GenericViewController : UIViewController {
    IBOutlet UILabel *deviceType;
}

@property (nonatomic,retain) UILabel *deviceType;

@end
```

Open GenericViewController.m and add a `@synthesize` directive for `deviceType` after the `@implementation` line:

```
@synthesize deviceType;
```

Clean up by releasing `deviceType` in the `dealloc` method:

```
- (void)dealloc {
    [deviceType release];
    [super dealloc];
}
```

Complete the class by implementing the `viewDidLoad` method just as we did in the last tutorial:

```
- (void)viewDidLoad {
    deviceType.text=[[UIDevice currentDevice] model];
    [super viewDidLoad];
}
```

Implementing the iPhone and iPad Views

Finish this second project by opening and implementing the iPhoneView.xib and iPadView.xib files exactly as you did in the first project. Add a `UILabel`, if you want, that states what type of device the view is for, and then a second label that will be connected to the `deviceType` outlet.

Control-drag from the File's Owner icon to the device type label you want to use to display the device type. Choose `deviceType` from the pop-up window when prompted.

Watch
Out!

> Last time I'll say this: Make sure that you've built the views for both iPadView.xib and iPhoneView.xib!

If you Build and Run the UniversalToo application, it should appear exactly the same as the first application. There is, however, one very important difference. This application shares a view controller between the iPhone and the iPad. Any logic that is implemented in the view controller (such as the display of the device type in the `deviceType` label) needs to be implemented only *once*!

The Takeaway

Granted, both Universal and UniversalToo required work. Although UniversalToo required more time setting up the XIB files, those configuration changes never need to change once put into place.

Imagine what would happen if the application we were building included thousands of lines in the view controller. In UniversalToo, the code only has to be maintained in one place. In the Universal app, however, any changes to the iPad view controller would have to be copied into the iPhone view controller, and vice versa.

Extend this approach across multiple classes and you'll quickly see how the maintenance of an application like Universal could spiral out of control.

In short, look for opportunities to consolidate classes and share code within your
iPad and iPhone applications. You'll almost always need to create multiple XIB files,
but there's a big difference between keeping and maintaining different interface files
and maintaining the same methods repeated over and over and over.

Other Universal Application Tools

There are a few additional tools within Interface Builder and Xcode that you'll want
to take advantage of. Within Xcode, for example, you can quickly prepare a universal application—or automate the conversion of an iPhone application to the iPad.

Upgrading an iPhone Target

To do this, open your project file in Xcode, expand the Targets group, selecting the
enclosed target. Next, choose Upgrade Current Target for iPad from the Project
menu. The upgrade dialog will appear, as shown in Figure 22.12.

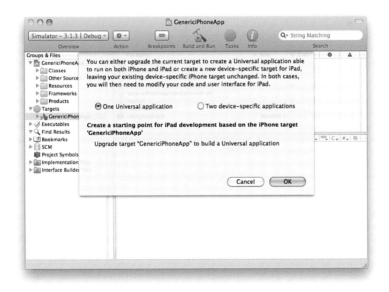

FIGURE 22.12
Xcode can help
you upgrade
your iPhone
apps to run on
the iPad.

You can choose between One Universal Application and Two Device-Specific
Applications. The first choice will create iPad resources, including views, with the
same split delegate approach that we used earlier this hour. The second option
again creates iPad resources, but they are segregated from the iPhone application.

While you can share resources and classes, you will choose between an iPhone and iPad target when building, thus creating distinct executables for both platforms.

Click OK to complete the conversion and upgrade your iPhone project for the iPad.

Converting Interfaces

Another helpful tool is Interface Builder's Create iPhone/iPod Touch Version and Create iPad Version features. When viewing an interface for the iPad or iPhone, you can convert to the other device type using these options, found under the File menu. A new copy of the XIB will be created with an auto "magically" generated view, as shown in Figure 22.13.

FIGURE 22.13
Create iPhone versions of an interface from an iPad view or vice versa.

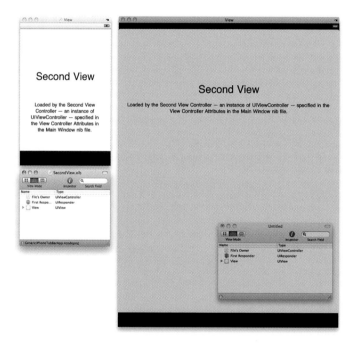

You'll notice that there are two variations of interface conversion function: one that uses autosizing masks and one that doesn't. Autosizing masks will attempt to resize objects within the view in a way that "makes sense" for the various screen sizes. Try each option, view the results, and choose the one that comes closest to what you want.

Further Exploration

The best way to learn more about universal applications is to start building them. Apple's developer documentation, "iPad Human Interface Guidelines" and "iPhone Human Interface Guidelines," will help you understand how your application's interface can be presented on each device.

These documents are also important because what is "acceptable" on one platform (according to Apple) might not be acceptable on the other. UI classes such as UIPickerView and UIActionSheet, for example, cannot be displayed outside of a popover on the iPad. On the iPhone, popovers don't even (currently) exist. Be sure to have a plan of how to present your interface on both devices before even attempting to create a universal app.

Summary

This hour's lesson covered the process of building universal applications on the iPhone and iPad platforms. Using the Universal Window-based Application template, you can quickly create an application that is customized to the device that it is running on. As you (somewhat painfully) learned, one of the problems in developing a universal application is avoiding duplicating code. In the first example, multiple view controllers were used, resulting in essentially two different applications within a single executable. The second tutorial, however, combined the application logic into a single view controller that displayed either a iPhone or iPad view.

The lesson ended with a quick look at a few tools built in to Xcode and Interface Builder that can help convert your existing applications and views so that they can target both iPhone and iPad platforms.

Q&A

Q. *Why isn't everyone building universal applications?*

A. Surprisingly, many people are creating versions of their iPhone applications that run only on the iPad. In my opinion, this is being driven by two things. First, many applications, when expanded for the iPad, are "different" enough that a separate application is warranted. Second, I think that many developers are the potential for higher profits by selling multiple copies of their apps!

Q. *I want to share code, but my views are too different to share a controller. What do I do?*

A. Look for opportunities to create other shared classes. View controllers aren't the only opportunity for shared code. Any application logic that is shared between the iPad and iPhone could potentially be placed in its own class.

Workshop

Quiz

1. Universal apps run on the Mac, iPad, and iPhone. True or false?

2. Apple requires that any app available for both the iPhone and iPad be submitted as a universal application. True or false?

3. Only a single icon is required for universal applications. True or false?

Answers

1. False. Universal apps run only on the iPhone and iPad platforms (not including the iPhone simulator on the Mac).

2. False. You can create separate applications for iPad and iPhone platforms, or a universal app. Apple does not take this into account during evaluation.

3. False. You must add a `CFBundleIconFiles` array to the project's plist file containing icons for both the iPad and iPhone.

Activities

1. Return to a project in an earlier hour and create an iPhone-ready version!

HOUR 23

Application Debugging and Optimization

What You'll Learn in this Hour:

▶ Debugging in Xcode

▶ Monitoring with Instruments

▶ Profiling with Shark

Despite our best efforts, no application is ever bug-free. The ability to find and eliminate bugs quickly is an essential skill.

This hour covers the debugging, tracing, and profiling tools included in the iPhone OS SDK. You'll learn how to use Xcode's debugger to find and correct errors. We also delve into the Instruments and Shark tools to profile an application's resource usage and performance. This potent combination of tools can help you deliver applications that run more efficiently and with fewer bugs.

> With the term *debugging*, it is assumed your project builds with no errors but then encounters an error or otherwise fails to work as designed when it's executed. If there is an error in your code that prevents it from building, then you are still coding, not debugging. The tools in this hour are for improving applications that build but then have errors or resource-utilization problems.

Debugging in Xcode

Xcode brings together the five basic tools of the software developer's trade into a single application: the text editor, compiler, linker, debugger, and reference documentation. Xcode has debugging tools integrated within it, and so all your debugging activities can take place from within the now-familiar confines of Xcode.

Debugging with NSLog

The first, and most primitive, debugging tool in your Xcode arsenal is the humble NSLog function. Many a gnarly bug has been slain with just this function alone. At any point in your application, you can embed a call to NSLog to confirm the flow of your application into and out of methods or to check the current value of a variable. Any statement you log with NSLog is echoed to Xcode's Debugger Console.

> To show the Debugger Console, choose Run, Console from the Xcode menu bar or press Command+Shift+R.

The NSLog function takes an NSString argument that can optionally contain string format specifiers. NSLog then takes a variable number of arguments that are inserted into the string at the location of the specifiers. This is colloquially known as "printf style" from the C printf function.

A string format specifier is nothing more than a percent sign (%) followed by one or two characters. The characters after the % sign indicate the type of the variable that will be displayed. You can get the full list of string format specifiers from the "String Format Specifier" section of the *String Programming Guide for Cocoa* in Xcode's Help. Three string format specifiers to learn and know are %i for integers (often used to debug loop counters and array offsets), %f for floats, and %@ for any Objective-C object, including NSString objects. Here are a few examples of typical NSLog function calls:

```
NSLog(@"Entering method");

int foo = 42;
float bar = 99.9;
NSLog(@"Value of foo: %i, Value of bar: %f", foo, bar);

NSString *name = [[NSString alloc]initWithString: @"Prince"];
NSDate *date = [NSDate distantPast];
NSLog(@"Value of name: %@, Value of date: %@", name, date);
[name release];
```

And here is what the output from these calls looks like in the Debugger Console:

```
[Session started at 2010-03-29 19:18:56 -0400.]
2010-03-29 19:19:29.289 TestLogger[15755:207] Entering method
2010-03-29 19:19:29.291 TestLogger [15755:207] Value of foo: 42, Value of bar:
➡99.900002
2010-03-29 19:19:29.356 TestLogger [15755:207] Value of name: Prince, Value of
➡date: 0001-12-31 19:00:00 -0500
```

> When the %@ string format specifier is used with an Objective-C object, the object's description method is called—this can provide additional information to about the object within the debugging output. Many of Apple's classes include an implementation of description that is useful for debugging. If you need to debug your own objects with NSLog, you can implement description, which returns an NSString variable.

By the Way

> As its name implies, the NSLog function is actually intended for logging, not debugging. In addition to printing the statements to Xcode's console, the statements are written out to a file on the file system. Logging to the file system is not what you're intending, it's just a side effect of using NSLog for debugging. It's easy to accidentally leave old NSLog statements in your code after you've finished debugging, which means your application is taking time to write out statements to the file system and is wasting space on the user's device. Search through your project and remove or comment old NSLog statements in your application before you build a release to distribute.

Watch Out!

Building a Project for Debugging

NSLog is a good quick-and-dirty approach to debugging, but it is not the best tool for debugging more complex issues. It's often more productive to use a debugger, which is a tool that lets you examine a running program and inspect its state. It's been said that what separates true software development professionals from weekend hackers is the ability to proficiently use a debugger. If this statement is true, then you are in luck, because using Xcode's debugger is not hard.

Normally an application executes at computer speeds, which on an iPad is millions of instructions per second. A debugger acts like the developer's brake, slowing the progress of the application down to human speeds and letting the developer control the progress of the program from one instruction to the next. At each step in the program, the developer can use the debugger to examine the values of the variables in the program to help determine what's gone wrong.

Debuggers work on the machine instructions that are compiled from an application's source code. With a source-level debugger, however, the compiler provides data to the debugger about which lines of source code generated which instructions.

Using this data, the source-level debugger insulates the developer from the machine instructions generated by the compiler and lets the developer work with the source code he has written.

Xcode's debugger, called gdb (GNU Debugger), is a source-level debugger. The compiler doesn't always generate the data needed for source-level debugging. It can amount to a lot of data, and it provides no benefit to an application's users, so the data is not generated in a release build configuration. Before you can benefit from source-level debugging, you need to build your application in a debug build configuration that will generate the debug symbols.

By default, a new Xcode project comes with two build configurations, Debug and Release. The Debug build configuration includes debug symbols, whereas the Release build configuration does not. Whenever you are working on developing your application, use the Debug configuration so that you can drop into the debugger whenever you need to. Because Debug is usually the build configuration you want to work with, it's the default configuration, too. To switch back and forth between the Debug and Release configurations, use the Overview drop-down menu, demonstrated in Figure 23.1, or chose Project, Set Active Build Configuration, Debug from the menu.

FIGURE 23.1
Set the Configuration in the Overview drop-down menu.

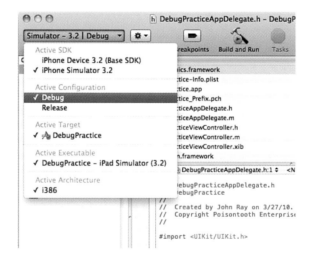

Make sure you remember to use the Release build configuration when you create a version of your application for distribution. See Hour 24, "Distributing Applications Through the App Store," for details on preparing your application for distribution.

Setting Breakpoints and Stepping Through Code

Create a new Xcode project with the View-Based Application template and call it
DebuggerPractice. Many of Xcode's debugging features are located in the left side
of the content area, called the "gutter," shown in Figure 23.2.

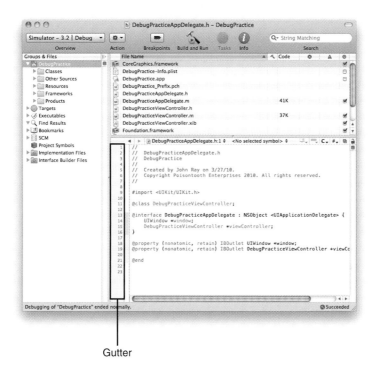

FIGURE 23.2
Xcode's gutter
contains useful
features for
debugging.

Gutter

The debugger frequently references source code line numbers, and it is helpful to
have these displayed in the gutter.

> If you don't see the gutter or if your gutter is not displaying line numbers, open
> the Xcode, Preferences menu and check the Show Gutter and Show Line Numbers
> check boxes in the Text Editing tab.

Did you Know?

Open the DebugPracticeViewController.m file in the Classes group and uncomment
the viewDidLoad method. Add a for loop that uses NSLog to display the numbers
between 1 and 10 in Xcode's debugger console. Next, add a describeInteger
method with a conditional to return a string that describes the number as odd or
even, as shown in Listing 23.1.

LISTING 23.1

```
-(NSString *)describeInteger:(int)i {

    if (i % 2 == 0) {
        return @"even";
    } else {
        return0 @"odd";
    }

}

- (void)viewDidLoad {
    [super viewDidLoad];

    NSString *description;

    NSLog(@"Start");
    for (int i = 1;i <= 10;i++) {
        description = [self describeInteger:i];
        NSLog(@"Variables: i - %i and description - %@", i, description);
    }
    NSLog(@"Done");
}
```

Click the Breakpoints button in the Xcode toolbar, and then choose Run, Debug
from the menu. The program starts up and brings us to our application's empty
view. The output from our NSLog statements are in the Debugger Console. As shown
in Figure 23.3, there is some extra, unbolded output from gdb, and a gdb prompt,
but nothing else indicates that we are running in the debugger.

FIGURE 23.3
The debugger is
waiting...

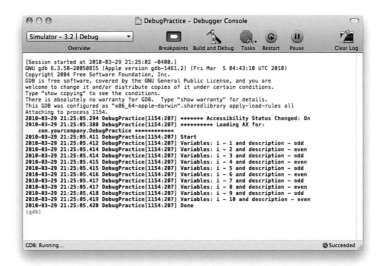

The gdb debugger is running; we just haven't told it that we want it to do anything. The most common way to start interacting with the debugger is to set a breakpoint in your application's source code.

Setting a Breakpoint

A breakpoint is an instruction to the debugger letting it know you want the program execution to pause at that point. To set a breakpoint, click once in the gutter next to the line where you want the application to pause. A breakpoint will appear as a blue arrow, demonstrated in Figure 23.4. Click the blue arrow to toggle the breakpoint off and on. When the breakpoint is on, it is displayed as dark blue. When it is off, it is light blue, and the debugger ignores it. To remove a breakpoint, right-click it and select Remove Breakpoint from the contextual menu, or simply drag it out of the Xcode gutter and it will disappear.

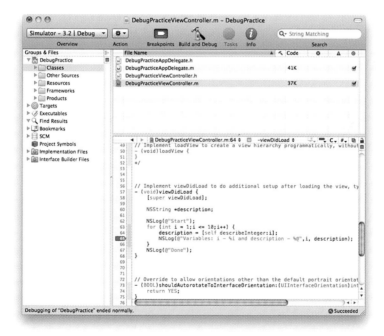

FIGURE 23.4
Set a breakpoint by clicking in the gutter.

Let's create and use a breakpoint. Quit the execution of the application and click the gutter to set a breakpoint next to this line:

```
NSLog(@"Variables: i - %i and description - %@", i, description);
```

Make sure the Breakpoints icon is highlighted in the toolbar (this enables/disables debugging breakpoints), and then click the Build and Debug icon. Notice that the application stops after printing just one log statement to the Debugger Console:

`2010-03-29 21:28:13.115 DebugPractice[1257:207]`

The debugger has paused the execution of the application at our breakpoint and is awaiting further direction, as shown in Figure 23.5.

FIGURE 23.5
The debugger pauses at breakpoints.

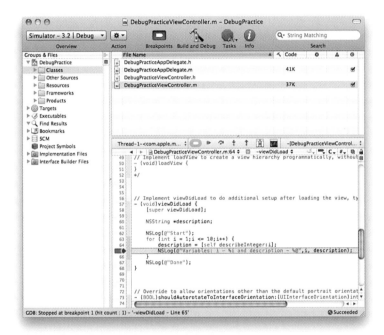

Examining and Changing Variable States

Now that the execution of the program is paused in the debugger, we can look at the value of any variables that are in scope. One of the easiest ways Xcode provides to examine variables is the debugger *datatip*. Simply hover over a variable in the source code of the paused method and Xcode will display a cascading pop-up menu, visible in Figure 23.6. The type, name, memory address, and value of the variable are displayed. Hover over the i loop counter in the for statement, and then the description variable. Notice that the datatip for i is just one level, but the datatip for the more complex NSString object has three levels. (Click the disclosure triangles to see the additional levels.)

FIGURE 23.6
You can display the datatip for the description variable by hovering over the variable.

Datatips can also be used to change the value of a variable. Again, hover over the i variable in the for loop statement and click the value in the datatip. It is currently 1, but you can change it to 4 by typing 4 and pressing Enter. The value in the running program is immediately changed, so this trip through the loop will log to the console with a value of 4, and there won't be a logged statement with a value of 2 or 3. To confirm that the program does execute as if the i variable has a value of 4, we need to continue the execution of the program.

Stepping Through Code

By far, the most common debugging activity is watching the flow of your application and following what it does while it's running. To do this, you need to be able to control the flow of execution, pausing at the interesting parts, and skipping over the mundane.

The debugger provides four icons for controlling program execution (see Figure 23.7):

▶ **Continue**: Resumes execution of the paused program, pausing again at the next error or active breakpoint.

▶ **Step Over**: Steps to the next line of code in the same method.

▶ **Step Into**: Steps into the method that is being called. If a method isn't being called on the current line of code, it acts like Step Over.

▶ **Step Out**: Steps out of the current method back to the caller of the current method.

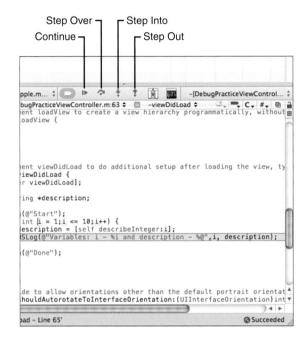

Whereas the global breakpoint control is obvious (and useful!) the other options might not be so clear. Let's take a look at how each of these works to control the flow of our application. First click the Continue icon a couple of times. Control returns back to the same breakpoint each time you continue, but if you hover over the i and description variables, you'll see that i is incrementing and description is switching between even and odd.

Add a breakpoint to this line of code by clicking the gutter:

```
description = [self describeInteger:i];
```

Click the Continue icon again, and this time you'll see the program stops at the new breakpoint because it's the next breakpoint the program encounters. This break-point is on a line of source where we are calling the describeInteger method. If we want to see what's going on inside that method, we need to step into it. Click the Step Into icon, and the program stops on the first line of the describeInteger method, demonstrated in Figure 23.8.

To step line by line through a method without entering any of the methods that might be called, use the step over task. Click the Step Over icon three times to step through the describeInteger method and return to the viewDidLoad method.

Click the Continue icon to return to the breakpoint on the describeInteger
method, and click the Step Into icon to step into the method a second time. This
time, rather than stepping all the way through describeInteger, click the Step Out
icon, and you'll be stopped back at the line where the describeInteger method
was called. The rest of the describeInteger method still executed, you just didn't
watch each step of it. You are stopped where the program flow has just exited the
describeInteger method.

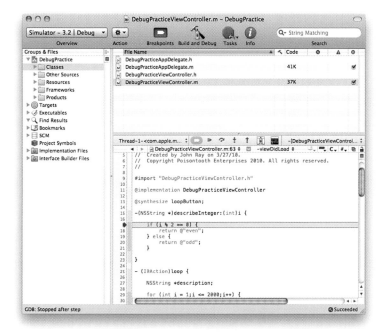

FIGURE 23.8
Program execu-
tion after step-
ping into the
describeInteger
method.

In addition to these program control tasks, another important option is hidden in
the gutter. It's called Continue to Here. Continue to Here works on the line of code
you select it on, and it works like a combination of the continue task and a temporary breakpoint. Program flow continues until it reaches an error, an active breakpoint, or it reaches the line of code you continued to.

To try this, right-click in the gutter next to this line:

```
NSLog(@"Done");
```

Click Continue to Here in the contextual menu, as shown in Figure 23.9. Notice that
we didn't make it to the line of code we continued to; we stopped on one of the two
existing breakpoints inside the for loop.

FIGURE 23.9
The Continue to
Here option of
the gutter con-
text menu.

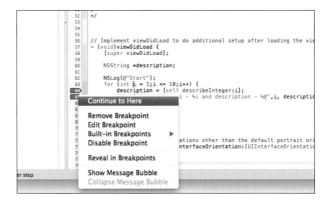

FIGURE 23.9
The Continue to
Here option of
the gutter con-
text menu.

Click each breakpoint once to make it inactive, and click Continue to Here on the
gutter next to the final line of the method one more time. This time we make it to
the end of the method. Inspect the i and description variables with the hover
datatip and notice that description's value is even but i is no longer in scope and
can't be inspected. The i variable was scoped only to the for loop, and now that
we have exited the for loop, it no longer exists. You can now quit the application.

Setting a Watch Point

Let's suppose now that there is a tricky bug in your application that only occurs on
the 1,000th time through the loop. You wouldn't want to put a breakpoint in the
loop and have to click the continue icon 1,000 times! That's where a watchpoint
comes in handy. A watchpoint is a conditional breakpoint; it doesn't stop execution
every time, it only stops when a condition you define is true.

To test this out, update the for loop to execute 2,000 times rather than 10 times.
Your viewDidLoad method should now resemble Listing 23.2.

LISTING 23.2

```
- (void)viewDidLoad {
    [super viewDidLoad];

    NSString *description;

    NSLog(@"Start");
    for (int i = 1;i <= 2000;i++) {
        description = [self describeInteger:i];
        NSLog(@"Variables: i - %i and description - %@", i, description);
    }
    NSLog(@"Done");
}
```

Now let's set a watchpoint that'll stop execution when the loop counter is equal to 1,000. First, right-click the two existing breakpoints and remove them with the Remove Breakpoint option in the context menu. Add a normal breakpoint by clicking in the gutter next to this line:

```
NSLog(@"Start");
```

Right-click the gutter next to this line to add a watchpoint:

```
NSLog(@"Variables: i - %i and description - %@", i, description);
```

To add the watchpoint, click the Add & Edit Breakpoint menu option in the context menu. The Breakpoints window will open and you'll see a table containing two breakpoints in the `viewDidLoad` method. There is a column called Condition. Click in the cell for this column in the second row and type **i == 1000** (as shown in Figure 23.10).

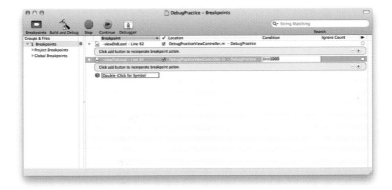

FIGURE 23.10
Program execution stops on the 1,000th iteration.

Click the Build and Debug icon to execute the application. The program will stop at the first breakpoint. Click the Continue icon and the application will go through the loop 999 times before stopping on the watchpoint on the 1,000th trip through the loop when the loop counter i is equal to 1,000. You can confirm this by looking at the 999 log messages in the Debugger Console or by hovering over the i variable in the source and looking at its value in the datatip.

Debugging in the Debugger View

We first looked at the debugger in the Debugger Console and since then we've been debugging in the Text Editor window. There is also a window dedicated to debugging that has some helpful benefits. With the application still paused on the 1,000th trip through the loop, open the Debugger window by choosing Run, Debugger from the menu (Shift+Command+Y) or by clicking the Show Debugger icon immediately following the Step Out icon.

Flow controls, just as you've been using, are present in this window, as shown in Figure 23.11. The window is divided into three panels. The lower-middle panel is the same view we've been working with in the Editor and so should be familiar. The upper-left panel is the application's call stack listed by thread. A call stack is the list of all the subroutines (methods and functions) currently being executed.

Each method in the call stack has been called by the method below it. Notice that the `viewDidLoad` method of our view controller is at the top of the stack and it was called by the superclass's (`UIViewController`) view method. Also notice that two of the methods, `viewDidLoad` and the app delegate's `applicationDidFinishLaunching:WithOptions`, are listed in bold. The bold listing indicates the debugger has source code symbols for those methods and can display them as source. Click the row for the app delegate's `applicationDidFinishLaunching:WithOptions` method and you'll see the code and you'll see that program execution is waiting for this line of code to return from executing:

```
[window addSubview:viewController.view];
```

FIGURE 23.11
The Debugger
window.

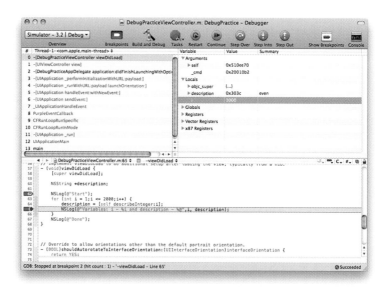

The rows in the call stack that are not in bold are for methods where the debugger only has assembly language available. Click the row for the `UIViewController`'s view method to see some assembly code. (Doesn't that make you thankful that we have the gdb source-level debugger?)

The upper-right panel contains the variable list. This is a list of all the variables that are in scope in the current method. Click back on the row in the call stack for the viewDidLoad method and you'll see that both the i and description variables we've been inspecting with datatips are listed in the variable list under the Locals disclosure, as shown in Figure 23.11. The Locals designation means these variables are declared locally in the method. The other disclosure in the variable list that you'll be most interested in is the Arguments scope for variables that have been passed into the current method as arguments.

You've done enough now to start getting the hang of using the debugger. With just these few simple steps for controlling program flow and inspecting and changing program state, you are able to debug many of the issues you may run into.

Monitoring with Instruments

The next tool we'll look at is called Instruments. Instruments is used for profiling various aspects of an application, and helps you to understand the runtime behavior of the application and the iPhone OS.

Instruments is a flexible container for plug-ins (also known as instruments) that each record and display a different aspect of an application's behavior. You choose the instruments you want to use to capture the particular aspects of the application you want to examine. The user interface is modeled after timeline editors such as Apple's GarageBand and iMovie, with the different instruments forming a vertical list, and the time expanding horizontally left to right demonstrated in Figure 23.12.

Each execution of an application that is monitored by Instruments is called a run and contains all the traces collected by the various instruments. A trace document can contain the traces from multiple instruments across multiple runs. Typically you'll work with traces immediately, but you can also save trace documents and open them again later.

Tracing an Application

Let's take one common use for Instruments, memory leak detection, and walk through a scenario.

As a quick reminder, a memory leak occurs when memory is allocated by an application but never released. One of the instruments available in Instruments is a leak detector called Leaks. How does Leaks know when an application has leaked memory? It tracks all memory allocation by the application, and it tracks the pointers to that memory. At the point where an application no longer has a valid pointer to memory it has allocated, Leaks knows the application can never free the memory, and therefore a leak has occurred.

By the Way

An application can simply use too much memory by never freeing the memory it allocates, even after it no longer needs it, but as long as a pointer to the memory exists in the application then there is at least the possibility that the application will free the memory, and so a leak does not yet exist. You'd use the Object Allocations instrument to detect this scenario of using too much memory without every actually leaking any. It's typical, when debugging memory issues, to use these two instruments together.

To test the Leaks instrument, we are going to purposely leak memory. Let's first trace the application as is to confirm there are no leaks yet. There are many ways to start a trace session with Instruments: You can run Instruments and have it launch the iPad application on the device or in the simulator, or you can have Instruments attach to an already running application on the device or in the simulator.

By the Way

Instruments is located in /Developer/Applications. You can launch it from there using Finder, or you can drag it to the Dock for quicker access.

For this scenario, we'll use a third and more straightforward method: launching Instruments from within Xcode. When launching Instruments from Xcode, we need to decide if we want to trace the application on the device or in the simulator. The device provides a much more accurate picture of how our application is going to perform and should be your default choice in most cases, but for the purposes of detecting leaks, the simulator works just fine, so let's trace from there.

Open the Debugger window with the Run, Debugger menu option (Shift+Command+Y) and use the Active SDK drop-down to target the iPhone Simulator. To launch the DebugPractice application in Instruments from Xcode, select Run, Run with Performance Tool, Leaks from the Xcode menu as shown in Figure 23.12.

The Instruments application will launch, and it will start the DebugPractice application in the iPhone Simulator. Our (very sparse) application will launch in the simulator, and after the initial object allocations involved in getting the application started, displaying the UI, and iterating through our odd/even loop, there is no other activity for Instruments to trace.

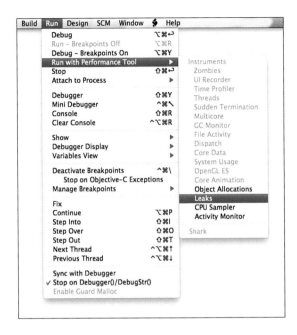

FIGURE 23.12
Launching the application with Instruments tracing.

When you are convinced of this, click the Stop button. Notice that this also stops the application in the simulator. We've now completed one run in Instruments. Click the row for the Leaks instrument and you can see, as in Figure 23.13, that it has no leaks to report.

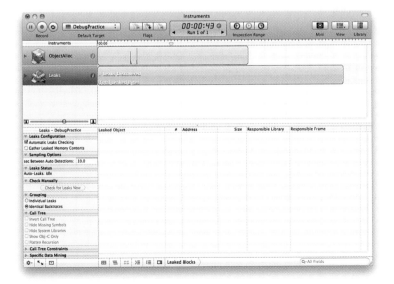

FIGURE 23.13
No leaks during the first run.

Now let's be nefarious and introduce a memory leak into the application. Allocate memory for a new string each time through the loop and let the pointer to the string go out of scope at the end of each loop iteration. Update the `viewDidLoad` method of the DebugPracticeViewController.m file as shown in Listing 23.3.

LISTING 23.3

```
- (void)viewDidLoad {
    [super viewDidLoad];

    NSString *description;

    NSLog(@"Start");
    for (int i = 1;i <= 2000;i++) {
        description = [self describeInteger:i];

        // Don't try this at home!
        NSString *status = [[NSString alloc]initWithUTF8String:"leaking"];

        NSLog(@"Variables: i - %i and description - %@ and status - %@",
            i, description, status);
    }
    NSLog(@"Done");
}
```

Now we are ready to give the application a second run. Because we last ran the application with Instruments, Xcode keeps that as the default. This time we can start the application with the Build and Run icon.

You can't use Xcode's gdb debugger and Instruments at the same time. Their use is mutually exclusive. When we run the DebugPractice application with Instruments tracing, breakpoints are ignored, and there is no output to the Debugger Console. Whereas Xcode's first option in the Run menu had been called Run, Go (Debug), after running with Instruments tracing, the default option becomes Run, Go (Leaks). To stop running with Instruments tracing and to go back to running in the debugger, use the Run, Debugger menu option.

After about 10 seconds you'll see a red spike in the output of the leaks application. You can see this effect in Figure 23.14. The spike represents our leaking of 2,000 strings. After you see the spike you can stop the application with the iPhone Simulator's Home button.

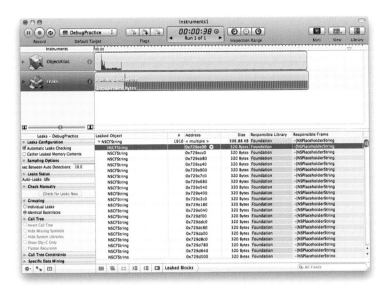

FIGURE 23.14
Oh no! In this run we are leaking like a sieve!

It didn't actually take 10 seconds for the DebugPractice application to leak the memory. This happened within the first second. The Leaks instrument is trying to keep out of the way of our application and is only sampling every 10 seconds; it was 10 seconds into the run before Leaks had its first chance to notice our leakage. We can increase or decrease the sample rate using the Sec. Between Auto Detections text box (see Figure 23.14). While the application is running, you can also force a check for leaks at any time by clicking the Check for Leaks Now button.

By the Way

Knowing we have leaked some objects is helpful, but unlike in this artificial case, we usually won't know where the leak is coming from. Remember that we said the Leaks instrument works by tracking all the application's memory allocations. The Leaks instrument knows where in the application we allocated the memory that was leaked.

Click the View drop-down list in the upper-right corner and select Extended Detail. This opens a new panel on the right of the Instruments application, as seen in Figure 23.15. Now click the first leaked object in the list and you'll see a color-coded stack trace. The colors indicate the library that each method belongs to, and our application's code is purple. We can see that our application's DebugPracticeViewController's viewDidLoad method allocated the leaked NSString objects. Double-clicking the stack trace even takes us to the specific line that leaked!

FIGURE 23.15
Details on the
leak.

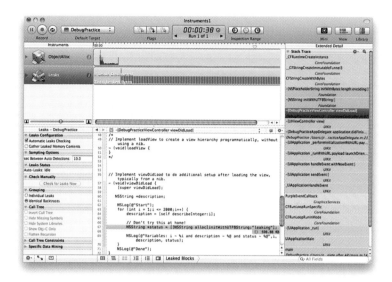

Available Instruments

Tracking down excess memory consumption and leaks is one use for Instruments,
but it's really just the tip of the iceberg. There are other instruments besides Leak
and Object Allocations that can quickly shed light on aspects of your application
that would be difficult and very time-consuming to explore with just NSLog and the
debugger. Not every instrument works with iPad applications. Table 23.1 is a list of
default instruments sets that are useful with iPad applications. When you need an
instrument, choose File, New, within Instruments, then pick the appropriate instrument template from the iPhone or iPhone Simulator categories on the left, as seen in
Figure 23.16.

You can also add instruments directly from the Instruments Library (Window,
Library), but by opening a new template, you automatically get a set of preconfig-
ured instruments rather than having to add the appropriate combinations yourself.

FIGURE 23.16
Instruments
Library.

TABLE 23.1   Available Instruments

Instrument	Function
Activity Monitor	Monitors overall CPU, memory, disk, and network activity
CPU Sampler	Precise time-based sampling of CPU usage
Leaks	Detects memory leaks
Object Allocations	Measures memory usage by class
Core Data	Monitors Core Data activity and performance, including writes to the data repository and cache efficiency
File Activity	Monitors an application's interaction with the file system
Core Animation	Measures Core Animation graphics performance and the resulting CPU load
Open GL ES	Measures Open GL ES graphics performance and the resulting CPU load
System Usage	Monitors file, network, and memory I/O use and duration for each method

Profiling with Shark

The last tool we'll look at in this hour is the Shark profiler. A profiler is a tool for better understanding application performance so that you know where to make targeted optimizations in the application. A profiler like Shark polls the application while it's running to see where it is spending time. The result of a profiling session with Shark is a report on which methods and lines of code your application is spending its time on. These lines of code and methods where you application is spending the bulk of its time are referred to as hot spots, and are where you should direct your optimization efforts.

Many applications are going to spend the bulk of their time waiting on user input or a network response, and will not benefit at all from optimization or from using a profiler. In fact, a classic sin of application development is premature optimization. Premature optimization is spending time improving the performance of your code before you know a particular section of code has a real and significant impact on the user's experience. A profiler can be a dangerous tool in this regard, because it tells you where your application is spending its time and there can be temptation to blindly optimize according to the profiler's results. Don't profile your application looking for slow spots. This is a mistake. Instead, find the slow spots by using your application as the user will use it, and then profile those slow spots to determine what's causing the slow down.

Attaching to Your Application

Using Shark for iPad applications is a little tricky because to get data that has any value, you need to remotely profile the application running on the device. Profiling your application in the simulator usually doesn't make sense because the performance characteristics will be completely different.

Also, it can be especially tricky to use Shark to profile application startup time because Shark must attach to an already running application. To avoid this problem, let's go ahead and make a small adjustment to the DebugPractice application so that there will be something interesting happening after startup for Shark to profile. Add an IBOutlet called loopButton and an IBAction called loop to the DebugPracticeViewController.h file in the Classes group, as shown in Listing 23.4.

LISTING 23.4

```
#import <UIKit/UIKit.h>

@interface DebugPracticeViewController : UIViewController {
    IBOutlet UIButton *loopButton;
}

@property (nonatomic, retain) UIButton *loopButton;
-(IBAction)loop;

@end
```

In the DebugPracticeViewController.m file in the Classes group, synthesize the loopButton property and add a loop method that does the same thing as the nonleaking version of the loop from the viewDidLoad. Remove the for loop from viewDidLoad. The methods, following the @implementation line in the DebugPracticeViewController implementation file should now be similar to Listing 23.5.

LISTING 23.5

```
@synthesize loopButton;

- (void)viewDidLoad {
    [super viewDidLoad];
}

- (IBAction)loop {

    NSString *description;

    for (int i = 1;i <= 2000;i++) {
        description = [self describeInteger:i];
        NSLog(@"Variables: i - %i and description - %@", i, description);
    }

    [loopButton setTitleColor:[UIColor redColor]
        forState:UIControlStateNormal];
}
```

Perform the following steps to add the button to the view and connect the outlet and action for the button:

1. Double-click the DebugPracticeViewController.xib file in the Resources group to launch Interface Builder.

2. Open the Library and drag a UIButton to the center of the view.

3. Click the new button and open the Attribute Inspector (Command+1). Click the Title field and type **Loop**. Change the color of the text to green.

4. Switch to the Connections Inspector for the button, and drag-click from the circle beside "Touch Up Inside" to the File's Owner icon. Choose loop when prompted for the action.

5. Press Control; then click and drag from the File's Owner icon to the button within the view. Connect to the loopButton outlet when prompted.

6. Your view should now look like Figure 23.17. Save the XIB file and return to Xcode.

FIGURE 23.17
The
DebugPractice
view in Interface
Builder.

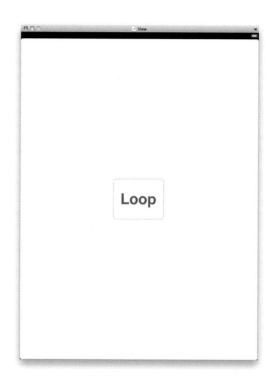

To use Shark to profile the modified DebugPractice application, follow these steps:

1. Set the Active SDK to the device with the Project, Set Active SDK, iPhone Device menu option.

2. Click the Build and Run icon to build the application and install it on the device. We want to run without gdb attached, so once the application starts, press the Home button on the device to stop it. Find the application on the device (it will have a completely white icon) and start it back up again. This time, leave it running on the device.

3. Use Finder to navigate to /Developer/Applications/Performance Tools and double-click the Shark application.

4. Once Shark starts up, make sure iPhone profiling is enabled by selecting the Sampling, Network/iPhone Profiling menu option (Shift+Command+N).

5. Select the Control Network Profiling of Shared Computers radio button, and the devices you have connected to your Mac will appear.

6. Click the Use check box beside the mobile device where the DebugPractice application is running. After a small delay, the Target column will populate with a list of the processes running on the device. "Everything" will be the initially selected value.

   Profiling everything running on the iPad will result in a lot of data, and it will take a long time to gather and analyze it. We are just interested in data for the DebugPractice application, and so that's the only process we'll profile.

7. Click the Target drop-down menu for the device and select DebugPractice from the list, as seen in Figure 23.18.

8. Press the Start button in the upper-left corner of the Shark UI, and Shark will start sampling where DebugPractice is spending its time.

9. Click the Loop button in the DebugPractice application on the device and wait until the button text turns red to let you know the loop is complete (a few seconds). Press the Stop button in the upper-left corner of the Shark UI. Shark will spend a couple of minutes or more analyzing the samples.

> Shark data is computationally expensive to collect and analyze. If you sample 20 minutes of your application, prepare to wait a *long* time before you'll be able to see the results. Try to keep your shark samples small and focused and under a minute long.

By the Way

FIGURE 23.18
Connecting
Shark to a run-
ning application.

Understanding Profile Results

When Shark finishes analyzing the profile data, it displays the Session window, shown in Figure 23.19. By default, data from the session is ordered by where the most time was spent, which is called the Heavy (Bottom-Up) view. The heaviest methods are often not your own code, but are code from the various frameworks that make up the iPhone OS SDK, such as UIKit and Core Foundation. It can also be hard to correlate this view to any sense of how your application works, because the methods are inverse of the normal call stack order; the sense of the program's flow of execution can become lost.

There is another view called Tree (Top-Down) that provides the call stack order of methods and will likely seem more familiar. Tree view starts with the application's main, then UIApplicationMain, and the tree progresses from there on into the methods of your application that you coded yourself. Figure 23.20 shows an example of the tree view in action.

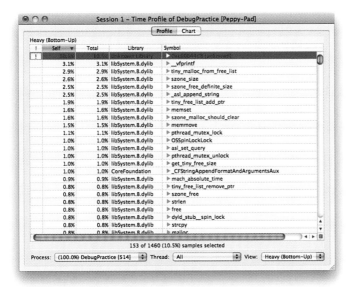

FIGURE 23.19
Profile results in
the Heavy view.

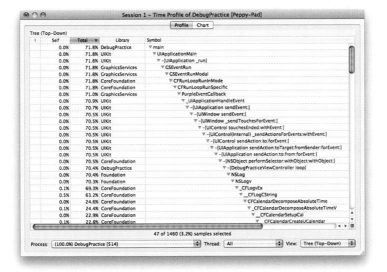

FIGURE 23.20
Profile results in
the Tree view.

Finally, there is a Heavy and Tree view that stacks the Heavy view above the Tree
view and let's you see both at the same time. Change the view with the View drop-
down in the lower-right corner. At any point, you can look at a method's implementation by double-clicking the method name in the Symbol column. Like the debugger, Shark will show you the source of the method if it has the debug symbols for

that method, as is the case in Figure 23.21, and will otherwise show the assembly code. Shark also has some built-in optimization tips that will display.

The key data point to consider in the Shark profile data is the total and self percentages for each of your methods. The Total column tells you approximately how much of the application's time (during the window of time that was profiled) was spent in that method, and the Self column tells you how much of the time was spent in the method itself rather than in the other methods that were called by the method.

The majority of the time, the methods you write yourself will have fairly small self percentages, because often the heavy computation in your application is done by the iPhone SDK frameworks on your behalf. Consider how a single line of your code can dismiss a complex model view with a flip transition and return to displaying the parent view. A huge amount of code in Core Animation and Quartz must then execute to make this one line of your code happen. Optimizing iPad applications usually means changing your application to make a more informed use of the SDK, once you understand the expense of the operations you're asking be performed.

FIGURE 23.21
An optimization
hint from Shark.

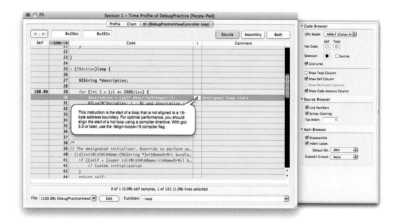

There is more art than science in profiling and optimizing, and I can't begin to tell you the exact way to proceed. The overall approach is to look through the Shark data for the things that surprise you the most. When writing your application, you have some sense of how it is going to perform. You expect certain operations you are calling to be expensive and others to be computationally cheap. When you find something in the data that breaks your mental model and surprises you, follow your nose and get to the bottom of it.

Remain patient and resist the urge to jump into optimizing. It's usually best to try a little test first to fake any optimization you are contemplating making. Make sure that if you succeeded in the optimization, there is a noticeable impact in the user experience of the application before you invest the time in implementing the optimization.

Further Exploration

Investing some time into becoming proficient with Xcode debugging, Instruments, and Shark can really pay off toward the end of a development project when you are trying to get a product release out the door, or when you are trying to quickly turn around a fix to an embarrassing bug or performance problem. In these cases, time is short and the stress level is high, so it's not the ideal circumstances to be learning these applications for the first time. Become comfortable with these tools now, and they'll provide a significant productivity boost when you need it the most.

To start to master the iPhone OS SDK toolset, and to delve deeper into debugging, Instruments, and Shark, you should read Fritz Anderson's excellent book *Xcode 3 Unleashed*. If instead you want to focus in on just one of these tools, you can find Apple's *Xcode Debugging Guide, Instruments User Guide* and *Shark User Guide* in the iPhone OS Reference Library.

If you want to start interacting with the debugger directly, I recommend Richard Stallman's *Debugging with GDB: The GNU Source-Level Debugger* and Arnold Robbin's *GDB Pocket Reference*.

Summary

In this hour, we used three important tools of the iPhone OS SDK: Xcode's gdb debugger, the Instruments tracing tool, and the Shark profiler. It takes much longer than an hour to understand everything these powerful tools can do for you, but the goal has been to give you enough exposure to them that you recognize when you need the benefits of each of these tools. You also know enough to start using each tool and exploring further what it can do for you.

Workshop

Quiz

1. What is a breakpoint? What is a watchpoint?

2. Name some useful things you can monitor with Instruments.

3. Shark helps track down application performance problems when running in the iPhone Simulator. True or false?

Answers

1. A breakpoint tells the debugger to stop execution at the start of a particular line of source code so that the developer can inspect and possibly change the state of the running application and control and monitor the application's progress. A watchpoint is a conditional breakpoint that only stops execution if a specified condition is true.

2. Answers will vary. In this hour, we used Instruments to look at memory allocation and leakage. Read through Table 23.1 again if you couldn't remember any other uses.

3. False. You're really interested in using Shark to see how an application performs on the targeted device hardware. In some cases, applications will perform better in the simulator than on the actual device.

Activities

Use the tools discussed in this chapter to analyze the implementation of other hours' projects. What did you find? Does any of your analysis identify potential optimizations that could be made to improve performance or memory usage?

HOUR 24

Distributing Applications Through the App Store

What You'll Learn in This Hour:

▶ How to prepare and build a version of your application for distribution
▶ The different ways an application can be distributed
▶ How to market your application

You've done it! Your application is built, tested, and ready for prime time. Now you need to decide how to deploy and market it. More than 150,000 applications are available for download via Apple's iTunes App Store. The trick to success is to stand out from the crowd. This hour provides step-by-step instructions to submit your application and examines how to most effectively get your application to those who need it.

By the Way

Keep a close eye on how your app is managed in the App Store. If Apple makes changes, such as requiring support for the latest OS, ensure that you application supports the latest requirements. (Otherwise, you risk your application being dropped from the App Store.) Also, give Apple plenty of time to evaluate your updates. Typically, Apple takes about a week to evaluate an update or new submission before posting it to the App Store. Apple does continue to tweak and evaluate their process, but it is still far from perfect. Part of the problem is the massive number of new applications posted to the App Store each day. So, if Apple mandates specific changes, get to them fast.

Preparing an Application for the App Store

You're almost there: Your application has been developed and tested, and now you want to share it. However, before you can sell on the App Store, you must complete a few finishing touches.

Creating Artwork

Remember that admonition to never judge a book by its cover? Unfortunately, that sage advice doesn't apply to iPad applications. Artwork for your application is important. People browsing the iTunes App Store are presented with thousands of applications. You need to have artwork that stands out from the crowd.

You have tight control over two pieces of artwork: the artwork used to present your application in your iTunes Applications Library, and the icon used to present your application on your iPad.

Open the Applications Library in your copy of iTunes to see how iTunes artwork is used to visually identify applications (see Figure 24.1). Many companies extend their company brand to the colors, images, and treatment of their artwork used by their applications.

FIGURE 24.1
You can see iTunes artwork used by every application in your Applications Library in your copy of iTunes.

The artwork used in the iTunes Applications Library is 512x512 pixels in size, and the final exported PNG image must be named iTunesArtwork, with no file extension.

As you learned at the beginning of our journey through iPad development, your application must also have an icon that is 72x72 pixels.

Let's quickly review the steps needed to add these resources to your projects.

You can use any of the dozens of available image-editing tools to create the icons and iTunes artwork for your application. The PNG file format is a noncommercial file format that most popular tools support.

By the Way

We use a simple Hello World project here to demonstrate how to add artwork to your application. You can follow these same steps for your own application:

1. Open the Welcome project for Hour 1, "Preparing Your System and iPad for Development." Included in the Images folder within the project are two PNG files that have been formatted for use as the iTunes artwork and as the default icon for your application.

2. To add the image resources to your project, drag the files in the Images folder into the Resources group of the project. Choose to copy the resources to the project, when prompted.

3. Open Welcome-Info.plist. Find the key labeled `icon` and add the value **icon.png**, as shown in Figure 24.2. By default, Apple will add glossy image treatment to the icon to keep it consistent with other icons as they appear on your iPad.

FIGURE 24.2
Add the icon filename to your project's plist.

4. That's it! You'll want to take some screenshots of the app for later, but they won't be needed within the project itself.

Did you Know?

If you want, you can override Apple's effects on your icon image by using a special key added to the plist called `UIPrerenderedIcon`.

Just create a new key and enter **UIPrerenderedIcon** as the key value. The name will change to Icon Already Includes Gloss and Bevel Effects. Check the box to activate the feature. Save all your work.

Watch Out!

The rules for icons change if you are building a universal application. Be sure to read Hour 22, "Building Universal Applications," for more details on creating icons for applications that run on both the iPhone and iPad platforms.

Creating an iPad Distribution Certificate

The person responsible for submitting final applications to the iTunes store is called the team agent. For the team agent to be able to submit any solutions, he or she must have an approved Distribution Certificate. This section discusses how to obtain this certificate.

If you followed the steps in Hour 1, you should already have a personal certificate loaded on your machine. If you are part of a larger team, you'll need to generate a new certificate for the person who will submit the app to the App Store. Let's revisit that process again.

From the Applications folder on your Mac, launch the Keychain Access utility. You are going to request a certificate from a certificate authority (CA). To do this, you must change some of the settings in the Keychain Access utility (see Figure 24.3). Select the Preferences menu, and then set Online Certificate Status Protocol (OSCP) and Certificate Revocation List (CRL) to Off in the Certificates section.

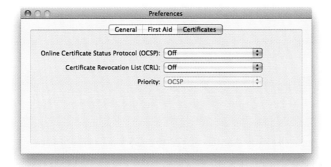

FIGURE 24.3
Modifying the settings for the Keychain Access utility.

To request a new certificate, complete the following steps:

1. Choose Certificate Assistant, Request a Certificate from a Certificate Authority (see Figure 24.4).

2. Enter the team agent's email address and the name of your company as it appears in the iPhone Developer Program. You do not need a CA email address.

3. Save the data to disk and select Let Me Specify Key Pair Information. Click Continue.

4. Choose Key Size and Algorithm. Select 2048 bits and RSA for the algorithm. Save the certificate as a CSR file to your desktop.

5. Navigate to the Provisioning Portal (http://developer.apple.com/iphone/manage/overview/index.action) Click the Certificates category (left side), and then the Distribution tab. All active certificates you have will be listed in the Distribution window. To obtain a certificate, select Request Certificate and upload the CSR file you just created.

6. After your certificate has been approved, you can download a CER file to your computer. The CER file is the Distribution Certificate associated with your computer. Double-click the CER file to add it to your keychain.

You should save your Distribution Certificate somewhere safe. The certificate ties your development environment directly to your solutions. Without the Distribution Certificate, you cannot deploy your applications. Best practice is to burn the certificate to a CD and store that CD somewhere safe.

Setting an App ID

When you distribute an app, you'll need to provide a unique identifier for it; this is known as the App ID. The App ID is necessary for providing push notifications and for sharing keychain information between multiple apps that you push. In Hour 1, you created an App ID for all the tutorial projects in this book. Chances are, you'll want a new App ID for distributing your final creation.

1. Within the Provisioning Portal, click the App IDs category on the left side.

2. Click New App ID to create a new identifier for this project you will be publishing to the App Store.

3. On the Create App ID screen, shown in Figure 24.5, provide a description for the App ID.

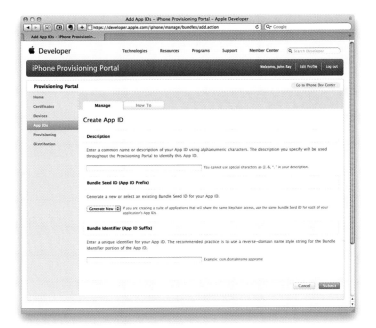

FIGURE 24.5
Create a new App ID for the apps you are publishing.

4. Choose Generate New for the Bundle Seed ID, unless you want to share a keychain between multiple applications.

5. Set a unique ID for the Bundle Identifier. Apple prefers a format that follows *com.domainname.appname* (substituting your own domain and app name).

6. Click Submit to create the new App ID.

> Push notifications and in-app purchases are beyond the scope of this book, but if you intend to support them, you'll need to view the list of App IDs, and then click the Configure link beside the ID that you want to enable for use with these features.

Did you Know?

Creating a Distribution Provisioning Profile

You next need to create a Distribution Provisioning Profile, which will associate your distribution certificate, App ID, and distribution method within Xcode:

1. In the Provisioning Portal, choose Provisioning, Distribution (http://developer.apple.com/iphone/manage/provisioningprofiles/viewDistributionProfiles.action). Then click the New Profile button.

2. Choose whether the application will be uploaded to the App Store or will be deployed ad hoc, as shown in Figure 24.6. We discuss ad hoc distribution a bit later.

FIGURE 24.6
Create a provisioning profile that describes how your app will be distributed.

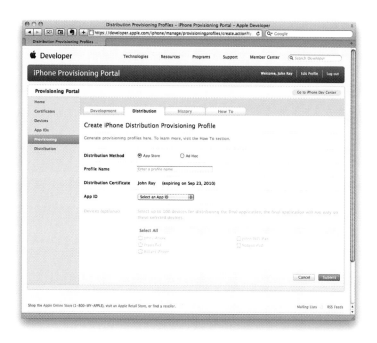

3. Give your profile a meaningful name.

4. Double-check that the certificate and App ID is correct, and then select Submit. The profile is generated and, after a few moments, can be downloaded. The file you will download has the extension .mobileprovision.

5. To install the profile, double-click or drag the .mobileprovision file onto either iTunes or Xcode in your dock.

Configuring a Project for Distribution

The final thing you need to do is to create a version of your application that you can submit to the App Store. Follow these steps to prepare your app:

1. Open the project in Xcode. Double-click the main project file within the Xcode Groups & Files pane to open the Information panel, and then Click the Configurations button (see Figure 24.7).

FIGURE 24.7
Create a new distribution configuration.

2. Select the Release Configuration option, click the Duplicate button in the lower-left corner, and rename the new copy **Distribution**.

3. Close the Info window, and then choose Edit Active Target from the Project menu. The Target Info window appears.

4. Click the Build button, and select Distribution from the Configuration menu options.

5. You now need to associate your Distribution Certificate and Provisioning Profile with the build. Within the Code Signing section, shown in Figure 24.8, under Code Signing Identity, select Any iPhone Device, and choose your certificate from the drop-down list. Within the list, your certificate will be in bold, with your Provisioning Profile in gray. Without a valid certificate, you cannot upload your applications to the App Store.

FIGURE 24.8
Choose your
team agent cer-
tificate.

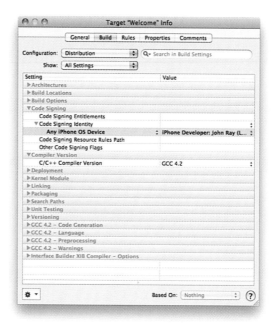

6. Display the Properties tab so that you can enter the bundle identifier for your
   application (see Figure 24.9). The bundle identifier is the same as your App
   ID, without the unique string at the beginning. (For example, if your App ID
   is 123456789.com.yourcompany.yourappname, you would enter **com.your-
   company.yourappname**.) Close the Target Info window.

7. Next, you create an entitlement plist, a file that provides the code signing for
   the app, as shown in Figure 24.10. Choose New File, iPhone OS, Code Signing,
   Entitlements.

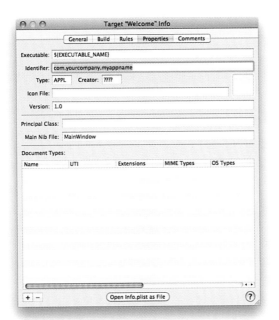

FIGURE 24.9
Set the bundle
identifier for
your application.

FIGURE 24.10
Create an enti-
tlement plist.

8. Name the entitlement file **Entitlements.plist**. The file is saved to the root of your application. The Entitlements.plist has one property called `get-task-allow`. Uncheck the Boolean value of this property, as shown in Figure 24.11.

9. Open the Target Info panel for your application again (Project, Edit Target). Click the Build button and select Code Signing Entitlements from the Code Signing section. Type in **entitlements.plist** and save your work.

FIGURE 24.11
The
Entitlement's
`get-task-allow` property
must be
unchecked.

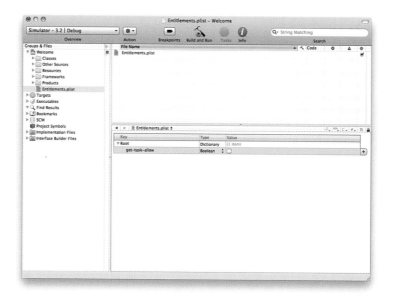

10. Now change the application's active configuration to Distribution and choose Build and Archive from the Xcode Build menu. The application is now ready for submission to the App Store.

Submitting an Application for Approval

The Apple iTunes App Store is a dazzling success. Now duplicated by RIM, Palm, Nokia, Google, and Microsoft, the iTunes App Store boasts more than 185,000 unique applications, 3 billion (that's with a *b*, not an *m*) downloads, and an audience of more than 50 million users.

The success of the App Store is built on making the user experience easy. For many people, the hardest part of running an application is installing it. With the App Store, Apple has introduced a one-click installation process that makes it easy to install any solution. Users just click an application's price button to start the buying and installing process. The application's price display is red. Click that button and the wording on the button changes to Purchase. To actually purchase the application, you must click the button again and then enter your account password. That's it. After that, iPhone OS does the rest.

This simple process enables every developer to easily deploy a solution and know that it will be installed correctly. In addition, the customer can apply updates to your application via a one-click download from the App Store app.

Apple is also upfront about the charges. Apple charges just one rate: 30% of the price of your application (or nothing if the app is given away for free). So, if you are selling an application for $2.99, 30% goes to Apple and 70% to you. In this case, you get $2.00 for each sale.

At first it might seem that Apple is gouging you of your profits; but if you have developed content for the Nintendo DS, Microsoft Xbox 360, or Sony PlayStation, you know that Apple's fee is reasonable. After all, it is Apple that is hosting the applications in their own server farms, managing the 40 million accounts, and giving you access to tools to effectively control how you sell your applications. Yes, the 30% cost is *very* reasonable.

Apple strives for transparency about how well your application is selling. In fact, they created iTunes Connect to help you manage your account. You should log in to the iTunes Connect site at https://itunesconnect.apple.com and make sure that your company information is properly entered before proceeding.

Preparing Your Application Profile

When you have your accounts set up, you will want to start uploading your applications to the store through the itunesconnect.apple.com website. Only a release version of your application can be uploaded. In iTunes Connect, click the Manage Your Applications link, and then start the process by clicking the Add New Application link, shown in Figure 24.12.

FIGURE 24.12
Upload an appli-
cation to the
App Store.

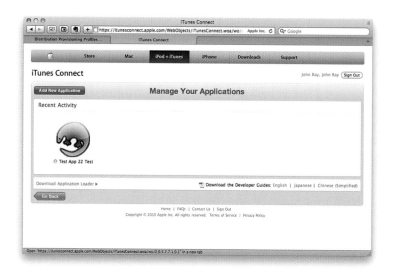

If this is the first app you've uploaded, you'll be prompted to select your language
and company name. Enter this information, and then click Continue.

Next, iTunes Connect will prompt to verify that you aren't exporting encryption software. Answer the question and click Continue.

The fourth screen gets to the application details, as shown in Figure 24.13. Here
you'll need to enter all the information about the application:

- ▶ Application Name.

- ▶ Application Description (limit 4,000 characters).

- ▶ Device Requirements.

- ▶ Primary Category. There are 20 primary categories, including Games,
  Entertainment, Business, Books, and News. Some categories, such as Games,
  have subcategories to help organize the content more effectively.

- ▶ Secondary Category. You can choose a second category for your application.

- ▶ Copyright (the person who owns the code).

- ▶ Version Number. You can use your own schema for version number.

- ▶ SKU Number (a unique identifier that you create). A simple way to create an
  SKU is to insert the date, such 08312010 for August 31, 2010. When you
  update the application, just apply a new date.

▶ Keywords. Keywords are used to help return results when a customer is searching for an application.

▶ Application URL. The application URL links to the application's website.

▶ Support URL. The support URL links to the support site for the application.

▶ Support Email Address.

▶ Demo Account. If the app accesses any online services, this input area gives you a place to provide testing accounts that Apple can use to validate your software.

FIGURE 24.13
Accurately describe your application before submitting it.

Click Continue when you have finished describing your application.

Next, you'll need to rate your application so that parental controls can be applied (see Figure 24.14). The age limit will change depending on how you rate your application. Make sure you enter information correctly. During an audit process, Apple reviews how you score your application.

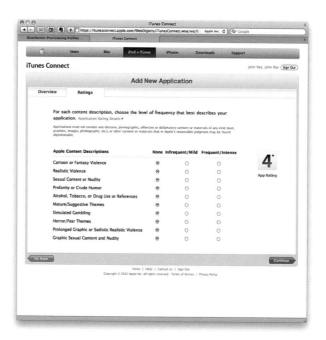

Click Continue to proceed. You will be asked whether your application should be visible in the Game Center (Apple's new social gaming portal). Game Center integration is not available in the initial release of the iPad OS, and is beyond the scope of this book. Click Continue to skip this step.

In the next step, you'll submit your application and its associated artwork (see Figure 24.15). Along with the iTunes artwork and application, you should have screen shots of the application to promote the application in iTunes. The screen shots should be 1024x768, 748x1024, or 1004x768 pixels.

Click Choose File and then Upload File for each file section within the Upload screen, *but choose to upload the application binary later.* Click Continue when you have finished uploading all the application resources with the exception of the application itself.

You'll now be prompted for localization information. Click Continue to skip this step unless you've added support for multiple languages in your app.

The Pricing screen lets you select when the application will go on sale, what pricing tier you prefer, and even which stores can carry your app, as shown in Figure 24.16. Click Continue to finalize your submission.

FIGURE 24.15
You can easily add artwork for your application.

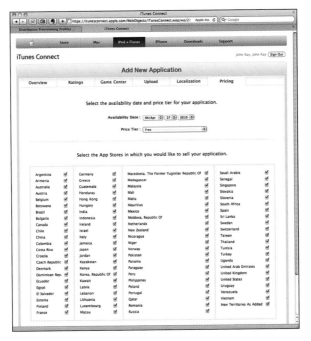

FIGURE 24.16
Manage when your app goes on sale and how much it will cost.

Did you
Know?

If you're staring at the pricing screen wondering where the tiers are actually defined, all you need to do is select a tier other than Free. Once you've picked a tier, the pricing will appear along with a link to a full pricing tier matrix.

On a Summary screen, you can double-check everything about your application before you submit it for Apple's approval. Review the information and then continue. You'll be taken back to the main iTunes Connect page where you can view the status of your application submission. Because no application binary has been submitted yet, your application status will read "Waiting for Upload."

Uploading an Application Binary

After you've configured an application profile in iTunes Connect, you can return to the comfort of Xcode to complete the upload. Open the application project in Xcode, and then switch to the Organizer (Window, Organizer).

Click the Archived Applications category to show the applications that are ready to be uploaded. You'll need to expand the disclosure arrow in front of the application to show the different binaries (listed by date) that you can upload.

Select the date that corresponds to the version you want to submit, and then Click the Submit Application to iTunesConnect button at the bottom of the window. You will be prompted for your iTunes Connect login information, as shown in Figure 24.17.

FIGURE 24.17
Enter your iTunesConnect login credentials.

After you enter your information and click OK, Xcode will chug away for a little while and then show a screen where you can choose your distribution signing identity (you can choose Don't Re-sign since you already picked the correct information prior to building) and the application profiles awaiting an upload. Choose the application that you entered information for, and then click Submit to iTunesConnect, as shown in Figure 24.18. Your application will be uploaded to Apple's servers.

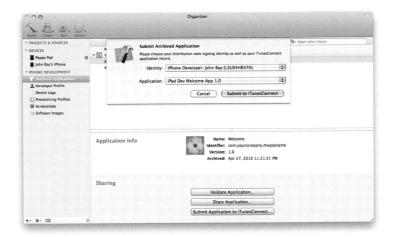

FIGURE 24.18
Choose the application profile that you entered in iTunes Connect.

If you want to make sure that everything is in order with your application before submitting, you can use the Validate Application button in the organizer. The application will also be validated during submission, and Xcode will display any errors that occur.

Did you Know?

After submitting the app, you can track its progress from the Manage Your Applications link within iTunes Connect (http://itunesconnect.apple.com/).

Promoting Your Application

You've done it. Your application is installed in the App Store. You have heard all the "rags to riches" stories of developers who have made tens of thousands from sales of apps, and now you are waiting for your pot of gold to arrive. But, you might be waiting for a while. Although you can make a lot of money from selling your application, you must be willing to expend a bit of effort.

To sell any piece of software, you want to take advantage of all the traditional ways software has been sold in the past. In addition, we now have some seriously focused tools (and tactics) that can really help your sales, including the following:

▶ Use Apple's iTunes Connect to monitor/manage sales.

▶ Exploit websites and social networks.

▶ Update your application.

▶ Change your price.

Any or all of the "tools" listed here can help build interest and drive sales of your application.

Using iTunes Connect to Monitor/Manage Sales

As you've learned, iTunes Connect provides tools for managing and uploading applications, but can also help you monitor your sales. Via iTunes Connect, you can do the following:

▶ Assess sales/trends

▶ Review your contracts, tax, and banking information

▶ Download financial reports

▶ Request promotional codes

▶ Contact Apple support with any questions you may have

When you log in to iTunes Connect, ensure that your banking information is correct. After all, if you are selling something, you want to make sure that you get paid.

Then, set up accounts for those persons in your company who need access to iTunes Connect. Three user types can access the iTunes Connect account in addition to the original person who set up the account (called the Legal account), as follows:

▶ The Admin account has the right to view, add, and delete additional accounts and manage the whole iTunes Connect environment.

▶ The Finance account gives the user access to financial reports and contracts, tax and banking information, and sales/trend reports modules.

▶ The Technical account allows the user to manage applications and manage users' modules.

Generally, you will add multiple accounts only if you have a large organization that requires different levels of access to the iTunes Connect service.

A feature that you will want to use to promote your applications is Request Promotional Codes. This feature, located on iTunes Connect (in the Request Promotional Codes section), allows you to send promo codes to users who can then download and use your application for free. The promotional code cannot be shared after it has been used.

> If you have a lot of applications for sale in a lot of countries, managing all the Apple-provided data can get confusing. However, a number of companies provide tools to sift through all the iTunes Connect data. Check out the Developer Tools section of Apple's website for the latest solutions (http://www.apple.com/downloads/macosx/development_tools/).

By the Way

Arguably, the most important feature in iTunes Connect is Sales Trends Analysis. This tool tells you how your sales are going (by date and by country).

Exploiting Websites and Social Networks

It might seem very turn of the millennium, but websites work well to advertise your applications. A website can be built very quickly using tools such as Adobe Dreamweaver, WordPress, Joomla, or even iWeb if you are pressed for resources.

The key is to build a website that's easy to view on any device (including via Safari on the iPad). In addition, test your site on Windows and Mac computers.

As mentioned earlier, you must associate a website with your application during the submission process. Therefore, every application available via the App Store has a web address. Customers should be able to use Safari, the iPad's own web browser, to view your application's website.

Mobile Safari is one of the most advanced web browsers available, and therefore you can add many of the latest HTML tricks to your website. For instance, Mobile Safari supports HTML 5, and so you can add rich transition and animation effects to your website.

From your website, you can advertise and link back to applications you are selling in the App Store. You can find the URL for any application in the App Store by right-clicking the link inside of iTunes. The cryptic URL you are given will look something like this:

```
http://itunes.apple.com/WebObjects/MZStore.woa/wa/viewSoftware?id=306220440&mt=8
```

Add this link to your web page. When potential customers click it, they will be taken directly to the page in iTunes where they can purchase your application. Similarly, if a potential customer is using Mobile Safari and clicks a link to your app, Mobile Safari will close and the App Store app will open and go directly to your application.

The really long URL link is great to add to your own website, but it doesn't work if you want to use social networking sites such as Twitter and Facebook. Twitter, in particular, limits the number of characters you can type to 140, and thus prevents long URLs from being entered. To resolve this problem, use URL-shortening services such as bit.ly so that you can post a URL that has fewer than a dozen characters.

You can also build social networking directly into your application. Many social networking sites have their own API. For example, with Facebook's API, you can post the latest high score or challenge your Facebook friends to a game. Freeverse's Postman enables you to send custom postcards directly to Facebook, Twitter, or Tumblr.

In addition to social networks, you will also want to contact the editors of websites that cover iPhone OS applications. You can often get a boost in sales by working with these editors and getting a link to your app from their website. Good sites to contact and work with include the following:

- ▶ AppStoreApps.com
- ▶ AppAdvice.com
- ▶ iLounge.com
- ▶ 148apps.com
- ▶ AppCraver.com
- ▶ AppSafari.com
- ▶ AppleiPhoneApps.com
- ▶ iPhoneApplicationList.com
- ▶ NativeiPhoneApps.com
- ▶ iPhoneApps.co.uk
- ▶ Apptism.com
- ▶ AppShopper.com
- ▶ Apprater.com

When you contact these sites, be courteous and give the editors a promotional code for your application so that they can test it and write a review.

As you build your website, think about how web search engines such as Google and Bing see your site. There are lots of great websites that lay out the search engine optimization techniques. Adding search engine optimization to your site can increase the number of times the site is presented on a search engine results page.

In addition to relying on organic placement on a search engine results page, you can purchase paid advertising. The goal of paid advertising is to appear alongside results similar to your product. Google's paid advertising allows your results to show on both their Google.com website and through their affiliate sites.

Finally, add analytical tools such as Google Analytics to your website. These tools provide information about how people are using your website, how often they return, and how they came to your site.

Updating Your Application

Unlike traditional computer-based software, applying updates to iPad applications is very easy, and you will find that your customers will have few problems updating their apps. There are tactical benefits to releasing updates to an application on a regular, scheduled basis:

▶ The first benefit is that customers think that they are getting something for free. The update is a bonus.

▶ The second benefit is that the update brings the user's attention back to the app. An update is an opportunity to rediscover an application.

▶ The final benefit is each update gets separate reviews in the App Store.

A final thought as you update your apps: Add good, descriptive explanations for the update. Frequently, developers list "bug fixes" as the only reason for the update. Although this is important to the developer and the users experiencing problems with the application, for the rest of your users it is not a very exciting update. A different approach is to add one or two new features with the bug fixes. This way a customer can get excited about installing the update and trying out a new feature.

Changing Your Price

How much should you charge for your application? This is a tough question for all developers and companies selling applications on the App Store. With hundreds of new applications being added each week, you can easily become lost in the melee.

A tactic that many developers adopt is to start selling at $4.99 and then, shortly after release, temporarily drop the price by a couple of dollars for a specified period. The effect is to create a fire sale, and thus drive urgency to purchase.

Dropping your price can also increase the number of sales in the iTunes App Store. Your goal is to break into the Top 100. Often referred to as racing to the bottom, the result of dropping your price as far you can go is to devalue your product just to get to number 1. Companies such as Electronic Arts and 2K Games, however, recognize that you can make more profit by keeping your price higher and not hitting number 1. For instance, EA's Scrabble spent several weeks in the Top 10 without changing its price of $4.99. The Scrabble app did not sell as many units as the number 1 app, but at 5x the price, it most likely made more profit.

Ultimately, how you choose and manage the price for your application depends on your marketing plan.

Exploring Other Distribution Methods

In addition to the App Store, Apple provides two other ways to distribute your application: ad hoc deployment and enterprise delivery.

Ad Hoc Deployment

Sometimes you do not want to deploy an application immediately to the App Store. Sometimes you just want to send it directly to some friends and coworkers to get feedback.

Ad hoc deployment allows you to package a release version of your application into a zip file and give it to whomever you want to via email, website download, or USB drive.

Packaging an application for ad hoc deployment is easy. After you have created a release build of your application in Xcode, using Build and Archive, find the version that you want to distribute within the Archived Applications section of the Xcode organizer.

Select the build you want to distribute, and then click Share. You will be prompted for an ad hoc provisioning profile to associate with the build, and then given the option of emailing the application or saving it to disk, as shown in Figure 24.19.

FIGURE 24.19
Distribute your
application to
your friends via
ad hoc distribu-
tion.

The setup for an ad hoc version of the Distribution Provisioning Profile is the same one for an app that will be deployed to the iTunes store. The only difference is that you choose Ad Hoc as the distribution type.

Did you Know?

To load the application, all your friends/coworkers/testers need to do is double-click the file they receive to load it into iTunes and begin using it.

Regarding the ad hoc process, be aware of the following caveats:

▶ Apple states that you are limited to only 100 people per release version of an app when you want to share the app ad hoc. Of course, there are ways around this limitation. You can change the version number each time you want to create an ad hoc deployment or even change the name of the application.

▶ This method should be used only for early releases and testing of your application. The ad hoc deployment method can in no way reach the number of people you can reach using the iTunes App Store (unless, of course, you have 40+ million users' email addresses in your Contacts folder).

Enterprise Provisioning

Some of the most prolific users of iPhone OS devices are businesses, and the iPad will likely continue this trend. Within days of the iPad going on sale, a TV station purchased iPads for its reporters. A local communications company (Hi Julie!) purchased iPads for all of its employees. Companies such as these can take advantage of Enterprise Deployment to simplify the distribution of custom applications. To take advantage of this…

▶ You must have an Enterprise subscription to Apple's Dev Center ($299/yr).

▶ Each custom application your company develops must be signed using your own digital certificate.

▶ An Enterprise Provisioning Profile must be created allowing authorized devices to install applications with your certificate.

▶ You then deploy your applications to authorized desktops.

Authorized users can drag and drop a deployed application into their iTunes and sync the next time they connect their device to their computer. The process is the same for Mac, Windows XP, Vista, and Windows 7 versions of iTunes.

Summary

In this hour, you learned how to prepare and submit your iPad application to the App Store for publication. Although waiting for your application to be approved can be nerve wracking, marketing the final product might be the biggest challenge you face. When this book hits the shelves, there will likely be more than 10,000 iPad-specific apps available. You need to work to make yours stand out!

Q&A

Q. *What type of applications are the most popular in the iTunes App Store?*

A. Games. You can choose to write a game for this popular group or review the other categories in the App Store and look for areas where there appears to be missing applications. Ultimately, a great solution will always sell as long as your customers know that it exists.

Q. *Should I only develop solutions for the iPad?*

A. If your application doesn't adapt to a smaller screen, yes, concentrate on the iPad. If you can offer a compelling experience across the iPhone OS platforms, do so! A bigger audience will result in larger sales.

Workshop

Quiz

1. What does an App ID do?

2. Where can you modify the settings for iPad icons?

3. What is iTunes Connect?

Answers

1. An App ID uniquely identifies an application or suite of applications that you're building. Applications that share App IDs can also share keychain information.

2. The icon settings can be modified in the application's plist file.

3. iTunes Connect is Apple's online site for managing your application submissions and sales.

Activities

1. Build a deployable version of your application and send it to some friends and have them test it on their iPads. When you are sure the application is good to be published, submit it to the iTunes App Store.

2. Develop a marketing strategy and start letting people know that your application exists. Easy ways to promote your application include contacting iPhone OS fan sites and asking whether they can review your app, posting to forums, and updating your Facebook and Twitter accounts.

Index

converting (universal
applications), 598
creating with Interface
Builder, 112-117
custom picker views, 303-304
customization, 117-120
Date Pickers, 294-295
flash card application,
438-446
flashlight application,
419-420
gesture recognition, 494-497
Hop button, 201-202
input/output techniques. *See*
input techniques; output
techniques
labels, 200
main view (modal views),
331-332
Media Playground application,
532-533
modal UI elements, 245
object release, 206
Orientation application,
513-515
popovers. *See* popovers
resizable. *See* resizable
interfaces
ReturnMe application,
426-427
rotatable. *See* rotatable
interfaces
simulation, 120
Split View-based Application
template. *See* Split-View
based Application template
table views. *See* table views
user notifications. *See* user
notifications
view controller logic
animation speed, 204-206
implementation, 203-204
**iPad Human Interface
Guidelines, 130**
**iPad view (GenericViewController
class), 596**
iPadViewController class, 584

**iPhone Dev Center (Apple
website), 9**
iPhone OS
developer tools, 12-13
frameworks, 100-103
SDK (Software Development
Kit), 8
technology layers, 85
Cocoa Touch, 86-87
Core OS, 89
Core Services, 88-89
Media, 87-88
**iPhone Simulator, testing
applications, 47, 152-153**
esoteric conditions, 51-52
generating multitouch
events, 50
Interface Builder, 120
launching applications, 48-49
rotation simulation, 50
iPhone target, 597-598
**iPhone view (GenericView-
Controller class), 596**
iPhoneViewController class, 585
**iPod Library, Media Picker,
548-549**
cleanup, 551
implementation, 549-550
Music Player, 552-553
playlists, 551
iPodMusicPlayer method, 548
isAnimating property, 197
isOn method, 212, 228
iTunes Applications Library, 632
**iTunes Connect, application
promotion, 650-651**

J–K

keyboard
customization, 165-166
hiding, 160, 179-182
input process, 159
buttons, 172-179
implementation, 159-160
preparation of outlets and
actions, 161-162

project setup, 160-161
text fields, 162-167
text views, 167-172
Keyboard (text input trait), 165
keychain, 16
Keychain Access utility, 635
keys, Launch image, 583

L

labels, 97, 159, 200
action sheets, 317-318
adding to views, 163
SimpleSpin, 469
landscape left orientation, 463
landscape right orientation, 463
landscapeView outlet, 482
lastAction outlet, 303
launch images
Launch image (iPad) key, 583
modifying project
properties, 47
universal applications, 583
launching
applications in iPhone
Simulator, 48-49
Development Provisioning
Assistant, 15
Mac OS X Installer, 13
layers (iPhone OS), 85
Cocoa Touch, 86-87
Core OS, 89
Core Services, 88-89
Media, 87-88
Layout menu commands, 115
layout tools (Interface Builder)
alignment, 115-116
guides, 114-115
selection handles, 115
Size Inspector, 116-117
**leak detector (Instruments tool),
616-619**
Leaks instrument, 621
**Library command (Tools menu),
112, 162**
Library/Caches directory, 435
Library/Preferences directory, 434
life cycle (applications), 89-91

How can we make this index more useful? Email us at indexes@samspublishing.com

settings (application preferences)

How can we make this index more useful? Email us at indexes@samspublishing.com

FREE Online Edition

Your purchase of **Sams Teach Yourself iPad™ Application Development in 24 Hours** includes access to a free online edition for 45 days through the Safari Books Online subscription service. Nearly every Sams book is available online through Safari Books Online, along with more than 5,000 other technical books and videos from publishers such as Addison-Wesley Professional, Cisco Press, Exam Cram, IBM Press, O'Reilly, Prentice Hall, and Que.

SAFARI BOOKS ONLINE allows you to search for a specific answer, cut and paste code, download chapters, and stay current with emerging technologies.

Activate your FREE Online Edition at www.informit.com/safarifree

> **STEP 1:** Enter the coupon code: UCSOHAA.

> **STEP 2:** New Safari users, complete the brief registration form.
> Safari subscribers, just log in.